MEDICAL SOCIOLOGY

MEDICAL
SOCIOLOGY

William C. Cockerham
University of Illinois

PRENTICE-HALL, INC., ENGLEWOOD CLIFFS, NEW JERSEY 07632

Library of Congress Cataloging in Publication Data

COCKERHAM, WILLIAM C
    Medical sociology.
    (Prentice-Hall series in sociology)
    Bibliography: p.
    Includes index.
    1. Social medicine.   I. Title.
RA418.C657   301.5   77–13162
ISBN 0–13–573402–9

Prentice-Hall Series in Sociology
Neil J. Smelser, *Editor*

© 1978 by Prentice-Hall, Inc., Englewood Cliffs, N.J. 07632

*All rights reserved. No part of this book may be reproduced
in any form or by any means
without permission in writing from the publisher.*

Printed in the United States of America

10 9 8 7 6 5 4 3

PRENTICE-HALL INTERNATIONAL, INC., *London*
PRENTICE-HALL OF AUSTRALIA PTY. LIMITED, *Sydney*
PRENTICE-HALL OF CANADA, LTD., *Toronto*
PRENTICE-HALL OF INDIA PRIVATE LIMITED, *New Delhi*
PRENTICE-HALL OF JAPAN, INC., *Tokyo*
PRENTICE-HALL OF SOUTHEAST ASIA PTE. LTD., *Singapore*
WHITEHALL BOOKS LIMITED, *Wellington, New Zealand*

TO MY CHILDREN

Laura, Geoffrey, and Sean

00064

CONTENTS

ACKNOWLEDGMENTS

There were several good textbooks in medical sociology available in 1970, but as the 1970s wore on, these books were not revised nor were new ones forthcoming. In this, one of the most dynamic fields in sociology, very few people appeared to be interested in writing a textbook, although there was general agreement that it was needed. Aware that the primary task of the sociologist is to produce social knowledge, I felt that rather than simply apologize to the students in my medical sociology classes for the use of outdated textbooks, I should do something about it. This book is the result of that decision.

While I alone am responsible for the conclusions rendered in this material, I would like to thank and acknowledge those who were especially helpful to me in the completion of the work. I began writing this book while a member of the faculty at the University of Wyoming and finished the manuscript at the University of Illinois at Urbana-Champaign, where I hold a joint appointment in the Department of Sociology and the School of Basic Medical Sciences.

At Wyoming, I would like to express my thanks to Marshall Jones, Professor Emeritus of Sociology, who made many helpful comments on some of the early chapters. I would also like to thank students Catherine Frazee and Betty Wells for their assistance in conducting literature reviews and securing citations.

There are several people at the University of Illinois to whom I am greatly indebted; I would like to particularly acknowledge the assistance of three individuals. Norman Denzin, Professor of Sociology, read several chapters and provided advice throughout the writing of this book. As a person whom I regard as a first-rate sociologist and friend, Professor Denzin has been a continual source of sound sociological insight, and I appreciate his counsel, both on this book and on other work. Morton Creditor, Associate Dean of the School of Basic Medical Sciences, was extremely helpful in the synthesis of viewpoints requiring a medical as well as a sociological perspective. Dr. Creditor also read large portions of the manuscript and made several important suggestions for improvement. In addition, I would like to thank my colleague Jeffrey Salloway, Assistant Professor of Sociology and Basic Medical Sciences, who not only read several chapters, but also acted as a good "sounding-board" to test my ideas about the book.

Gerry Swift and the staff at the Word Processing Center of the School of Basic Medical Sciences provided prompt and professional service in the typing of the manuscript; their work was indispensable. Besides Ms. Swift, other staff members who worked on the manuscript were Carol Hay, Deborah Heavner, Cynthia Parker, Connie Parsley, Geri Nugent, Linda Sherry, Irva Good, and Joan Jividen. I would also like to thank Pat Talbot and Janice Young of the Dean's Office, School of Basic Medical Sciences, for their administrative help. In addition to all of the above, sociology graduate students Michael Roach, Nina Stuart, and Patricia Ulbricht provided important assistance in the library.

Finally, I would like to acknowledge the services of Prentice-Hall, Inc. Edward Stanford, Social Science Executive Editor, provided extremely helpful advice over a period of many months, while Serena Hoffman, Production Editor, and Jean Thumm did an excellent job of copyediting. I would like to thank, too, those sociologists who reviewed the manuscript for Prentice-Hall—Professor of Sociology Neil Smelser of the University of California at Berkeley, Professor of Sociology Spencer Condie of Brigham Young University, and several anonymous readers.

My wife, Cynthia, was helpful in editing the manuscript, and I would like to thank her and the rest of my family—particularly my mother, Louise Mail; my father and step-mother, Carl and Jewel Cockerham; and my cousin, Sarah Bottoms—for their support in this and other projects.

WILLIAM COCKERHAM
Champaign, Illinois

PART I

HEALTH
AND SOCIETY

1

MEDICAL SOCIOLOGY

The relationship between social conditions and factors that influence health and the development of disease has long been a major interest of humankind. Throughout history people have generally tended to view health problems from the perspective of their own particular societies and cultures. As a result, they have usually responded to the threat of disease in predictable ways. Knowledge about norms, values, beliefs, social structures, and life styles has provided insight not only about the social organization of human resources designed to cope with health hazards, but also about the nature and causes of illness. The recognition, therefore, of the significance of the complex relationship between social factors and the level of health characteristic of specific social groups has led to the development of medical sociology as an important substantive area within the general field of sociology. As an academic discipline, sociology is concerned with the function, structure, and roles of social institutions and social processes, and with the social behavior of persons and groups. Thus it follows that medical sociology is concerned with the social facets of health and illness, the social functions of health institutions and organizations, the relationship of systems of health care delivery to other social systems, and the social behavior of health personnel and those people who are consumers of health care.

Robert Straus (1957) has made a significant observation about medical sociology that helps to explain its current orientation. Straus suggested that medical sociology was divided into two separate but closely interrelated areas: sociology *in* medicine and sociology *of* medicine.

The sociologist in medicine is a sociologist who collaborates directly with the physician and other health personnel in studying the social factors that are relevant to a particular health disorder. The work of the sociologist in medicine is intended to be directly applicable to patient care or to the solving of a public health problem. Some of the tasks of the sociologist in medicine are to analyze the etiology or causes of health disorders, the differences in social attitudes as they relate to health, and the way in which the incidence and prevalence of a specific health disorder is related to such social variables as age, sex, socioeconomic status, racial/ethnic group identity, education, and occupation. Such an analysis is then intended to be made available to health practitioners to assist them in treating health problems. Thus, sociology in medicine can be characterized as *applied research and analysis primarily motivated by a medical problem* rather than a sociological problem. Sociologists in medicine usually work in medical schools, nursing schools, public health schools, teaching hospitals, public health agencies, and other health organizations. They may also work for a governmental agency like the U.S. Department of Health, Education, and Welfare in the capacity of biostatisticians, health planners, administrators, and advisors.

The sociology *of* medicine, on the other hand, has a different emphasis. It deals with such factors as the organization, role relationships, norms, values, and beliefs of medical practice as a form of human behavior. The emphasis is upon the social processes that occur in the medical setting and how these contribute to our understanding of medical sociology in particular and to our understanding of social life in general. With few exceptions, there are no unique or special theories that pertain exclusively to the sociology of medicine; instead, the sociology of medicine shares the same goals as all other areas of sociology and may consequently be characterized as *research and analysis of the medical environment from a sociological perspective.* Although some sociologists of medicine are employed in health institutions, the majority work as professors in the sociology departments of universities and colleges.

THE EMERGING RELATIONSHIP
BETWEEN MEDICINE AND SOCIOLOGY

Good health is a prerequisite for the adequate functioning of any individual or society. If our health is sound we can engage in numerous types of activities. But if we are ill or injured, we may face the curtailment of our usual round of daily life and we may also become so preoccupied with our state of health that other pursuits are of secondary importance or quite meaningless. Obviously, nobody likes to feel unequal to his or her daily schedule. This natural concern with the healthy functioning of our bodies has probably been with us throughout our existence on this planet. René DuBos has suggested in *Man, Medicine, and Environment* (1969) that primitive human beings were closer to the animals in that they, too, relied upon their instincts to stay healthy. Yet some primitive humans recognized a cause and effect relationship between doing certain things and alleviating symptoms of a disease or improving the condition of a wound.

Since there was so much that primitive humans did not understand about the functioning of the body, *magic* became an integral component of the beliefs about the causes and cures of health disorders. Actually, an uncritical acceptance of magic and the supernatural pervaded practically every aspect of primitive life. So it is not surprising that early humans thought that illness was caused by evil spirits. Primitive medicines made from vegetables or animals were invariably used in combination with some form of ritual to expel the harmful spirit from a diseased body. During the Neolithic age, some 4,000 to 5,000 years ago, people living in what is today the Eastern Mediterranean and North Africa are known to have even engaged in a surgical procedure called *trepanation* or trephining, which consists of a hole being bored in the skull in order to liberate the evil spirit supposedly contained in a person's head. The finding by anthropologists of more than one hole in some skulls and the lack of signs of osteomyelitis (erosion of bone tissue) suggests that the operation was not always fatal. Some estimates indicate that the mortality rate from trepanation was as low as ten percent, an amazing accomplishment considering the difficulty of the procedure and the crude conditions under which it must have been performed (Mora, 1975).

Therefore, as DuBos explains, medicine has had a dual nature from its very inception in that it included knowledge about definite medical procedures and a belief in some magic or religious power involving forces beyond human comprehension. This dual nature of medicine is still with us today, as a patient's family and friends will attempt to supplement the modern physician's skill and experience with prayer. The prevailing structure of medical science, regardless of a society's level of medical knowledge and technology, still functions within the context of the values, attitudes, and beliefs of the people who comprise that society.

Hippocrates

One of the earliest attempts in the Western world to formulate principles of health care based upon rational thought and the rejection of supernatural phenomena is found in the work of the Greek physician Hippocrates. Little is known of Hippocrates the man, who lived around

400 B.C., not even whether he actually authored the collection of books that bears his name. Nevertheless, the writings attributed to him have provided a number of principles underlying modern medical practice. One of his most famous contributions, the Hippocratic Oath, is the foundation of contemporary medical morality and ethics. Among other things, it requires the physician to swear that he or she will help the sick, refrain from intentional wrongdoing or harm, and keep confidential all matters pertaining to the doctor–patient relationship.

Hippocrates also argued that medical knowledge should be derived from an understanding of the natural sciences and the logic of cause and effect relationships. In his classic treatise, *On Airs, Waters, and Places,* Hippocrates pointed out that human well-being is influenced by the totality of environmental factors: living habits or life style, climate, topography of the land, and the quality of air, water, and food. Interestingly enough, concerns about our health and the quality of airs, waters, and places are still very much with us in the twentieth century.

Another influential Hippocratic work was *The Book of Prognostics,* in which the author set forth his theory of medicine. Hippocrates believed that good health resulted from the equilibrium within the body of four humors (blood, phlegm, black bile, and yellow bile) and the harmony of the body itself with living habits and the environment. As long as the four humors were in balance, the body was healthy. If an imbalance occurred, that is, if there was more of one type of humor than another, a person was sick. Although wrong, Hippocrates' humoral theory of disease has persisted even to this day as a basic belief in the folk medicine of many cultures. For example, the practice of traditional folk medicine among Mexican-Americans in the twentieth-century United States is clearly based upon Hippocrates' notions of equilibrium and involves, among other remedies, the use of hot foods for a chill and cold foods for a fever. But what is more relevant for modern medicine is the Hippocratic demand for a *rational and systematic approach to patient care.* This approach, to be based upon thorough observation of the patient's symptoms and a logical plan of treatment according to proven procedures, remains central to contemporary medical practice.

Besides his other contributions, Hippocrates maintained that both the mind and the body profoundly affect each other and cannot be considered as independent entities. Health consisted of a healthy mind in a healthy body. Thus, a basic precept of the Hippocratic orientation was the recognition that the social environment was an important factor in understanding illness. In the treatment of patients, it was necessary to consider the "whole" person under the Hippocratic system.

Paracelsus

In their intellectual orientation toward disease, the ancient Greeks displayed a frame of reference that was more similar to contemporary medicine than to the subsequent practices of the Middle Ages and the Renaissance. Much of the medical knowledge of the ancient world was lost during the Dark Ages after the fall of Rome and what knowledge remained was preserved by the Roman Catholic Church. It was the position of the Church that it, not medicine, was responsible for the study of the mind and the treatment of social problems. A few physicians, such as Paracelsus, a famous Swiss doctor who lived in the early sixteenth century, did continue to show concern with health and social conditions. Paracelsus demonstrated that diseases common to certain occupations (such as mining) were related to the work environment. He also argued that mentally ill persons were neither criminals nor sinners but sick persons in need of medical assistance. However, the Middle Ages and the Renaissance saw few systematic measures undertaken to explain the relationship between the mind and the body and the effect of adverse social conditions upon health.

Descartes

The lack of understanding of social and psychological factors in illness continued during the seventeenth century. The French philosopher René Descartes, considered the most outstanding representative of seventeenth-century rationalism, helped to shape the direction of philosophical thought for nearly three centuries, profoundly influencing the direction of both psychology and medicine (DuBos, 1969; Mora, 1975). Descartes laid the basis for a philosophical orientation consisting of mathematical axioms and correlates that failed to take human emotions into account. He also reinforced the mind–body dichotomy by insisting that each was an entirely different type of entity. The mind, identified by Descartes as being in the pineal gland, was supposedly an expression of God, too mysterious to be approached as the object of scientific study. By contrast, Descartes defined the body as a physical machine whose operation was within the scope of human knowledge and therefore could be studied. The implication of Descartes' work for medicine was that physicians should not attempt to understand the person as a whole, but should concentrate exclusively upon the physical functioning of the body. DuBos states:

> Descartes' philosophy led scientists to neglect questions pertaining to the nature of the mind and the soul and encouraged them to

focus their efforts on the much simpler, more concrete, problems of body structure and operation. They could apply knowledge of physics and chemistry, derived from the study of inanimate matter, to the problems of the body without fear of debasing the more lofty manifestations of man's nature, those of his soul. The self-imposed limitations and intellectual freedom that biologists derived from Cartesian dualism gave them a general tendency to study man as a nonthinking, nonfeeling entity.[1]

The approach of Descartes and his followers was in keeping with the Christian notion of the human body as a weak and imperfect vessel intended to transfer the soul from this world to the next (Engel, 1977; Rasmussen, 1975). As long as there was a tacit understanding that the investigation of the mind was a religious matter, the Church did not object to the scientific study of the body. The result was that both Western religion and science sponsored the idea "of the body as a machine, of disease as a breakdown of the machine, and of the doctor's task as repair of the machine" (Engel, 1977:131).

Progress in Public Health

Although many of Descartes' theories were discarded in the twentieth century, they nonetheless provided a philosophical framework for the emphasis two centuries of scientists placed upon understanding the physical and chemical processes of the human body. The mind–body relationship was not a fruitful topic of scientific investigation well into the nineteenth century, but occasional observations continued to link social and cultural factors to the general state of health of a patricular community. An awareness of the social etiology of disease dawned through common sense and practical experience. A most significant development occurred in the field of public health when it was accepted that uncontaminated food, water, and air, as well as sanitary living conditions, could reduce the onset and spread of communicable diseases. Prior to the advent of modern medicine, the high mortality rates from communicable diseases such as typhus, tuberculosis, scarlet fever, measles, and cholera were significantly lowered in both Europe and North America. Thus the late eighteenth and early nineteenth centuries are conspicuous for the implementation of improved public hygiene and sanitation.

Noting the link between life style and health, some nineteenth-century European physicians argued that improvement was necessary in the living conditions of the poor. They advocated governmental recognition of the social as well as medical nature of measures undertaken to

[1] René DuBos, *Man, Medicine, and Environment* (New York: Mentor, 1969), p. 77.

promote health. Rudolf Virchow, for instance, a prominent physician known in clinical medicine for the development of cellular pathology, insisted that medicine was a social science. Virchow, a German, argued strongly that the poor should have not only quality medical care, but also that they should have free choice of a physician. Improved medical care was also to go hand in hand with changed social conditions leading to a better life (Rosen, 1972). However, these proposals had little effect outside Virchow's small circle of colleagues.

The Germ Theory of Disease

Most members of the medical profession in the 1800s were primarily interested in improving the state of medical technology. They were not necessarily concerned with social reform. The success during this century of Louis Pasteur, Robert Koch, and others in bacteriological research that led to the conceptualization of the germ theory of disease, along with tremendous progress in the development of internal medicine, anesthesiology, pathology, immunology, and surgical techniques, convinced physicians to focus exclusively upon a clinical medicine grounded in exact scientific laboratory procedures. The practice of medicine in the twentieth century thus rested solidly upon the premise that every disease had a specific pathogenic cause whose treatment could best be accomplished by removing or controlling that cause within a biomedical framework. DuBos (1969) has pointed out that modern medicine's thinking has been dominated by the search for drugs as "magic bullets" that can be shot into the body to kill or control all health disorders. Because research in microbiology, biochemistry, and related fields has resulted in the discovery and production of a large variety of drugs and drug-based techniques for treating many diseases, this approach has been generally successful.

Return to the "Whole Person"

As medicine moves into the twenty-first century, it is increasingly called upon to return to the health problems of the whole person, which extend well beyond singular causes of disease. Contemporary physicians are often required to deal with health disorders more aptly described as "problems in living," dysfunctions that involve multiple factors of causation, not all of them biological in nature. The evidence is now quite striking that the manner in which people respond to social, psychological, and cultural influences has much to do not only with whether they become sick, but also with the form, duration, and intensity of their symptoms and disabilities. Thus it has become clear that modern medicine must develop insight into the behaviors characteristic of the people it treats.

To illustrate this point, consider that the major health disorders in urban-industrial countries are no longer a result of communicable diseases, but instead are the problems of chronic or long-term illnesses such as heart disease and cancer. Because chronic disorder can be influenced by many causes, health personnel should consider all aspects (social, psychological, and physiological) of a chronic condition.

Also, it is not uncommon for an individual suffering from a chronic disease to feel perfectly normal, even when irreversible damage to organs and tissues has already occurred. Because of the irremediable damage done to the body by a chronic disease, patients may be required to permanently change their style of living and modify their social relationships. So, as Anselm Strauss (1975) has pointed out, health practitioners should know how patients with chronic disorders:

1. manage medical crises
2. control their symptoms
3. carry out their prescribed regimens
4. adjust to changes in the course of the disorder
5. attempt to normalize their interaction with others
6. cope with the social isolation caused by reduced contact with others, and
7. seek the necessary money to pay for their treatment and possibly to support themselves and their dependents.

This is in addition to all else that physicians need to know about the behavior and life styles of individuals that influences whether or not they are likely to develop chronic disorders in the first place.

And as Strauss has also observed, many physicians and allied health personnel are not well trained in the behavioral sciences, nor do they know very much about the personal lives of their patients and their families. While they fully recognize that chronic disease is the most prevalent health problem in the United States, they continue to deal with it in the same way they formerly dealt with communicable diseases—by focusing on a particular category (heart, cancer, neurological disorder) of chronic illness rather than on chronic illness in general or on the patient. A probable explanation for the persistence of this type of approach may be the way in which physicians have been selected and trained. Kerr White (1972) explains that, in the past, medical schools selected students who were motivated primarily by curiosity about disease, instead of students motivated by humanistic concern for people. Although both types of physicians are needed, the emphasis upon the former has tended to exclude the latter. Additionally, the experience of medical school itself appears to encourage medical students to take a detached view of their patients and become less idealistic (see Chapter Six). In a recent study of the manner in which medical students and physicians learn to cope with their personal emotions about death and dying, Robert Coombs and Pauline Powers (1975:258) found that physicians would intellectually dissect their patient into physical parts and concentrate upon treating only the pathological part. According to one of the more experienced physicians in their study, this was known as the "old scientific fragmentalization method," which allowed the doctor to deal only with the parts and not with the whole. Murray Wexler has aptly described this situation:

> In essence, this concept is characterized by a form of communication in which the patient is identified by the disease rather than by his human qualities. This attitude is characterized (perhaps caricatured) in a play about physicians, produced in the 1930's, in which one intern reminds his associate, "You'll have to check the gallbladder in 321."[2]

Objectivity in treating a disease may not necessarily be a bad thing. But some critics of medical education contend that medical schools are merely "trade" schools that train doctors to be little more than "technicians" or "mechanics" who work on the human body.

Medicine and Sociology

As Howard Rasmussen (1975) has made clear, medicine is now faced with two distinct alternatives. It can either redefine disease and restrict its treatment to specifically medical conditions, or it can accept a broad concept of disease (which includes problems in living) and change medical education programs to deal effectively with the wider spectrum of illness. This latter alternative forecasts a close association between medicine and the behavioral sciences of sociology, anthropology, and psychology, the beginnings of which are already in evidence. In 1969 a study originated within the American Sociological Association that reviewed behavioral science programs in nine major medical schools and found that such programs were well accepted.[3] Wexler characterized the findings of this study by noting that:

[2] Murray Wexler, "The Behavioral Sciences in Medical Education," *American Psychologist*, 3 (April 1976), 276.

[3] The nine medical schools included in the study were the University of Connecticut, Duke University, Harvard University, the University of Kentucky, Michigan State University, the University of Missouri, the Pennsylvania State University Hershey Medical Center, Stanford University, and the University of Toronto. For the full report, see C. R. Fletcher et al., *A Study for Teaching Behavioral Sciences in Schools of Medicine*, 3 vols. (Rockville, Md.: National Center for Health Services Research and Development, 1972).

The case studies are impressive documents. They describe in detail the enormous amount of effort that has been expended in trying to effect a major change in medical education and thinking. It would be necessary to have been a participant in medical education prior to 1960 to appreciate how drastically the scene has changed for the behavioral sciences. Anthropologists, psychologists, and sociologists are increasingly familiar figures in the lecture halls and seminar rooms, on ward walks, at grand rounds, on admissions committees, etc.[4]

As for sociologists, many hold joint teaching and research appointments between departments of sociology and health institutions, or are employed full-time in these institutions. Medical, nursing, pharmacy, and public health schools are all expanding the number of faculty positions for sociologists and adding courses in the behavioral sciences at a significant rate. The growing interest of medicine in human behavior is also reflected in the much larger proportion of questions dealing with the behavioral sciences on national board examinations taken by medical students. In addition to courses in the behavioral sciences, sociologists lecture on medical sociology, social psychiatry, epidemiology, preventive medicine, community medicine, public health, and the social aspects of pharmacy. They also participate in studies of the utilization and evaluation of health services and the development of health policies on local, state, and national levels.

Some premedical students who major in sociology are now being admitted to medical schools (compared to practically none in the 1950s).[5] And one physician, George Reader, has argued that medical schools should require a background in sociology of all students who apply for admission on the grounds that sociological principles are basic to understanding how to be a better medical student and a better practicing physician. According to Reader:

Interviewing patients can be made more of a science and less an art; obstacles to compliance with a therapeutic regime can be more easily recognized; quality of care can be measured more accurately; effects of health legislation can be made more predictable; and epidemiology gains new dimensions.[6]

4 Wexler, "The Behavioral Sciences," p. 279.

5 Of the 274 persons with undergraduate majors in sociology who applied for admission to U.S. medical schools for the 1974–1975 year, 85, or 31 percent, of the total were accepted. See *Medical School Admissions Requirements, 1977–78,* 27th ed. (Washington, D.C.: Association of American Medical Colleges, 1976), p. 5.

6 George G. Reader, "Should Medical Schools Require a Sociology Background?" *AAMC Education News,* 4 (December 1976): 3,8.

This is not to say, however, that the growing acceptance of the behavioral sciences in medicine is proceeding without any serious problems. Not all medical educators and physicians agree about the importance of the behavioral sciences in the medical school curriculum, and the behavioral scientists themselves have yet to identify those aspects of their subject matter best suited for solving practical medical problems (Wexler, 1976:283). Nevertheless, the indication is that inclusion of the behavioral sciences in medical education is here and will continue for some time.

Sociology and Medicine

While the development of modern medicine emphasized the biological and neglected the behavioral sciences (with the exception of medically oriented psychiatry), the development of sociology, in turn, originally spurned the influence of biological elements upon human social behavior. For that matter, a case can be made that modern sociology developed largely in opposition to biological theories that explained differences in human behavior on the basis of innate biological characteristics. One of the most significant factors in the thought of the French sociologist Emile Durkheim (1858–1917), whose theories have dominated a large portion of sociology's approach to human behavior, was his strong rejection of biology (see Nisbet, 1974). Neither in the gene pool of a particular race nor in the genetic composition of an individual did Durkheim find relevant evidence for sociology. Although recognizing that biological explanations of human behavior contribute to our understanding of human interaction, Durkheim argued that they can never be *totally* sufficient explanations. Instead, the basis for sound explanations of social behavior were to be found in the *social processes of culture, environment, and human thought.* Thus social behavior must be explained from the standpoint of such social elements as norms, values, and statuses that comprise the basis of human group life. The persuasiveness of Durkheim's argument and its support by other sociologists led to the nearly total disregard of biology by social theorists. Only within the past few years have the contributions of biology once again been given serious sociological consideration; today the field of social biology represents a promising but still highly underdeveloped area of study.

What prompted sociologists to organize medical sociology as an area of sociological inquiry in its own right was neither medicine nor biology, but the realization that medical practice represented a distinct segment of society with its own unique social institutions, social processes, occupations, problems, and behavioral settings. The development of the sociology of medicine was greatly influenced by the expansion of the

National Institutes of Health in the United States during the late 1940s, especially the establishment of the National Institute of Mental Health, which provided the funding and encouraged the interaction of researchers from both the social and the medical sciences. According to August Hollingshead (1973), one of the early participants, a major result of this interaction was the stimulus to both social and medical scientists to formulate and implement joint projects. Thereafter, the growth of medical sociology proceeded at such a rate that since 1960 it has become one of the largest and most active sections of the American Sociological Association. The position of medical sociology was further strengthened in 1966 when the *Journal of Health and Social Behavior* became an official American Sociological Association publication (for a history of medical sociology see Freeman et al., 1972; Hollingshead, 1973).

The preceding discussion has briefly outlined the convergence of medicine and sociology in contemporary American society. John McKinlay (1971) has ventured to suggest that the time may come when the research contributions of medical sociology will stand in the same relation to medicine as do those of physiology, endocrinology, and biology as a body of knowledge explaining human functioning in the medical sphere. It is too early to surmise whether or not McKinlay's prediction will prove true, because medical sociology is a relatively new field and a considerable amount of research still needs to be compiled and precisely formulated. However, the work to date has been most impressive and promises even more exciting contributions in the future. John Knowles (1972) is correct when he states that medicine is a social science as well as a biological science and that it needs the social sciences as never before.

PLAN OF THIS BOOK

The intent of this book is to provide an overview of the general field of medical sociology from the standpoint of both the sociologist of medicine and the sociologist in medicine. A survey of medical sociology is long overdue because many changes have taken place during the 1970s that are not covered in existing textbooks. Then, too, many social factors in health care that medical sociologists and others have long taken for granted are no longer accurate. For instance, it can not be assumed that the poor in American society underutilize physician services, nor that the race differential in life expectancy between whites and blacks in American society is more significant than sexual patterns of longevity.

As late as 1970, Eliot Freidson (1970b) was noting that sociologists have been reluctant to criticize the medical profession because they agreed that medicine represents a positive value in society intended to eliminate human suffering. (This is known as medicine's "halo effect.") Yet there have recently been a number of sociological criticisms of both physicians and medical organizations and a growing awareness not only among sociologists, but also among the general public, that medical science has not delivered the quality of health care throughout American society of which it is capable.

Furthermore, the interests of a majority of medical sociologists have begun to shift away from studies of medical students, nurses, and ethnic differences in attitudes toward health care, toward understanding the changing role of the health practitioner and the sick person as a consumer of health care services. Medical sociologists are expanding the scope of their interests to include the assessment of the quality of health care delivery systems and the need for national health insurance, plus an understanding of the social psychology of help-seeking behavior, aging, and death and dying. These and other issues will be examined in this book.

Accordingly, the material in this text has been organized into four major parts dealing with the following general topics: (1) Health and Society, (2) Health Practitioners, (3) Health Institutions, and (4) Health and Social Problems.

Part I (Health and Society) is concerned with the relationship between social factors, illness, and the behavior of persons who define themselves as being sick and in need of medical attention. Chapter Two (Social Epidemiology) discusses the role of the epidemiologist and the social variables of age, sex, race, and socioeconomic status upon the overall health profile of persons living in the United States. Broadly speaking, the epidemiologist's function is to explore the relationship between the environment and groups of people. Chapter Three (Mind, Body, and Society) is concerned primarily with the concept of stress and how social influences contribute to the development of stress-induced physical and mental disorders. Chapter Four examines the various theories and concepts that have been advanced to explain whether or not certain people will seek out a physician for assistance, utilize the other services of a health care delivery system, or treat their health problem without professional assistance. Chapter Five discusses Talcott Parsons' concept of the sick role, which has become a central theory in medical sociology. The sick role represents a temporary exemption from normal social functioning that is granted to certain individuals upon the condition that they seek professional care in order to get well. This theory has been a source of considerable controversy in medical sociology and this chapter will assess its validity.

Part II (Health Practitioners) looks at research findings in medical sociology pertaining to physicians, nurses, and other health personnel. Chapter Six deals with the physician's traditional role of professional dominance in the health occupations and the manner in which this dominant position is being challenged by laypersons who are changing their status from that of "patient" to that of health care "consumer"— with all that implies in terms of a different type of social relationship. Chapter Seven on nurses and the emerging paramedical practitioners likewise examines the changing nature of occupational roles in medicine and the reverberations of these new concepts both, within and outside the profession.

In Part III (Health Institutions), Chapter Eight explores the social development and structure of the hospital as a formal institution. This discussion includes an examination of the dual nature of its authority system and the effect of the organization of its services upon the interaction between patients and staff. Chapter Nine considers health care delivery systems and their interface with social policy.

Part IV (Health and Social Problems), will examine selected social problems as they relate to health care. Chapter Ten explores changing concepts in mental health and social factors that have been found to be important indicators of mental disorders. Chapter Eleven discusses the social psychology of aging and the role of the aged in contemporary society. Chapter Twelve examines the fears and anxieties people express in regard to their own personal mortality and the manner in which they cope with the inevitability of their deaths. Evidence will also be discussed that suggests that the attitudes toward death and dying may be changing in American society.

SUMMARY

Throughout history human beings have been interested in and, in fact, deeply concerned with the effects of the social environment upon the health of individuals and the groups to which they belong. Despite a promising beginning in ancient Greece, medicine developed in such a way that it ignored sociology. Much later, the formal beginnings of sociology dictated an opposition to biological and medical contributions. Yet sociology's interest in medicine as a unique system of human social behavior, and medicine's recognition that sociology can help health practitioners to better understand their patients and provide improved forms of health care, has begun to bring about a convergence of mutual interest between the two disciplines. More and more medical sociologists are being invited to join the staffs of medical institutions and to participate in medical research projects. Medical sociology courses and degrees are now more frequently offered by universities and colleges. The extensive growth of sociological literature in academic medicine is further evidence of the rising status of the medical sociologist. Although a considerable amount of work remains to be done, the medical sociologist at this time is in the enviable position of participating in, and influencing the development of, an exciting, significant, and relatively new field.

2

SOCIAL EPIDEMIOLOGY

Many sociologists working in the field of medicine are epidemiologists. In its strictest sense, epidemiology is the science of epidemics; however, present day epidemiologists have broadened their field to include not only epidemic diseases, but also all other forms of disease and bodily injury such as cancer, heart disease, alcoholism, drug addiction, suicide, and automobile accidents. Epidemiology can thus be defined as "measurements of the circumstances where diseases occur, where diseases tend to flourish, and where they do not" (Paul, 1966:4). The epidemiologist or sociologist as epidemiologist is, therefore, concerned with exploring human ecology as it relates to the health of human beings and their environment.

The primary focus of the epidemiologist is not on the individual, but on *the health problems of social aggregates or large groups of people.* The epidemiologist studies both the origin and the distribution of health problems in a population through the collection of data from many different sources. He or she then constructs a logical chain of inferences to explain the various factors in a society or segment of a society that cause a particular health problem to exist. Epidemiology is one of the most important investigative techniques in the study of health and disease.

The role of the epidemiologist can probably be best likened to that of a detective investigating the scene of a crime for clues. The epidemiologist usually begins by examining the sick person or persons and then extends the investigation to the setting where the patient (s) first became ill and is likely to become ill again. What the epidemiologist is looking for is the common denominator that links all the victims of a health problem together so that the cause of the problem can be identified and eliminated or controlled.

THE DEVELOPMENT OF SOCIAL EPIDEMIOLOGY

As a method of measuring diseases in human aggregates, epidemiology has been a relatively recent development. So long as human beings lived as nomads or in widely scattered and isolated communities, the danger from epidemics and infectious disease was relatively slight. However, once people began to crowd into primitive cities with unsanitary living conditions and an abundance of rats and lice, the probabilities favoring the development of communicable diseases greatly increased. The crowded conditions of urban living also insured that infectious diseases would spread more quickly and that disease-causing microorganisms would persist within the community for longer periods of time. In additon, the migration of peoples from one region of the world to another spread disease from geographic area to geographic area. Bubonic plague, for example, apparently reached Europe from China during the fourteenth century, cholera entered Great Britain by way of India in the seventeenth century, while Europeans brought smallpox to the Western Hemisphere during the exploration and settlement of the New World. History reveals numerous examples of explorers and travelers introducing the microorganisms of a dreaded disease to a community of unsuspecting people.

The bubonic plague which ravaged Europe between 1340 and 1750 marks one of the worst epidemic afflictions in all human history. It is estimated that one-quarter of the population of Europe died during its greatest prevalence (Paul, 1966). During one single month (September, 1665) in one city (London), approximately 30,000 people died from the plague. The cause of the plague was thought by many to be God's wrath upon sinners; however, the realization eventually came that diseases could be transmitted from person to person or between animals and people. The origin of the plague turned out to be the flea of the black rat, but the pneumonic plague, the most deadly form of the bubonic plague, was transmitted from person to person. What actually ended the plague about 1750 was the appearance in cities of the aggressive brown rat. The brown rat tended to avoid humans, had fleas that were less effective carriers, and drove most of Europe's black rats out of urban areas. Another very important factor was the development of improved housing and sanitation.

One of the earliest epidemiological studies was conducted by Sir Percival Pott in England in 1775 (Graham, 1972). Pott observed that English chimney sweeps seemed to have a high incidence of cancer of the scrotum. He reasoned that the chimney sweep's occupation, which placed him in close and frequent contact with soot, might be the cause of cancer of the scrotum among those individuals who were susceptible to the disease. Pott suggested a relationship between a behavior (chimney sweeping) and a disease of a specific organ (cancer of the scrotum). He demonstrated that if behavior were changed by increased bathing, the incidence of the disease could be reduced. Pott's work showed that social activities can significantly affect susceptibility to a particular disease.

However, epidemiology as a form of systematic analysis did not develop until the nineteenth century. It was not until 1854 that the work of John Snow established the foundation of modern epidemiology. Snow was an English physician who plotted the geographic location of all reported cholera cases in London. He then went out into the neighborhoods of these victims and inquired into their day-to-day behavior. He wanted to know what they ate, what they drank, where they went, and the nature of all their activities. Eventually Snow began to suspect that cholera was transmitted by water, since the common factor in the daily lives of the victims was getting their water from the Broad Street pump. At that time, London obtained drinking water from several water companies, and a few of these companies apparently were providing water contaminated with cholera bacteria. By closing down the pump on Broad Street, Snow was able to stop the epidemic. He not only established a mode of investigation, but also demonstrated that research could lead to positive action.

At the time of Snow's research, the development of scientific medicine was well underway. The work of Pasteur and his immediate followers during the latter part of the nineteenth century revolutionized medical thought with the germ theory of disease, stipulating that bacteria were the source of infection in the human body. The findings of Snow, Pasteur, and others provided the epidemiologist with a framework of analysis. Recognition that germs were causal agents of disease served as a precursor to scientific determination that causal agents included: (1) biological agents, such as bacteria, viruses, or insects; (2) nutritional agents, such as fats and carbohydrates as producers of cholesterol; (3) chemical agents, such as dust, gases, or particles in the air; (4) physical agents, such as climate or vegetation, and (5) social agents, such as occupation, social class, or location of residence. What a person does, who a person is, and where a person lives can specify what health hazards are most likely to exist in that individual's life. The epidemiologist then identifies a particular host (person or group of persons or animals) most susceptible to these causal agents. The human host is also defined in terms of age, sex, life style, and general physical condition. Next, the physical and social environment of the causal agent and the host is explored. The end result is intended to be an identification of *what* is causing a group of people to become sick or suffer injury.

When we use the term *social environment* in epidemiological research, we are referring to actual living conditions, such as poverty or crowding, and the norms, values, and attitudes that reflect a particular social and cultural context. Societies have socially prescribed patterns of living arrangements, as well as standards pertaining to the use of water, food and food handling, and household and personal hygiene. Therefore, the social environment provides information that can be used not only to identify causal agents and to trace the transmission process, but also to assist in ascertaining the most effective means of treatment and prevention within that particular environment.

For example, in 1944 a well-known epidemiological study took place on Manhattan's skid row, an environment of poverty and alcoholism (Roueché, 1967). Known as the case of the "Eleven Blue Men," it involved eleven alcoholics who were admitted to a hospital with the skin of their extremities turning a blue color. At first the hospital physicians and local health authorities surmised that carbon monoxide poisoning had caused the skin condition, but the men lacked other symptoms of gas poisoning. By interviewing the patients, it was discovered that each of the victims had eaten breakfast in the same cafe on the same day. It was also noted that all had eaten oatmeal for breakfast. A further discovery that the cook had used sodium nitrite, a mild poison, in the oatmeal instead of salt suggested food poisoning. Yet numerous people had eaten the poisoned oatmeal and only eleven had been affected, so an important question was left unanswered. The case was finally solved when an epidemiologist remembered that sometimes alcoholics use salt instead of sugar on oatmeal because of a salt deficiency in their blood. The amount of sodium nitrite in the oatmeal had not been enough to poison anyone, but a busboy or someone who had the job of filling the salt shakers had made the same mistake the cook had, and put sodium nitrite in the shakers. It was this double dosage of sodium nitrite that produced the strong toxic effect. Knowledge concerning the behavior of alcoholics had provided the most significant clue in solving the case and providing the hospital doctors with the information they needed to help the men.

COMPLEX SOCIETIES

Not all health disorders in today's urban and industrialized societies lend themselves to such direct cause and effect relationships as the case of the "Eleven Blue Men." Many contemporary epidemiological problems are extremely complex, as the major health threat to contemporary society is from a variety of chronic and degenerative ills related to aging and the effects of man-made environments.

An illustration of the role of multi-causality in modern social epidemiology is the Framingham, Massachusetts research project (Dawber et al., 1963). Begun during the 1950s, this study has shown in preliminary data that arteriosclerosis does not strike people at random as they age, but that highly susceptible individuals can be identified in advance. Some 5,000 persons were selected, mostly at random, to participate in the study. They were all between the ages of thirty and sixty and were free from any form of heart disease at the time of their initial examination. They were given relatively complete physical examinations every two years for a twenty-year period. Although the final report has not been released, the direction of the data clearly suggests that male sex, advancing age, high blood pressure, cigarette smoking, diabetes, and obesity constitute significant risk factors in whether or not a person develops heart disease.

Although heart disease joins cancer, stroke, accidents, and mental disorders as the leading causes of disability and death in advanced industrial societies, the underdeveloped nations of the world show different patterns of major health problems. In these societies, the traditional diseases of human history, influenced by poor sanitation and malnutrition, still prevail. Underdeveloped nations usually are characterized by a high birth rate and a high death rate and a relatively young population because infectious diseases do not allow large numbers of people to live long enough to develop chronic disorders. A major distinction, therefore, in how diseases are distributed among population groups becomes apparent when the health profiles of industrialized societies are compared to those of underdeveloped nations. Although malnutrition may occur in the United States and heart disease may occur in rural India, these cases do not follow general societal patterns. Many epidemiologists insist that there is a regular sequence of health problems corresponding to each stage of a nation's change in social organization from a rural to an urban society and from an agricultural to an industrial producer. For example, the leading causes of death in the United States in 1900 were infant diarrhea, pneumonia, and tuberculosis. By 1977 these disorders had been replaced by heart disease, cancer, and accidents as the major causes of deaths in an increasingly urban and industrialized society.

The complexity of health disorders in modern nations has spurred the development of social epidemiology toward the concept that physical and psychological living systems are invariably linked together in a cause and effect relationship (Wilson, 1970). It appears that a psychological event, for example, a thwarted need for love or affection, may not only affect an individual's personality but also have biological consequences due to excessive stress and tension within the body. Then, too, causes and effects are not necessarily contained within a particular living system, but may branch out into all areas of life in which an individual is involved. The loss of a limb can affect a person's concept of self and social relations with other people, and, conversely, remorse attributable to a social event may "cause" insomnia or the secretion of excessive hydrochloric acid within the stomach.

A study by Thomas Holmes (1962) and his associates in Seattle, Washington, serves to illustrate the interplay between mind, body, and disease in epidemiological research. Like John Snow's study of cholera in London, Holmes' investigation involved the distribution of a particular disease in a large urban area. Holmes discovered a high concentration of tuberculosis among men living alone in the center of Seattle. A study of those individuals who were hospitalized suggest that the onset of tuberculosis was closely associated with alcoholism, divorce, and/or the experience of relatively stressful life events, such as loss of a job or separation from a loved one. Another significant factor was social isolation. Not only was tuberculosis prevalent among skid row residents, but also among blacks who lived in otherwise all-white neighborhoods. This research suggested that the activation of tuberculosis was highly dependent upon a variety of circumstances. Susceptibility to the disease apparently increased when individuals were removed from their normal environments and were exposed to the stress of isolation and a possible accompanying change for the worse in self-concept.

THE LEGIONNAIRES' DISEASE

The most widely publicized and baffling epidemiological case in recent years was the mysterious Legionnaires' disease, which appeared without warning in Pennsylvania in July 1976. The common denominator in this episode was that all of the victims had either attended a state American Legion convention held at the Bellevue-Stratford Hotel in Philadelphia, intermingled with the legionnaires during the convention, or were delegates to a Eucharistic Congress of the Roman Catholic Church held at the same hotel a few days later. Eventually some twenty-nine persons were to die and over 150 persons were hospitalized from the disease.

The American Legion Convention started out like most other such gatherings in the past: meetings, speeches, banquets, drinking, and making the rounds of nearby bars and night clubs. As the convention went on, some people began to feel ill, but most of those becoming sick did not experience the symptoms of headaches, muscle and chest pains, fever as high as 107, and pneumonia until after they returned to homes located throughout the state.

The first evidence of a possible epidemic came a week after the Legionnaires had returned home. It came from a physician who suspected the possibility of an outbreak of typhoid. One of his patients had come to him complaining of fever and a loss of weight. Fearing cancer, the physician ordered laboratory tests which suggested typhoid (many of the legionnaires had typhoid antibodies in their blood due to typhoid vaccinations). Upon hearing that he might have typhoid, the patient informed the physician that two other of his friends (also legionnaires who attended the convention) were in the same hospital (one of these men died a few hours later). Laboratory tests on these two men also produced results suggesting typhoid, and the physician notified a state public health center of his findings. Shortly thereafter, reports of persons showing similar symptoms were made from other communities in the state; some of these persons died.

As there was no information to link these people together, state health authorities had no idea that they were all legionnaires and had attended the state convention the week before. The realization that something terrible was happening occurred first to the legionnaires themselves when the news began to spread around the state about illnesses and untimely deaths among some of their fellows. One of the legionnaires became alarmed and began making telephone calls to various Legion posts to ascertain where else legionnaires were sick. By the Monday of the second week after the convention, enough information had been obtained that the Pennsylvania Department of Health issued a statewide alert on the mystery disease and its existence became prime news in the mass media. Teams of epidemiologists from the Federal Center for Disease Control in Atlanta, Georgia, and from the Pennsylvania Department of Health were rushed to various hospitals and towns where they interviewed the victims and their physicians, talked to family members, neighbors, and friends of the victims, and collected specimens for laboratory analysis. There was great relief when no new cases were reported, nor were there any secondary infections among persons having contact with the victims after they had returned home.

But there was no explanation of what had caused the disease. Several theories were advanced, but none of them provided the answer.

Initially, it was thought that swine flu or some other type of influenza virus was the culprit. Laboratory tests showed, however, that it was not a virus; nor was it salmonella, a typhoid-like organism transmitted by food or water, or psittacosis, a respiratory disease carried by birds. Other diseases known to be transmitted by monkeys and hamsters were ruled out as was food poisoning (because it is seldom linked with pneumonia). Some persons even suggested deliberate sabotage or germ warfare. At one point, epidemiologists focused on a fifty-foot water hose that connected the drinking water in the hotel with the cold water lines for air conditioning. A workman assigned to adjusting the air conditioners had come down with symptoms of the disease, and the possibility that chemically tainted water was responsible for spreading germs through the air was quickly investigated. This theory likewise failed, as did the possibility of nickel carbonyl gas poisoning, a substance used in the manufacture of plastics and synthetic rubber. The discovery of potentially fatal levels of nickel in tissue samples taken from some of the victims had suggested this lead.

When none of the theories was found to be adequate, the investigation was broadened to include further measures. Organs and other tissue specimens from the dead victims were subjected to extensive laboratory analysis and reanalysis. At the same time, questionnaires were administered to all persons known to have attended the convention who did not become ill. This was done in order to draw comparisons with those who were sick. The medical detectives sought to find the common link as they asked the legionnaires again and again what they ate, what they drank, where they went, what they did when they got there, what time they did it, and so forth.

For a time, it appeared that the answer might never be forthcoming. But finally in January 1977, about six months after the first reports of the disease, the cause was discovered. It took thousands of laboratory tests, several epidemiologists, and several dozen eggs to find out what happened. Two epidemiologists at the Federal Center for Disease Control, Dr. Charles Shepard and Joseph McDade, had quietly tested a theory that rickettsia, organisms of a class between viruses and bacteria had been involved. The first tests were negative, but the researchers continued looking. Finally they tried injecting lung tissue from one of the victims into guinea pigs, and it produced a fever that suggested bacterial infection. Known bacteria were dismissed when they failed to react to the antibodies found in blood samples of the victims. Thus it appeared that the researchers were on to some type of new organism. The guinea pigs were again injected with the lung tissue material and again became sick. The spleens from the sick animals were next ground up and injected into the yolk sacs of fertilized chicken eggs. The egg embryos died. The bacteria found in the eggs were larger than rickettsia but smaller than known bacteria. Tests were repeated yet, unlike bacteria, the new organisms were extremely difficult to grow under artificial conditions. Eventually enough of the organisms were grown, and they were found to react against the antibodies from samples of the victims' blood. This meant that the new organism was the one that the victims' bodies were trying to fight off. What the organism is, how it kills people, and the biological and social factors explaining how people catch the disease are still unknown as this book goes to press. Nevertheless, as work continues, the Legionnaires' disease investigation already stands as one of the most challenging epidemiological problems of our time.

EPIDEMIOLOGICAL MEASURES

There are several important analytic concepts that assist the epidemiologist in describing the health problems of human groups. Two of the most commonly employed concepts are those of *incidence* and *prevalence*. *Incidence* refers to the frequency with which a specific health disorder occurs within a given population during a stated period of time. In other words, incidence describes the rate of development of a disorder over time. The incidence of new cases of German measles during a particular week would be the proportion of persons within a population who are reported as having developed the illness during the week in question. *Prevalence*, in contrast, would be the total number of cases of a health disorder that exist at any given time. Prevalence might also be thought of as the accumulated incidence of new cases. To illustrate the difference between incidence and prevalence, consider that the incidence of swine flu in a community might be low because no new cases had developed. Yet a measure of the disease's prevalence could be a larger figure because it would represent all persons who are currently sick from the illness.

Regardless of the size of the group under investigation, the epidemiologist is concerned with the computing of ratios. This is done in order to develop an accurate description of a particular health disorder in relation to a particular population. The epidemiologist accomplishes this task by collecting data from various sources such as face-to-face interviews or reports rendered by various health practitioners, institutions, and agencies. Once the relevant data are gathered, the epidemiologist computes a ratio which demonstrates the incidence and/or prevalence of the health problem. The ratio is always expressed as the total number of cases of a disease compared to the total number of people within a population:

$$\frac{\text{cases}}{\text{population}}$$

The simplest ratio computed by the epidemiologist is called the *crude rate,* which is the number of persons (cases) who have the characteristics being measured during a specific unit of time. Typical types of crude rates are birth rates and mortality rates. For example, the crude *mortality* (death) *rate* for a particular year is computed by using the number of deaths in that year as the numerator and the total number of residents in a specific population as the denominator. The results are then multiplied by either 1,000, 10,000 or 100,000 depending on whether the mortality rate being figured is for the number of deaths per 1,000, per 10,000, or per 100,000 people. To illustrate how crude death rates are calculated, consider that the United States in 1976 had a population of 214,500,000 people with 1,901,000 deaths occurring during that year. The formula for computing the crude death rate in the United States for 1976 per 1,000 people would be as follows:

$$\frac{1,901,000 \ (\text{cases})}{214,500,000 \ (\text{population})} \times 1,000 = 1976 \ \text{crude death rate}$$

or

$$\frac{1,901,000}{214,500,000} \times 1,000 = 8.9$$

Therefore, in 1976 the United States had 8.9 deaths per every 1,000 persons. Birth rates would be computed in the same manner, except that the number of cases would refer to births instead of deaths.

Crude death and birth rates, however, are usually too gross a measure to be meaningful for most sociological purposes. Sociologists are typically concerned with the effects of specific variables or social characteristics within a population such as age, sex, race, occupation, or any other measure of significant social differences. *Age-specific rates* are an example of rates used to show differences by age. Age-specific rates are computed in the same way as crude rates, except the numerator and the denominator are confined to a specific age group (a similar method can be used to determine sex-specific rates, race-specific rates, etc.). In order to calculate an age-specific rate, the procedure is to subdivide a population by age and then compare the number of cases in this subpopulation by the total number of persons within the subpopulation. If you wanted to compute the age-specific mortality rate for all infants for a particular year in the United States, for example, you would need to know how many infants there were in that year and the number of deaths that occurred in this age-specific group. The *infant mortality rate,* a measure of the deaths of all infants in a geographical area under the age of one year, is a very common age-specific rate in epidemiology. Consider that in 1976 some 47,700 infants died in the United States out of a total infant population of 3,140,000. You would compute the 1976 U.S. infant mortality rate in the following manner:

$$\frac{47,700 \text{ (cases)}}{3,140,000 \text{ (population)}} \times 1,000 = 1976 \text{ U.S. infant mortality rate}$$

or

$$\frac{47,000}{3,140,000} \times 1,000 = 15.2$$

Therefore, the 1976 U.S. infant mortality rate was 15.2 deaths per 1,000 infants.

The infant mortality rate has special significance for a society because it is traditionally used as an approximate measure of a society's sanitary and medical standards. For instance, the infant mortality rate in the United States in 1900 per 1,000 infants was 162.4; by 1940 this rate had been reduced to 47.0 as a result of improvements in medical techniques and facilities. After World War II further medical advances reduced infant mortality rates per 1,000 infants to 29.2 in 1950, 27.0 in 1960, 21.5 in 1969, and 15.2 in 1976. Infant mortality rates during the twentieth century have traditionally been lowest in technologically advanced societies such as Great Britain, Denmark, Sweden, and the United States. The highest rates have usually been in the underdeveloped countries of Asia, Africa, and South America.

Among the other major rates employed by social epidemiologists are *life expectancy rates,* the average number of years from birth to death that a person with particular social characteristics, e.g., according to age, sex, and race, can be expected to live. Life expectancy rates are expressed in two types of tables, the *generation* or *cohort life table* and the *current life table.* The *generation life table* presents life expectancy rates based upon the mortality experience of a particular cohort, such as all persons born in 1890, from moment of birth through consecutive ages in successive years. This table reflects the mortality experience of a cohort from birth until all members of the cohort have died.

The most frequently used life table is the *current life table,* which assumes that a hypothetical cohort is subject throughout its lifetime to the age-specific death rate prevailing for an actual population during a particular calendar year. Figure 2-2 in this chapter is an example of a current life table reflecting the expectation of life statistics for males and females in the United States in 1974. Life tables are commonly used by insurance companies to determine premiums and other information regarding applicants for life insurance.

AGE, SEX, RACE, AND SOCIAL CLASS

The basic variables in social epidemiological research are age, sex, race, and social class or socioeconomic background. It has been found that each of these four variables represents differences among people that can be correlated with health and life expectancy.

Age

The most striking fact about age in the United States is the great increase in life expectancy. In 1900 the average number of years that an American could expect to live was 47.3; by 1974 this had increased to 71.9 years. The decline in mortality rates in this country has been influenced by two major factors: (1) the quantity and quality of available health services and (2) the rise in the American standard of living, which promoted significant improvements in living and work environments as well as in diet and recreational opportunities. The overall result has been that most Americans today die not from infectious diseases, but from biological decay and the effects of aging.

Considering only the period between 1960 and 1974, there has been a lowering of the death rates for practically all age groups in the United States. Figure 2–1 shows that the largest decreases have occurred for persons 75 to 84 years of age and especially for those persons over 85. The slight (0.1) increase in death rates for 15- to 24-year-olds—who should be enjoying the most healthy period in their lives—is related to a rise in deaths from accidents, particularly automobile accidents. With the exception of accidents, it would appear that most Americans share a healthy childhood and young adulthood.

Also according to Figure 2–1, the infant mortality rates for the years 1960 and 1974 show a decline which has been a consistent trend in the United States since 1900 when, as previously noted, the infant mortality rate was 162.4 deaths per 1,000 infants. These figures lend support to the assumption that if a person survives the first year of life in the United States, that person is likely to reach old age. From ages five to fifteen, the human body is at its highest stage of ability to resist disease and repair injury. The ability of the human body to maintain itself remains at a high level during the twenties, but then begins to decline slowly until the age of fifty when the aging process begins to accelerate.

FIGURE 2–1. AGE SPECIFIC MORTALITY RATES PER 1,000 PERSONS IN THE UNITED STATES, 1960 AND 1974

Ages	1960 Death Rate	1974 Death Rate	Change
Under 1 years	27.0	17.6	− 9.4
1–4 years	1.1	0.7	− 0.4
5–14 years	0.5	0.4	− 0.1
15–24 years	1.1	1.2	+ 0.1
25–34 years	1.5	1.5	0.0
35–44 years	3.0	2.8	− 0.2
45–54 years	7.6	6.8	− 0.8
55–64 years	17.4	15.5	− 1.9
65–74 years	38.2	33.2	− 5.0
75–84 years	87.5	76.5	− 11.0
85 years and over	198.6	165.3	− 33.3

SOURCE: U.S. National Center for Health Statistics, *Monthly Vital Statistics Report, Advance Report—Final Mortality Statistics, 1974,* Vol. 24, No. 11 (Washington D.C.: U.S. Department of Health, Education, and Welfare, February 3, 1976).

As more and more Americans live to old age, aging has become a social problem in American society that manifests itself in the devalued social role of the aged, particularly with regard to older persons' self-concept and feelings of uselessness and isolation. The stress of daily living, especially that associated with maintaining valued adult status, has a definite effect upon the well-being of the elderly (Rosow, 1967, 1974). Recent studies of elderly subjects have demonstrated that the presence of an intimate and stable relationship with a close relative or friend is important in maintaining adjustment and psychological well-being (Lowenthal and Haven, 1968; Moriwaki, 1973). Yet this is a period of life when many people are alone.

Sociologists concerned with aging usually work in social gerontology, a subfield of gerontology that deals primarily with the nonphysical aspects of aging. These specialists study the ways in which the elderly adjust to their society and how society adapts to the elderly. As larger numbers of people live longer, new social and psychological questions relating to the aged must be answered. Chapter Eleven will consider the problems of aging in greater detail.

Sex

Sex differences in illness and death are highly significant in American society. The most striking generalization is that the life expectancy of the American female is much higher than that of the male. Male death rates exceed female death rates at all ages and for all causes except diabetes. The result is that, as of 1974, the average life expectancy in the United States of white females was 76.6 years compared to 68.9 years for white males. The same advantage also applies to the non-white female, who in 1974 had an average life expectancy of 71.2 years compared to 62.9 years for the non-white male.

While mortality rates for American females have not risen, the death rates for males, not counting military deaths in Vietnam, have increased during the 1960s. A rising mortality rate among young civilian males, for example, can be attributed to a greater proportion of violent deaths, again mostly from automobile accidents. In addition, for both white and non-white males, such health disorders as lung cancer, cirrhosis of the liver, and circulatory diseases caused death at progressively lower ages. The principal effect of rising male mortality rates in American society has been to increase the deficit in numbers of adult men. In 1910 because of increased immigration, there were approximately 106 men for every 100 women in the United States. By 1940, however, the ratio was even with about 100 men for every 100 women. From 1968 until the present, there have been about 95 men for every 100 women, a ratio that represents the lowest point in a steady decline since 1910.

Figure 2–2 also demonstrates female superiority in life expectancy. In 1974, the U.S. National Center for Health Statistics projected that 98.7 percent of all females and 98.3 percent of all white males would survive to age one from birth; by age sixty-five, however, only 68.5 percent of the white males would be alive compared to 82.7 percent of the white females. The lowest level of life expectancy belongs to the non-white male. Figure 2–2 shows that 97.3 percent of the non-white males will survive from birth to age one compared to 97.8 percent of the non-white females; by age sixty-five the percent of surviving non-white males is 52.9 and the percent of surviving non-white females is 69.9. Although the non-

FIGURE 2–2. PERCENT OF MALES AND FEMALES SURVIVING FROM BIRTH IN THE UNITED STATES, 1974

Percent Surviving from Birth	White Males	White Females	Non-White Males	Non-White Females
To age 1	98.3	98.7	97.3	97.8
To age 20	96.9	97.9	95.4	96.7
To age 65	68.5	82.7	52.9	69.9

SOURCE: U.S. National Center for Health Statistics, *Monthly Vital Statistics Report, Advance Report—Final Mortality Statistics, 1974*, Vol. 24, No. 11 (Washington, D.C.: U.S. Department of Health, Education, and Welfare, February 3, 1976).

white female has a definite advantage in longevity over the non-white male, her life expectancy is only slightly higher than that of the white male. Thus despite the female advantage, life expectancy in the United States is strongly affected by racial background. For a long life in the United States it is best to be female and to be white.

Men have a substantial health inferiority in terms of life expectancy because of the combined result of two major effects: (1) biological and (2) social–psychological. The male of the human species is at a biological disadvantage to the female. The fact that the male is weaker physiologically than the female is demonstrated by higher mortality rates from the prenatal and neonatal stages of life onward. Although the percentages may vary somewhat from year to year, the chances of dying during the prenatal stage are approximately 12 percent greater among males than females and 130 percent greater during the neonatal (new born) stage. Examples of neonatal disorders common to male rather than female babies are such afflictions as hyaline membrane disease (a respiratory disease) and pyloric stenosis (a disorder of the pyloric muscle affecting the emptying of the stomach). Neonatal males are also more prone to certain circulatory disorders of the aorta and pulmonary artery. As an organism, it appears that the male is more vulnerable than the female, even before being exposed to the differential social roles and stress situations of later life.

While the evidence is not conclusive, it is nonetheless presumed that social and psychological influences play an important part in the determination of life expectancy (Mechanic, 1968; Coe, 1970; Wilson, 1970). Accidents, for example, are a major cause of deaths among males of certain age groups but not among females, which strongly suggests a difference in sex roles. Men in general are expected to be more aggressive than women in both work and play. High accident rates among males may be attributed to the male's increased exposure to dangerous activities, especially those arising from high-risk occupations. The most dangerous job in the United States (according to the Metropolitan Life Insurance Company) is sponge diving, followed by (in order) motorcycle racing, trapeze and high-wire artists, structural steel workers, lumbermen, bank guards, munitions and explosive workers, anthracite coal miners, and state policemen. Being President of the United States is also hazardous. About one out of three U.S. Presidents has lived to enjoy his normal life expectancy.

Another factor contributing to excess male mortality rates may be occupational competition and the pressure associated with a job. The life style of the business executive or professional with his orientation toward "career" and his drive toward "success," marks of the upwardly mobile middle-class male in American society, is thought to contribute strongly to the development of stress among such men. Middle-aged professional males in the United States today are noted by life insurance companies as a high-risk group, particularly if they smoke, are overweight, and tend to overwork. It would thus seem that both the male sex role and the psychodynamics of male competitiveness are significant factors affecting male longevity.

While men have a higher rate of mortality, women appear to have a higher morbidity. That is, the female is sick more often; or at least the act of defining one's self as ill and recognizing the symptoms of being sick seem to be more appropriate to the social role of the woman. Data from the National Health Survey for 1957 through 1972 show that females tend to have higher rates of acute illnesses, chronic illnesses, and disability due to acute illnesses than males of the same age. Excluding maternity, females also exhibit greater use of health services than males (Anderson and Andersen, 1972). Robert Wilson (1970) believes that there may be an inverse relationship between patterns of mortality and morbidity in regard to sex differences. Women may be sick more often, but live longer. Men may be sick less often, but die sooner.

Although women are more fit biologically and less often exposed to the social and psychological hazards of dangerous and stressful occupational roles, the female advantage in life expectancy is a mixed blessing. Many studies confirm that depression is more frequent among females than males (see Warheit et al., 1973) and that rates for manic-depressive psychoses and neuroses are higher among women (see Bruce Dohrenwend, 1975). Female longevity has also resulted in a growing social problem, an increasing number of widows who are faced with important decisions about remarriage, employment, and loneliness.

Race

One reflection of social inequality in the United States is the differences among the health profiles of racial groups. Non-white infants have traditionally had almost twice as high an infant mortality rate as white infants in American society. In 1960, for example, there were 43.2 infant deaths per 1,000 non-white infants compared to an infant mortality rate of 22.9 among whites. Although the spread in infant mortality rates has declined to a 10 percent margin as of 1974 (24.9 for non-whites versus 14.9 for whites), the difference is still significant. The effect of social inequality upon infant mortality is most apparent when it is realized that race as a factor does not actually come into play until the postnatal period, when adverse environmental conditions threaten life chances. Non-white infant mortality rates, on a par with those for white infants at birth, increase threefold during the first three to eight months of life.

As previously indicated in our discussion of sex differences, the non-

FIGURE 2–3. AVERAGE NUMBER OF YEARS OF LIFE EXPECTANCY IN THE UNITED STATES BY RACE AND SEX, SINCE 1900

Life Expectancy at Birth by Year	White Males	White Females	Non-White Males	Non-White Females
1900	46.6	48.7	32.5	33.5
1950	66.5	72.2	59.1	62.9
1960	67.4	74.1	61.1	66.3
1970	68.0	75.6	61.3	69.4
1974	68.9	76.6	62.9	71.2

SOURCE: U.S. National Center for Health Statistics, *Monthly Vital Statistics Report, Advance Report—Final Mortality Statistics, 1974*, Vol. 24, No. 11 (Washington, D.C.: U.S. Department of Health, Education, and Welfare, February 3, 1976).

white male clearly has the lowest life expectancy of any racial sex category. Figure 2–3 shows that in 1974 the non-white male in the United States with a life expectancy of 62.9 years will generally live nearly six years less than the white male (68.9 years) and approximately thirteen years less than the white female (76.6 years). The white female has a life expectancy 5.4 years greater than the non-white female.

The majority of persons represented by health data on non-white Americans are black. The improvement in the social status of the black American has been related to a significant improvement in health status. However, as is evident from Figure 2–3, advances in life expectancy have not been uniform for all segments of the U.S. population. A particular health problem for black Americans has been that of hypertension or high blood pressure. While twenty-two million Americans suffer from hypertension, some five to six million of these are black. Thus, although blacks constitute approximately 10 percent of the American population, they have over 20 percent of the diagnosed hypertension. Between the ages of twenty-five and forty-four years, hypertension kills black males 15.5 times more frequently than it does white males. The ratio of black to white females dying from hypertension in the same age category is seventeen to one.

Various hypotheses have been suggested to explain racial differences in the incidence of hypertension:

1. The genetic hypothesis argues that blacks are genetically different from whites in ways that predispose them to hypertension.
2. The physical exertion hypothesis postulates that blacks are more likely than whites to be engaged in manual labor, and that greater physical exertion leads to higher mortality from hypertension.

3. The associated disorder hypothesis asserts that blacks are more prone to diseases such as pyelonephritis and syphilis that may result in secondary hypertension.
4. The psychological stress hypothesis theorizes that blacks are severely frustrated by racial discrimination and that this stress and the repressed aggression associated with it lead to a higher prevalence of hypertension.
5. The diet hypothesis emphasizes that blacks may have dietary patterns that increase their susceptibility to hypertension.
6. The medical care hypothesis argues that blacks receive poorer medical care than whites and that this results in greater morbidity and mortality from hypertensive disease, and perhaps a higher prevalence of secondary hypertension.

At the present time the exact causes of the higher rates of hypertension among blacks is not known. A 1970 analysis by Jan Howard and Barbara Holman of U.S. Public Health data strongly suggests that the disparity between blacks and whites cannot be explained solely upon the basis of socioeconomic factors. Instead they indicate that the genetic hypothesis and the psychological stress hypothesis seem to contribute most to an understanding of the phenomenon. They base their findings upon the observation that even the highest status blacks have substantially higher mortality rates from hypertension than do lower status whites. However, the Howard and Holman study is not conclusive and it would be premature to favor either the genetic or the discrimination hypothesis at this time. The importance of their study is the relevance of an approach based on genetics or racial discrimination for future research.

Another major problem faced by blacks in the United States is the small number of black physicians. While the ratio among whites is one physician for every 750 persons, that among blacks is one to 3,500. The black-white physician differential may thus be a significant factor in the lower quality of health care provided blacks (see Hines, 1972).

Adverse differences in levels of a positive health profile are not limited to blacks, but also include Mexican-Americans and American Indians. Health data on Mexican-Americans are difficult to obtain because federal, state, and local agencies generally include Mexican-Americans with Anglos in the white category. The few existing studies on the health of Mexican-Americans suggest, however, that Mexican-Americans have a higher infant mortality rate, a shorter life expectancy, and higher mortality rates from influenza, pneumonia, and tuberculosis than Anglo-Americans (Moustafa and Weiss, 1968). It should also be noted that Mexican-Americans appear to have lower mortality rates than Anglos from heart disease and cancer.

Joan Moore (1970) believes that the high prevalence of tuberculosis and pneumonia and the relative absence of deaths from heart disease and cancer among Mexican-Americans are consequences of poverty. Heart disease and cancer usually strike the more affluent upper classes, while both tuberculosis and pneumonia are typical diseases of the poor segments of American society.

The same pattern is repeated for the American Indian as exists for the other U.S. minorities. In fact, American Indians may have the poorest health of all Americans. While Indians have low mortality rates for cancer and heart disease, they have very high mortality rates for diabetes and tuberculosis. The incidence of tuberculosis among Indians is ten times greater than that within the population as a whole. Indians also suffer sixty times more dysentery, thirty times more strep throat, and eleven times more hepatitis than other Americans. Other significant health problems of American Indians are alcoholism, dietary deficiency, cirrhosis of the liver, and gastrointestinal bleeding. In addition, chronic otitis media, a severe ear ailment that arises when simple ear infections are not treated, occurs among ten percent of all Indian children, according to statistics gathered in 1974 by the U.S. Senate Subcommittee on Permanent Investigations.

Although the infant mortality rate for American Indians and native Alaskans declined from 62.5 in 1955 to 32.9 in 1968, this rate is still significantly higher than that of whites. Death rates for Indians of all age groups for all causes are 40 percent higher than the death rates for other Americans. Indians do show low mortality rates for heart disease and cancer; as previously noted these health problems are generally related to high socioeconomic status. They are also associated with old age and proportionately fewer Indians reach the higher age groups where these diseases are prevalent.

Two health problems commonly linked with American Indians are drinking and suicide. Although drinking appears to be a recognized evil in Indian communities (Dozier, 1966), it has generally remained the dominant mode of social activity for males (Waddell, 1973). A study of a tri-ethnic community in Colorado (Jessor et al., 1968) found that, in comparison to Anglos and Mexican-Americans, Indians not only drank more frequently and became drunk more often, but they also had more drinking-related problems. Indians were also more apt to drink to solve personal problems. Although not all studies agree that Indian drinking involves a high level of alcoholism, there is a consensus that Indians drink a lot and that they frequently get into trouble as a result (Levy and Kunitz, 1973; Cockerham, 1975). The overwhelming majority of crimes committed by Indians in the Southwest United States are committed under the influence of alcohol, and the proportion of Indians arrested for alcohol-related crimes in comparison to other ethnic groups is the highest in the nation (Stewart, 1964; FBI, 1975).

While a strong case can be made for excessive drinking among American Indians as a group, existing data on suicides among and within various ethnic groups do not support any general prevalence of suicide among Indians. According to Estelle Fuchs and Robert Havighurst (1972), who have made an extensive review of the literature pertaining to Indian suicide rates, the overall suicide rates for Indians of all ages are about the same as for non-Indians of all ages. For 1968, U.S. Public Health figures show that approximately eleven Indians per 100,000 committed suicide compared to a rate of 10.8 suicides per 100,000 for all Americans. Although *overall* suicide rates are comparable, there are significant differences in Indian suicide by sex and age. Indian females in general and both Indian males and females over the age of forty-five show low rates of suicide. Yet Indian males between the ages of fifteen and forty-five show a suicide rate which is four times that of non-Indians. The problem of Indian suicides is, therefore, largely concentrated among young Indian males. Fuchs and Havighurst (1972:154) warn: "The relatively high suicide rate of young Indian men should be taken as a symptom of something wrong with the society in which they live."

Another possible threat to the health of the American Indian, one that has yet to be adequately researched, is drug abuse. Within some Indian tribal cultures there has existed a traditional use of drugs such as peyote and mescaline in religious rituals and folk medicine, but the general extent of Indian drug use remains relatively unknown at present. What little research does exist shows that, in comparison to all other ethnic groups, American Indian college students report a higher level of contact with drugs (Strimbu et al., 1973). This same pattern has also been found in a comparison of Indian and white high school students (Cockerham et al., 1976; Cockerham, 1977).

Indian health problems are further complicated by poor communication between Indians and white health professionals and by Indian mistrust of the white medical bureaucracy. A report on urban Indians living in a northern Arizona bordertown (Allen and Tollivier, 1974) discloses that Indians had difficulty in understanding white financial procedures and resented white attitudes of superiority. This latter complaint usually resulted from professionals' admonishing them about personal hygiene, degree of child care, and delay in seeking health care until an illness reached an emergency state. When Indians showed an inability to pay for services, they were often referred to reservation medical facilities, several miles away, that provided free services for Indians. Reservation authorities, on the other hand, were sometimes reluctant to provide health care to urban Indians who were not viewed as being their responsibility. As a result, urban Indians were left either seeking health services on the reservation or choosing to utilize only emergency care and free health clinics in town.

Besides the problems faced by urban Indians, reservation Indians are often subject to health care inferior to that of whites because of understaffing, underfunding, and poor facilities. A 1974 U.S. Senate study disclosed that only half of the fifty-one Indian Health Service Hospitals have been accredited as meeting minimum national standards by the Joint Commission on the Accreditation of Hospitals, and a mere sixteen were able to meet national fire and safety codes.

Therefore, despite the increase in life expectancy among American Indians, their overall health profile is far worse than that of whites or of the other U.S. minority groups, including blacks living in urban slums and Mexican-Americans in the Southwest.

Although there are some afflictions such as hypertension and sickle cell anemia that appears to have a genetic basis, the great majority of health disorders among minority groups in American society are the result of environmental factors related to poverty. Alcoholism, drug addiction, suicide, lead poisoning, rat-bite fever, influenza, pneumonia, and tuberculosis are health disorders more common to the poor. Race becomes a significant health variable in the United States primarily *because* racial minorities typically occupy disadvantaged socioeconomic positions. A study by George Warheit et al. (1973) discloses, for example, that blacks, females, the aged, the poor, and those with the least formal education have the highest rates of symptoms of depression. However, when race, sex, age, and socioeconomic status were correlated, only sex and socioeconomic status were statistically significant. The major difference in depression scores between whites and blacks was accounted for by the socioeconomic variable, with most blacks occupying the lowest socioeconomic level. Poor health for non-whites in general may largely be accounted for by the fact of being both non-white and lower class.

Social Class

The uneven distribution of health among racial groups in American society repeats itself when the distribution of health among socioeconomic groups or social classes is considered. On nearly every measure, membership in lower social classes carries health penalties similar to those of non-whites. To be poor is by definition to have less of the things (including health care) produced by society.

Before the 1930s, the medically indigent patient was dependent largely upon the charity of medical institutions and private physicians.

Many times this charity was erratic. In addition, many of the urban clinics providing treatment for the poor were established and maintained as teaching facilities for medical and nursing students. Hence, treatment was sometimes oriented more toward educational needs than toward patient needs. Since the 1930s, however, there has been a considerable increase in the number and types of facilities as well as an improvement in the quality of medical care available to the poor. Yet as Charles H. Goodrich et al. (1972) explain, there has been little change in the organizational structure of welfare medicine.

A long-standing impediment to the sound application and control of medical care for the poor has been inadequate coordination and unnecessary duplication of many services. Anselm Strauss (1970) points out that medical systems in the United States have not met the needs of the poor because they have never been designed to do so. The manner in which the poor live and perceive their social environment has not been considered in the organization and norms of American medical care. Strauss believes that the parochial nature of modern medical organizations is at fault because the poor lack experience in organizational life and middle-class norms. For example, Strauss discusses the breakdown in communication between middle-class health professionals and the poor by noting that many health professionals assume that the poor (like themselves) have regular meals, lead regular lives, try to support families, keep healthy, and plan for the future. To prescribe the same type of treatment for all diseases for all people does not take into account the fact that people live their lives differently. Strauss (1970:16) illustrates this point by asking, "What does 'take with each meal' mean to a family that eats irregularly, seldom together, and usually less than three times a day?"

A review of relevant research discloses that a number of studies substantiate the relationship between poverty and lack of access to *quality* medical care in the United States (see Elam, 1969; Kosa et al., 1969; Hurley, 1971; Mechanic, 1972). Despite evidence of more frequent visits to physicians made possible by greater health insurance coverage through Medicaid and Medicare, lower-class persons are still treated within the framework of welfare medicine and still live on a day-to-day basis within the environment of poverty. It appears also that professional health practitioners are likely to "prefer" upper-class patients or at least to provide more personalized care for the upper-class sick (Miller, 1973). Strauss (1970:11–12) summarizes the position of the poor in American medicine by stating, "The poor definitely get second-rate medical care. This is self-evident to anyone who has worked either with them or in public medical facilities."

An interesting study by Aaron Antonovsky (1972) on life expectancy and social class further reinforces the importance of the socioeconomic differential by suggesting that, on every measure, social class position influences one's opportunity for longevity. Antonovsky conducted a statistical investigation of approximately thirty studies of mortality rates in the United States and Europe. Other than rates for coronary heart disease, which is prevalent among achieving and affluent males, Antonovsky found that the upper socioeconomic classes were favored in all dimensions of life expectancy.[1] "The inescapable conclusion," stated Antonovsky (1972:28), "is that class influences one's chances of staying alive." The only major contradiction found by Antonovsky involved a Dutch study (DeWolff and Meerdink, 1954); however, the population in this study demonstrated few social class differences and, as a whole, had one of the lowest death rates ever recorded. This research by the Dutch scientists suggests the important hypothesis that as differences between social classes decline, overall mortality rates of a population may similarly decline.

Since many health disorders appear related to poverty, it is a logical assumption that if poverty were not a factor retarding the availability of quality medical care, the incidence and prevalence of illness in the lower social classes would be reduced. Following World War II, socialized medicine was introduced in Great Britain to provide the lower classes with the same medical care available to the upper classes. It should be noted, however, that poverty and social class differences remained—only health care was equalized. Results have shown that the equalization of health care alone has not reduced the disparity in health between social classes. Mortality rates remained higher for the lower classes, and class differences in infant mortality actually increased. According to Marvin Susser and William Watson (1971), Britain's experiment failed to reduce health disparities precisely because living conditions and life style could not be equalized; the physical environment of poverty and poor nutrition continued to adversely affect lower-class health. In addition, Susser and Watson believe that a "cultural lag" exists in that the lower classes persist in their traditional attitudes and norms regarding medical care even though improved health services are available.

As has already been indicated, types of health disorders seem to vary by social class. Heart disease is more prevalent among the upper classes and tuberculosis and influenza frequent the lower classes. There is also evidence that, in the case of cancer, location of the disease in the body may

[1] Fuchs (1974) reminds us of an opposite conclusion. He says that high income can harm health as well if it is reflected in a rich diet, heavy smoking, lack of exercise, automobile accidents, and other expressions of "high" living. All things considered, however, the greatest disadvantage in life expectancy for most people seems to be low income when considered in terms that are strictly socioeconomic.

have a social class relationship. Saxon Graham (1972), for instance, reports on several studies that suggest lower-class females are more likely than upper-class females to develop cancer of the cervix because of an earlier and higher frequency of sexual intercourse and multiple pregnancies. In turn, breast cancer has been found to be more prevalent among upper-class women who have nursed fewer children than their lower-class counterparts.

While social class can be an important factor in health, cultural considerations also may be relevant. Graham found the cross-cultural distribution of cancer of the stomach to be of particular significance as a result of studies on male mortality rates. The highest male mortality rates from cancer of the stomach were in Japan, Finland, Austria, and Poland. The lowest mortality rates were in England, Canada, Australia, New Zealand, and among American whites. Although convincing evidence is lacking, perhaps the lower mortality rates for this disease among countries of English origin are due to some protective feature of English culture.

Citing Japanese studies, Graham also pointed to the cultural differential of stomach cancer among genetically similar Japanese. The mortality rates from cancer of the stomach were highest in Japan, somewhat lower among full-blooded Japanese living in Hawaii, and even lower among full-blooded Japanese living on the West Coast of the United States. Apparently as Japanese become more Americanized, the incidence of stomach cancer is reduced. Y. Scott Matsumoto (1971), on the other hand, reported on an inverse relationship between Japan and the United States in regard to coronary heart disease. Japanese living in the United States have a higher mortality rate from heart disease than Japanese living in Hawaii and a much higher rate than Japanese living in Japan. Recognizing that diet is an important socioeconomic variable, although dietary studies concerning heart disease are not conclusive (see Susser and Watson, 1971), Matsumoto focused upon the stress factor. Japan is the only non-Western nation to achieve extensive industrialization and urbanization and also to have a low rate of coronary heart disease. Matsumoto suggested that the difference in coronary disease rates might be due to the stronger feelings of group solidarity among Japanese workers strengthened by the widespread paternalism of Japanese corporations and stress-reducing group activities, such as after-work socializing and periodic group vacations.

A significant group activity among Japanese male workers is the after-work socializing on a daily or weekly basis with close friends in bars or tea and coffee shops. These drinking places are designed to encourage relaxation and to allow temporary escape from the tensions of modern living. The activity seems to have been fully incorporated into the life style of industrial Japan despite the Japanese preference for a highly structured society.

Cultural influences upon health point toward interesting and perhaps highly significant variables; however, to date, there is no conclusive evidence to explain the differences.

SUMMARY

This chapter has been concerned with social epidemiology and the basic sociological variables of age, sex, race, and social class as indicators of health differences. The social epidemiologist is like a detective, investigating the scene of a crime in which the criminal is a disease or some other form of health menace. The epidemiologist is primarily concerned not with individuals, but with the health profiles of social aggregates or large populations of people. Important tools of the epidemiologist are the ratios used to compute descriptions of mortality, incidence, and prevalence. These rates can be either crude rates or standardized rates reflecting age-specific data, sex-specific data and so on.

The section on age disclosed that as more and more persons live to older ages in American society, there emerge some very serious problems concerning the social role of the elderly. As for sex differences, in general females have a very definite advantage over males with regard to life expectancy. This advantage involves both biological and social–psychological factors. White Americans also have a definite advantage in health over non-white Americans. Other than race, however, the most significant socioeconomic variable affecting non-whites is that they are likely to be poor, and poverty, as far as medical care is concerned, may be equated with second-rate treatment. Socialized medicine in Great Britain failed to reduce health differentials between the social classes because social class differences themselves were not reduced. Thus, the environment of poverty continued to influence a higher prevalence of disease among the British lower classes.

3

THE INTERACTION
OF MIND, BODY,
AND SOCIETY

Social influences upon the onset and the subsequent course of a particular disease are not limited to such variables as age, sex, race, social class,
and the conditions of poverty as they relate to life style, habits, and
customs. It is also important to recognize that interaction between the
human mind and body represents a critical factor in regard to health.
Although the evidence is not conclusive, there is a considerable amount
of literature in both medicine and the social sciences that maintains that
psychological responses to social events can cause stress (see, for example,
Levine and Scotch, 1970; McGrath, 1970; Moss, 1973; House, 1974).
Accordingly, stress can be defined as an emotional–psychophysiological
state of an organism that occurs in a situational context, involving
stimuli which serve as cues to elicit fear or anxiety responses (Janis,
1958).

   Usually stress is thought to occur when individuals are faced with a
situation where their usual modes of behavior are not adequate and the
consequences of not adapting to the situation are perceived as serious
(McGrath, 1970). In general, it appears that there are four possible types
of reactions to stress: (1) the normal, where anxiety is followed by an
effective defensive reaction; (2) the neurotic, where anxiety is so great
that the defense is rendered ineffective; (3) the psychotic, where anxiety
is misperceived or possibly ignored; and (4) the pyschophysiological,
where defense fails and anxiety results in changes in body tissues
(Kaplan, 1975). The majority of the studies on stress indicate that most,

if not all, stress is socially induced as a result of interaction between people (Moss, 1973). A review of selected sociological theories developed by Emile Durkheim, Charles Cooley, William I. Thomas, and Erving Goffman will serve to demonstrate how social processes, from the standpoint of both the wider society and the individual, can produce social conditions considered stressful by the individuals involved.

Durkheim: Functionalism

Emile Durkheim (1858–1917), who formulated the functionalist approach in sociology, was primarily interested in the characteristics of groups and social structures. He was most concerned with those social processes and constraints that integrate individuals into the larger social community. He believed that when a society was strongly integrated, it held individuals firmly under its control (Durkheim, 1950, 1956). Individuals were integrated into a society as a result of their participation in a consensus of community values and through social interaction in accord with this value consensus. Especially important were participation in rituals celebrating a society's traditions and also involvement in work activities.

As members of society, individuals were constrained in their behavior by laws and customs. These constraints were "social facts," which Durkheim (1950:13) defined as "every way of acting, fixed or not, capable of exercising on the individual an external constraint." Robert Nisbet (1966) has suggested that the import of Durkheim's analysis is to give society an existence outside of and above the individual. Social control is, therefore, real and external to the individual.

Among Durkheim's works, the most pertinent to an understanding of the social determinants of stress is his 1897 study, *Suicide* (1951). In explaining the differential rates of suicide among various religious and occupational groupings, Durkheim suggested that suicide was not entirely a matter of free choice by individuals. He believed that suicide was a social fact explainable in terms of social causes. Durkheim distinguished between three major types of suicide, each dependent upon the relationship of the individual to society. These three types were (1) egoistic suicide, in which individuals become detached from society and, suddenly on their own, are overwhelmed by the resulting stress; (2) anomic suicide, in which individuals suffer a sudden dislocation of normative systems where their norms and values are no longer relevant, so that controls of society no longer restrain them from taking their lives; and (3) altruistic suicide, in which individuals feel themselves so strongly integrated into a demanding society that their only escape seems to be suicide.

Durkheim's typology of suicide suggests how a society might induce enough stress among individuals to cause them to take their lives. Egoistic suicide is a result of stress brought about by the separation of a strongly integrated individual from his or her group. Durkheim uses the example of the military officer who is suddenly retired and left without the group ties which typically regulated his behavior. Egoistic suicide is based upon the overstimulation of an individual's intelligence by the realization that he or she has been deprived of collective activity and meaning. Anomic suicide is characterized by an overstimulation of emotion and a corresponding freedom from society's restraints. It is a result of sudden change that includes the breakdown of values and norms by which an individual has lived his or her life. Sudden wealth or sudden poverty, for example, could disrupt the usual normative patterns and induce a state of anomie or normlessness. In this situation a chronic lack of regulation results in a state of restlessness, unbounded ambition, or perhaps crisis, in which an individual's norms no longer bind him or her to society.

Whereas egoistic and anomic forms of suicide are both due to "society's insufficient presence in individuals" (Durkheim, 1951:256), altruistic suicide represents the strong presence of a social system encouraging suicide among certain groups. Suicide in the altruistic form could be characterized as the avoidance of stress on the part of individuals who prefer to conform to a society's normative system rather than risk the stress of opposing it. Examples of altruistic suicide are the practice of hara-kiri in Japan, where certain social failures on the part of an individual are expected to be properly redressed by the individual's suicide, or the traditional Hindu custom of the widow's committing ritual suicide at her husband's funeral.

Although altruistic suicide is relatively rare in Western society, stories commonly appear in daily newspapers of individuals killing themselves for reasons that could be considered egoistic or anomic. Yet the significance of Durkheim's orientation toward social processes for the understanding of the stress phenomenon extends well beyond the issue of suicide, since this is only one of many possible ways a person might find to cope with social and psychological problems. What is particularly insightful is Durkheim's notion of the capability of the larger society to create stressful situations where people are forced to respond to conditions not of their own choosing.

For example, in a 1976 Federal Government report, M. Harvey Brenner linked increased incidence of heart disease, stroke, kidney failure, mental illness, and even infant mortality to rising unemployment. Brenner's thesis is that there are few areas of our lives not intimately affected by the state of the economy. He demonstrates that economic recession increases the amount of stress on an individual by comparing economic cycles with health statistics for approximately seventy years prior to the publication of his work. Brenner found that heart attacks increase during periods of recession. Usually the first wave of deaths follows the recession by three years, with a second wave occurring five to seven years after the recession. The lag was thought to be due to the length of time it takes heart disease to cause death. Waves of kidney failure deaths generally lagged two years behind a recession, while death from strokes took about two to four years to follow an economic downturn. Infant mortality rates were particularly striking during periods of recession according to Brenner. Mothers suffering from the stresses of the recession tended to have higher blood pressure and be less healthy themselves, thereby giving birth to a child whose chances for survival had likewise been weakened.

What causes stress during an economic recession was the intensified struggle for the basic necessities of life (food, clothing, shelter, health care, and education for children) and a possible loss of self-satisfaction and social status associated with unemployment while trying to survive on savings, welfare, and unemployment insurance. These stresses were often found to be enhanced by a rise in drinking and smoking at the same time. What is happening, suggests Brenner, is that social stress from economic conditions increases exposure to the major risk factors known to accompany many health disorders.

Cooley, Thomas, and Goffman: Symbolic Interaction

While Durkheim emphasized the influence of the larger society upon the individual, Cooley, Thomas, and Goffman reflect the symbolic interactionist approach to human behavior which views human group life from the perspective of the individual. This approach sees the individual as a creative, thinking organism who is able to choose his or her behavior instead of reacting more or less mechanically to the influence of social processes. It assumes that all behavior is self-directed upon the basis of symbolic meanings which are shared, communicated, and manipulated by interacting human beings in social situations. Of special relevance to a sociological understanding of stress is Charles H. Cooley's (1864–1929) theory of the "Looking-Glass Self." Cooley (1964) maintained that our self-concepts are the result of social interaction in which we see ourselves reflected in the meanings other people attach to us as social objects. Cooley compares the reflection of our self in others to our reflections in a looking glass:

Each to each a looking glass
Reflects the other that dot!ı pass.

Cooley's looking-glass self concept has three basic components: (1) we see ourselves in our imagination as we think we appear to the other person; (2) we see in our imagination the other person's judgment of our appearance; and (3) as a result of what we see in our imagination about how we are viewed by the other person, we experience some sort of self-feeling, such as pride or humiliation. The contribution of this theory to an understanding of stress is that an individual's perception of himself as a social object is related to the reaction of other people. Quite obviously stress could result from the failure of the observer to reflect a self-image consistent with that of the subject. Thus, stress can be seen as having a very definite social and personal component based upon perception of a social event.

The work of William I. Thomas (1863–1947) is also relevant for its understanding of crisis as residing in the individual's "definition of the situation" (Volkart, 1951). Thomas stated that so long as definitions of a social situation remain relatively constant, behavior will generally be orderly. However, when rival definitions appear and habitual behavior becomes disrupted, social disorganization and personal demoralization may be anticipated. The ability of an individual to cope with a crisis situation will be strongly related to socialization experiences that have taught the person how to cope with new events in general.

Consequently, Thomas makes two particularly important contributions concerning stress. First, he notes that the same crisis will not produce the *same effect uniformly in all persons,* and second, he explains that adjustment and control of a crisis situation results from an individual's ability to compare a present situation with similar ones in the past and to revise judgment and action upon the basis of past experience. The outcome of a particular situation depends, therefore, upon an individual's definition of a situation and upon how that individual comes to terms with that situation. As David Mechanic (1968:302) states, "Thomas' concept of crisis is important because it emphasizes that crises lie not in situations, but rather in the interaction between a situation and a person's capacities to meet it." Saxon Graham and Leo Reeder (1972:91) add that in Thomas' notion of adaptation ". . . the individual's repertoire of coping behavior is a crucial element in understanding the ways in which people come to terms with a given stressful situation."

Erving Goffman, a contemporary figure in American sociology, is noted for the dramaturgical or "life as theatre" approach. The symbolic interactionist orientation is obvious in Goffman's (1959) belief that in order for social interaction to be viable, individuals need information about the other participants in a joint act. Such information is communicated through (1) a person's appearance, (2) a person's experience with other similar individuals, (3) the social setting, and (4) most important, the information a person communicates about himself or herself through words and actions. This fourth category of information is decisive because it is subject to control by the individual and represents the impression the person is trying to project—which others may come to accept. This information is significant because it helps to define a situation by enabling others to know in advance what a person expects of them and what they may expect of him. Goffman calls this process "impression management."

Goffman says people live in worlds of social encounters in which they act out a line of behavior, a pattern of verbal and nonverbal acts by which individuals express their view of a situation and their evaluation of the participants, particularly themselves. The positive social value individuals claim for themselves by the line that others assume they have taken during a particular encounter is termed a "face." This face is an image of self projected to other people who may share that face. One's face is one's most personal possession and is the center of security and pleasure, but Goffman is quick to point out that a person's face is only on loan to him from society and can be withdrawn if the person conducts himself in a manner others deem as being unworthy. A person may be in the "wrong face" when information about one's social worth cannot be integrated into his line of behavior or a person may be "out of face" when the person participates in an encounter without the line of behavior of the type that participants in that particular situation would be expected to take.

Goffman further explains that the maintenance of face is a condition of interaction, not its objective. This is so because one's face is a constant factor taken for granted in interaction. When a person engages in "face-work," he is taking action to make his activities consistent with the face he is projecting. This is important because every member of a social group is expected to have some knowledge of face-work and some experience in its use, such as the exercise of social skills like tact. Goffman sees almost all acts involving other people as being influenced by considerations of face; for example, an individual is given a chance to quit a job rather than be fired. A person must be aware of the interpretations that others have placed upon his behavior and the interpretations that he should place upon their behavior. Therefore, Goffman's view of the self is that it has two distinct roles in social interaction: first, the self as an image of a person formed from the flow of events in an encounter and second, the self as a kind of player in a ritual game who copes judgmentally with a situation.

Goffman's principal contribution to our understanding of stress arises from his claim that the self is a sacred object. The self is more important than anything else to us because it is always with us and represents who we are. For someone to challenge the integrity of that self as a social object is an embarrassing situation. Each self is special, and in social relationships that very special self we have tried to nourish and protect for a lifetime is put on display. Goffman has said that role-specific behavior is based not upon the functional requirements of a particular role, but upon the *appearance* of having discharged a role's requirements. Thus, stress could be induced when an individual perceives his chosen face or performance in a given situation to be inconsistent with the concept of self he tries to maintain for himself and others in that situation. Otherwise, people might not be so willing to take such great care that they act out lines of behavior considered appropriate to their setting.

STRESS

The theories of Durkheim, Cooley, Thomas, and Goffman demonstrate a relationship between social interaction and stress, but they do not explain the effect of stress upon the human body. Embarrassment and psychological discomfort can be socially painful, yet the effects of stress can transcend the social situation and cause physiological damage as well. Hence, a physiological perspective of stress must be considered.

Walter Cannon (1932) believed that the real measure of health is not the absence of disease, but the ability of the human organism to function effectively within a given environment. This belief was based upon the observation that the human body undergoes continuous adaptation to its environment in response to weather, microorganisms, chemical irritants and pollutants, and the psychological pressures of daily life. Cannon called this process of physiological adaptation *homeostasis,* which is derived from the Greek and means "staying the same." Homeostasis refers to the maintenance of a relatively constant condition; for example, when the body becomes cold, heat is produced; when the body is threatened by bacteria, antibodies are produced to fight the germs; and when the body is threatened by an attack from another human being, the body prepares itself either to fight or to run.

As an organism the human body is thus prepared to meet both internal and external threats to survival, whether these threats are real or symbolic. A person may react with fear to an actual object or to a symbol of that object—for example a bear versus a bear's footprint. In the second case, the fear is not of the footprint, but of the bear that the footprint represents. Symbolic threats in contemporary urban societies could include types of stimuli such as heavy traffic, loud noises, or competition at work, all of which can produce emotional stress related more to a social situation than to a specific person or object.

Whether or not the stressful situation actually induces physiological change depends upon an individual's perception of the stress stimulus and the meaning that the stimulus holds for him or her. A person's reaction, for instance, may not correspond to the actual reality of the dangers that the stimulus represents; that is, a person may overreact or underreact. Thus there is considerable agreement that an individual's subjective interpretation of a social situation is the trigger that produces physiological responses (see Moss, 1973). Situations themselves cannot usually be assumed beforehand to produce physiological changes.

Physiological Responses to Stress

Cannon (1932) formulated the concept of the "fight or flight" pattern of physiological change to illustrate how the body copes with stress resulting from a social situation. When a person experiences fear or anxiety, the body undergoes physiological changes that prepare it for vigorous effort and the effect of possible injury. Physiological changes in the body as a result of stress situations primarily involve the autonomic and neuroendocrine systems. The autonomic nervous system controls heart rate, blood pressure, and gastrointestinal functions—processes that occur automatically and are not under the voluntary control of the central nervous system. The autonomic nervous system is delicately balanced between relaxation and stimulation and is activated primarily through the hypothalamus, which is located in the central ventral portion of the brain. It is composed of two major divisions, the parasympathetic and the sympathetic systems. The parasympathetic system is dominant when there is no emergency and regulates the vegetative processes of the body such as the storing of sugar in the liver, the constriction of the pupil of the eye in response to intense light, and the decreasing of heart rate. When there is an emergency, the sympathetic system governs the body's autonomic functions and increases heart rate so that blood flows swiftly to the organs and muscles that are needed in defense. It also inhibits bowel movements and dilates the pupil of the eye in order to improve sight.

Besides the autonomic nervous system, the endocrine glands perform an important role in the body's physiological reaction to stress. The neuroendocrine system consists of the adrenal and pituitary glands, the parathyroids, the islets of Langerhans, and the gonads. They secrete hormones directly into the blood stream because they lack ducts to carry their hormones to particular glands. The two glands that are the most responsive to stress situations are the adrenal and pituitary glands. The adrenal gland secretes two hormones, epinephrine and norepinephrine, under stimulation from the hypothalamus. Epinephrine accelerates the heart rate and helps to distribute blood to the heart, lungs, central nervous system, and limbs; also it makes the blood coagulate more readily so that as little blood as possible will be lost in case of injury. Norepinephrine raises blood pressure and joins with epinephrine to mobilize fatty acids in the blood stream for use as energy. The function of the pituitary gland is, upon stimulation by the hypothalamus, to secrete hormones that, in turn, stimulate other endocrine glands to secrete their hormones.

At first, most medical scientists believed that only the adrenal gland was involved in stress reaction; however, in 1936 Hans Selye demonstrated the existence of a pituitary-adrenal cortical axis as having a profound effect upon body metabolism. Selye (1956) developed a theory known as the *general adaptation syndrome.* He believed that after an initial alarm reaction, a second stage of resistance to prolonged stress was accomplished primarily through increased activity of the anterior pituitary and adrenal cortex. If stress continued and pituitary and adrenal defenses were consumed, Selye indicated that a person would enter a third stage of exhaustion. He described this third stage as a kind of premature aging due to wear and tear on the body. However, it now seems that the entire endocrine system, not just the pituitary and adrenal glands, are involved in some manner in stress reaction. Under acute stimulus, hormone secretions by the endocrine glands increase; under calming influences, secretions decrease.

Most threats in modern society are symbolic, not physical, and they do not usually require a physical response. Today the human organism faces emotional threats with the same physical system used to fight enemies. Yet modern society disapproves of such physical responses as fighting. Socially, the human organism is often left with no course of action except verbal insults; this inability to respond externally leaves the body physiologically mobilized for action, a readiness that can result in damage to the body. For example, fat which has been mobilized for energy in defense may not be burned up in response, but instead may be left as deposits in the arteries and contribute to the development of arteriosclerosis.

A number of studies have shown that the human organism's inability to manage the social, psychological, and emotional aspects of life—to respond suitably to a social situation—can lead to the development of cardiovascular complications and hypertension, peptic ulcers, muscular pain, compulsive vomiting, asthma, migraine headaches, and other health problems (see, for example, McNeil, 1970; Moss, 1973; House, 1974). Some research suggests that even the onset of cancer is related to changes and disappointments in social relationships (LeShan, 1966).

A classic study demonstrating the interaction of mind and body was conducted in 1943 by Stewart Wolf and Harold Wolff. This study was based upon a patient known as "Tom" whose stomach protruded through his abdomen, providing his physicians with a "window" into his stomach. It was found that the lining of the stomach responded to emotional disturbances by stomach secretions of hydrochloric acid. The authors speculated that perhaps during an early evolutionary period people met threats by killing and eating their enemies, or that somehow they developed a possible physiological relationship between social conflict and eating. When Tom was depressed or withdrawn from other people, the opposite effect occurred and his stomach was pale, bloodless, and generally empty of digestive secretions. Wolf and Wolff's research clearly suggested a strong relationship between the functioning of the stomach and emotional states. Often Tom's stomach revealed emotional conflict before Tom's behavior did.

While there are few studies that actually correlate physiological responses with social activity in specific social situations, existing research does support the claim that physiological change can be related to social interaction. It has been shown, for example, that the verbal discussion of events for which a person subjectively feels fear, dread, anxiety, or anger may act to increase fatty acids in the blood (Back and Bogdonoff, 1964); that new or unexpected information may produce a physiological response (Oken, 1967); and that the anticipation of dreaded events that have been previously experienced can produce physiological responses similar to those experienced during the actual event itself (Oken, 1967). Uncertainty of behavior and the blocking of goal aspirations have also been found to be important causes of adverse physiological responses (Henry and Cassell, 1969).

PSYCHOPHYSIOLOGICAL MEDICINE

The belief that mind and body interact has led to the development of psychophysiological medicine. This branch of medicine rests on the premise that discomforting social situations produce stress, which plays a role in causing or contributing to the occurrences of a physiological disorder or illness. The reader is reminded that although the concept of stress-related illness and disease is generally accepted, the literature on stress remains characterized by disagreement and uncertainty.

A major problem is that stress is a subjective phenomenon and difficult to measure except for a few external physiological indicators such as galvanic skin response (GSR), electroencephalograph (EEG), and electromyograph (EMG); and internal indicators such as changes in the secretion and excretion of hormone levels in the blood and urine. Yet the external physiological indicators do not always represent reliable measures of internal bodily states; and while internal indicators of hormone levels may provide more exact measures of rapid change within the body, they are difficult to generalize to other individuals in the same circumstances. Gordon Moss (1973) notes that the wide range of individual physiological responses to a social situation cannot be adequately explained without considering an individual's *subjective* understanding of the situation. Nevertheless, psychophysiological medicine represents a definite attempt by medicine to cope with the interplay of mind and body. Three of the major psychophysiological approaches to the mind—body problem are outlined below.

The Psychoanalytic Perspective

The development of a psychoanalytic approach to psychophysiological medicine is due primarily to the work of Franz Alexander and his colleagues at the Chicago Psychoanalytic Institute during the 1930s. Alexander relied heavily upon Sigmund Freud's studies of hysteria conversion. As a result of his work with hypnosis, Freud observed that hysterical symptoms disappeared under hypnosis in patients who had repressed their emotions. Freud believed that hysterical symptoms in his patients were converted into symbolic expression in disturbed bodily functions. An intense emotion would disappear from consciousness and reappear with a physiological effect, such as paralysis of a limb. Freud called this process the hysterical conversion symptom because emotional tension was converted into an organic effect, since it was unable to find other symbolic expression.

Several clinical studies have supported Freud's explanation for hysteria, although it should be noted that such studies have been able to account only for pathogenic symptoms occurring in muscles under voluntary control (Alexander and Selesnick, 1966). Other research has suggested that much more than simple repression is needed to explain the full effect of hysteria (Shapiro, 1965). Yet the significant insight for future research was that mind and body do interact.

While Freud and many of his associates continued to concern themselves with questions regarding conflict within the structure of the personality and the nature of the id, the ego, and the superego, Alexander explored his theory that personality conflicts were not problems of structure, but instead represented emotional tensions. Alexander was particularly concerned with the tendency of the human personality to chastise itself as a primary component of neurotic symptoms (Wyss, 1973). Based upon Freud's oral and anal stages of psychosexual development, Alexander and his associates identified three main conflicts within the personality as being responsible for psychophysiological disorders: (1) the wish to receive or incorporate; (2) the wish to eliminate, to give or to accomplish something; and (3) the wish to retain and accumulate. Failure to achieve gratification early in a person's psychosexual development was thought to weaken the capacity of the individual to tolerate anxiety and depression during adulthood, and to predispose the individual to ego regression and conversion to physiological disorders during stress situations. Alexander believed that *specific* psychological conflicts within the personality could be the basis for explaining *specific* physiological manifestations. For example, diarrhea was thought to be caused by an oral-dependent longing to give, while ulcers were related to oral-receptive longings from a reaction to an excessive effort to accomplish.

Disagreement among psychoanalysts about the correlation between specific personality and organic disorders has resulted in a further clarification of the psychoanalytic position on psychophysiological medicine. Roy Grinker (1953) has revised the contemporary basic assumptions of the psychoanalytic approach by explaining that stress can manifest itself in a number of linked open systems. Stress that occurs in one system may be transferred to other systems, so that several systems are involved in the process of the human organism's adaptation to stress. Grinker maintains that five essential systems are involved in handling stress: (1) the enzymatic system, which includes the endocrine system, (2) the organic system, (3) the nervous system, (4) the psychological system, and (5) the sociocultural system. When anxiety becomes too intense within one system, other systems intervene to absorb the effects. These other systems do not become involved until the anxiety is too much for one particular system.

Despite the fact that psychoanalysis offers some very appealing conceptualizations about the mind-body relationship, its approach suffers some serious limitations. For one thing, there is at present no reliable correlation between specific psychological problems and predisposition to a particular illness (Ludwig et al., 1969). Also important is the criticism that psychoanalytic theory is too abstract, poorly specified, and not always dependent upon controlled scientific research (Mechanic, 1968;

Moss, 1973) ; additionally, it views people as unusually weak and in-effectual against the biological and social forces that act upon them.

The Attitude Specificity Perspective

The theory of attitude specificity is the result of the work of David Graham and his colleagues (1962) on the question of whether or not certain personalities are associated with particular diseases, as Alexander tried to demonstrate. On the basis of patient interviews, Graham found that hypertension could be correlated with a feeling of being always prepared to meet all threats, and hives could be correlated with a feeling of being mistreated. Graham obtained some interesting results through hypnotic suggestion. He induced attitudes in patients during hypnosis that resulted in symptoms of hypertension and hives. The symptoms were very mild and did not persist, but appeared nevertheless. While specific attitudes cannot at this time be conclusively linked to specific physiologi-cal responses, Graham and his colleagues have opened the door to some interesting future research.

The Life Situation Perspective

The life situation approach to psychophysiological disease is based upon the work of Harold Wolff (Wolf and Goodell, 1968), whose theories are drawn largely from laboratory and clinical observations, such as his classical study of "Tom's" stomach and its reaction to stress. Wolff believed that stress resulted from interaction between the external en-vironment and the human organism, with the major variable being the past experience of the organism. Both physically and socially threatening life situations called forth reactions in the human organism whose ability to maintain homeostasis was based upon the capacity to withstand these threats. Wolff felt that all the organic systems could be involved in a response to threats, and he insisted that a person's attitudes determined the extent of a physiological response. Stress, therefore, was derived largely from an individual's perception of the social situation and that individual's perception was based upon several factors, particularly past experience, but also attitudes, cultural pressures, psychological needs, early conditioning influences, and genetic background.

Wolff's work is generally considered to be reasonably sound and he has made a valuable contribution by noting that many organic systems can be influenced by a social situation to the point that susceptibility to disease is enhanced and organs themselves are perhaps damaged through hyperactivity. Mechanic (1968) notes that the principal advantage of

Wolff's approach is that it is relatively simple to understand and that his research procedures are closely related to his theory. However, Mechanic feels that Wolff's theory, while useful, has not been substantiated. Mechanic (1968:316) states, "Wolff is no doubt correct that physiological adaptive responses can be generalized to symbolic threats, but the true extent of this process and its role in a wide variety of disease states are unknown."

In fact, definite conclusions concerning the specific mind–body relationships in psychophysiological medicine generally must await further research and clarification. The best that psychophysiological medicine offers us at the present time are a few guidelines for the direction of future research.

SOCIAL FACTORS AND STRESS

There is a considerable amount of empirical research in medical sociology dealing with stress and stress-related topics. Selected findings from the work of Schwab and Pritchard (1950), Mechanic (1968), and Moss (1973) will be reviewed here. Also relevant research on group influences and changes in life events will be considered. The intent of this section is to show how contemporary sociologists are helping to improve our understanding of stress.

Stress Situations

Robert Schwab and John Pritchard (1950) classified types of situations they believe may lead to physiological disorders and chronic disease. Their classification system was based not only upon the type of situation, but also the duration of the influence of the situation and the degree of stress induced by that situation.

Stress situations were typed as either (1) short stress situations, in which mild stress occurred whose effects lasted from seconds to hours; (2) moderate stress situations, in which the effects lasted from days to weeks; and (3) severe stress situations, in which the effects lasted from weeks to months and even years. Examples of a short stress situation are annoying insects, public appearances before large audiences, and doors slamming. In other words, these are the so-called minor burdens and annoyances of everyday life which probably do not produce the onset of stress-related disease. Moderate stress situations are characterized by overwork, temporary absence of loved ones, gastric upsets, or minor psychological setbacks during social interaction. Severe stress situations would be death of loved ones, severe financial reverses, perpetuation of intolerable social situations, illness, or perhaps prolonged absence from loved ones. The moderate and particularly the severe stress situation would be capable of producing a serious physiological response.

Specific types of stress formulated by Schwab and Pritchard were those of (1) trauma, such as fear in armed combat; (2) infection from disease; (3) financial reverses and the feeling of frustration; (4) death of a loved one; (5) fear of an unknown situation such as recovery from surgery; (6) fright; (7) chronic worry; (8) fatigue from overwork; (9) fatigue from extensive travel; (10) rejection and the feeling of isolation; (11) disappointment; and (12) conflict.

Schwab and Pritchard believe that the common element in their typology of stress situations, other than duration, is that of the disruption of social relationships, either threatened or actual. Other research agrees that the greatest source of potential stress is the disruption or threat of disruption of an individual's social ties to another person or persons (Dodge and Martin, 1970).

Stress Adaptation

Mechanic (1962b, 1968) attempts to explain the social determinants of stress from the standpoint of the social structure of the community rather than from the personal experiences of the individual alone. He draws on the work of William I. Thomas (Volkart, 1951), who pointed out that the meaning of a crisis lies not in the situation, but rather in the interaction between the situation and the person's ability to rise above it. The outcome or effect of a crisis depends upon how well a person comes to terms with the situation. Stress, therefore, refers to difficulties experienced by the individual as a result of perceived challenges.

Mechanic believes that in social situations people have different skills and abilities in coping with problems; not everyone has an equal degree of control in managing emotional defenses nor the same motivation and personal involvement in a situation. In analyzing any particular situation, an observer must consider not only whether an individual is prepared to meet a threat, but also whether or not he is motivated to meet it.

Extending his concept of stress from the individual to societal components, Mechanic states that an individual's ability to cope with problems is influenced by a society's preparatory institutions, such as schools and the family, two organizations designed to develop skills and competencies in dealing with society's needs. An individual's emotional control and ability to defend are also related to society's incentive systems

—that is, society's rewards (or punishments) for those who did (or did not) control their behavior in accordance with societal norms. As for an individual's involvement or motivation in a situation, Mechanic explains that society's evaluative institutions provide norms of approval or disapproval for following particular courses of action.

Hence, the extent of physiological damage or change within an individual depends upon (1) the stimulus situation, which includes the importance of the situation to the individual and the extent of his or her motivation; (2) an individual's capacity to deal with the stimulus situation, such as the influence of genetic factors, personal skills, innate abilities, and past experiences; (3) the individual's preparation by society to meet problems; and (4) the influence of society's approved modes of behavior. Mechanic (1962b:8) emphasizes the contribution of society toward an individual's adaptation to stress by stating, ". . . that whether or not a person experiences stress will depend on the means, largely learned, that he has available to deal with his life situation."

Mechanic's model represents an important contribution toward our understanding of stress by showing the importance of adaptation and explaining how that adaptation is based upon an individual's perception of life situations combined with his or her degree of preparation by society to cope with stressful circumstances. Mechanic thus identifies adaptablity as the key variable in whether or not a person will eventually suffer organic damage. The major criticism of Mechanic's work, however, is that he fails to deal adequately with the relationship between social processes and specific physiological responses (Moss, 1973). This leaves his theory too general to be of specific utility, but it provides considerable insight into the social factors involved in coping with stress.

Biosocial Resonation

Moss (1973) has conceptualized a highly promising model of stress which he calls *biosocial resonation*. The significance of this model lies in its sophisticated attempt to link sociology with body physiology. Moss (1973:241) defines biosocial resonation as "the continuing reciprocal influences of physiological and social behavior in social interaction." He suggests that human beings are biosocial resonating beings living in a social world of communication networks that enable them to perceive the environment. A communication network is composed of a group or configuration of interacting people who transmit and modify a body of social information—conceptions of the environment and the norms and values that delineate preferred patterns of social interaction. As long as the information of a communication network is perceived by the individual as being both accurate and effective, that person is likely to identify with the communication network. If most members of the network identify with it, there will be little social change.

Moss believes that conformance to the norms of the communication network and participation within that network will reduce the opportunity of an individual to come into contact with members of other networks and their information which might be of an incongruous nature. Information incongruity has the effect of invalidating that part of an individual's repertoire of information that represents a mismatch between neural representations of information and current perceptions. However, in modern society it is difficult, if not impossible, not to come into contact with incompatible networks and incongruous information. If the information from an incompatible network is judged acceptable, then change is likely to occur within the individual and possibly among other persons in the communication network.

Stress and physiological change are likely to occur when a person experiences information incongruities. Based upon a thorough review of the literature on stress research, Moss has determined that information processing leads to changes in the central nervous system, the autonomic nervous system, and the neuroendocrine system, all of which can alter the susceptibility to disease among "tuned" people. Tuning is defined as disruption of the sympathetic-imbalance in autonomic functioning. It is found in certain persons and is a result of genetic inheritance or of experiences. Moss states:

> Perception of information incongruities that are highly salient and/or remain unresolved can produce pronounced, repeated, and/or prolonged general physiological responses that may establish tuning. Tuned individuals' general susceptibility is greater than that of balanced individuals because more general physiological responses are more easily elicited and likely to be more pronounced and prolonged for tuned individuals than for balanced individuals.[1]

Moss believes that a communication network can take steps to reduce stress reactions among the network's membership through the processes of social immunity, social cure, and social therapy. *Social immunity* is the ability of a communication network to prevent members from encountering information incongruities by providing correct information, or through the isolation of its members. *Social cure* is the ability of a communication network to satisfy a member's concern about the encountered information incongruities, while *social therapy* refers to the activities and information of a network in relieving a member's symptoms accompanying encounters with information incongruities. A

[1] Gordon E. Moss, *Illness, Immunity, and Social Interaction* (New York: Wiley, 1973), p. 245.

communication network's social immunity, social cure, and social therapy are most effective when a member strongly identifies with the network. When the first two of these devices are inadequate, information incongruities are likely to remain unresolved and increase the probability of a prolonged physiological response, which will in turn increase an individual's susceptibility to disease.

To date, Moss' theory of biosocial resonation has not been empirically tested. In the absence of research applications of his model, the primary weakness of Moss' theory lies in its failure to account adequately for a lack of consensus within the information network itself. Even though Moss recognizes intra-network conflict is possible, he seems to assume that a network will generally be cohesive, and he does not adequately explain what happens when it is not. Moss is also somewhat vague as to the effects of information incongruities between several networks within which an individual may participate and the problems that may arise when a particular subgroup's information is incongruous with the wider society, as in the case of a deviant subgroup.

The merit of Moss' theory, however, lies in its important emphasis upon the advantages of group membership in providing social support for the individual. Subjective feelings of belonging, being accepted, and being needed have consistently shown themselves to be crucial in the development of feelings of well-being and the relieving of symptoms of tension. The vagueness of a few facets of Moss' theory should not detract from its overall potential utility. Theoretically, Moss' model represents the most extensive and concise synthesis yet developed of sociological and biological processes incorporated in the stress experience.

Stress and the Social Group

An individual's perception of an event may be influenced by his or her intelligence, past experience, socialization, and awareness of stimuli, but the influence of group membership is also important. Moss has indicated that the significance of a group or communication network in influencing physiological responses lies in its providing corrective information to counteract incongruities and in isolating members from opposing information perspectives. There is often a tendency among members of small groups to develop a consensus about how social events should be perceived; this both minimizes individual differences and maintains group conformity and ideological purity (Hare, 1976). Conformity to group-approved attitudes and definitions has long been hypothesized in sociology and social psychology as reducing anxiety by ensuring acceptance from persons and groups important to the individual (Presthus, 1962).

For example, research on combat motivation during wartime has shown primary group relations to be a decisive factor in determining whether or not a soldier will fight. The primary group, according to Cooley (1962), is characterized by intimate association and cooperation, and is primary in the sense that it is fundamental in forming the social nature and ideals of the individual. The importance of the primary group in combat was that it set and emphasized group standards of behavior and supported and sustained the individual in difficult situations (Stouffer et al., 1949). The group was able to enforce its standards by offering or withholding recognition, respect, and approval. The subjective reward of following group norms also enhanced the individual soldier's resources in dealing with the combat situation. What motivated him to fight was to show other members of his group that he supported them, so that he in turn would be supported by other group members.

A study conducted by Peter Bourne (1970) in Vietnam failed to find significant physiological changes occurring in some soldiers during life-endangering situations. Bourne found that these individuals ignored the danger by "hardening" themselves to become insensitive persons. They interpreted combat not as a continued threat of personal injury or death, but as a sequence of demands to be responded to by precise military performances. Bourne believed that by losing identity to the group, the individual allowed his behavior under stress to be modified by social influences that significantly affected physiological responses to objective threats from the environment.

Life Changes

Another important factor in the production of stress is the occurrence of significant changes in a person's life. Selye (1956) has suggested that any type of environmental change, either pleasant or unpleasant, requiring the individual to adapt can produce a specific stress response. Past research has demonstrated that unpleasant events like earthquakes, tornados, and presidential assassinations can induce stress (Barbara Dohrenwend, 1973). It has also been shown that rapid urbanization and industrialization are stress-inducing agents both in the United States (Marks, 1967) and in South America (Henry and Cassel, 1969). However, research on heads of families and life change by Barbara Dohrenwend (1973) has confirmed Selye's hypothesis that change itself, not necessarily the unpleasantness or undesirability of the change, is the primary component influencing change-induced stress. S. Leonard Syme (1975) has reported on studies in North Dakota and California where it was found that rates of coronary heart disease were twice as high among men who had experienced several lifetime job changes and geographic moves as compared to men with no such changes. The findings were not attributable to differences in diet, smoking habits, obesity, blood pressure, physical activity, age, or familial longevity, but to changes in the situations in which people lived.

Thomas Holmes and Robert Rahe (1967) devised a social readjustment rating scale that reflects the assumption that change, no matter how good or how bad, demands a certain degree of adjustment on the part of an individual: the greater the adjustment, the greater the stress. Holmes and Rahe have carried their analysis one step further and have suggested that changes in life events occur in a cumulative pattern that can eventually build to a stressful impact.

The Holmes and Rahe Social Readjustment Rating Scale, an adaptation of which is shown in Figure 3–1, lists certain life events that are associated with varying amounts of disruption in the life of an average person. It was constructed by having hundreds of persons of

FIGURE 3–1. LIFE EVENTS AND WEIGHTED VALUES

Life Event	Value	Life Event	Value
Death of spouse	100	Son or daughter leaving home	29
Divorce	73	Trouble with in-laws	29
Marital separation	65	Outstanding personal	
Jail term	63	achievement	28
Death of close family member	63	Wife beginning or stopping	
Personal injury or illness	53	work	26
Marriage	50	Beginning or ending school	26
Fired at work	47	Revision of habits	24
Marital reconciliation	45	Trouble with boss	23
Retirement	45	Change in work hours	20
Change in health of family	44	Change in residence	20
Pregnancy	40	Change in schools	20
Sex difficulties	39	Change in recreation	19
Gain of new family member	39	Change in social activity	18
Change in financial state	38	Change in sleeping habits	16
Death of close friend	37	Change in number of family	
Change of work	36	get-togethers	15
Change in number of		Change in eating habits	15
arguments with spouse	35	Vacation	13
Foreclosure of mortgage	30	Minor violations of law	11
Change of responsibility			
at work	29		

SOURCE: Adapted from T. H. Holmes and R. H. Rahe, "The Social Readjustment Rating Scale," *Journal of Psychosomatic Research*, 11 (August 1967), Table 3–1, 213. Reprinted with permission from the authors and Pergamon Press Ltd.

different social backgrounds rank the relative amount of adjustment accompanying a particular life experience. Death of a spouse is ranked highest, with a relative stress value of 100; marriage ranks seventh with a value of 50, retirement tenth with a value of 45, taking a vacation is ranked forty-first with a value of 13, and so forth. Holmes and Rahe call each stress value a "life change" unit. They suggest that as the total value of life change units mounts, the probability of having a serious illness also increases, particularly if a person accumulates too many life change units in too short a time. If an individual accumulates 200 or more life change units within the period of a year, Holmes and Rahe believe such a person will risk a serious disorder.

Although the majority of life change studies agree that change itself, not necessarily the type of change, is what is important in inducing stress, Robert Lauer (1974) has suggested that the rate of change is also a significant variable. Using the Social Readjustment Rating Scale of Holmes and Rahe, Lauer tested a "future shock" hypothesis on college students that indicated that the rate or speed of change and the type of change, either positive or negative, were the most important variables in stress produced by change. Though stress was directly related to the perceived rate of change, his findings indicated that the effect of rapid change can be moderated by whether or not the change was perceived to be desirable.

The Holmes and Rahe Social Readjustment Scale has been one of the most influential instruments shaping the direction of research concerned with change and stress. Unfortunately the scale has some disadvantages which need to be overcome in future studies. The scale fails to account for cultural variation among respondents (Hough et al., 1976) and some of the life events, such as divorce, can be regarded as a *consequence* of stress rather than a *cause* (Hudgens, 1974). Furthermore, the combination of life events like divorce with others such as death of spouse (which are clearly independent of a person's mental state prior to the event's occurrence) is highly likely to confound the relationships being measured (Barbara Dohrenwend, 1974, 1975).

However, in a review of the relevant literature, Bruce and Barbara Dohrenwend (1975) indicate that clarification of the methodological problems traditionally involved in life events research is forthcoming. More attention is being given to the problems involved in defining relevant life events, obtaining accurate samples from representative populations, and improving measurement techniques. Investigation is now underway, according to Barbara Dohrenwend (1975), of intrinsic differences between types of events and cultural differences between people who interpret those events. Also under study are different styles of coping with both expected and unexpected events and the extent to which life events are experienced as within or outside an individual's control. This type of research suggests that the life change approach to the study of stress will become increasingly significant in the near future.

SUMMARY

The study of the relationship between social factors and stress-related diseases has advanced significantly in the past fifteen years, but the precise nature of this relationship is not yet fully understood. It is clear from existing studies, however, that the experience of stress is a subjective response on the part of an individual as a result of exposure to certain social experiences. Before an assessment can be made of the effect of stress upon an individual, it will be necessary to know: (1) the nature of the threat itself; (2) the objective social environment within which the threat appears; (3) the psychological style and personality of the individual involved; (4) the subjective definition of the threat by the individual; (5) the social influences acting upon the individual, particularly the psychological supports offered by group membership; and (6) the duration of the threat. Obviously stress research represents a very complex investigative effort. But the potential contribution of such research to both the social and medical sciences is great. As James House (1974) has pointed out, stress research offers opportunities to learn more about a generic phenomenon which has implications not only for understanding disease processes, but also for understanding a wide range of human behavior, such as suicide, delinquency, social movements, family violence, child abuse, mental health, and many other important social problems.

4

THE PROCESS
OF SEEKING
MEDICAL CARE

Just as certain persons perceive specific social conditions to be stressful and others do not, so too will some individuals recognize particular physical symptoms such as pain, a high fever, or nausea, and seek out a physician for treatment; others with similar symptoms may attempt self-medication or dismiss the symptoms as not needing attention. These differences in deciding whether or not to seek medical care have been and are continuing to be the subject of extensive investigation in medical sociology. Although the exact processes involved in making the decision to obtain medical care are not fully identified or understood at present, enough data have been collected in recent years to support a relationship between individual interpretation of deviation in physical functioning and social and psychological factors.

For those individuals and groups concerned with the planning, organization, and implementation of health care delivery systems, the question of what social influences encourage or discourage a person from seeking medical treatment is of great significance. An understanding of the help-seeking process in medicine can have a tremendous impact upon the structuring of health services for maximum utilization by persons living in a community, both in terms of providing better medical care and making that care more accessible to the people who need it.

Medical sociologists and other behavioral scientists also want to find out how help-seeking behavior for medical care relates to the wider range of behaviors in which people attempt to obtain services generally. This type of research is essential to understanding what makes social life possible. The focus of this chapter, however, will be upon reviewing the social processes influencing the decisions of individuals to use professional medical services. First, relevant sociodemographic variables will be examined. These, however, explain only that variations in health services utilization exist, rather than *why* they exist. Thus our second topic will be selected social–psychological models of medical help-seeking. Only when certain conditions are satisfied in the mind of an individual can we expect him or her to go to the doctor.

SOCIODEMOGRAPHIC VARIABLES

A significant portion of past research in medical sociology has concerned itself with the effect of sociodemographic variables on the utilization of health care services. The reader should keep in mind that help-seeking behavior often involves interaction between several variables acting in combination to influence specific outcomes in specific social situations. Nonetheless, attempts to isolate some sociodemographic variables have resulted in studies of such factors as age, sex, ethnicity, and socioeconomic status, explaining how they relate to the behavior of persons seeking medical care.

Age and Sex

The findings for age and sex have been fairly consistent: utilization of health services is greater for females than for males and is greatest for the elderly. As indicated in Chapter Two on social epidemiology, it is clear from existing data that females report a higher morbidity and, even after correcting for maternity, have a higher rate of hospital admissions (Anderson and Andersen, 1972). If extent of knowledge about the symptoms of an illness is considered, it also appears that women generally know more about health matters than men (Feldman, 1966). In addition, it appears that the proportion of females in a household is causally linked to the number of physician visits for that household. It has been shown, for instance, that the larger the proportion of females in a particular household, the greater the demand or requirement for physicians (Wan and Soifer, 1974).

Perhaps it is obvious to say that persons over sixty-five years of age are in poorer health and are hospitalized more often than other age groups (Susser and Watson, 1971; Anderson and Andersen, 1972). But the general literature on health care utilization as well as recent studies in Rhode Island (Monteiro, 1973a), Los Angeles County (Galvin and Fan, 1975), and in five New York and Pennsylvania counties (Wan and

Soifer, 1974) substantiates the supposition that elderly persons are more likely to visit a physician. In Los Angeles County, Michael Galvin and Margaret Fan (1975) found public insurance and disability were directly related to the frequency of physician visits. Thus since older persons were more likely both to be physically disabled and to have public insurance (Medicare or Medicaid) coverage, they tended to visit a doctor fairly often.

The relationship of physical symptoms to help–seeking behavior for persons under sixty-five years of age has also been studied. D. Garth Taylor et al. (1975) looked at the number of physician visits made in response to symptoms that actually occurred in a national sample of the United States population. They compared these totals with the number of visits that a panel of physicians on the University of Chicago Medical School faculty recommended for these same symptoms. Children and adolescents were apt to see (or be taken to see) a physician more often than the severity of their symptoms required, while young adults (age eighteen to thirty-four) visited doctors in response to symptoms at rates generally suggested by the panel of doctors. But older adults, those between the ages of thirty-five and sixty-four visited a doctor less often than the panel recommended. Men were also less likely to see a doctor when they needed to than women.

One of the clearest indicators of the public's contact with the medical profession is the portion of the population who visit physicians. Figure 4–1 shows the number of physician visits per person in the United States by sex and age for 1971. Except for birth through age fourteen, females exhibited a lifelong pattern of visiting doctors more often than males. Figure 4–1 indicates three peaks in the visitation pattern for females. Initially, there are high rates during childhood, followed by a decline until a second rise during the childbearing years. After thirty-five, there is once again a decline, but physician visits by females steadily increases after age forty-five. For males, there are high rates of visits during childhood, followed by comparatively low rates of physician services until a gradual increase begins at age forty-five. For the entire period under review, females saw a physician 5.5 times a year compared to 4.3 visits for males.

Ethnicity

Several studies in medical sociology have attempted to relate a person's utilization of health care services to his or her cultural background. One of the most systematic studies has been Edward A. Suchman's (1965a) study of the extent of the belief in and acceptance of modern medicine among several ethnic groups in New York City. Such-

FIGURE 4–1. NUMBER OF PHYSICIAN VISITS
PER PERSON IN THE UNITED
STATES BY SEX AND AGE, 1971

Age in Years	Males	Females
Under 5	7.2	6.4
5–14	3.5	3.1
15–24	3.4	5.5
25–34	3.4	6.7
35–44	3.6	5.4
45–54	4.1	6.0
55–64	5.5	6.2
65–74	6.0	6.7
75 and over	6.5	7.6
All ages:	4.3	5.5

SOURCE: National Center for Health Statistics.
*Physician Visits, Volume and Interval Since
Last Visit, United States—1971*, Series 10,
No. 97 (Washington, D.C.: Department of
Health, Education and Welfare, 1975), p. 18.

man sought to relate individual medical orientations and behaviors to
specific types of social relationships and their corresponding group structures. He believed the interplay of group relationships with an individual's personal orientation toward medicine affected his or her health-
seeking behavior.

To measure the influence of group structure, scales were developed
to assess three levels of group involvement: the community level (the
tendency of persons to interact with other persons of their own ethnic
background), the social group level (the degree to which individuals
belonged to limited friendship groups of long duration), and the family
level (the dominance of family ties in an individual's life according to
submissiveness to family authority and tradition). Group structures were
further classified as either cosmopolitan or parochial. To measure individual medical orientations, three scales were also designed to assess the
cognitive (knowledge of disease), the affective (skepticism of the ability
of health professionals to treat disease), and the behavioral (dependency
in illness and need for help) aspects of dealing with sickness and medical
care. A person's individual attitudes were regarded as either scientific or
popular.

Suchman felt that individual medical orientations and group structures were related in that members of cosmopolitan groups would hold
scientific attitudes and parochial group members would hold popular

and nonscientific beliefs. Although a serious question exists concerning the validity of combining different levels of group structure and aspects of individual medical beliefs into two gross, summary classifications of cosmopolitan-parochial and scientific-popular (see Reeder and Berkanovic, 1973) —and not all of Suchman's hypotheses were supported by his data—there was substantial confirmation.

Members of parochial groups did appear to subscribe to popular beliefs about medicine instead of scientific views. Persons in a parochial group were also found to have close and exclusive relationships with family, friends, and members of their ethnic group, and to display limited knowledge of disease, skepticism of medical care, and high dependency in illness. They were more likely than the cosmopolitan group to delay in seeking medical care and more likely to rely upon a "lay-referral system" in coping with their symptoms of illness. A lay-referral system consists of nonprofessionals—family members, friends, neighbors, etc.—who assist an individual in interpreting his or her symptoms and in recommending a course of action. The concept of the lay-referral system originated with Eliot Freidson (1960), who described the process of seeking medical help as involving a group of potential consultants, beginning in the nuclear family and extending outward to more select, authoritative lay persons, until the "professional" practitioner is reached. Freidson suggests that when cultural definitions of illness contradict professional definitions, the referral process will often not lead to the professional practitioner. The highest degree of resistance to using medical services in a lay-referral structure is found in lower-class neighborhoods characterized by a strong ethnic identification and extended family relationships.

By contrast, the cosmopolitan group demonstrated low ethnic exclusivity, less limited friendship systems, and fewer authoritarian family relationships. Additionally, they were more likely than the parochial group to know something about disease, to trust health professionals, and to be less dependent upon others while sick.

Studies of racial/ethnic minorities in the U.S., such as blacks and Mexican-Americans, seem to support Suchman's theory. Ralph Hines (1972) claims that preventive medicine is largely a white middle-class concept which provides a patient with an elaborate structure of routine prenatal and postnatal care, pediatric services, dental care, immunizations, and screening for the presence of disease. Even today it may be exceptional for many blacks to seek contact with health professionals without first turning to pseudo- and paramedical healers among friends and relatives or to consult with druggists and practical nurses. Only after a series of successive failures at treatment, does Hines believe that many blacks turn to official health agencies for help. The failure to use preventive health facilities by blacks is blamed by Hines on a lack of value orientation regarding such services. It can probably be attributed to a lack of financial resources as well. For those blacks living at a subsistence level, the only option seems to be welfare medicine, which by its very nature is often bureaucratic and impersonal. Thus being black—and especially being poor—appears to militate against the utilization of certain health services.

Many Mexican-Americans are also prone to utilize the services of nonprofessionals in health care matters. Taher Moustafa and Gertrud Weiss (1968) state that low-income Mexican-Americans often consult physicians only late in their illness and in general demonstrate a lack of confidence in professional health personnel. Instead they tend to favor the use of "folk" medicine, which involves treatment by friends, relatives, or neighbors who employ patent medicine and home cures for ailments.

Some Mexican-Americans subscribe to a theory of balanced relationships within the body that determine health or illness (Clark, 1959; Madsen, 1973). A healthy body is seen as a temperate blend of "hot" and "cold" components; an illness results when an imbalance occurs. This theory derives from principles of Hippocratic medicine the Spaniards introduced in Mexico during the sixteenth century. According to the Hippocratic view, four humors of blood, phlegm, choler (yellow bile of depression), and melancholia (black bile of depression) are balanced within the body. In Mexican folklore, an imbalance of these humors can cause sickness as a result of strong emotions or the excessive consumption of either hot or cold foods. Also certain periods of life are believed to produce extreme body temperatures. Hence, adolescents should be fed cold foods because of their strong passions and the elderly should be fed hot foods because of a declining life force. Although some foods such as chile and onions are generally known to be "hot" and watermelons and cucumbers are "cold," only a few people classified as healers have the knowledge to prescribe the right foods in the right proportions for specific ailments.

In San Jose, California, Margaret Clark (1959) observed that physicians or nurses who denied the existence of the "evil eye" or other syndromes of "folk" medicine were regarded as either "liars" or "fools." William Madsen (1973) found in south Texas that even when Mexican-American patients consulted a physician, they would terminate the relationship unless the response to treatment was rapid. Yet when modern medicine produced a cure, Madsen observed that credit for that cure was often attributed to folk treatments which preceded, accompanied, or followed scientific treatment. Hospitalization, except in time of crisis, was also avoided like a "plague." "To be separated from the family," Madsen

(1973:95) states, "and isolated in an Anglo world is well-nigh intolerable for the conservative Mexican-American. Next to prison, the hospital is most dreaded as a place of isolation in an impersonal and enigmatic world."

However, a study in Nebraska (Welch et al., 1973) suggests that some Mexican-Americans are not exceptionally different from Anglos in their attitudes toward health care. This study found that Mexican-Americans have family doctors, go regularly to the dentist, and freely utilize other official health services. Madsen, too, mentions a greater frequency of physician visits among Mexican-Americans, particularly for the treatment of children. In south Texas, reliance upon modern medicine was most likely among the upper classes and those with the highest level of education. The assimilation of Anglo norms and values by Mexican-Americans apparently includes a tendency toward increased physician contact. Yet, folk medicine is still a viable form of help-seeking behavior for lower-income Mexican-Americans.

What is suggested by Suchman's (1965a) study and the other studies of blacks and Mexican-Americans is that, under certain conditions, close and ethnically exclusive social relationships tend to channel help-seeking behavior, at least initially, toward the group rather than professional health care delivery systems. However, Reed Geertsen et al. (1975) replicated Suchman's study in Salt Lake City and found an opposite trend. They observed that the Mormon community, with its strong value on good health and education, and its emphasis upon family authority and tradition, demonstrated that group closeness and exclusivity can increase, rather than decrease, the likelihood of an individual responding to professional health resources. They concluded that persons who belong to close and exclusive groups, especially tradition- and authority-oriented families are (1) more likely to respond to a health problem by seeking medical care if it is consistent with their cultural beliefs and practices, or are (2) less likely to seek medical care if their cultural beliefs support skepticism and distrust of professional medicine.

Geertsen et al. focused on the family rather than the ethnic group as the critical social unit in determining help-seeking behavior; the family is the person's first significant social group and usually the primary source of societal values. Thus knowledge of disease and family authority appear as the key intervening variables in a person's medical orientation, as knowledge assists in recognition of symptoms, while family authority impels the sick person into the professional health care system. Alternatively, low knowledge about disease and/or weak family authority could act as inhibiting factors in obtaining professional treatment.

In Boston, Jeffrey Salloway (1973) observed similar processes in the help-seeking behavior of the gypsy community. Gypsies, according to Salloway, are among the poor, uneducated, and ethnically distinct of American society whom most studies have found to exhibit the lowest rates of health care utilization. Salloway's study demonstrated, to the contrary, that gypsies were rather sophisticated when it came to obtaining treatment in Boston's complex, urban medical system. Although nonliterate or semiliterate, gypsies operated an extensive communication network in their community through which they informed each other on a regular basis who was sick, where they were being treated, who was treating them, and how pleased or displeased the patient, family, and other interested parties were with the treatment. Visits of gypsies to health practitioners or a visit by a practitioner to the gypsies was invariably a public affair. Information about the problem and its treatment were shared and became part of a general fund of community knowledge.

Salloway points out the existence of an extensive accumulation of data among family and friends concerning past diagnoses, the treating agency, the prescription, and the prognosis for specific disorders. Gypsies were also very much aware of the differences in the quality of care available at local hospitals and out-patient clinics, including the specialities they offered, and the identity of care providers receptive to their needs. They were thus able to utilize available health care services more extensively than many disadvantaged minority groups because of an unusual intra-group network of communication.

What is suggested by these studies of health care utilization and ethnicity is not that ethnicity per se is important, but that ethnicity represents a social experience that influences how a particular person perceives his or her health situation. Individuals are born into a family of significant others—significant because they provide the child with a specific social identity. This identity includes not only an appraisal of physical and intellectual characteristics, but knowledge concerning the social history of a particular family and group with all that means in terms of social status, perspective, and cultural background. As the child becomes older and takes as his own the values and opinions of the immediate family or group, or those of the wider society as presented through the mediating perspective of the family, the child is considered to be properly socialized in that he or she behaves in accordance with group-approved views.

Admittedly, the child can either accept or reject the social perspective put forth by his family as representative of his own social reality; yet the choices offered to him in the process of his socialization are set by adults who determine what information is provided and in what form it is presented. Thus, although the child may not be entirely passive in the socialization experience, what is important, as Peter Berger and Thomas

Luckmann (1967) explain, is that the child has no choice in the selection of his significant others so that identification with them is quasi-automatic. This further means that the child's internalization of his family's interpretation of social reality is quasi-inevitable. While this initial social world presented to the child by his or her significant others may be weakened by later social relationships, it can nevertheless be a lasting influence on a person.

Therefore, it is not surprising that a person's family or social group often guides the perceptual process or signals the perspective from which the total society is viewed. For this reason, medical sociologists like McKinlay (1972) and Salloway (1973) have emphasized the social network as a determining factor in help-seeking behavior. A social network refers to the social relationships a person has during day-to-day interaction which serve as the normal avenue for the exchange of opinion, information, and affection. Typically, the social network is composed of family, relatives, and friends that comprise the individual's immediate social world, although the concept of a social network can be expanded to include increasingly larger units of society.

In the case of health care utilization, the role of the social network and its specific values, opinions, attitudes, and cultural background act to suggest, advise, or coerce an individual into taking or not taking particular courses of action regarding health care. Conformity with the social network's recommendations could reduce a person's anxiety by ensuring the approval of significant others. McKinlay (1973) found, for example, that persons with close-knit and interlocking social networks tended to display greater conformity with these reference groups than those with loose-knit, differentiated social networks.

To return to our discussion of ethnicity, patterns of help-seeking behavior among lower-class ethnic groups appear to be strongly influenced by both the conditions of poverty and the existence of tightly knit social networks. Another variable which confounds the effect of ethnicity is that of socioeconomic status. August Hollingshead and Frederick Redlich's (1958) influential study of social stratification and mental illness clearly points out that the higher a person's socioeconomic position, the more white middle-class the person appears to be. In other words, middle-class blacks, Mexican-Americans, Oriental-Americans, etc. tend to take on white or Anglo middle-class norms and values as part of their participation in middle-class society. Included in this process of socialization, and the obtainment of status through the sharing of common norms, values, and life style, is the adoption of middle-class perspectives toward health care utilization. Social networks, common throughout all social strata, seem to be a much stronger predictor of health services utilization than ethnicity. Ethnicity as a predictor of help-seeking behavior is thus apparently limited to its role in providing a cultural context for decision making within social networks.

Socioeconomic Status

Another major approach to the study of help-seeking behavior has been its correlation with socioeconomic status. Until recently, it was generally believed that lower-class persons tended to underutilize health services because of the financial cost and/or a subculture of poverty that failed to emphasize the importance of good health. The seminal study in this regard was Earl Koos' *The Health of Regionville* (1954). Koos conducted his study in a small community in New York where he found it possible to rank the local residents into three distinct socioeconomic classes. Class I consisted of the most successful people in town in terms of financial assets. Class II represented middle-class wage earners who were the majority of citizens, while Class III represented the least skilled workers and poorest members of the community.

The relationship of socioeconomic status on the seeking of medical care by Regionville's people is shown in Figure 4–2. Here are summarized the responses by socioeconomic class to indicate whether each of a selected list of easily recognized symptoms were considered to be significant enough to be brought to the attention of a doctor.

Figure 4–2 shows that Class I respondents demonstrated a much higher level of recognition of the importance of symptoms than either Class II or Class III. Only two of the symptoms, loss of appetite and backache, were reported by less than three-fourths of Class I as needing medical attention. Otherwise, almost all Class I respondents were prepared to go to a physician if a symptom appeared. For only one symptom, persistent coughing, did Class I respondents not rank highest percentage-wise and this difference was negligible.

Class III respondents, on the other hand, showed a marked indifference to most symptoms. Seventy-five percent of the lower-class respondents considered ten of the seventeen symptoms not serious enough to warrant medical attention. Only three symptoms (excessive vaginal bleeding and blood in stool and urine) achieved a response of fifty percent or more, and all of these were associated with unexplained bleeding.

Thus, in Regionville at the time of Koos' study in the early 1950s, symptoms did not necessarily lead to seeking medical treatment, especially among the lower class. In addition, Class III persons were also inhibited from seeking treatment because of cost, fear, and relative need as related to age and the role of the sick person. The very young, the elderly, and breadwinners were most likely to receive medical attention

**FIGURE 4–2. PERCENT OF RESPONDENTS IN EACH SOCIAL CLASS RECOGNIZ-
ING SELECTED SYMPTOMS AS REQUIRING MEDICAL TREATMENT**

Symptom	Class I (N = 51)	Class II (N = 335)	Class III (N = 128)
Loss of appetite	57	50	20
Persistent backache	53	44	19
Continued coughing	77	78	23
Persistent joint and muscle pains	80	47	19
Blood in stool	98	89	60
Blood in urine	100	93	69
Excessive vaginal bleeding	92	83	54
Swelling of ankles	77	76	23
Loss of weight	80	51	21
Bleeding gums	79	51	20
Chronic fatigue	80	53	19
Shortness of breath	77	55	21
Persistent headaches	80	56	22
Fainting spells	80	51	33
Pain in chest	80	51	31
Lump in breast	94	71	44
Lump in abdomen	92	65	34

SOURCE: From Earl L. Koos, *The Health of Regionville* (New York: Columbia University Press, 1954), p. 32. Reprinted with permission of Columbia University Press.

NOTE: Percentages have been rounded to the nearest whole number.

among the poor. Another important factor in help-seeking behavior for Class III persons was group expectations about symptoms, further suggesting the importance of the social network. Backache, for example, was a symptom the poor commonly defined as not being a serious ailment.

For a time, Koos' study helped establish the premise that lower-class persons are less likely than others to recognize various symptoms as requiring medical treatment and that these beliefs contribute to differences in the actual use of services. This premise was supported by the conclusions of surveys by the National Center for Health Statistics in 1960 and 1965 which found a relationship by income in health care that higher income persons were utilizing the physician to a much greater extent than lower income persons.

In 1968, however, the National Center found a changing pattern of physician utilization. It was now the middle-income group consisting of those persons earning between $3,000 to $9,999 a year who had become the underutilizers. Highest rates of physician visits were either persons with the lowest (under $3,000) level of income or the highest level (over

$10,000). The higher rate for the low-income group was explainable by Medicaid and Medicare coverage for the elderly, who were overrepresented in the low-income group. Also, important was the availability of free care through physicians donating their time and the existence of public clinics available only to families at the subsistence level.

Since 1968 several studies (Bellin and Geiger, 1972; Bice et al., 1972; Monteiro, 1973a; Sparer and Okada, 1974; Galvin and Fan, 1975) have confirmed that it can no longer be assumed that low-income persons underutilize physician services. Lois Monteiro (1973a) completed an extensive comparison of the 1968 National Health Survey and a sample of Rhode Island residents. She concluded that: (1) when an illness is present, there is an equal tendency among all income groups to see a physician; (2) when an illness is not present, lower income residents tend to report higher physician utilization if "free" (Medicaid or Medicare) care is available; otherwise, lower income persons show about the same level of use as upper income persons who have no "free" care available; and (3) therefore, higher rates of demand for physicians and the availability of publicly financed care resulted in an increased use of health services by the poor.

Discussion

There are, of course, other variables related to help-seeking behavior—for example, education, marital status, and the time, energy, effort, and distance required to see a doctor. Generally, education has been found to be related to socioeconomic status in that well-educated persons, usually in the upper income group, tend to have more knowledge of disease and more sensitivity to symptoms. This may be changing, however, as the poor have shown evidence of a relatively high degree of sophistication with respect to those symptoms that should be brought to the attention of a physician (Bellin and Geiger, 1972). Findings regarding marital status vary, but generally it seems that the influence of a spouse encourages a married person to maintain a state of good health. Often single persons, widows, and widowers show lower rates of physician visits than married persons. The effects of time, energy, effort, and distance have also been found as significant barriers to physician utilization, but these factors may likewise be changing due to the impact of neighborhood health centers in low-income areas (Bellin and Geiger, 1972).

These trends have prompted some medical sociologists to suggest that perhaps sociodemographic variables are no longer so important in determining health care utilization as they were once thought to be (Bice et al., 1972; Anderson and Barktus, 1973). Where cost of care is not an inhibiting factor, differences in health care utilization by socioeconomic status have been generally reduced. Also, age has been found to lack significance in explaining the relationship between income and physician visits (Monteiro, 1973a). The sex variable may be significant only because women report more illnesses than do men. The masculine role probably dictates a "business as usual" attitude even though a man may feel sick. The influence of ethnicity upon health care utilization is largely due to the shared framework within which ethnic groups view the provision of health services. Because of the widespread influence of the mass media and the availability of increased upward social mobility, middle-class norms and values may become more important influences on health care utilization, regardless of ethnicity.

Nonetheless, sociodemographic variables should not be ignored as explanations for seeking medical care. American society has not become so homogenized that sociodemographic differences between people have totally disappeared, nor are they likely to in the foreseeable future. What is important now, as David Mechanic (1968:129–130) has pointed out, is that it is necessary to move beyond gross cultural and social differences in health care utilization toward the development of social–psychological models which can provide a clearer explanation of the processes involved in seeking medical help.

SOCIAL–PSYCHOLOGICAL MODELS
OF HEALTH CARE UTILIZATION

The major social psychological models of help-seeking behavior discussed in this chapter refer to the concepts of health behavior and illness behavior. Health behavior is the activity undertaken by a person who believes himself or herself to be healthy for the purpose of preventing disease, while illness behavior is the activity undertaken by a person who feels ill for the purpose of defining that illness and seeking relief from it (Kasl and Cobb, 1966).

Health Behavior and the Health Belief Model

One of the most influential social–psychological approaches designed to account for the ways in which healthy people seek to avoid illness is the Health Belief Model of Irwin Rosenstock (1966) and his colleagues (Becker, 1974). The Health Belief Model is derived to a great extent from the theories of Kurt Lewin and other psychologists who believe that people exist in a life space composed of regions with both positive and negative valences (values). An illness would be a negative valence and would have the effect of pushing a person away from that region, unless doing so would cause the person to enter a region of even greater negative valence (e.g., risking disease might be less negative than failing at an important task). While people are pushed away from regions with negative valences, they are attracted toward regions of positive valences. Thus, a person's behavior might be viewed as the result of seeking regions which offer the most attractive values.

Within this framework, human behavior is seen as being dependent upon two primary variables: (1) the value placed by a person upon a particular outcome and (2) the person's belief that a given action will result in that outcome. Accordingly, the Health Belief Model, shown in Figure 4–3, suggests that preventive action taken by an individual to avoid disease "X" is due to that particular individual's perception that he or she is personally susceptible and that the occurrence of the disease would have at least some severe implications of a personal nature.

Although not directly indicated in Figure 4–3, the assumption in this model is that by taking a particular action, susceptibility would be reduced, or if the disease occurred, severity would be reduced. The perception of the threat posed by disease "X," however, is affected by modifying factors. As shown in Figure 4–3, these factors are demographic, sociopsychological, and structural variables which can influence both perception and the corresponding cues necessary to instigate action. Action cues are required, says Rosenstock, because while an individual may perceive that a given action will be effective in reducing the threat of disease, that action may not be taken if it is further defined as too expensive, too unpleasant or painful, too inconvenient, or perhaps too traumatic.

So despite recognition that action is necessary and the presence of energy to take that action, a person may still not be sufficiently motivated to do something. Thus, the likelihood of action also involves a weighing of the perceived benefits to action contrasted to the perceived barriers. Therefore, Rosenstock believed that a stimulus in the form of an action cue was required to "trigger" the appropriate behavior. Such a stimulus could be either internal (perception of bodily states) or external (interpersonal interaction, mass media communication, or personal knowledge of someone affected by the health problem).

The Health Belief Model has been employed successfully in several studies of (preventive) health behavior, such as the taking of penicillin prophylaxis for heart disease (Heinzelman, 1962), vaccination against Asian influenza (Leventhal et al., 1960), and the seeking of dental care

FIGURE 4–3. THE HEALTH BELIEF MODEL

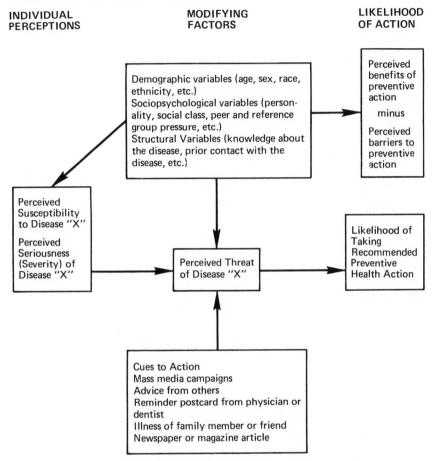

INDIVIDUAL
PERCEPTIONS

MODIFYING
FACTORS

LIKELIHOOD
OF ACTION

Demographic variables (age, sex, race, ethnicity, etc.)
Sociopsychological variables (personality, social class, peer and reference group pressure, etc.)
Structural Variables (knowledge about the disease, prior contact with the disease, etc.)

Perceived benefits of preventive action
minus
Perceived barriers to preventive action

Perceived Susceptibility to Disease "X"

Perceived Seriousness (Severity) of Disease "X"

Perceived Threat of Disease "X"

Likelihood of Taking Recommended Preventive Health Action

Cues to Action
Mass media campaigns
Advice from others
Reminder postcard from physician or dentist
Illness of family member or friend
Newspaper or magazine article

SOURCE: Marshall H. Becker (ed.), *The Health Belief Model and Personal Health Behavior* (San Francisco: Society for Public Health Education, Inc., 1974), p. 334. Reprinted with permission of Marshall H. Becker.

(Kegeles, 1963; Gochman, 1971). Help-seeking behavior was observed in each of these studies to be based upon the value of the perceived outcome (avoidance of personal vulnerability) and the expectation that preventive action would result in that outcome. For example, the Gochman (1971) study found that if children are motivated to have good health in general, their perception of vulnerability to tooth disease and the benefits of visiting the dentist would result in their intentions to seek future dental care. Conversely, those children with low health motivation were not as likely to have the future intention of seeing a dentist.

Unfortunately, the usefulness of the Health Belief Model is limited in that it has been applied mostly to preventive situations in which the behavior studied is voluntary. Obviously, however, many persons who seek health services are motivated to take action by the appearance of clear and definite symptoms. Therefore, it remains to be seen whether an improvement in health and the avoidance of future disease are strong enough motivating factors for healthy persons to utilize health care delivery systems.

Nevertheless, the Health Belief Model has demonstrated considerable utility in the study of health behavior and may yet be modified to account for illness behavior as well (see Kirscht, 1974). The merit of the model is that even when an individual recognizes personal susceptibility, he or she may not take action *unless* the individual also perceives that being ill will result in serious difficulty. Thus, the individual's subjective assessment of the health situation becomes the critical variable in the utilization of health services. In fact, a person's subjective assessment may be more important than an objective medical diagnosis. There are several studies that show no (sometimes even a negative) correlation between medical estimates of health and patient compliance (see, for example, Becker and Maiman, 1975). Mechanic (1972) has noted that the difficulty in preventive medicine is that common sense approaches do not necessarily match clinical approaches, and common sense often determines whether or not health services are sought. Furthermore, once a patient subjectively feels well, physicians may be faced with the additional problem of encouraging the patient to continue to follow medical advice.

Illness Behavior

In contrast to health behavior, illness behavior pertains to persons who perceive themselves as being sick. Mechanic and Volkart (1961:52) describe illness behavior as "the way in which symptoms are perceived, evaluated and acted upon by a person who recognizes some pain, discomfort or other signs of organic malfunction."

Several studies have suggested that laypersons generally define illness in terms of the ability or non-ability to carry out activities. Dorrian Apple (1960), for instance, noted that laypersons' judgments about whether or not a person is sick were based upon two criteria: (1) the recency or novelty of the experience, behavior, or attribute, and (2) the degree to which the experience interferes with normal activities. Barbara Baumann (1961) found that laypersons distinguish between health states according to three major factors: (1) feelings of well-being, (2) an absence of symptoms, and (3) a state of being able to perform those activities that a person in good health should be able to do. Conversely, to be sick would mean feeling bad, the presence of symptoms, and not being able to engage in usual activities. Andrew Twaddle (1969) also identified three signs perceived as illness among persons: (1) changes in feeling states, the most important being the occurrence of pain and weakness; (2) incapacity for normal role performance; and (3) other symptoms or changes in the biological state of the organism regarded as important because of their presumed implications for future activities.

Thus, what laypersons recognize as illness is in part deviance from a standard of normality established by common sense and everyday experience. Especially important is the capacity to act out one's social roles in a normal fashion. However, other factors are also important. Mechanic and Volkart (1961) have suggested that a given illness manifests specific characteristics with regard to symptom recognition and the extent of danger. Illness recognition is determined by how common the occurrence of the illness is in a given population and how familiar people are with its symptoms. Illness danger refers to the relative predictability of the outcome of the illness and the amount of threat or loss that is likely to result. When a particular symptom is easily recognizable and relatively devoid of danger, it is likely to be defined as a routine illness. When a symptom occurs infrequently, making identification more difficult, and is combined with an increasing perception of danger, there is likely to be a greater sense of concern.

Yet, as Mechanic (1968) has noted, recognition of a symptom, while certainly a necessary condition to motivate help-seeking behavior, is not in itself sufficient for a definition of illness. Some illnesses, such as appendicitis, may have obvious symptoms, while other illnesses, such as the early stages of cancer, may have little visibility. Also there are cases of persons who, despite symptoms, delay seeking health care. Cancer patients have been known to avoid cancer screening procedures because of their anxiety about learning the truth and being forced to confront what it means to have cancer (Becker and Maiman, 1975). Therefore, the characteristics of illness recognition and illness danger can be significant influences on the manner in which persons perceive a disease.

Another important contribution to the understanding of illness behavior is Suchman's (1965b) description of the stages of illness experience. According to Suchman, when individuals perceive themselves becoming sick they can pass through as many as five different response stages, depending upon their interpretation of their particular illness experience. These stages, shown in Figure 4–4, are (1) the symptom experience, (2) the assumption of the sick role, (3) medical care contact, (4) the dependent-patient role, and (5) recovery and rehabilitation.

The illness experience begins with the symptom stage, in which the

FIGURE 4-4. SUCHMAN'S STAGES OF ILLNESS EXPERIENCE

	I Symptom Experience	II Assumption of the Sick Role	III Medical Care Contact	IV Dependent-Patient Role	V Recovery and Rehabilitation
Decision	Something is wrong	Relinquish normal roles	Seek professional advice	Accept professional treatment	Relinquish sick role
Behaviors	Application of folk medicine, self-medication	Request provisional validation for sick role from members of lay referral system-continue lay remedies	Seek authoritative legitimation for sick role—negotiate treatment procedures	Undergo treatment procedures for illness—follow regimen	Resume normal roles
Outcomes	Denial (flight into health) → Delay → Acceptance	Denial → Acceptance	Denial → Shopping → Confirmation	Rejection → Secondary gain → Acceptance	Refusal (chronic sick role) → Malingerer → Acceptance

SOURCE: Rodney M. Coe, *Sociology of Medicine* (New York: McGraw-Hill, Inc., 1970), p. 108. Reprinted with permission of McGraw-Hill, Inc.

individual is confronted with a decision about whether or not "something is wrong." The decision of the person involved may be to deny the symptoms as not needing attention, to delay making a decision until the symptoms are more obvious, or to accept the symptoms as evidence of a health disorder. The person may also attempt to treat himself or herself through the application of folk medicine or self-medication.

If the decision is made to accept the symptom experience as indicative of an illness, the person is likely to enter Suchman's second stage of the sick role. Here the person is allowed to relinquish normal social obligations provided permission is obtained from the person's lay-referral system. The lay-referral system can grant the individual provisional permission to assume the sick role. "Official" permission to adopt the sick role, however, can come only from the physician, who acts as society's agent as the authority on illness. Thus, while lay remedies may continue, the individual is again faced with a decision to deny the illness and abandon the illness experience or accept the provisional sick role and perhaps seek medical treatment.

If professional assistance is sought, the person enters the third stage of medical care contact. At this stage, the person attempts to obtain legitimation of his or her sick role status and to negotiate the treatment procedure. The illness experience may be confirmed or denied by the physician. If there is a disagreement between physician and patient, the patient may go "shopping" for another physician's diagnosis which might prove more acceptable.

If both patient and physician agree that treatment is necessary, the person passes into the dependent-patient stage. Here the person undergoes the prescribed treatment, but still has the option either to terminate or to continue the treatment. Sometimes patients settle for the "secondary gain" of enjoying the privileges accorded to a sick person, such as taking time off from work, and do not seriously try to get well. Or both patient and physician may cooperate to allow the patient to enter the fifth and final stage of recovery and rehabilitation. In this stage the patient is expected to relinquish the sick role and resume normal social roles. This may not happen, as in the case of a chronic illness or when the patient chooses to malinger in an illness experience even though technically well.

Although an illness experience may not involve all of the stages described by Suchman and can be terminated at any particular stage through denial, the significance of Suchman's model is that each stage requires the sick person to take different kinds of decisions and actions. In evaluating the experience of illness, the sick person must interpret not only his or her symptoms, but also what is necessary in terms of available resources, alternative behaviors, and the probability of success. Suchman's model is similar in its approach to the positions advocated by both Rosenstock (1966) and Mechanic and Volkart (1961) who likewise agree that individual perception is the key variable in assessing modes of coping with problems of health and illness. Rosenstock's Health Belief Model stressed the perception of personal susceptibility and the benefits of taking preventive action; whereas, Mechanic and Volkart emphasized perception from the standpoint of illness recognition and illness danger.

SUMMARY

This chapter has reviewed the major theories and findings of medical sociology concerning the process of seeking medical care and the utilization of health care services. While there is no single theory or approach that has earned general consensus, the existing literature reveals the two most important variables in health care utilization to be the perceived severity of symptoms and the ability to pay for the rendering of services.

Social-psychological models of help-seeking behavior have emphasized the importance of self-perception as this relates to a person's understanding of a particular symptom. Especially important is whether or not the person perceives himself or herself as able to perform normal social roles. Studies concentrating on ethnicity as a factor have pointed to the role of the social network in influencing the perceptual process according to the network's own sociocultural orientation. Social networks have been shown to be either barriers to the seeking of professional treatment, as in the case of blacks (Hines, 1972) and Mexican-Americans (Clark, 1959; Madsen, 1973), or as important forces channeling the sick into professional health care delivery systems as in the case of gypsies (Salloway, 1973) and Mormons (Geertsen et al., 1975). Although some patients, notably cancer patients, may delay seeing a doctor because they are fearful about having their perceptions confirmed (Becker and Maiman, 1975), the generalization can be made that the more symptoms are perceived as representing a serious illness, the more likely it is that a person will seek professional services.

The ability to pay for health services has traditionally accounted for significant socioeconomic differences in health care utilization. Today it appears that public health insurance and social welfare monies have enabled the poor to visit physicians as frequently as the upper income groups. However, whether increased physician visitation has resulted in a corresponding rise in the quality of health care provided the poor remains to be determined. Then, too, the poor still reside in an environment of poverty that perpetuates their increased risk to health hazards.

Among those persons without public health insurance—those covered by private health insurance plans that still leave considerable cost for the individual consumer, or those without any health insurance—the ability to pay remains an important obstacle to help-seeking behavior.

This chapter also discussed the sociodemographic variables of age and sex, which were found to be consistent predictors of seeking medical care. Elderly persons and females generally report more illness than younger persons and males, so it is not surprising that they tend to consult physicians more readily. Although some researchers have suggested that the significance of sociodemographic variables has been reduced to the point where they are no longer of major importance in analyzing help-seeking behavior, sociodemographic differences in health care utilization still exist and probably will continue to do so for some time to come.

Two other aspects of help-seeking behavior not considered in this chapter require further study: (1) the analysis of the organizational characteristics of health care services themselves, and (2) the relationship of seeking health care to other forms of help-seeking behavior. As John McKinlay (1972) has noted, the social organization of services is another factor highly related to help-seeking behavior. There are several studies on organizational structure and processes that point to the tendency of bureaucracies to develop particular orientations toward their clients. These may result from the structure of rules and regulations or from differing social values, norms, beliefs, and lifestyles between the providers and the consumers; in any case, many of these orientations have been shown to limit services and perhaps neglect those clients in greatest need (for a review, see McKinlay, 1972).

The organizational nature of health care institutions will be considered more fully in Chapter Nine, but it is important to note at this point that the full impact of bureaucratic processes on help-seeking behavior has not yet been documented. This is despite the fact that medical sociologists have condemned the structure of welfare medicine for its impersonal nature (Strauss, 1970) and have warned that cultural antagonism between health care providers and consumers may increase the psychological cost to the consumer of using the services (Berkanovic and Reeder, 1974).

Further research is also needed in the area of relating action to seek medical care to help-seeking behavior in general. It appears that the initial step in help-seeking behavior is the individual's perception that something is either lacking or amiss. The next step is to decide whether a particular problem should be handled medically by visiting a physician or in some other way—by visiting a bartender, a friend or relative, a minister, or a lawyer. In other words, how does the decision to utilize health care services fit into the wider range of help-seeking behaviors for different types of problems? In the case of health care, there should be a belief that a cure can be obtained and that the cost in terms of time, money, effort, and energy is worth the total expenditure. Do people go to their bartenders, lawyers, or ministers for the same reasons? Until a general understanding of what motivates people to seek help of any type is developed, theories of health care utilization will be limited explanations of human behavior.

5

THE SICK ROLE

Each society's definition of illness becomes institutionalized within its cultural patterns, so that one measure of social development is a culture's conception of illness. In primitive societies illness was defined as an autonomous force or "being," such as an evil spirit, which attacked people and settled within their bodies in order to cause them pain or death. During the Middle Ages illness came to be defined as a punishment for sins, and care of the sick was regarded as religious charity. Today illness is defined as a state or condition of suffering as the result of a disease or sickness. This definition is based upon the modern scientific view that an illness is an abnormal biological affliction or mental disorder with a cause, a characteristic train of symptoms, and a method of treatment.

ILLNESS AS DEVIANCE

The medical view of illness is that of deviance from a biological norm of health and feelings of well-being. This view involves the presence of a pathogenic mechanism within the body that can be objectively documented. The diagnosis of a disease, for example, results from a correlation of observable symptoms with knowledge about the physiological functioning of the human being. Ideally, a person is defined as ill when his or her symptoms, complaints, or the results of a physical examination and/or laboratory tests indicate an abnormality. The traditional identifying criteria for disease are: (1) the patient's experience of subjective feelings of sickness; (2) the finding by the physician that the patient has a disordered function of the body; and (3) the patient's symptoms hopefully conforming to a recognizable clinical pattern. The clinical pattern is a representation of a model or theory of disease held by the diagnostician. In diagnosis, logic is the basic tool.

The physician's function in the treatment of illness involves, first, arriving at a diagnosis and, second, applying remedial action to the health disorder in such a way as to return the human organism to as normal a state as possible. The evaluation of illness by the physician contains the medical definition of what is good, desirable, and normal as opposed to what is bad, undesirable, and abnormal. This evaluation is interpreted within the context of existing medical knowledge and the physician's experience. On this basis the medical profession formulates medical rules defining biological deviance and seeks to enforce them by virtue of its authority to treat those persons defined as sick.

In medical sociology, illness may be viewed as a deviant social state brought about by disruption of normal behavior through disease (a biological state). Sociologists generally prefer describing illness as a social rather than a biological event because the condition of suffering denoted by illness is a subjective experience that usually results in individuals' modifying their behavior. Therefore, while a disease represents a medical entity that can be defined in terms of biological, physiological, and psychological functioning, an illness can be regarded as a social entity definable in terms of social functioning (Suchman, 1965a).

The sociological view of illness as deviance was initially formulated by Talcott Parsons (1951) in his concept of the sick role—characteristic behaviors a sick person adopts in accordance with the normative demands of the situation. Parsons saw being sick as a disturbance in the "normal" condition of the human being, both biologically *and* socially. Previously, the sociological study of health and illness had relied upon the medical perspective; efforts were in fact limited to correlating social factors with biological factors based upon references provided solely by the health practitioner. This medically-oriented approach emphasized the physiological reality of the human organism, but neglected the sociological reality that a person is sick when he or she *acts* sick.

The basis for describing illness as a form of deviant behavior lies in the sociological definition of deviance as any act or behavior that violates the social norms within a given social system. Thus deviant behavior is not simply a variation from a statistical average. The statistical view of deviance, as Howard Becker (1963) has explained, is far too limited because it would define left-handed, red-headed persons as deviant only because they would vary from the majority of people who are right-handed brunettes.

Instead, a pronouncement of deviant behavior involves making a *social judgment* about what is right and proper behavior according to a social norm. Norms reflect expectations of appropriate behavior shared by people in specific social settings, or they may be more general expectations of behavior common to a wide variety of social situations. Conformity to prevailing norms is generally rewarded by group acceptance and approval of behavior; deviation from a norm, however, can lead to disapproval of behavior, punishment, or other forms of social sanctions being applied against the offender. Many norms allow for variation of behavior within a permissible range, but deviant behavior typically violates the range of permissible behavior and elicits a response from other people intended to control that behavior. Most theories of deviant behavior in sociology are concerned with behavior common in crime, delinquency, mental disorders, alcoholism, and drug addiction. These forms of behavior typically offend someone.

It is important to note that not all forms of deviant behavior produce undesirable consequences for a society. Deviance from the usual norms in such fields as art, music, theatre, literature, and the dance often provides very positive rewards both for the creative deviant and the society. However, illness as deviance is typically regarded as an undesirable circumstance for both the sick person and for society. For the sick person, an illness obviously can mean discomfort and either permanent or temporary disruption of normal biological and social functioning, including death. Illness also entails the risk of economic hardship for the sick person's family. For society, illness can mean a reduction in the ability of a social group or organization to carry out its usual tasks and perform its normal social functions.

While sociologists have suggested that the explanation for illness as a social event can be found outside of biology and medicine by including illness within the general category of deviant behavior, this approach has been relatively recent. The early causal theories of deviance in sociology were essentially biological models that defined the source of deviance as something inherent in certain individuals. Undesirable behavior was thought to be caused by the genetic inheritance of criminal traits or perhaps a capricious genetic combination. The biological view of deviance has been generally rejected by contemporary sociologists as concentrating exclusively on the physiology of the individual and completely overlooking the implications of social norms and social judgments about an individual's behavior.

In turn, these social judgments are influenced by various aspects of social change. For example, in our past agrarian society, illness occurred largely in small-group contexts such as the family. It was a common occurrence and the roles of being sick or attending sick people were part of a role-set that included expectable variations in behavior as well as "normal" behavior. The routine nature of illness and its occurrence in primary group constellations (as well as the relatively limited scope of treatment techniques) tended to draw illness into the area of expectable, non-deviant behavior. However, far-reaching changes have occurred in industrialized society: the decline of family cohesiveness, changing theories in the treatment of disease, and the evolution of complex medical techniques that often require hospitalization. These developments have tended to draw disease out of the area of the expectable into a highly specialized, institutionalized, somewhat mysterious context. Similarly, our attitudes toward sick people have increasingly tended to alienate them, transferring them to the care of specialists who operate outside the context of the familiar and over whom ordinary people have few powers of control. This transfer itself, coupled with our submission to hospital routines and medical "wonders," creates a specialized set of circumstances that lead to a definition of illness as deviance. The physically sick, like the insane and criminals, represent a social category of persons removed from the mainstream of society if their illness is judged severe enough. Of course, the insane and criminals are much more stigmatized by society than the physically sick, but the point is that the pattern of treatment (removal from society and treatment by specialists) allows the person who is physically sick to be similar—though not identical—with the insane who go to asylums or criminals who go to prisons. Since the methods for dealing with ill persons and criminals or the insane are in certain respects similar, we can see a basis for defining illness as deviance.

THE FUNCTIONALIST APPROACH TO DEVIANCE

While sociologists reject biological models of deviance, present-day functionalism, stressing societal process, systems, equilibrium, and interrelationships, represents a modern version of a homeostatic theory of deviance. This model is not organic or physiological. It does not find the causes of deviant behavior in individual needs, drives, instincts, genetic combinations, or any other purely individual patterns. It does find the sources of deviant behavior in the interactions of individuals with social systems. Authority figures define certain behavior as deviant because they perceive the consequences of that behavior as destructive of the social system. Conversely, of course, they define other behaviors as non-deviant, "normal," acceptable, because they perceive the consequences of those behaviors as maintaining the system.

Two points are important here. First, the perceptions of authority figures, and the resulting evaluation of behaviors as deviant or non-deviant, may be faulty. There is thus no guarantee of essential "rightness" or of successful results from the application of their judgments. Second, since functionalists view social systems as closely interconnected entities, changes, decisions, and definitions made in one part of the system inevitably affect to some degree all other parts of the system. Hence a person's position within the social system subjects him or her to pressures (of judgment, of "labeling," of sanctions) originating in remote areas of the system. Behavior that is adaptive from one's own perspective may be labeled deviant, "wrong," intolerable by authority figures. The individual then has the choice of continuing the adaptive behavior (to which there may appear to be no alternative) and being labeled deviant, or of changing the adaptive behavior and disrupting patterns of social relationships that mean survival to them. Not unexpectedly, many persons continue the disapproved behavior and are thus pressured into deviance by the social system.

Thus the functionalist approach sees deviance as a stable and objective state, not within an individual but within a dynamic social system. An analogy may be drawn between the biological concept of homeostasis (the regulation of internal conditions within a relatively constant range in order to secure adequate bodily functioning) and the self-maintenance of society. In the case of a social system, the functionalist perspective sees society held in a cohesive range of equilibrium by harmonious patterns of common norms and values which are reinforced by mutually supporting behavioral expectations. These are "functional" processes because they make social order possible and offset "dysfunctional" processes, such as crime, which promote deviant behavior. Deviancy in a social system is thus reduced through the application of social sanctions.

According to functionalist theory, illness is dysfunctional because it threatens to interfere with the stability of the social system. The medical profession functions to offset the dysfunctional aspects of illness by both curing and preventing disease and by establishing patterns of relationships by which handicapped persons can assist in self-maintenance and in system maintenance. This analytical approach is the basis for Parsons' theory of the sick role, a central concept in medical sociology today.

THE SICK ROLE

Talcott Parsons' (1951) concept of the sick role represents the most consistent approach to explaining the behavior characteristic of sick persons in Western society. It is based upon the assumption that being sick is not a deliberate and knowing choice of the sick person, though illness may occur as a result of motivated exposure to infection or injury. Thus, while the criminal is thought to violate social norms because he "wants to," the sick person is considered deviant only because he "cannot help it." Parsons warns, however, that some persons may be attracted to the sick role in order to be socially sanctioned in their lapse of normal responsibilities. Generally society accounts for the distinction between deviant roles by punishing the criminal and providing therapeutic care for the sick. Both processes function to reduce deviancy and change conditions that interfere with conformity to social norms. Both processes also require the intervention of social agencies, law enforcement or medicine, in order to control deviant behavior. Being sick, Parsons argues, is not just experiencing the physical condition of a sick state; rather it constitutes a social role because it involves behavior based on institutional expectations and reinforced by the norms of society corresponding to these expectations.

A major expectation concerning the sick is that they are unable to take care of themselves. It thus becomes necessary for the sick to seek medical advice and cooperate with medical experts. This behavior is predicated upon the assumption made by Parsons that being sick is an undesirable state and the sick person wants to get well. By engaging in help-seeking behavior, the role of the sick person becomes involved with the role of the physician in a complementary but asymmetrical role relationship.

Parsons insists that illness is dysfunctional because it represents a mode of response to social pressure that permits the evasion of social responsibilities. A person may desire to retain the sick role more or less permanently because of what Parsons calls a "secondary gain," which is the exemption from normal obligations and the gaining of other privileges commonly accorded to the sick. Hence, medical practice becomes a mechanism by which a social system seeks to control the illnesses of its deviant sick by returning them to as normal a state of functioning as possible.

The specific aspects of Parsons' concept of the sick role can be described in four basic categories:

1. *The sick person is exempt from "normal" social roles.* An individual's illness is grounds for his exemption from normal role performance and social responsibilities. This exemption, however, is relative to the nature and severity of the illness. The more severe the illness, the greater the exemption. Exemption requires legitimation by the physician as the authority on what constitutes sickness. Legitimation serves the social function of protecting society against malingering.

2. *The sick person is not responsible for his or her condition.* An individual's illness is usually thought to be beyond his own control. A morbid condition of the body needs to be changed and some curative process apart from personal will power or motivation is needed to get well.

3. *The sick person should try to get well.* The first two aspects of the sick role are conditional on the third aspect, which is recognition by the sick person that being sick is undesirable. Exemption from normal responsibilities is temporary and conditional upon the desire to regain normal health. Thus, the sick person has an obligation to get well.

4. *The sick person should seek technically competent help and cooperate with the physician.* The obligation to get well involves a further obligation on the part of the sick person to seek technically competent help, usually from a physician. The sick person is also expected to cooperate with the physician in the process of trying to get well.

The Patient–Physician Role Relationship

Parsons' concept of the sick role is a useful sociological approach to illness because it views the patient–physician relationship within a framework of social roles, attitudes, and activities that both parties bring to the situation. The patient–physician role, like all other roles, involves a basic mutuality; that is, each participant in the social situation is expected to be familiar with both his own and others' expectations of behavior and the probable sequence of social acts to be followed. *The sick role evokes a set of patterned expectations that define the norms and values appropriate to being sick, both for the individual and for others who interact with the person.* Neither party can define his role independently of his role partner. The full meaning of "acting like a physician" is dependent upon the patient's conception of what a physician is in terms of the social role. The physician's role is, as Parsons tells us, to return the sick person to his normal state of functioning.

The role of the patient is likewise dependent upon the conception the physician holds of the patient's role. According to Parsons, the patient is expected to recognize that being sick is unpleasant and that he has an obligation to get well by seeking the physician's help. The patient–physician role relationship is therefore not a spontaneous form of social interaction. It is a well-defined encounter consisting of two or more persons whose object is the health of a single individual. It is also a situation that is too important to be left to undefined forms of behavior; for this reason, patients and physicians tend to act in a stable and predictable manner.

The patient–physician relationship is intended by society to be therapeutic in nature. The patient has a need for technical services from the physician, and the physician is the technical expert who is qualified and defined by society as prepared to help the patient. The goal of the patient–physician encounter is thus to promote some significant change for the better in the health of the patient.

Although the patient–physician relationship involves mutuality in the form of behavioral expectations, the status and power of the parties are not equal. The role of the physician is based upon an imbalance of power and technical expertise favorable exclusively to the physician. This imbalance is necessary because the physician needs leverage in his or her relationship with the patient in order to promote positive changes in the patient's health. Accomplishment of this goal sometimes requires procedures that can be painful or discomforting to the patient, yet the patient must accept and follow the treatment plan if the physician is to be effective. The physician exercises leverage through three basic techniques: (1) professional prestige, (2) situational authority, and (3) situational dependency of the patient. A physician's professional prestige rests upon technical qualifications and certification by society as a healer. The physician's situational power, on the other hand, refers to the physician's having what the patient wants and needs. By contrast, the patient is dependent because he or she lacks the expertise required to treat the health disorder.

The role of the physician is also enhanced by a certain mystique reflecting faith in the power to heal. This aspect of the physician role results from the dependence of the patient upon the physician for life and death decisions. Since the physician has the responsibility to "do everything possible" and because the survival of the patient may be at issue, the patient may be likely to regard the physician with a strong emotional attachment and the hope or belief that the physician has a "gift" or natural skill in the healing arts. Since medical practice is sometimes characterized by uncertainty, a physician's presumed talent can be a very important dimension in the patient–physician relationship. Exact proof of the existence of many minor ailments and most chronic diseases is either not possible, or attempts to establish such proof may not be justifiable because of the hazards to the patient involved in the investigation (Pappworth, 1971). Despite the great advancement of the science of medicine during the twentieth century, the physician must still sometimes act on the basis of a "hunch."

An interesting analog to the patient–physician relationship is the child–parent relationship. For some people an illness can foster a child-like state of dependency. However, while the role of the child is an immature role, the role of the patient represents a "disturbed" maturity (Wilson, 1970). Both the child and the sick person lack the capacity to perform the usual functions of the adult in everyday life, and both are dependent upon a stronger and more adequate person to take care of them. Also the physician can be like a parent figure in that the physician provides support and controls rewards significant to the dependent party. The primary reward for the child would be approval, while the primary reward for the sick person would be to get well. Yet the physician and the parent are unlike in the magnitude of their involvement with the dependent party and the depth of their emotional feelings. Obviously, the states of childhood and patienthood are not totally similar, yet the similarity is a striking one because the extremely sick person who is helpless, technically incompetent in treating his disorder, and perhaps emotionally disturbed over his condition of illness can be very dependent and fully capable of acting in childlike ways.

Medicine as an Institution of Social Control

Besides Parsons' analytical insight into the ramifications of the patient–physician relationship, implicit in his concept of the sick role is the idea that medicine is (and should be) an institution for the social control of deviant behavior. Some medical sociologists (Twaddle, 1969; Freidson, 1970a) have expressed concern that medicine is indeed an institution for the control of deviance and is taking responsibility for an ever greater proportion of behaviors defined as deviant. In other words, acts that might have been defined as sin or crime and controlled by the church or the law are increasingly regarded as illnesses to be controlled through medical care. Thomas Szasz explains this trend as follows:

Starting with such things as syphilis, tuberculosis, typhoid fever, and carcinomas and fractures we have created the class, "illness." At first, this class was composed of only a few items all of which shared the common feature of reference to a state of disordered structure or function of the human body as a physical–chemical machine. As time went on additional items were added to this class. They were not added, however, because they were newly discovered bodily disorders. The physician's attention has been deflected from this criterion and has become focused instead on disability and suffering as new criteria for selection. Thus, at first slowly, such things as hysteria, hypochondriasis, obsessive-compulsive neurosis and depression were added to the category of illness. Then with increasing zeal, physicians and especially psychiatrists began to call "illness" . . . anything and everything in which they could detect any sign of malfunctioning, based on no matter what the norm. Hence, agoraphobia is illness because one should not be afraid of open spaces. Homosexuality is an illness because heterosexuality is the social norm. Divorce is illness because it signals failure of marriage.[1]

If Szasz's view is correct, then there appears to be a long-term trend toward making illness and deviance not only synonymous, but also toward treating deviance exclusively in a medical mode. Eliot Freidson (1970a) has argued that medicine has established a jurisdiction far wider than justified by its demonstrable capacity to "cure." Nonetheless, the medical profession has been highly successful in gaining authority to define deviant behavior as illness—behavior properly handled only by the physician. Andrew Twaddle (1973:756) points out that "today there are few, if any, problems of human behavior that some group does not think of as medical problems." Therefore, to the extent that the control of human behavior is the basis of social organization and to the extent that the control of deviant behavior is becoming the function of the medical profession, Parsons' concept of the sick role helps us understand contemporary mechanisms of social stability.

Research Applications of the Sick Role

Parsons' concept of the sick role, as Freidson (1970a:228) has explained, represents "a penetrating and apt analysis of sickness from a distinctly sociological point of view." This comment is particularly appropriate when it is recognized that the sick role has stimulated a considerable body of research in medical sociology. To mention only a few such studies, Paul Chalfant and Richard Kurtz (1971) utilized Parsons' sick role concept in explaining social workers' denial of the sick role to alcoholics. Social workers in this study felt that drinking was motivated behavior and that the alcoholic could avoid his disorder if he desired to do so. Hence, the alcoholic was not entitled to exemption from normal responsibilities.

Howard Waitzkin (1971) hypothesized that adoption of the sick role: (1) in the family can lead to the prevention of disruptive strains in family relationships; (2) in mental hospitals can reduce conflict between patients and staff; (3) in totalitarian countries can permit limited deviant behavior that satisfies frustrations capable of threatening the stability of the regime; (4) in penal institutions can allow a prisoner to deviate temporarily within a carefully controlled environment; (5) in the armed

[1] Thomas S. Szasz, *The Myth of Mental Illness* (New York: Harper & Row, 1964), pp. 44–45.

forces allows an individual the only authorized escape route from his normal duty; and (6) can allow some individuals to escape military service altogether through certification as being physically unsuitable.

Another application of the sick role is found in Sephen Cole and Robert LeJeune's (1972) study of welfare mothers. Cole and LeJeune observed that among welfare mothers in New York City the general norm was to accept the dominant cultural view that being on welfare is a result of personal failure. Welfare mothers who had given up hope of getting off welfare were prone to adopt the sick role in order to legitimize their self-defined failure. This study concluded that the sick role may provide a "substitute" status by way of exemption from normal role responsibilities for persons who lack other socially approved statuses. What is implied here is that certain persons may seek out the sick role in society so they can legitimize their failure to perform adequately.

CRITICISM OF THE SICK ROLE

Although Parsons' concept of the sick role has demonstrated research utility as a framework for explaining illness-related behavior and has become a basic concept in medical sociology, the model has some serious defects which have led a few sociologists to suggest that it should be abandoned entirely (see Kosa and Robertson, 1969; Berkanovic, 1972). Gerald Gordon (1966) has pointed out that, although widely accepted, Parsons' sick role concept is not based upon systematic observation and has not been empirically validated. Gordon states that the sick role concept has been accepted primarily because of its prima facie reasonableness and logical construction.

Parsons' sick role theory can be criticized because of (1) behavioral variation; (2) types of illnesses; (3) the patient–physician relationship; and (4) the sick role's middle-class orientation.

Behavioral Variation

Much of the criticism of the sick role has been directed toward its lack of uniformity among various persons and social groups. David Mechanic (1962a), for example, has suggested that age, sex, and the importance of social roles and learned responses to symptoms vary among individuals. In a 1964 study of illness behavior among children, he found important sex and age differences among children pertaining to attitudes toward illness. Boys appeared to have more stoical attitudes toward illness than girls, and older children appeared to have more stoical attitudes than younger children.

In a random sample of persons living in New York City, Gordon (1966) found at least two distinct and unrelated statuses and complementary role expectations associated with being sick. When a prognosis was believed to be serious and uncertain, expectations of behavior generally conformed to Parsons' description of the sick role; however, when a prognosis was known and not serious, the notion of an "impaired role" emerged from Gordon's data, which required normal role responsibilities and rejected role exemptions despite sickness.

Twaddle (1969) reported at least seven configurations of the sick role, with Parsons' model being only one, in a study of Rhode Island married couples in late middle age. The exact configuration of the alternative sick roles discovered by Twaddle depended in part on cultural values and whether or not a person defined himself or herself as "sick." Not only were there differing personal definitions of "being sick," but also not all of the respondents stated they expected to get well and not all of them cooperated with the physician. Twaddle found that the sick role, as defined by Parsons, was much more applicable to Jews than to either Protestants or Italian Catholics. Jews were more likely to see themselves as being sick, as expecting to get well, and as cooperating with the physician. Protestants were the most resistant to seeing a physician, and Italian Catholics were generally the least cooperative with the physician. There were also other important ethno-cultural differences in the Twaddle study. Protestants, for example, were much more likely to regard functional incapacity (usually an inability to work) as the first sign of illness, while Italian Catholics were more likely to emphasize changes in feeling states such as pain. Jews, however, tended to emphasize fear of eventual outcomes rather than feeling states or functional incapacities.

A well-known study by Mark Zborowski (1952) demonstrated important group differences pertaining to pain. While pain is clearly a biological phenomenon, Zborowski observed that responses to pain are not always biological but vary among ethno-cultural groups. Zborowski's sample consisted of eighty-seven male patients and sixteen healthy males in New York City who were primarily of Jewish, Italian, and "Old American" ethnic backgrounds. The so-called "Old Americans" were defined as white, native-born, and usually Protestant patients whose family had lived at least two generations in the United States; they also did not identify with any particular foreign nationality. All of the patients suffered from neurological ailments, such as herniated discs or spinal lesions, which represented disorders where the pain involved would vary only within fairly narrow limits.

Although the level of pain was thought to be generally similar, Zborowski found significant variation in the responses to pain. Jews and

Italians tended to be more sensitive to pain and more prone to exaggerate the experience of pain than Old Americans. While Jews and Italians were similar in responding to pain in the hospital, the two ethnic groups differed in the home setting. At home the Italian was masculine and authoritative, but in the hospital he was emotional. The Jewish patient was emotional in both settings. Zborowski observed that Jewish patients also used their suffering as a device for manipulating the behavior of others. But once satisfied that adequate care was being provided, the Jewish patient tended to become more restrained in his response.

In contrast, the Old American patients tried to conform to the medical image of the ideal patient. They cooperated with hospital personnel and avoided being a nuisance as much as possible. The Old American patients also avoided expressing pain in public, and when examined by the physician they tended to assume the role of a detached observer by becoming unemotional and attempting to provide an efficient description of their internal state to aid in a correct diagnosis. If their pain was too much for them to control, they would withdraw to their rooms and express their pain privately.

The attitudes toward pain also varied. Zborowski reported that Italians were more concerned with the discomfort of the pain itself and were relatively satisfied and happy when immediate relief was provided. The Italian patient also tended to display a confident attitude toward the physician. The Jewish patient, however, was not particularly confident about his physician, and he seemed to be more concerned about the significance of his pain for his general state of health rather than about any specific and immediate discomfort. While Italian patients sought pain killers, Jewish patients were reluctant to take drugs because they were apprehensive about the habit-forming characteristics of the drugs. The Old Americans, like the Jews, were also primarily concerned about what pain signified for their general state of health, but unlike the Jews, they were optimistic about the power of medicine and its ability to provide a cure. Hence, they displayed great confidence in the decisions made by the physicians.

In an effort to explain these ethno-cultural differences, Zborowski believed that Jewish and Italian mothers demonstrated overprotective and over-emotional attitudes about their sons' health and that this socialization experience fostered the development of anxieties regarding pain among the Jewish and Italian patients. Zborowski also noted that Jewish and Italian parents had tended to favor their sons' avoiding physical injury by prohibiting them from playing rough games and sports. On the other hand, Old American parents had socialized their sons to expect to get hurt in sports and to fight back. Old American boys were taught "not to be sissies," "not to cry," and "to take pain like a man." If such a child were actually injured, he was expected not to get emotional but to seek proper treatment immediately.

Besides ethnic variation, laypersons may have different interpretations of the sick role. A study of Rhode Island heart patients (Monteiro, 1973b) found differing expectations of behavior between patients and laypersons. Heart patients believed that laypersons exempted them from normal role responsibilities following a heart attack. Laypersons, however, reported an opposite expectation and said that heart patients should not be exempt from normal responsibilities. Instead laypersons believed that heart patients should resume their normal activities after a heart attack while being careful to "not overdo it."

A study by Louise Blackwell (1967) on healthy and well-educated adults between the ages of twenty-five and forty-four suggested that upper- and upper-middle-class persons expect to cope with physical and psychiatric health disorders by themselves prior to seeking professional help. The study shows that these persons may have strong feelings of responsibility for coping with their own health conditions, depending upon the manifestation of the illness and the explicitness of the pathology.

Emil Berkanovic (1972) came to a similar conclusion in his research on sick role conceptions among Los Angeles city employees. Although his sample cannot claim to be representative of city employees generally, his findings do suggest that some people feel they are able to define appropriate illness behavior under certain circumstances. These persons do not reject medical theories of illness, but simply feel competent to decide what is the correct behavior for the sick person, provided the symptoms are recognized and the outcome of the illness is known. Berkanovic points out that often the physician is consulted only as a last resort and only after all other sources of health information fail to provide an adequate explanation.

What is indicated by all of these studies is that Parsons' concept of the sick role does not account for all of the considerable variations in the way people view sickness and define appropriate sick role behavior for themselves and others.

Type of Illness

The second major category of criticism regarding Parsons' concept of the sick role is that it seems to apply only to acute illnesses, which by their nature are temporary, usually recognizable by laypersons, and readily overcome with a physician's help. Yet chronic illnesses, such as cancer and heart disease, are by definition not temporary, and often the patient cannot be expected to get well as Parsons' model suggests, no matter how willing the patient may be to cooperate with the physician. Therefore, temporary exemptions from normal role responsibilities for the chronic patient are both inappropriate and perhaps impossible.

Research on patients with chronic disorders (Kassebaum and Baumann, 1965) has shown that they perceive the sick role differently from patients with acute illnesses. Chronic patients were faced with the impossibility of resuming normal roles and the necessity of adjusting their activities to a permanent health disorder. However, in a recent reconsideration of the sick role, Parsons (1975) argued that even if the goal of a complete recovery is impractical, many chronic diseases can be "managed" so that the patient is able to maintain a relatively normal pattern of physiological and social functioning. While diabetes, for example, cannot be cured in the sense that pneumonia can, Parsons insists that a chronic disease like diabetes should not be placed in a totally different category from that of "curable" illnesses if the patient can be returned to a normal range of functioning. True, this explanation may allow the sick role concept to account for some chronic disorders; still it cannot be applied to a wide range of illness situations such as the bedridden patient or the terminally ill patient.

Patient–Physician Role Relationship

A third major area of criticism of Parsons' sick role model is that it is based upon a traditional one-to-one interaction between a patient and a physician. This form of interaction is common because the usual setting is the physician's office where Parsons' version of the sick role is conceptualized. It is the setting where the physician has maximum control. Yet quite different patterns of interaction may emerge in the hospital, where perhaps a team of physicians and other members of the hospital staff are involved. In the hospital the physician is one of several physicians and is subject to organizational constraints and policies. If the patient is at home, the patient–physician relationship may also again vary because the patient and his family can much more clearly influence the interaction.

In addition, the pattern of relationships outlined in Parsons' sick role is modified if the client is a target of preventive techniques rather than strictly therapeutic measures. A considerable portion of contemporary medical practice is concerned not with restoring a single patient to his normal social functioning, but with maintaining and improving public health. The patient–physician relationship is different when the target is a group of individuals, particularly if the health problem is not a disabling illness but a behavioral problem such as smoking cigarettes, or an environmental problem such as water or air pollution. In this situation the physician or health agent must usually be persuasive rather than authoritative, since he or she lacks the leverage to control the client group. The physician must convince the group that certain actions, such as physical examinations or x-ray examinations for tuberculosis, are good for them. In defense of Parsons' sick role, however, it should be noted that the behavior involved in such cases is often "normal" rather than "sick."

Middle-Class Orientation

Finally, it should be noted that Parsons' sick role model is a middle-class pattern of behavior. It emphasizes the merits of individual responsibility and the deliberate striving toward good health and a return to normality. It is oriented to the middle-class assumption that rational problem solving is the only viable behavior in the face of difficulty and that effort will result in positive gain. It fails to take into account what it is like to live in an environment of poverty where success is the exception to the rule.

Also, many persons in the lower socioeconomic classes may tend to deny the sick role, not only because they may not have the opportunity to enjoy typically middle-class secondary gains, but also because the functional incapacity of the poor person may render him or her less likely to be able to earn a living or survive in conditions of poverty (Kassebaum and Baumann, 1965; Kosa et al., 1969). Therefore, persons living in a poverty environment might work, regardless of how sick they might be, so long as they feel able to perform some of their work activities.

Parsons' Sick Role: Conclusion

Despite the considerable criticism of Parsons' sick role concept in recent sociological literature, the reader should note that this model represents a significant contribution to medical sociology. Parsons insists that illness is a form of deviance and that as such it is necessary for a society to return the sick to their normal social functioning. Thus, Parsons views medicine as a mechanism by which a society attempts to control deviance and maintain social stability. In light of the trend toward classifying more and more social problems as medical problems, Parsons' explanation of the function of medicine has broad implications for the future treatment of deviants in our society.

While recognizing that some criticisms of Parsons' theory are valid, we should note that at least some of this criticism is based upon a misunderstanding of Parsons. Apparently some critics incorrectly assume that Parsons viewed the sick role as a fixed, mechanical kind of "cage" that would produce similarities of behavior among sick people regardless of variant cultural backgrounds and differing personal learning experiences. Instead what Parsons has given us is an "ideal type" of the sick role (see also Segall, 1976). By definition, ideal types do not exist in reality. They are abstractions, erected by emphasizing selected aspects of behavior typical in certain contexts, and they serve as bases for comparing and differentiating concrete behaviors occurring in similar situations in different sociocultural circumstances.

Therefore, it can be concluded that Parsons' model is a useful and viable framework of sociological analysis within certain contexts. Although the theory is an insufficient explanation of all illness behavior, it does describe many general similarities and should not be abandoned. In fact, writing in a later article, Parsons (1975) admitted that he did not believe it was ever his intention to make his concept cover the whole range of phenomena associated with the sick role. Two possibilities exist: (1) using the model as an "ideal type" with which various forms of illness behavior can be contrasted or (2) expanding the concept to account for conditions generally common to most illness situations.

LABELING THEORY

By failing to account for the behavioral variations within the sick role, the functionalist approach to illness has neglected the problematic aspects of being sick. Chapter Four on the process of seeking medical care pointed out that two persons having much the same symptoms may behave quite differently. One person may become concerned and seek medical treatment, while another person may ignore the symptoms completely. Z. Lipowski (1970) has noted that individual strategies in coping with illness vary from passive cooperation to positive action to get well and from fear at being diagnosed as ill to actual pleasure in anticipation of secondary gains. Several writers, Freidson (1970a) in particular, have taken the position that illness as deviant behavior is relative and must be seen as such; this is the perspective of labeling theory.

Labeling theory is based upon the concept that what is regarded as deviant behavior by one person or social group may not be so regarded by other persons or social groups. Howard Becker (1963), one of the leading proponents of labeling theory, illustrates the concept in his study of marijuana users. His analysis reveals a discrepancy in American society between those persons who insist that smoking marijuana is harmful and that use of the drug should be illegal, and those who support a norm favoring marijuana smoking and who believe that use of the drug should be legalized. While the wider society views marijuana smoking as devi-

ant, groups of marijuana smokers view their behavior as socially acceptable within their own particular group.

Becker's position is that deviance is therefore created by social
groups who make rules or norms. Infractions of these rules or norms
constitute deviant behavior. Accordingly, deviance is not a quality of the
act a person commits, but instead is a consequence of the definition
applied to that act by other persons. The critical variable in understanding deviance is the social audience, because the audience determines
what is and what is not deviant behavior.

The applicability of labeling theory as a vehicle for explaining
illness behavior is that while sickness may be a biological state existing
independently of human knowledge, illness is a social state created and
formed by human perception. Thus, as Freidson (1970a) has pointed
out, when a veterinarian diagnoses a cow's condition as an illness, the
diagnosis itself does not change the cow's behavior. But when a physician
diagnoses a human's condition as illness, the diagnosis can and often does
change the sick person's behavior. Thus, illness is seen by labeling theorists as a condition created by human beings in accordance with their
understanding of the situation.

For example, among the Kuba people of Sumatra, skin diseases and
injuries to the skin are quite common because of a difficult jungle
environment (Sigerist, 1960). A person suffering from a skin disease
would not be considered to be sick among the Kuba because the condition, while unhealthy, is not considered abnormal. In parts of Africa,
such afflictions as hookworms and yaws may not be considered abnormal
because of their prevalence. Margaret Clark (1959) points out that
among the Mexican-Americans in her study conducted in the southwestern United States, such disorders as diarrhea and coughing were so
common, they were considered "normal," though not necessarily good.
Examples such as these have led to the realization that an essentially
unhealthy state may not always be equated with illness when the persons
involved are able to function effectively and the presence of the disorder
does not affect the normal rhythm of daily life. Therefore, judgments
concerning what is illness and what is deviant behavior are relative and
cannot be separated from the social situations in which people live.

Labeling Theory and Illness Behavior

Labeling theory has so far failed to develop a theory of illness
behavior comparable to Parsons' model. The closest equivalent deriving
from the symbolic interactionist view (labeling theory) is that of Eliot
Freidson (1970a). Freidson indicates that the key to distinguishing
among sick roles is the notion of legitimacy. As shown in Figure 5–1, he

maintains that in illness states, there are three types of legitimacy: (1) *conditional legitimacy,* where the deviant is temporarily exempted from normal obligations and gains some extra privileges on the proviso that he seek help in order to rid himself of his deviance; (2) *unconditional legitimacy,* where the deviant is exempted permanently from normal obligations and is granted additional privileges in view of the hopeless nature of his deviance; and (3) *illegitimacy,* where the deviant is exempted from some normal obligations by virtue of his deviance, for which he is technically not responsible, but gains few if any privileges and takes on new handicapping obligations.

Although the health professional would argue that there is no such thing as an illegitimate illness, Freidson suggests that there are illegitimate ways of acting sick. Applying the distinction of "minor" and "serious" deviations to this typology of legitimacy, Freidson constructs an

FIGURE 5–1. FREIDSON'S TYPES OF DEVIANCE FOR WHICH THE INDIVIDUAL IS NOT HELD RESPONSIBLE, BY IMPUTED LEGITIMACY AND SERIOUSNESS

Imputed Seriousness	Illegitimate (Stigmatized)	Conditionally Legitimate	Unconditionally Legitimate
Minor Deviation	Cell 1. "Stammer" Partial suspension of some ordinary obligations; few or no new privileges; adoption of a few new obligations.	Cell 2. "A Cold" Temporary suspension of few ordinary obligations; temporary enhancement of ordinary privileges. Obligation to get well.	Cell 3. "Pockmarks" No special change in obligations or privileges.
Serious Deviation	Cell 4. "Epilepsy" Suspension of some ordinary obligations; adoption of new obligations; few or no new privileges.	Cell 5. "Pneumonia" Temporary release from ordinary obligations; addition to ordinary privileges. Obligation to cooperate and seek help treatment.	Cell 6. "Cancer" Permanent suspension of many ordinary obligations; marked addition to privileges.

SOURCE: From Eliot Freidson, *The Profession of Medicine,* p. 239. Copyright © 1970 by Harper & Row, Publishers, Inc. Reprinted by permission of the publishers. (Formerly published by Dodd, Mead.)

illustrative framework for his theory (see Figure 5–1). Cells 1 and 4 demonstrate the condition of illegitimacy in its minor (a stammer) and serious (epilepsy) modes. In these illness states, an individual may be exempted from normal obligations but gains few if any privileges—and takes on an additional handicap, stigma. Cells 2 and 5 suggest the situation of conditional legitimacy where a cold (minor) and pneumonia (serious) represent conditions that temporarily exempt the individual from normal obligations and grant him privileges on the grounds that he seeks help. With a cold, a few obligations are suspended, but with pneumonia there is release from all ordinary obligations. Cell 5 would thus be the only illness state corresponding to Parsons' sick role. Cells 3 and 6 represent situations of unconditional legitimacy; the minor varia- tion in Cell 3 (pockmarks) gains no special privileges or obligations. Cell 6, chronic illness in the form of cancer (serious), also represents a permanent condition, but here the deviant gains permanent exemptions from normal obligations because of the terminal nature of his deviance.

Freidson's classification of six distinct varieties of deviance as illness implies different consequences for both the individual and for his society. The management of the deviant and his treatment by other people is dependent upon the label or definition applied to the deviant's health disorder by the social audience. Freidson's model accounts for the proble- matic aspects of illness relative to social situations. A person with a skin disease in the Kuba tribe or a person with hookworms in Africa could be classified in Cell 3 as unconditionally legitimate, because the afflicted person would gain no special privileges or changes in obligations since the disorder would be common to most people who functioned normally in their society.

Freidson's concept, however, is strictly theoretical and has not been extensively tested. Whether it can account for variations in illness be- havior is therefore still a matter of speculation. While Freidson's model is useful in categorizing illness behavior according to prevailing American middle-class norms, it fails to explain differences in the way people define themselves as being sick and in need of professional medical care. The merit of Freidson's model, on the other hand, is that it does go beyond Parsons' concept of the sick role by describing differing types of illness and by pointing out that illness is a socially created label.

Criticism of Labeling Theory

The inadequacy of labeling theory as an explanation of illness behavior lies in its restricted approach to the nature of illness. Labeling theorists choose one (perhaps obvious) element of a complex interactive pattern and stress the unique importance of that element to the neglect of other factors involved. Few would deny that groups create deviance when they establish norms. Admittedly, the reaction of an "audience" to variant types of behavior influences the individual's self-concept and also influences society's counter-behavior. Yet, from a scientific viewpoint, behavior does not become deviant because it is so labeled by an audience but rather on account of its observable consequences. Audiences may label the drinking of cyanide in a variety of interesting ways, but the hard and observable fact is that drinking cyanide results in the death of the drinker, regardless of how it is labeled. Thus it might be argued that the relative deviance of, say, smoking marijuana occurs because there is no scientifically verifiable knowledge of the consequences of smoking marijuana. The same statement may be made with respect to other deviances such as homosexuality.

Certainly all of this is *not* to deny the importance of labeling as an influence on behavior. Studies directed toward an analysis of the influence of labeling in specific situations can guide our thoughts from a vague and general approach to the subject toward an organized framework. But there is the danger that interest in, and enthusiasm for, the labeling approach may turn it into dogma rather than hypothesis, a result obviously to be avoided. The central assertion of labeling theory is that acts termed deviant are so defined only with reference to the character of the reaction to them by the social audience. Thus, the essential feature of a deviant act is external both to the act itself and to the actor. As Jack Gibbs (1971) has pointed out, if deviant acts and actors share common characteristics other than societal reaction, these common characteristics have yet to be defined or explained. Nor does labeling theory explain why certain people commit deviant acts and others in the same circumstances do not. All this seems to pose the question of whether or not societal reaction alone is sufficient to explain deviant behavior; the answer seems to be that it is not. In a later reconsideration, Becker (1973:179) agreed that labeling theory "cannot possibly be considered as the sole explanation of what alleged deviants actually do."

Labeling Theory: Conclusion

When compared to Parsons' concept of the sick role, labeling theory does address itself to the specific variations in illness behavior that seem to be present among differing socioeconomic and ethno-cultural groups in American society. It also provides a framework of analysis for illness behavior according to the definition and perception of particular social groups, and allows the social scientist to account for differences between social settings and types of illnesses as well. Over and against these advantages, labeling theory suffers from vagueness in its conceptualization; it also remains to be seen whether the concept of illness as deviance can be explained to rival the Parsonian concept. While Freidson's model has potential, it has not attracted the attention accorded to Parsons' sick role. But most important, there is serious doubt whether societal reactions in and of themselves are sufficient to explain the generalities of behavior occurring among the sick.

ILLNESS AS SOCIAL DEVIANCE?

This chapter has discussed the various approaches to illness as deviance. The question remains whether this perspective of illness is useful or adequate for sociological studies. The conceptualization of illness as deviant behavior does make illness a sociologically relevant variable; but it also restricts the analysis of illness to the framework of a social event. This is in accord with the major intention of the illness-as-deviance perspective in sociology: to focus exclusively upon the social properties of illness and thus to exclude biological properties definable only by the physician. Yet by dwelling exclusively upon the social properties of illness, the deviance perspective severely limits its capacity to deal with questions of disease etiology and the biological aspects of illness as a condition of suffering, both of which are necessary for a thorough conceptualization of illness behavior.

It can also be argued that while deviance is behavior contrary to the normative expectations of society, sickness itself does not counteract social norms (Pflanz and Rohde, 1970). The members of any society are expected to become ill now and then during their lives. Accordingly, if illness is deviance and since deviance is regarded as a violation of expectations of behavior, it would be necessary to assume that society expects people not to become ill, just as it expects them not to commit a crime or become a homosexual or drug addict.

The illness-as-deviance approach may, therefore, not be particularly suitable in understanding and defining the behavior of the sick. Instead it may be more appropriate for sociologists to integrate their perspective with the medical definition of illness and disease in order to provide a more comprehensive explanation of illness behavior. As Freidson (1970a: 206) has indicated, by virtue of being the authority on what "illness really is," medicine does indeed create the social possibilities for acting sick and medicine's perspectives should be considered.

Twaddle (1973) has suggested that the concept of illness-as-deviance be replaced, or at least supplemented, by a concept of illness as evidence of maladaptation. This is a useful concept if we recall that sociologists are concerned primarily with collective (group, societal) rather than with individual maladaptation. Thus both illness and deviant behavior can be viewed as evidence of maladaptation by social systems—evidence of the system's failure to maintain adaptive processes that enable it to continue functioning.

Twaddle bases his suggestion on Parsons' (Parsons et al., 1953) theory of "functional imperatives," which holds that there are certain processes all systems must maintain if they are to survive. Functional imperatives are thus the solutions a society offers to certain basic problems that must be handled before any cultural elaboration is possible. They include (1) *adaptation* to the external environment, (2) *goal attainment* with reference to priorities among goals and the allocation of resources to obtain the goals, (3) *integration* of system units, and (4) *latency*, which embraces the related problems of tension management and pattern maintenance. Parsons did not include a consideration of illness or the sick role in this general theoretical explanation of social action. However, it can be surmised that the concept of illness within this framework would be viewed as evidence of a system's failure to meet a potential threat to its ability to survive. Good health would be seen as evidence of society's or an individual's continuous activity to adapt with relative success at least to the "imperative" portions of its environment.

Donald Kennedy (1973) has identified seven types of adaptive behavior in which society engages in order to cope with illness and other health hazards. These behaviors are (1) *escape behavior,* patterns of flight from threats to health, usually undertaken by either individuals or families; (2) *precautionary behavior,* protection against health hazards afforded most commonly by vaccination and regulation of migration, but also including proper diet, shelter, and such; (3) *emergency response,* mobilization of a community's resources to deal with a threat to health; (4) *curative health services,* organized activity of scientific medicine designed to eliminate or reduce the effects of health hazards; (5) *rehabilitative services,* designed to increase the level of behavioral functioning where cures are not available; (6) *scientific research,* mobilization of scientific effort to improve ways of dealing with illness; and (7) *acceptance behavior,* tolerance for accepting the problems produced by health hazards.

Kennedy's thesis is that within any aggregate setting human beings have discovered patterns of behavior that represent a workable adaptation to the threat of disease and other health-related problems. Social action in response to a health threat is thus perceived as a coherent pattern providing for the survival of both individuals and the system.

The merit of the illness-as-maladaption approach is that it provides a greater range for the analysis of illness behavior than is currently provided by the illness-as-deviance approach. This more comprehensive approach would allow sociologists and health practitioners to see the sick person as attempting to cope with his biological deviance within the structure of a particular society; it also takes into account the manner in which a society utilizes its resources to cope with illness. The adaptation perspective could thus serve as a unifying framework for the biological and sociological components of illness by correlating specific *biological* dysfunctions with specific forms of *social* maladaptation. Certainly this approach would be more useful to the health professional than the contemporary illness-as-deviance explanation, which neglects disease etiology. The maladaptation approach also avoids placing the physically sick within the general category of social deviants, a categorization that tends to make laypersons, sociologists, and health practitioners uncomfortable because it shifts the innocent sick into the category of rule breakers and criminals (Pflanz and Rohde, 1970).

To date, however, a maladaptation theory of illness has not been formulated or empirically tested in medical sociology. In fact, many contemporary sociologists remain content with the illness-as-deviance approach to illness. Yet the inadequacies of both Parsons' concept of the sick role and of labeling theory clearly suggest that a new and more comprehensive concept of illness behavior is needed. This problem remains an important area of future concern for medical sociologists.

SUMMARY

This chapter has dealt with theories that attempt to explain the relationship between illness and society. Not surprisingly, no single, comprehensive theory has been either devised or received general acceptance. Medical sociology therefore takes its place with the other branches of sociology in exhibiting a number of interesting hypotheses, all of which must be tested with regard to method and aim of research, validity of conclusions, and tendency to reality-obscuring enthusiasm. Is all of this evidence of conflict in sociology itself? It could be, and has been called so, but the present author prefers to view it as positive evidence that the discipline is alive and struggling to arrive at some consensus about certain aspects of human group life.

Parsons' concept of the sick role included the following postulates: (1) an individual's illness is grounds for exemption from normal responsibilities and obligations; (2) an individual's illness is not his fault and he needs help in order to get well; (3) the sick person has an obligation to get well because being sick is undesirable; and (4) the obligation to get well subsumes the more specific obligation of the sick person to seek technically competent help. Parsons also demonstrated the utility of medicine as an institution of social control by virtue of its mission of treating the deviant sick.

Although Parsons' concept of the sick role has provided a useful framework for understanding illness behavior, it has not been generally sufficient because of its failure (1) to explain the variation within illness behavior; (2) to apply to chronic illness; (3) to account for the variety of settings and situations affecting the patient–physician relationship; and (4) to explain the behavior of lower-class patients. Nonetheless, if we realize the limitations of Parsons' sick role theory, we can continue to apply it to behavior as an ideal-type model. Whatever knowledge we gain from such use must be supplemented by other approaches, including those discussed in this chapter. Human behavior is still variable beyond our present understanding and no alternative can be completely disregarded. Labeling theory, for instance, provides a useful approach for dealing with the problematic aspects of illness behavior. However, a definitive sick role concept utilizing labeling theory has yet to be developed. We also suggested that perhaps the illness-as-deviance approach is too limiting a perspective, since it fails adequately to incorporate biological notions of illness into its theoretical structure. A synthesis of biological and social factors might be achieved in an adaptation theory of illness, but such a theory still awaits meaningful formulation.

Note that there are points of agreement among all of the theories discussed. Admittedly, these are general viewpoints that require specific analysis and validation, but they do represent typically sociological approaches. Among them are:

1. *The idea that both health and illness are more than individual matters.* They depend on such social factors as the state of medical knowledge, cultural evaluation of behavior, awareness of relationships among different kinds of behavior, and the relative reward/ punishment conditions accompanying the fact of being sick. Thus health and illness are no longer purely biological phenomena but sociological events as well.

2. *The viewpoint that what a society does about illness depends on many sociocultural factors, by no means all of them logically based or scientifically validated.* Some of them—for example, the declining cohesiveness of the family and the increasing variability of family relationships—influence what we do about illness but they do not develop in connection with the fact of illness. They develop as a result of pressures from a changing economic system, shifts in population size and composition, changes in religious and ethical outlooks, among other things; yet they affect society's behaviors toward illness and the ill. We cannot understand this

changed behavior itself if we relate it only to illness; we must see it as part of a much broader series of social developments.

3. *Recognition that since social systems can function only through people, the health or illness of all members of society should be a matter of group concern.* Present methods of health delivery may be defective from a moral or ethical viewpoint because many segments of our population do not have access to medical procedures that are commonly available to other segments. One reason for this situation is that "underprivileged" segments of the population are perceived (very probably wrongly perceived) as being less important for the survival of the system than are the "privileged" segments. This then becomes a social problem and not a medical problem. Whether an individual is diagnosed as ill or not, how he considers the fact of his illness, the behavior of other people toward him as an ill person, all depend not on his individual characteristics, but on his position in the social system.

4. *The realization that group behavior results from the interaction of people within a specific context and that individual behavior in most of its expressions reflects group behavior.* Since our own society is a complex one, consisting of many different groups in which widely different behaviors are viewed as appropriate, we should expect (and we actually find) widely different attitudes to illness and many variant behaviors toward illness. Yet despite individual variations in behavior resulting from the confrontation by unique individuals of a multiplicity of situations, similarities of behavior among people are more common than differences within a given context.

PART II

HEALTH
PRACTITIONERS

6

THE PHYSICIAN IN
A CHANGING SOCIETY

There are over 350,000 medical doctors actively practicing medicine in the United States (National Center for Health Statistics, 1975).[1] They constitute less than 10 percent of the total health manpower, yet the entire health care industry in the United States is subordinate to their professional authority, regardless of whether the task is patient care, research, or administration. Physicians not only control the conditions of their own work, but also the work of most of the other members of the health profession as well. Consequently, the status and prestige accorded to the physician by the general public is recognition of the physician's monopoly of one of society's most essential functions: the definition and treatment of health disorders.

The Kingsley Davis and Wilbert Moore (1945) theory of social stratification partially explains the physician's status in American society. Davis and Moore suggest that differential rewards and prestige are necessary as a means of ensuring that essential tasks are accomplished. All societies, therefore, need some method of allocating members into important positions so they will be motivated to perform the duties these positions require. In complex societies, these positions usually require

---

[1] According to official U.S. government figures, there were 350,609 M.D.s in active practice in the United States in 1974; approximately 60 percent of these physicians provided office-based patient care. For every 100,000 Americans, it was estimated there were about 182 physicians. See National Center for Health Statistics, *Health Resources Statistics* (Washington, D.C.: U.S. Department of Health, Education and Welfare, 1975).

skilled personnel. Thus, arrangements must be made to ensure that not only motivated people, but also skilled people are available to fill these important positions, and the Davis-Moore argument is that it is necessary to make such positions attractive so that people will want to compete for them. Rewards are related to the social importance of a particular position and the relative availability of qualified persons. Thus the greatest rewards are associated with those roles that (1) have the greatest importance for society and (2) require the greatest training or talent. Accordingly, the status, prestige, and financial reward of the physician in American society is a result of society's need to place able persons in the critically important position of providing medical care.

THE PROFESSIONALIZATION OF THE PHYSICIAN

However, the social importance of the medical function and the limited number of persons with the training and talent to perform as physicians are not the only criteria explaining the professional dominance of the physician group. A particularly important factor is the organization of the medical profession itself. William Goode (1957, 1960), after eliminating such occupational traits as prestige, power, and income, has noted that two basic characteristics are sociologically relevant in explaining professionalism: prolonged training in a body of specialized, abstract knowledge and an orientation toward providing a service.

Moreover, once a professional group becomes established, Goode indicates that it begins further to consolidate its power by formalizing social relationships that govern the interaction of the professionals with their clients, their colleagues, and with official agencies outside the profession. Recognition on the part of both clients, outside agencies, and the wider society of the profession's claim to competence, as well as the profession's ability to control its own membership, is necessary if professional decisions are not to be reviewed by outside authorities. Once this situation (public acceptance of claims to competence and the profession's control of its membership) occurs, Goode believes that additional features of the profession can be established. Goode (1960:903) described these features as follows:

1. The profession determines its own standards of education and training.
2. The student professional goes through a more stringent socialization experience than the learner in other occupations.
3. Professional practice is often legally recognized by some form of licensure.

4. Licensing and admission boards are manned by members of the profession.
5. Most legislation concerned with the profession is shaped by that profession.
6. The occupation gains income, power, and prestige ranking, and can demand high-caliber students.
7. The practitioner is relatively free of lay evaluation and control.
8. The norms of practice enforced by the profession are more stringent than legal controls.
9. Members are more strongly identified and affiliated with the profession than are members of other occupations with theirs.
10. The profession is more likely to be a terminal occupation. Members do not care to leave it, and a higher proportion assert that if they had it to do over again, they would again choose that type of work.

What Goode has accomplished, for our purposes, is the development of guidelines for analyzing the development of the medical profession in American society. While physicians in the U.S. have traditionally shared a basic service orientation, the second requirement, that of lengthy training in a specialized and abstract body of knowledge, was initially lacking. Most American medical practitioners in the period before the American Revolution were ship's surgeons, apothecaries, or clergy who had obtained a familiarity with medical knowledge in Europe (see Coe, 1970; Major, 1954; Stevens, 1971). Few practitioners had been educated in either a university setting or a medical school. Anyone who wanted to practice medicine could do so and could claim the title of "doctor," which in Europe was reserved exclusively for persons educated at a university. The most distinguished early American physicians were those trained at the University of Edinburgh, Great Britain's foremost medical school in that era. From this small group of British-trained physicians came the impetus for establishment of the first American medical school in 1765 at the College of Philadelphia. This medical school, which later became part of the University of Pennsylvania, was subsequently joined in the years prior to 1800 by the organization of other medical schools at King's College (Columbia), Harvard, and Dartmouth.

After 1800, American medical schools virtually mushroomed, and an impressive body of scientific knowledge was formulated, both in Europe and the United States. Louis Pasteur's germ theory of disease, advanced during the mid-1800s, provided the foundation for the discovery, classification, and treatment of numerous health problems. Other significant medical improvements during the 1800s included René Laennec's (1816) invention of the stethoscope; the work of Crawford

Long (1842), Robert Liston (1846), and William Morton (1846) on ether as an anesthetic; Claude Bernard's (1849) discovery of glycogen and the development of a theory of hormonal secretions providing the basis for endocrinology; Rudolf Virchow's (1858) investigation of cellular pathology; Joseph Lister's (1866) use of antiseptic procedures in surgery; Robert Koch's work in bacteriology leading to the discovery of the bacillus for anthrax (1876), tuberculosis (1882), and cholera (1883); William Welch's (1892) discovery of staphylococcus; Wilhelm Roentgen's (1895) development of the x-ray; and Ronald Ross' (1895) research on the cause of malaria. Thus, by the beginning of the twentieth century, American medical doctors were clearly able to claim the two core characteristics of a profession as outlined by Goode—a service orientation and a body of specialized knowledge.

The American Medical Association

Another important step was necessary before physicians could take advantage of their evolving professional status—the organization of physicians into a professionally identifiable group. With the founding of the American Medical Association in Philadelphia in 1847 physicians could mark the beginning of a new era in medicine (see American Medical Association, 1951; Burrow, 1963; Coe, 1970; Fishbein, 1947; Freidson, 1970a; Hyde and Wolff, 1954; Stevens, 1971). Weak and ineffectual in the beginning, the American Medical Association gradually extended its authority to become the single greatest influence on the organization and practice of medicine in the United States.

Two internal organizational measures were highly significant in this process. First, in 1883 the *Journal of the American Medical Association* appeared. This journal not only disseminated the latest medical knowledge and contributed to the prestige of the association, but also developed an awareness among the members of the AMA of their primary allegiance to the medical profession. Second, in 1902 an important reorganization took place when the AMA was divided into component societies on the local level (district or county medical societies), constituent societies (state or territorial medical associations), a national House of Delegates, a Board of Trustees, and national officers.

As a result of this change, the basic unit of the AMA had become the local society. Most important, it had the authority to set its own qualifications for membership. In theory, all "reputable and ethical" licensed physicians were eligible to join the local society, but final approval of membership was dependent upon the local society's arbitrary discretion. The power of the local society was further enhanced because

AMA organizational structure permits no formal right to a hearing or right to appeal the local society's decisions. Thus threats of denial of membership or of expulsion from the local society represent powerful sanctions, since there is no alternative medical association and AMA membership can be critically important to a physician's career. Often such membership influences patient referrals, consultations, specialty ratings, and other professional and social contacts important to a highly successful medical practice.

In 1975 the AMA had a membership of 180,000 physicians. This figure represents less than 60 percent of all active and inactive doctors of medicine. Nonmembers include those who have retired, who have not satisfied local residence requirements, who have violated the AMA code of ethics, and who are employed by the government, the armed forces, research agencies, or universities and thus believe they do not need the benefits of membership. Other physicians may not belong because for some reason they are unacceptable to the local society or because they themselves disapprove of the AMA's policies. Often foreign doctors are excluded and sometimes racial/ethnic minority persons, especially black physicians in the South, have been denied membership. Although the AMA has tried to discourage this practice, it has not always been success-ful because of the authority of the local societies to determine member-ship qualifications. James Burrow (1963), in his political history of the AMA, has pointed out that local societies have the power to enforce conformity at their level, but the national organization is relatively weak in implementing national policies.

Despite the strength of local societies, there is little dispute within the AMA concerning its national objectives. As Eliot Freidson (1970a) and others have pointed out, the actual exercise of power in the Ameri-can Medical Association is concentrated in the hands of a relatively limited number of physicians. Many members have either not been interested in the association's internal politics or have been too busy with their own medical practices to devote time to professional problems. The vast majority has usually been content to let the AMA represent the medical profession with Congress and other governmental agencies. The association in turn keeps its membership informed about significant medical and health legislation on both state and national levels.

Additionally, there is no forum for effective dissent within the AMA because public debates are disapproved in order to project an image of a united profession in the association's interaction with outside agencies. Dissenting issues within the AMA must first win major support at the local level or they are not considered further. And the *Journal of the American Medical Association* seldom publishes views other than official policy. Opposition groups within the AMA are further prevented from gaining power because of the indirect system of elections for national officers. Only the House of Delegates, which consists of representatives from each state, elects persons to the top offices and to the Board of Trustees, which exercises day-to-day control over the association. Many influential appointments to AMA councils and committees are made directly by the Board of Trustees and are not voted upon by either the general membership or the House of Delegates.

In an examination of the American Medical Association by David Hyde and Payson Wolff in the *Yale Law Journal* (1954), the overall power base of the AMA was described as resulting from three primary sources: (1) power over the medical profession, (2) a strong economic position, and (3) the social status of the physician. The power of the AMA over the medical profession was described as the power of *consent*, *monopoly*, and *coercion*. Hyde and Wolff speculated that the AMA did have the consent of a majority of physicians to represent organized medicine. This consent was derived from an awareness among medical doctors that a formal organization was needed to enforce professional integrity, to advance professional interests, and to resist lay attempts to control medical matters. Monopoly resulted from the AMA's position as the only nationally recognized professional association available to the physician. The AMA's power of coercion was due to its authority to ostracize offending physicians and also to the incorporation of AMA guidelines into state medical practice laws and licensing procedures.

One of the most significant guiding principles of the AMA has been its view of the physician as an independent practitioner largely free of public control who engages in private medical practice on a fee-for-service basis. Since the 1920s a considerable portion of the AMA's energies have gone toward maintaining this situation, particularly in regard to the issue of national health insurance, which the AMA believes will inhibit the ability of the medical profession to provide quality medical care because it is likely to reduce the physician's freedom to control both the conditions of practice and the setting of fees. A more extensive discussion of the complex national health insurance controversy will be presented in Chapter Nine, but at this point it is important to note that the major public image of the American Medical Association has become that of a protective trade association seeking to ensure that challenges to the physician's position as an individual entrepreneur of health services is not hindered. With the majority of U.S. physicians (about 60 percent) represented in its membership, the AMA has been able to claim that it speaks for organized medicine. However, this claim may be misleading as there is increasing evidence that the AMA's membership is declining in numbers (AMA membership was 219,000 in 1973 compared to 180,000 in 1975) and that it does not represent the opinions and attitudes of a growing minority of physicians.

In two recent studies of Yale University School of Medicine students and graduates, Lee Goldman (1974a, 1974b) observed that support for reform legislation in health insurance went well beyond the AMA's compromise efforts. The strongest predictor of medical attitudes was political ideology. Physicians who identified themselves as politically conservative were more likely than liberals to be members of the AMA and to oppose national health insurance. But only 50 percent of the Yale sample either belonged to the AMA or planned to apply for membership·

While Yale physicians may not be typical of all other physicians, Goldman's studies do imply that perhaps a substantial portion of American physicians may not be represented by the views of the American Medical Association. Consequently, there may be considerably more variation in the medical and political attitudes of medical doctors in the United States than has been previously assumed. If this is the case, then the reputation of the AMA as a powerful lobby in Washington, D.C., may, to some extent, be spurious, despite conflicting evidence (see Burrow, 1963). David Mechanic (1972:28) seems to find for a weaker AMA when he explains that the idea of any particular political group's being able to dominate health policy is not consistent with the history of recent social legislation in health care. Although the AMA opposed both Medicare and the Regional Medical Program, these programs became law.

However, the evidence does not go so far as to conclude that the AMA no longer yields significant influence in health legislation. In fact, as Mechanic has also pointed out, even legislation that passed Congress over the objections of the AMA has taken those objections into account and attempted to protect the interests of the medical profession as much as possible. With its organization, influence, and financing, the AMA will likely remain a very important factor in future legislative battles in the health sector and will continue to be instrumental in shaping the overall direction of the medical profession. As Rosemary Stevens (1971:532) has surmised in her excellent analysis of the medical profession, the primary future role of the AMA seems likely to be that of a negotiating body with government and a governmental agent (by way of providing professional standards and discipline), rather than a protective trade association or the spokesman for medical education and health manpower development. While the AMA has apparently lost the battle for national health insurance, it still will have a critical role in policy development and administration of any national health care program.

The Control of Medical Education

The professionalization of medicine would not have been possible without control over the standards for medical education. At the beginning of the nineteenth century, the United States had seen the emergence of a vast number of proprietary medical schools. These schools, in the absence of any educational controls, were designed to offer medical degrees as part of a profit-making venture. It is estimated that about 400 proprietary medical schools existed during the 1800s; generally they had low standards of instruction, poor facilities, and admitted any student who could pay the required tuition. Since proprietary schools competed with other schools of this type and with schools affiliated with universities, they attempted to make their programs as attractive as possible. One school, for example, gave free trips to Europe upon graduation to any students who paid fees regularly and in cash for three years (see Stevens, 1971). Anyone who had the financial resources could obtain a medical degree and practice medicine, especially in the developing American West.

In 1904 the AMA established the Council on Medical Education to originate suggestions for the improvement of education and to become the association's agency for implementing educational change. The Council eventually became an important regulating agency that operated both to establish high standards in medical schools and to strengthen the AMA's influence in medical education. The subsequent success of this effort was stimulated by one of the most important events in the history of medical education: the Flexner Report.

Sponsored by the Carnegie Foundation for the Advancement of Teaching, Abraham Flexner visited every medical school in the country and issued his famous report in 1910. Hoping to obtain funds from the prestigious Carnegie Foundation, most medical schools were anxious to discuss their problems and shortcomings while extending their full cooperation to Flexner in assessing their particular situation. The Flexner Report came out as a devastating indictment of the lack of quality medical education in the United States. Only three medical schools—Harvard, Western Reserve, and Johns Hopkins—were given full approval; many other schools were characterized by Flexner as "plague spots," "utterly wretched," "out-and-out commercial enterprises," "wholly inadequate," and so forth (Stevens, 1971:67).

Flexner strongly recommended that medical schools consist of a full-time faculty and that both laboratory and hospital facilities be made available to medical students. He also urged that standards concerning the admission of students to medical schools be established and that the qualifications of medical school faculty be raised significantly. He likewise believed that medical education should be conducted by universities on a graduate level and that teaching and research functions be integrated within the institution offering the instruction. The example of a model medical school was Johns Hopkins University, with its medical education system containing a medical school, a nursing school, and a university hospital. Johns Hopkins required the bachelor's degree or its equivalent for admission as well as specific premedical college-level courses.

Although widespread protests arose from the affected schools, the Flexner Report induced considerable improvement in medical education. The better schools improved their programs and the lesser schools eventually closed because of the bad publicity, financial adversity, and failure to meet the requirements of state licensing boards. Many states refused to certify the graduates of inferior medical schools, and money from various foundations was usually channeled only into those schools with good reputations. Since the sole source of medical school ratings continued to be the AMA's Council on Medical Education, the medical profession was able to retain an effective monopoly over educational regulation.

In summary, by the mid-1920s, the medical profession had consolidated its professional position to the point that it clearly had become a model of professionalism. According to Goode's analysis of the characteristics of a profession, the medical profession had not only met the basic criteria of being a service occupation supported by prolonged training in a specialized knowledge, but furthermore, it had determined its own standards of education and training, had successfully demanded high-caliber students, had staffed its own licensing and admission boards, had shaped legislation in its own interests, had developed stringent professional sanctions, had become a terminal occupation, and was free of formal lay evaluation and control. Although threatened by current social legislation regarding reforms in health care, physicians constitute, and will in all probability remain, the dominant professional group in the rendering of medical service in the United States.

THE SOCIALIZATION OF THE PHYSICIAN

In order to understand the perspectives of physicians as a professional group, it is important also to consider the manner in which physicians are selected and trained as medical professionals. In the late 1970s, nearly 15,000 students will be selected annually out of some 45,000 applicants to begin training at 119 medical schools in the United States. Some 80 percent of these first-year students will be male; the remaining 20 percent represents a significant increase for females. In the 1960s only about 9 percent of all first-year medical students were female. There has also been an increase in the percentage of racial minority students, especially blacks. Since 1969, the percentage of racial minorities in first-year classes has risen from three to seven percent. Despite these changes, the majority of medical students in the United States remain white and male.

Typically, first-year medical students will be between the ages of twenty-one and twenty-three and will have at least a bachelor's degree with a 3.4 (on a 4.0 scale) premedical grade point average. Most likely the undergraduate college major will be in biology, chemistry, zoology, premedical, or psychology. Because these students are motivated and committed to a well-defined, terminal career goal, there is a high probability of successfully completing medical school once accepted; about 95 percent of all entering medical students currently attain the M.D. degree.

Several studies on the social origins of American medical students clearly show that most are from upper- and upper-middle-class families. Although there are signs that increasing numbers of lower-middle- and lower-class students are entering medical school, most medical students are homogeneous in terms of social class affiliation. For instance, Howard Becker et al. (1961), in a major study of students at the University of Kansas Medical School in the late 1950s, found that lower-class medical students, by virtue of their undergraduate education and commitment to becoming successful physicians, had clearly assimilated middle-class norms and values.

Family influence seems to be an important variable in encouraging and reinforcing the ambitions of the future recruit to the medical profession. Having a parent or close relative who is a physician also seems to be a distinct advantage. Natalie Rogoff (1957) observed in a study of medical students at the University of Pennsylvania that the more frequent the contact with a physician, the easier it was to form the idea of becoming a physician. Of those students with a physician father, 74 percent had made a decision to go to medical school before the age of fourteen. For medical students with either a distant relative as a physician or no family relationship to a physician, the percentage indicating a career decision under the age of fourteen was 52 percent and 40 percent respectively. In the Becker et al. study, a random sample of medical students disclosed that 48 percent of the sample had parents or other relatives who practiced medicine and another 23 percent were friendly with their family physician or knew other physicians as friends. Altogether, 71 percent of the total sample had some contact with members of the medical profession prior to making their decision about becoming a medical doctor. Samuel Bloom (1973) found that while medical students at the State University of New York Downstate Medical Center tended to make a career decision for medicine relatively late, those students having sustained contact with a physician through immediate or close family relationships likewise tended to consider medicine as a career earlier than other students. These findings support Oswald Hall's (1948) contention that the decision to study medicine is largely social in character, that is, it originates in a social group that is able to generate and nurture the medical ambition.

The reason given by most medical students for choosing a career in medicine has been generally that of wanting "to help people." At Tulane University Medical School, Leonard Reissman and Ralph Platou (1960) found that a majority of both junior and senior medical students could be described as "humanitarians," rather than "scientists" or "professionals." A major characteristic of the "humanitarian" student was a strong orientation toward working with patients and enjoying interpersonal relations. Becker et al. likewise found that first-year medical students had idealistic long-range perspectives about why they selected medicine as a career. These perspectives were summarized as follows (Becker et al., 1961:72) :

1. Medicine is the best of all professions.
2. When we begin to practice, we want to help people, have enjoyable, satisfying work while upholding medical ideals. We want to earn enough money to lead comfortable lives, but this is not our primary concern.

Some medical students no doubt enter medical school in order to make money or for the prestige of the M.D. degree, or both. According to John Columbotos (1969), physicians from a lower-class social origin were more likely than upper-class doctors to emphasize success values as reasons for going into medicine. But once in medical practice, social class background became less significant. Those physicians who were initially success oriented became less so after commencing their practices, while the reverse occurred with those who were less success oriented. Columbotos suggested this trend was most likely due to socialization by colleagues. Success oriented physicians were probably encouraged to be less obvious about their ambitions, and the less success oriented were most likely encouraged to strive for the level of status indicative of their professional group. Becker et al. noted that most entering medical students *assumed* they would be well-paid. Hence, making money was apparently secondary to helping patients. Many resented the notion that they were solely out to make money.

Once the medical student begins training, he or she is expected to acquire a foundation of knowledge in the basic medical sciences and the techniques employed in the actual practice of medicine. Included in this process is the internalization of ethical and moral principles that are essential if the physician is to be trusted by patients, colleagues, and the community and is to maintain professional autonomy. Most courses of study range from thirty-two to forty-five months, and the educational experience is usually divided into basic medical science studies and clinical studies. Basic medical science studies consist of courses in anatomy, biochemistry, physiology, pathology, pharmacology, microbiology, physical diagnosis, clinical laboratory procedures, and often behavioral science. The clinical programs consist of learning to use basic medical science to solve clinical problems by working with patients under the supervision of the faculty. The students also rotate through clerkships in various medical services, such as medicine, surgery, pediatrics, obstetrics-gynecology, psychiatry, and other specialties.

Much of the sociological research concerning medical education has focused on the consequences of that experience other than mastery of medical knowledge. Renée Fox (1957) found that medical students at Cornell Medical School acquired basically two traits as a result of their medical training: ability to be emotionally detached from the patient and to tolerate uncertainty. Fox, whose work was part of an extensive study of student physicians (see Merton et al., 1957), noted that the medical student experienced three types of uncertainty. First, there was uncertainty resulting from an awareness of not being able to learn everything about medicine. Second, there was the realization that limitations existed in current medical knowledge and techniques. The first two uncertainties led to a third type of uncertainty in which medical students had problems distinguishing between personal ignorance and the limits of available knowledge. However, Fox observed that as the student acquired medical knowledge and gained experience, along with a sense of personal adequacy in medicine, he or she learned to cope with the uncertainty and to assess conflicting evidence objectively in arriving at a diagnosis. This process was assisted by the realization that other medical students were coping with the same problems and that the faculty also experienced uncertainty in their everyday work.

At the University of Kansas Medical School, Becker et al. (1961) determined that the students developed a strong appreciation of clinical experience (actually working with patients rather than reading about disease and studying it in the laboratory) and that they acquired a sense of responsibility about patients. They also learned to view disease and death as medical problems rather than as emotional issues. The focal point of their passage through medical school was to graduate; since they could not learn everything they needed to know to practice medicine, they directed their efforts toward finding the most economical ways of learning. Generally, they tried to guess what the faculty wanted them to know, and then they studied this material for the examinations. Even so, they found that they put in an eight-hour day of classes and laboratories. They also studied four to five hours on week nights and continued studying on the weekends.

The Becker et al. study explored the charge that medical students become cynical as a result of their medical education. In reply, Becker and his colleagues noted that medical students did appear to enter medical school openly idealistic, but once in medical school, their idealism was replaced with a concern for getting through. Becker observed that medical students may in fact become cynical while in school, but he also pointed out that attitudes are often situational. Thus when graduation approached, idealism seemed to return as the students could set aside the immediate problem of completing their program of study. What had happened was that medical students had been isolated in an institutional setting and forced to adjust to the demands of that setting. But once the medical student was ready to return to the mainstream of society, the student again became concerned about service to humanity. In an earlier article, Becker and Blanche Greer (1958) had argued that cynicism on the part of medical students represented growth toward a more realistic perspective. What appeared as a harmful change of attitude was actually part of a functional learning process fitted to the physician's role of maintaining an objective perspective of health and disease.

In summary, the Fox and Becker et al. studies demonstrate that the experience of a medical education provides not only basic knowledge and techniques concerning the diagnosis and treatment of health disorders, but also inculcates the norms and values of the medical profession. Fox points out that medical students develop a tolerance for uncertainty and a detached concern for patients, while Becker et al. found that medical students developed an appreciation of clinical experience and medical responsibility for patients. A later study of Harvard interns (Miller, 1970) corroborated *clinical perspective* and *medical responsibility* as the enduring perspectives acquired by interns. Medical education does indeed seem to provide the professional perspectives needed by the physician.

There were, however, some differences between the Fox and Becker et al. studies. The most notable difference concerned Fox's impression that medical students were socialized into the physician role by anticipating their future behavior patterns as physicians during their student years. In contrast, Becker et al. did not find that medical students were socialized into a physician role. Kansas medical students were too busy trying to excel academically, and the faculty did not allow them to assume professional attitudes. Moreover, they had very low status in an apparently inflexible hierarchy. A major criticism of this finding is that even though Becker and his associates did not observe socialization taking place, that does not mean that the medical students did not recognize the dimensions of the physician role and did not incorporate these dimensions into their perspective for use at a future time.

Other research (Huntington, 1957; Lief, 1971) has clearly supported the thesis that the medical student goes through a process of anticipation, which is aided by increasing responsibility and competence during the clinical years of medical school. Thus, student self-image was gradually replaced by a professional self-image as "doctor" the nearer the medical student approached graduation. Mary Huntington (1957) discovered that medical students felt least like "doctors" around their fellow students or the medical school faculty, but their professional image was enhanced by their interaction with patients who attributed physician status to them.

However, in a later article Fox (1974) speculated that medical students in the 1970s are different from their 1950s counterparts. Although contemporary medical students are still likely to be white middle-class males, they are probably "late-deciders" for a career in medicine, with their decision coming during the second half of their undergraduate studies. The new medical student may be unsure as to whether he or she wants to be a physician even at the beginning of the medical school program. These new students are seen by Fox as staunchly egalitarian in their concept of the physician, the physician–patient relationship, and relationships with non-physician members of the health care team. In other words, they disapprove of the "physician as God" image and feel they are concerned about patients as people, not just as diseased specimens. They likewise hope to improve society by improving health care, especially for the poor.

There are data that support Fox's description of the "new" medical student. Daniel Funkenstein (1971), for example, in a study of consecutive classes at Harvard Medical School since 1957 found that the medical students of the early 1970s tended to show a stronger desire to be socially responsible and to believe that quality medical care had to be provided to all segments of society without regard for finances. At Yale University, Goldman (1974b) noted that medical students demonstrated more liberal attitudes toward political and medical issues than did older doctors. Another study by Goldman and Ebbert (1973) found, in addition, that Yale medical school graduates did not become more politically conservative as they became older. If these findings can be generalized beyond Yale students, the implications of Goldman's work are that the medical profession may receive a new generation of doctors with medically liberal views that may tend to persist over time. What is further indicated is that an increasing supply of new physicians receptive to the reorganization of health care delivery may influence the development of some profound changes in the American system of medical practice in the future.

THE POWER STRUCTURE OF AMERICAN MEDICINE

Before considering the possible sociological consequences of increased liberalism among members of the latest generation of medical doctors, it is important to examine the power structure of the medical profession in order to identify the factors with which any movement toward change will have to contend. One of the early influential studies concerning the power structure of the medical profession was done by Oswald Hall (1946, 1948) in an eastern American city. Subsequent to the ambition to be a doctor and the successful completion of medical school, Hall identified three additional stages in the career of a physician: (1) gaining admittance to various medical societies; (2) developing, retaining, and improving a clientele; and (3) developing a set of informal relationships with colleagues that facilitate the accomplishment of the other objectives.

The Hospital

A most significant factor in a successful urban medical career, according to Hall, was affiliation with a prestige hospital, because the more important hospital positions were usually associated with the more financially rewarding medical practices. Therefore, gaining an appointment at a prestige hospital represented a crucial point in the career development of the urban physician.

Of particular significance was the initial appointment because, as Hall (1948:330) explains, "the internship that a doctor has served is a distinctive badge; it is one of the most enduring criteria in the evaluation of his status." In a study of the Harvard Medical Unit at Boston City Hospital, Stephen Miller (1970) found that the "best" internship was not necessarily determined by the quality of teaching, the type of patient, or the range of responsibility interns were allowed to assume, though these factors were important. The "best" referred to the reputation of the program and its location.

Most medical specialists, scientists, and teachers, according to Miller, are trained in Chicago, New York, or Boston. So the reputation of an internship in the medical education and research institutions of these cities would serve as credentials to assist the candidate's entry into the academic medical circles of any particular urban center. For those physicians wishing to become general practitioners, the optimal setting for an internship would be in communities where they hoped to build a medical practice. Even at the local level, the initial hospital appointment was important in that it facilitated the formation of friendships and professional relationships that could help to enhance a career. Usually the location of an internship will determine the system of medical institutions and the group of physicians the intern will be associated with in the future.

For example, Miller observed that the Harvard program of graduate medical training was much more than a way to meet licensing requirements; it was a means by which an academic appointment at a "name" medical school could be secured. As one of the Harvard interns explained to Miller:

> I'm going into academic medicine, and I wanted the internship which was the best or very good; I think of the word "prestige," a great deal of prestige in being part of this group. It just has a very good reputation, you know. It will look good on paper.[2]

All interns, however, do not receive their first choice for an internship since there are usually many more applicants than positions in the programs with the best reputations. Hall found that the likelihood of gaining an appointment depended much less on superior technical competence than on the future intern's acceptability to the institution of choice. It was not the individual traits that were important, but whether those traits could be assimilated by the institution itself. The department head of a large Catholic hospital told Hall that:

> One of our most important problems here is picking interns. The main qualification as far as I can see is "personality." Now that is an intangible sort of thing. It means partly to mix well, to be humble to older doctors to the correct degree, and to be able to assume the proper degree of superiority toward the patient. Since all medical schools are now Grade A, there is no point in holding competitive examinations. So the main problem confronting the selection committee is that of getting interns who will fit well into the pattern of the hospital.[3]

[2] Stephen J. Miller, *Prescription for Leadership: Training for the Medical Elite* (Chicago: Aldine, 1970) , p. 81.

[3] Oswald Hall, "The Stages of a Medical Career," *American Journal of Sociology*, 53 (March 1948) , 330.

A similar pattern of attitudes toward applicants was apparent in the Miller study in Boston. One of the senior resident physicians in the study informed Miller that:

> . . . interviews here do not carry a great deal of weight, and people are accepted or rejected mostly in terms of where they stood in their medical school class and the kind of recommendations they get. But I suppose, in general, what we look for in the interview is some assurance that the fellow is reasonably mature and sensible. The people coming here obviously are all intelligent. We look for what their interests in the future might be. I think, by and large, people coming here are interested in academic careers, and somebody who is interested in general practice in Rudolph Junction, probably, this isn't the internship for him.[4]

Many of the interns in the Harvard Medical Unit at Boston City Hospital were graduates of "name" medical schools. About 50 percent had graduated from Harvard and another 30 percent were from schools like Cornell, Yale, and Johns Hopkins. The remaining 20 percent were from less well known medical schools. Thus, it was possible for the graduate of a "lesser" school to begin an internship with the Harvard group in order to acquire the background for an academic appointment at higher level medical institutions. As Miller explained, there were not enough "name" medical school graduates for all the internships available; then, too, the Harvard Medical Unit limited the number of Harvard graduates it would accept in order to avoid the "inbreeding" of its faculty.

Yet the process of selection for the Harvard Medical Unit was not entirely democratic. Since many graduates of the program had gone on to the faculties of other medical schools, a large number of schools featured alumni of the Unit, in effect a "colony" of physicians with the same medical background. Their letters of recommendation as former students, graduates, and people known to the Harvard Medical Unit greatly assisted the acceptability of applicants. Miller noted that all of the interns from lesser known schools in his study of the Harvard Medical Unit program were graduates of medical schools where Harvard alumni constitued a colony. Miller (1970:70) stated: "Most learned about the program from, discussed it with, and were advised to choose it by Harvard Medical Unit alumni." So not only were initial appointments important for the future careers of the interns, but also the gaining of these appointments was influenced to a certain degree by having recommendations from the "right" people. Hall found a similar trend in his study of the medical career.

4 Miller, *Prescription for Leadership*, pp. 59–60.

Another consideration in understanding the importance of the hospital is that within the hospital, physicians are arranged in a hierarchy of status—intern, resident, staff member, and associate staff member. Each level represents progress in a medical career and indicates the status and privileges of the doctors involved. There are differences in status not only within hospitals, but also between hospitals. Hall noted in his study that the major hospitals were organized according to social class and ethnic differentials. The leading physicians in the community were characterized by Hall as upper-class Yankees who attended expensive universities as undergraduates and the better known medical schools, especially Harvard. Then they held internships at the dominant Yankee hospital. These Yankee physicians entered the practice of medicine in their community from the vantage point of being associated with the "best" hospital.

In contrast, Hall found that Italian M.D.s found it difficult to gain a position at Yankee hospitals. Instead they sought an alternate route of career advancement in Catholic hospitals, which could both provide a good career and protect the Italian physician from Yankee competition. The point made by Hall was that the successful practice of medicine involved participation in a hospital system which in turn provided the physician with integration into the other medical institutions in the community. The marginal men in medical practice, according to Hall, were those who had abandoned the shelter of a hospital affiliation and had gone out on their own in the wider competitive field of medicine. This same pattern appeared in the Miller study. One of the Harvard Medical Unit interns, who was a native of Boston and wanted to practice medicine there, made it quite clear that being without "connections at the Harvard hospitals" was like being in "exile" (Miller, 1970:80).

The Clientele

The next stage described by Hall is that of acquiring a clientele and retaining and improving it. Hall likened this process to that of a commercial enterprise in that the physician needed to play the role of a promoter. In other words, the physician was required to interact with patients so as to secure their approval of the services provided. Freidson (1960) has pointed out that the lay referral system not only channels the patient to certain doctors, but also helps the patient to make a decision about returning to a particular doctor. Freidson notes that the first visit to a doctor is often tentative, especially in a community large enough to support more than one doctor. Freidson (1960:378) states: "Whether the physician's prescription will be followed or not, and whether the patient will come back, seems to rest at least partly on his retrospective assess-

ment of the professional consultation." Thus, the patient not only passes
through the lay referral system on the way to the physician, but also on
the way back by discussing the doctor's behavior, diagnosis, and prescription with family and friends. In a given community, certain doctors are
often chosen more frequently than others merely because they are fash-
ionable or popular. Most physicians become aware of lay expectations
and learn to deal with them if they expect patients to return.

Furthermore, Hall observed that success in medicine involves improving the practice by attracting the desired type of patient and discouraging those patients who do not fit into the physician's conception of
his or her practice. It may also be true that more affluent patients desire
to be treated with others of their kind; so a physician who treats both the
rich and the poor in the same setting and under the same circumstances
would run the risk of offending the rich. Michael Miller (1973) has
observed that upper-class patients will change physicians sooner than
lower-class patients.

Although the evidence is not conclusive, existing studies also generally suggest that physicians tend to favor upper- and middle-class
patients. Besides being perceived as more likely to pay their bills, upper-
and middle-class patients also reflect values, norms, and attitudes similar
to those of the physician. Raymond Duff and August Hollingshead
(1968), for example, found that physicians tended to be more attentive
to upper-class patients by "over-identifying" with them. Conversely, J. A.
Roth has described the manner in which he believes the poor are regarded by many physicians:

> They are considered the least desirable patients. The doctor has
> probably dealt with "their kind" during his years as a student and
> resident in outpatient and emergency clinics, and he has concluded
> that they are often dirty and smelly, follow poor health practices,
> fail to observe directions or meet appointments, and live in a situa-
> tion which makes it impossible to establish appropriate health
> regimes.[5]

This type of statement seems to imply that lower-class patients
receive inferior medical care not only because of differences in health
service availability, accessibility, comprehensiveness, and so forth, but
also because physicians themselves may be biased toward treating more
affluent patients. Some studies (Anderson and Sheatsley, 1967) support
this statement, but others do not (see Knowles, 1963), and the issue
remains unresolved at the present time. Hall found that the more successful physicians required a certain amount of "charity" work in order to

[5] J. A. Roth, "The Treatment of the Sick," in *Poverty and Health,* ed. J. Kosa, A.
Antonovsky, and I. Zola (Cambridge, Mass.: Harvard University Press, 1962), p. 227.

demonstrate a "serious" intent to practice medicine. Yet apparently few physicians desire to work in poverty programs on a full-time basis (Fredericks et al., 1974).

The best medical practice in Hall's study was the specialized practice because Hall believed the specialist was accorded superior status by others in the medical profession.[6] Other observers (Mechanic, 1972; Stevens, 1971) have also pointed toward the trend in specialization, which has resulted in the decline in number of general practitioners and the domination of the medical profession by specialty groups. A specialized practice, however, is dependent upon having a group of colleagues who refer patients to the specialist. Generally, referring physicians are reciprocated by fee-sharing or by the referral of patients back to the general practitioner. A specialized practice also requires access to hospital facilities, and hospital connections in themselves facilitate the development of referral relationships between physicians.

In a study of internists (specialists in internal medicine) in private practice in Chicago, Stephen Shortell (1973) found that they tended to refer their patients to other specialists on the hospital staff where they held a primary appointment. The influence of the hospital appointment was such that it provided both formal and informal channels of communication about who was available in the various specialties and what relative advantages they had to offer. Furthermore, the ability to follow up on a patient after care had been turned over to another specialist or specialists was dependent upon the internist's being on the same hospital staff.

Shortell's study traced the informal organization of medical practice by extensively examining the referral process. He found that patterns of referrals were related to the professional status of the physicians and operated according to the relative rewards and costs perceived by physicians at different levels of the status hierarchy. High status internists, for example, tended to refer their patients to other high status colleagues, while lower status internists also more often referred their patients to higher status physicians than to their peers. Higher status physicians thus tended to be the major recipients of referrals. High status physicians primarily choose each other as referral partners because the exchange helps validate their own personal status and maintains the status structure of their own group as well. Lower status physicians, however, tend to refer patients outside their group because of the prestige rewards of dealing with higher status physicians and because of a potential loss of

[6] The tremendous growth in the number of medical specialists has reduced the number of general practitioners and has made it more difficult to obtain primary care in the United States. This issue will be discussed in Chapter Nine, "Health Care Delivery and Social Policy."

clientele to fellow low status competitors. The reasoning was that low status physicians were much more likely to be concerned about building their medical practice and thereby might tend to retain patients sent to them. High status physicians, on the other hand, would already have a successful practice and would not be so desirous of acquiring more patients on a regular basis.

The "Inner Fraternity"

Hall's study pointed toward the existence of an "inner fraternity" in medicine that operated to recruit new members, to allocate these new members to positions in the various medical institutions, and to help them secure patients through referrals. Hall believed that the urban power structure of the medical profession consisted of four major groups of physicians. The first group was the "inner core," which Hall described as the specialists who have control of the major hospital positions. Immediately outside this inner core were the new recruits at various stages of their careers who were intended to inherit positions in the inner core at some time in the future. Next were the general practitioners who were linked to the inner core by the referral system. Besides these three groups were the marginal physicians, those who would remain on the fringes of the system because the inner core had its own methods of selecting recruits. According to Hall, the key to understanding the power structure of the medical profession was found in the system of control exercised by the inner core. The inner core displayed three major characteristics that enabled it to control the medical profession. First, it was a highly cohesive group of specialists with relatively identical educations and socioeconomic backgrounds, technical interdependence, and daily working relationships. Second, the social bonds between different specialists allowed these powerful physicians to integrate the various specialties into a cohesive body. And third, the inner core was able to organize the medical market by controlling the process in which patients were referred from one physician to another.

What Hall's analysis has provided in terms of understanding the power structure of the medical profession is the realization that a doctor's career takes place in a system of formal and informal relationships with colleagues. Formal relationships develop as a result of a physician's position within the prevailing medical institutions in a particular community. The control of the dominant posts within these institutions, especially hospital appointments, is the critical variable that distinguishes influential from noninfluential doctors. Informal relationships also develop over time as physicians interact with one another on a frequent basis and arrive at definitions of the quality of each other's work and personal characteristics. Thus, claims to position, status, and power become recognized and are perpetuated within the profession, and mechanisms for recruitment into the inner core become established in both formal and informal ways.

Hall's study took place during the 1940s. Whether or not the conditions he described at that time still hold true today is largely a matter of conjecture because recent studies of the power structure of the medical profession have been lacking. However, what data do exist seem to substantiate most of the major points made by Hall. Donald Freeborn and Benjamin Darsky's 1974 study of a medical community in a medium-sized Canadian city involved a sample of physicians who practiced medicine as private, fee-for-service practitioners similar to the majority of U.S. physicians. They also found that a definite power structure existed along the lines described by Hall—with one important exception. As in the Hall study, influence and power among physicians were related to control by a small group of the major medical institutional resources in the community. Influence and power were exercised in both a formal and informal fashion, but emanated from the same people. Generally, the top influentials were older physicians who had been able to gain control over the positions of power in the hospitals and medical association. But in contrast to the Hall study, the top influentials were not necessarily specialists (many were general practitioners) and they were not a closed "inner core." Instead a network of common friendships prevailed at all levels of influence; the most influential physicians were those who had gained their position of power as a result of long years of service to the community and the medical society. Over time they had developed extensive personal relationsips which allowed them to achieve and maintain key positions in the major medical institutions.

The most significant variable to emerge from this discussion of the power structure of the American medical profession is that of institutional position. The medical profession is based upon a variety of institutions—hospitals, clinics, medical schools, the AMA, and so forth. The policies and practices of these institutions are determined by those individuals who occupy decision-making positions within them. Power and influence among physicians (as in any other group) derive from being in a position to direct or at least share in a decision-making process that formulates significant professional policies.

An obvious but important factor is that the most important institutional positions are held by physicians who have pursued their career within the mainstream of the medical profession; they have achieved the best educational experiences and hospital appointments, as well as AMA membership, or vice versa. Most likely these individuals are specialists who occupy an institutional position such as administrator, faculty member, or researcher. If this is the case, and in all probability it is, what is further implied is that changes in the organization of medical practice in the United States would most likely not originate within the medical profession itself. This logical inference seems to derogate existing studies (Goldman and Ebbert, 1973; Goldman, 1974a, 1974b) which suggest liberal, change-oriented tendencies among the latest generation of medical doctors. Yet positions of power within the medical profession continue to be held by physicians who have succeeded in the present conservative system, a system that is oriented toward maintaining the private, fee-for-service, independent practitioner model. Perhaps the medical profession may eventually promote change if new physicians maintain their liberal tendencies until they reach positions of influence, but at this time it appears more probable that changes in the organization of medical care in the United States will have to occur as a result of pressure outside the system. The most likely source for this pressure is dissatisfied groups of health care consumers working to institute legislation limiting the control of physicians over medical practice.

THE PHYSICIAN AND SOCIAL CHANGE

Current public dissatisfaction with the delivery of health care in the United States results from two major issues: (1) failure of the medical profession to provide quality health care for all Americans despite the profession's publicly acknowledged claims to excellence and technological achievement, and (2) rising financial costs of health care. Both of these issues are related to the fact that most health care in the U.S. is organized around the economic concept of profit for health providers and health institutions within a free enterprise system. Accordingly, some argue that the present system should be changed because the profit motive discriminates against the poor, encourages the unnecessary duplication of many services, and introduces a dehumanizing connotation to the provision of a service intended to relieve human suffering. Others argue that the profit motive leads to greater efficiency in providing services, increased incentive for research and development, and more responsiveness to the patient. As previously noted, Chapter Nine will explore the financial issues involved in health care delivery, but it should be recognized that the issue of profit is an integral part of the structure of organized medicine in this country and the medical professional's lack of flexibility in confronting social issues.

Part of organized medicine's lack of social responsiveness may be attributed to medicine's development as a profession. Howard Rasmussen (1975) has pointed out that professionalism in American medicine has resulted in at least three undesirable consequences. First, it has fostered the development of a view of disease largely confined to specific organs or physiological systems, but which fails to consider a more holistic view of patients as persons. This conflicts directly with a major societal demand that contemporary practice come to terms with a wide spectrum of disorders related more to problems of living than to specific chemical and physical abnormalities of the body. Second, professionalism has led to the development of a highly rigid stratification system in medical practice which has promoted an increasingly large gap between physicians and non-physician medical personnel. And for certain functions the non-physician health worker may have a more important service to provide the patient than the physician. Third, professionalism has resulted in the separation of professional training so that a common educational base is lacking between physicians and paramedicals that might allow a health care team to work more effectively as a cohesive group. Overall, the physician has emerged in the role of a "super-physician" in a "super-hospital" where ultimate responsibility for the patient belongs to this deified being, who, as an individual, may not have the time, interest, training, or ability to cope with the entire range of modern patient care. Thus, while the health care needs of American society are those of the late twentieth century, organized medicine has continued to pursue a pattern of professional behavior based upon the image of medical practice at the turn of the century when the physician worked as an independent, fee-for-service, private general practitioner.

Social Control of Medical Practice

The social control of medical practice has traditionally presented special problems for American society. It has been argued that since physicians themselves have established the medical standards enforced by governmental regulating agencies and since lay-persons are generally unable to judge technical performance, the two most common forms of social control in an industrial society—bureaucratic supervision and judgment by the recipient of services—are lacking (see Rueschmeyer, 1972). However, the argument continues that the dilemma of controlling organized medicine is solved by the medical profession's emphasis upon the strong self-control of the individual physician, an ethical stance reinforced by both the formal and informal sanctions of a community of colleagues. Society is thus justified in granting the physician professional autonomy because he or she is a member of a self-controlled collectivity providing a vital function for society's general good. This argument contains three serious defects.

First of all, it is important to note that lay-persons do judge technical performance regardless of whether they are competent to do so. Freidson's (1960) discussion of the lay referral system made it quite clear that lay avenues of influence and authority exist independently of the physician and operate to guide the patient either toward or away from the services of a particular physician. This activity may not only determine the physician's success in attracting patients but also affect the physician's mode of medical practice. As Freidson (1960:379) has stated, "in being *relatively* free, the medical profession should not be mistaken for being *absolutely* free from control by patients." The choices of clients act as a form of social control over professionals and can militate against the survival of a group as a profession or the career success of particular professionals (Goode, 1957:198).

Several studies show that patients do terminate their relationships with physicians and actively "shop" around for other doctors who are more able to meet their expectations (cf. Ben-Sira, 1976; Hays-Bautista, 1976; Larson and Rootman, 1976; Kasteler et al., 1976). Besides lack of confidence in a physician's technical competence, other factors commonly identified as influencing patients to change doctors are the unwillingness of doctors to spend time talking to them, the high cost of services, the possible inconvenience of a particular doctor's office location and hours, and unfavorable assessments of the doctor's personality.

A second major defect in the argument legitimizing the medical profession's autonomy has to do with physicians' efforts at peer regulation. In a study of a medical group practice, Freidson (1975) found indeed that rules and standards existed to define the limits of acceptable performance by physicians associated with the group. However, norms governing colleague relations, essentially *rules of etiquette,* restricted the evaluation of work and discouraged the expression of criticism. Etiquette was a more important norm than accountability, and it undermined attempts at critical evaluation and control by overlooking fault in order to maintain group harmony. Confrontation with a colleague was considered distasteful even in private and was unthinkable in public. In this medical practice setting, the norms of etiquette had not only seriously limited the exercise of professional control, but had also reduced the scope of procedures colleagues were willing to review.

Marcia Millman (1977) noted a similar situation in her study of three private, university-affiliated hospitals. Many doctors in this study were willing to criticize their colleagues for errors in small group discussions and behind the other's back. But there was a strong reluctance to criticize another doctor's mistakes at any official meeting because of what Millman termed "a fear of reprisal" and "a recognition of common interests."

Millman's examination of medical mortality and morbidity conferences in which patient deaths were reviewed as a regular hospital procedure was particularly illustrative of the collective rationalization of mistakes. The atmosphere of these conferences was likened to such social events as weddings or funerals, in which the participants were expected to show tact and restraint in order to remain on friendly terms. Restricted to members of the hospital's medical staff, the conferences were intended to be educational, not punitive. Only certain cases (conspicuous was the absence of cases involving patient deaths by gross medical mismanagement) were picked for review because, as one hospital chief of medicine stated, "it's got to be a cordial affair." Millman described the meetings as follows:

> At Lakeside Hospital, the chief of medicine stands on the stage and presides as a master of ceremonies. As one member of the staff after another testifies about how he or she was led to the same mistaken diagnosis, the responsibility for the mistake is implicitly spread around. As in a good detective story, the case is reconstructed to show that there was evidence for suspecting an outcome different from the one that turned out to be the true circumstance. Responsibility for the error is also neutralized by making much of the unusual or misleading features of the case, or by showing how the patient was to blame because of uncooperative or neurotic behavior. Furthermore, by reviewing the case in fine detail, the physicians restore their images as careful, methodical practitioners, and thereby neutralize the sloppiness and carelessness that are made obvious by mistakes.[7]

Whether or not the lack of physician peer control described by Freidson and Millman is typical of most or even some medical practice settings is not known. However, if the so-called "malpractice crisis" in American medicine during the mid-1970s can be regarded as any kind of valid indicator, it would appear that incompetence in medicine, or at least a greater public awareness of medical malpractice, is not entirely uncommon. David Makofsky (1977) has estimated that approximately five percent of all practicing physicians are unfit for practice because of ignorance of modern medicine, drug addiction, or mental illness. He claims that 30,000 Americans die annually from faulty drug prescriptions and ten times that number suffer dangerous side effects. Unnecessary and poorly performed surgery is also regarded as a serious problem. To cite an extreme case, in 1973 a superior court in California awarded two million dollars to a patient for damages resulting from an unnecessary back fusion operation performed by a drug-addicted orthopedic surgeon.

[7] Marcia Millman, "Masking Doctors' Errors," *Human Behavior,* 6 (January 1977), 17.

The surgeon admitted to the court that he had performed unnecessary surgery on at least thirty-eight other persons because he needed the money.

In rebuttal it can be argued that physicians can be the victims of malpractice suits that have no merit in fact. Yet malpractice suits have risen dramatically in recent years (from a few hundred a year in the 1950s to about 10,000 a year in the 1970s), and so have the rates physicians pay for malpractice insurance. Some major malpractice insurance companies have refused to continue insuring doctors because of high losses resulting from malpractice settlements. In a vicious circle, physicians have charged increasingly higher prices for their services to cover the higher rates charged by those companies still writing malpractice policies. Many physicians are also practicing "defensive medicine," which is the ordering of unnecessary laboratory tests and procedures in order to make sure that they cannot be accused of carelessness, neglect, or incompetence. This practice likewise increases the cost to the patient of obtaining medical care.

In some states, emergency legislation has been passed to provide state-backed malpractice insurance coverage designed to protect both doctors and hospitals. At present, no single solution exists in any state, and the malpractice crisis remains one of the most significant issues affecting the doctor–patient relationship in the mid-1970s.

In addition to the malpractice crisis, another symptom of ineffective control of the medical practice is the high cost to the government of Medicare and Medicaid due to physician corruption. In 1975 and 1976, investigations of fraud in Medicare and Medicaid services in New York City disclosed that over 300 million dollars a year had been paid to doctors for false claims (Makofsky, 1977). Some physicians were arrested and sentenced to prison for misrepresenting care they supposedly gave Medicare and Medicaid patients.

This discussion is not intended to convey the impression that physicians are generally untrustworthy. Instances of corruption and fraud appear to be rare. In fact, Freidson (1975) argues that it can be assumed that physicians are usually dedicated to their patients. State medical societies do cooperate with state licensing agencies to remove the medical licenses of demonstratably incompetent physicians, thus preventing them from legally practicing medicine. Furthermore, Professional Standards Review Organizations were established in 1970 in conjunction with Medicaid and Medicare to review and evaluate the medical care given to patients eligible to use these services. PSROs are composed of licensed physicians and osteopaths who determine if the services rendered are medically necessary, meet professional standards of quality, and are provided as efficiently and effectively as possible (see Shindell et al., 1976). Although there is likely to be some latitude in the interpretation of standards in any diagnostic category, Freidson (1975:251) points out that a consensus of opinion will at least exclude "the blatant, gross, or obvious deviations from common knowledge and practice."

Nevertheless, it should be remembered that medical standards and practices continue to be regulated by the practitioners themselves. Thus it is generally difficult to find a physician who will be openly critical of another physician or to publicly testify against a colleague. Mistakes and errors in medical practice, either through neglect or ignorance, can sometimes be defended as "a difference of opinion." Millman (1977:18) suggests that possibly all doctors have at some time made a terrible mistake in their careers and realize that they may do so again. Therefore, in matters of peer regulation, they tend to follow the Golden Rule: "Do unto others as you would have them do unto you."

The third major defect in the professional autonomy argument arises from the fact that the autonomy granted the medical profession is granted *conditionally*, on the assumption that it will resolve significant issues in favor of the public interest. However, traditional AMA resistance to innovations in medical care that might threaten the fee-for-service pattern has been cited as an example of greater professional concern with matters of self-interest than with public welfare (Stevens, 1971). It therefore seems warranted for society to restrict the autonomy of the medical profession, and this claim has provided the basis for the present challenge to organized medicine launched by consumer groups working to enact legislative change.

Leo G. Reeder (1972) has formulated the clearest case to date that shows the changing relationship between physicians and their patients. He identifies three significant trends in contemporary society. One is the shift in medicine away from the treatment of acute diseases toward preventive health services intended to offset the effects of chronic disorders. Since the control of acute diseases has largely been accomplished, it is no longer the most important task for modern medical practice. Reeder explains:

> In a system dominated by curative or emergency care there is a "seller's market." The customer is suspect; client-professional relationships tend to be characterized by the traditional mode of interaction so well described in the literature. On the other hand, when prevention of illness is emphasized, the client has to be persuaded that he has a need for medical services such as periodic check-ups. The person has to be encouraged to come into the physician's office for medical care. Under these circumstances, there

are elements of a "buyer's market"; in such situations there is more of a tendency for the "customer to be right."[8]

The other two features of societal change noted by Reeder are the growing sophistication of the general public with bureaucracy and the development of consumerism. Reeder claims that the increased development of large-scale bureaucratic industrial systems has ensured a similarity of experiences and attitudes in contemporary society and this has tended to "level" or make more familiar the bureaucratic aspects of modern medicine. Also significant is the development of consumerism. Reeder states that during the 1960s, the concept of the person as a "consumer" rather than a patient became established; doctors were regarded as "health providers," so a new relationship of provider–consumer emerged in direct opposition to the old relationship of physician–patient with its emphasis upon patient dependency. The new concept places the consumer on a more equal basis with the physician in the health care interaction. It also provides the philosophy behind the increased consumer involvement in health legislation and other matters as consumer interest groups.

In an age of "consumerism," the social role of the physician and the overall physician–patient relationship can hardly escape modification. In general, this modification will take the form of physician and patient interacting on a more equal footing in terms of power dependency, reciprocity of expectations, and responsibility for outcome. There is already evidence, in such inherently uncertain areas of medical practice as genetic counseling, that the physician-patient relationship as a provider-consumer encounter has become more prevalent in health care interaction (see Sorenson, 1974).

SUMMARY

This chapter has examined the role of the physician in a changing society. From an initial service orientation and through the development of a body of specialized knowledge, the physician has been able to organize a professional group and control medical education in such a way as to dominate the entire health care industry in the United States. Yet there are increasing signs, such as the appearance of liberal tendencies among some members of the latest generation of medical doctors and

8 Leo G. Reeder, "The Patient-Client as a Consumer: Some Observations on the Changing Professional-Client Relationship," *Journal of Health and Social Behavior,* 13 (December 1972), 407.

the emergence of consumer interest groups in health affairs, that suggest that the professional dominance of the physician may be modified. Most likely the typical power dependency role of the physician-patient relationship will be transformed into more of a provider-consumer relationship in the future. This will mean, however, a basic change in the approach of traditional medicine toward health care delivery in contemporary social systems.

7

NURSING AND THE EMERGING PARAMEDICAL PRACTITIONERS

Although the dominant form of social interaction in the health care relationship has traditionally been that of the one-to-one encounter between the physician and the patient, the technical complexity and range of contemporary medical care has evolved well beyond this exclusive two-person social system. Modern medical treatment has come to involve a great variety of health personnel who specialize in treatment, laboratory procedures, therapy, rehabilitation, and administration. There are over four million persons in the United States currently employed in non-physician tasks related to health care.

Yet, as Robert Wilson (1970) has pointed out, many of the occupational roles that are synonymous with the practice of modern medicine have tended to be modelled on the ideal image of the physician, with its high standards of education, ethics, technical achievement, and independence of action. Wilson (1970:34) states: "In a sense, each variety of health worker gauges his status and professional selfhood in terms of how closely he approaches the doctor on a scale of privilege and responsibility." But the problem inherent in this imitative relationship is that while it may encourage physician-like aspirations and standards among paramedicals, it represents, as Wilson notes, an unrealistic and often frustrating situation. Almost all of these workers will never achieve professional equality with the physician within the existing framework of medical practice.

Other than physicians and a few consulting professions such as clinical psychology, most occupations performing tasks of patient care can be classified as paramedical because they are organized around the work of the physician and are usually under the physician's direct control. Eliot Freidson (1970a:49) claims that these paramedical occupations— nurse, pharmacist, laboratory technician, physical therapist—reflect four characteristic features that account for their subordinate position in the practice of medicine. First of all, Freidson notes that the technical knowledge employed by paramedical occupations tends to be discovered, developed, and approved by physicians. Second, paramedical tasks tend to assist physicians in their work rather than to replace the basic skills of diagnosis and treatment. Third, paramedical occupations are subordinate to the physician because their work largely occurs at the "request of" the physician; it is the "doctor's orders" that provide them with their work requirements. And fourth, among the various occupational roles in the health field, the American public ascribes considerably less prestige to non-physician workers than to physicians.

A related point concerning this prestige differential is that the social backgrounds of those persons recruited into paramedical work are generally lower than those of physicians. While physicians usually come from upper- and upper-middle-class social origins, persons in paramedical occupations frequently have lower-middle, working-class, and lower-class backgrounds. Also, women and members of racial/ethnic minority groups are found in a greater proportion among paramedical personnel than among medical doctors. However, if all the characteristics of the paramedical occupations, as outlined by Freidson, were reduced to the single most important distinction between these health care workers and physicians, that distinction would be the physician's ultimate control over their work, which effectively blocks their claims of professional autonomy.

One negative aspect of this situation is that physicians sometimes do not enjoy a good reputation with their co-workers (Bates, 1970). It has been pointed out that the physician is the "last of the autocrats" (Melick, 1959). He tends to regard other health personnel as working for him rather than working for the patient, while relegating them to a "non-professional limbo" in which he views them essentially as "servants rather than as associates or colleagues" (McGraw, 1966).

Just as the physician–patient relationship appears to be moving toward less dependency and increased equality for the patient, signs of a similar trend have begun to appear in the physician–registered nurse relationship. The time may come, as Wilson (1970) suggests, when patients will be treated by a medical team in which the physician is no longer an all-powerful figure, but collaborates with other health workers as first among equals. An examination of the physician–nurse relationship may therefore assist social scientists to determine more accurately the nature of the future role relationships among health personnel.

NURSING: PAST AND PRESENT

The licensed registered nurse ranks second in status only to the physician in the social organization of health providers in the United States. Many nurses consider themselves to be full-fledged professionals despite their lack of formal autonomy over their work role. Nursing represents the largest single group of health workers in the U.S., with an estimated 815,000 persons employed as licensed registered nurses in 1974; another 492,000 persons were estimated to be employed as licensed practical nurses (National Center for Health Statistics, 1975). About 75 percent of all licensed registered and practical nurses in the U.S. work in hospitals and nursing homes, while the remainder are employed in doctors' offices, public health agencies, schools, industrial plants, programs of nursing education, or as private duty nurses.

Registered nurses are responsible for the nature and quality of all nursing care patients receive, as well as for following the instructions of physicians regarding patients. In addition, they supervise practical nurses and other health personnel involved in providing patient care. The primary task of licensed practical nurses is the bedside care of patients; they may also assist in the supervision of auxiliary nursing workers such as nurse's aides, orderlies, and attendants. These auxiliary nursing personnel, who numbered about 936,000 persons in the U.S. as of 1974, assist registered and practical nurses by performing less skilled medical care tasks and by providing many services designed for the overall personal comfort and welfare of patients.

Whereas the licensed registered and practical nurses and nurse's aides are generally women, orderlies and attendants are usually men employed to care for male patients and perform whatever heavy duties are required in nursing care. What is obvious is that nursing tasks occur in a system of social relationships that are highly stratified by sex. The registered nurse, who has the most advanced training and professional qualifications of any of the nursing workers, is generally a female who is matched occupationally with a physician, whose role is dominant and who is usually a male. The registered nurse, in turn, supervises lesser trained females (practical nurses and nurse's aides) and lesser trained males (orderlies and attendants). Thus emerges the traditional stereotype of the physician as father figure and the nurse as mother figure. "This perception," according to Hans Mauksch (1972:217), "creates a woman who serves sacrificially, who supports and protects a dominant male, and who identifies her successes as a nurse with her successes as a woman."

The Early Development of Nursing as an Occupation

While males have been known historically to perform nursing tasks, the social role of the nurse has been profoundly affected by its identification with traditionally feminine functions (Davis, 1966, 1972; Freidson, 1970a, 1970b; Mauksch, 1972; Olesen and Whittaker, 1968; Schulman, 1972; Strauss, 1966, 1971). For instance, Mauksch (1972:208) has pointed out that in many European languages the very word *sister* not only refers to nuns but also generically identifies the nurse. In the English language, the word "nurse" carries with it a connotation of the mother's relationship to her child. Accordingly, the initial image of the nurse in Western society was that of a "mother-surrogate," in which nursing was equated with the mothering function (Schulman, 1972).

Following the rise of Christianity in the Western world, the practice of nursing as a formal occupation was significantly influenced by the presence of large numbers of nuns who performed nursing services under the auspices of the Roman Catholic Church. Prior to the late nineteenth century, hospitals were generally defined as places for the poor and lower social classes, often little more than "flophouses"; anyone who could afford it was usually cared for at home. Nursing activities in hospitals were thus viewed as acts of charity because they were typically carried out under difficult and unpleasant circumstances, as nurses served the personal needs of patients who were usually dirty and illiterate as well as diseased. Nursing under these conditions was regarded by the Church as a means by which those persons providing the services could attain spiritual salvation by helping those less fortunate. Hence the original concept of nursing was not as a formal occupation with its own body of knowledge and specialized training procedure; rather its primary focus as religious activity was in spiritual considerations. Nuns were not under the authority of doctors and they could refuse any orders they did not believe appropriate for themselves or their patients. Nuns were also reported to have refused to treat certain categories of patients such as unwed mothers or persons with venereal disease (Freidson, 1970a).

Beside nuns, there were secular nurses working in public hospitals. But these women were characterized as "women off the streets" or "of bad character," who were typically considered as little or no better than the low class of patients for whom they provided their services. Well into the nineteenth century, nursing could be described as an activity for women who lacked specialized training in medical care, a supportive work role that was not officially incorporated into the formal structure of medical services. Moreover, nursing was not an occupation held in high regard by the general public.

Florence Nightingale

The role of nursing in Western society was changed in the middle of the nineteenth century through the insight and effort of Florence Nightingale. Nightingale, an English Protestant from a respectable middle-class family, believed that God had called her to the service of Christianity as a result of a vision she had experienced in 1837. There was some confusion, however, on Nightingale's part as to exactly what service she was expected to render. Being a Protestant, she could not choose to become a Catholic nun. She solved her dilemma by deciding to become a nurse. Over the strong objections of her family and after a delay of several years, she was finally able to secure training as a nurse from a Protestant minister in Germany.

Returning to England in 1853, Nightingale established a hospital for "Sick Gentlewomen in Distressed Circumstances" and staffed it with trained nurses from good families. She insisted that nursing was intended to become an honorable and respected occupation and she sought to achieve this through a formal training program with recruits from upper- and middle-class social backgrounds. Good intentions notwithstanding, Nightingale's hospital was not entirely successful because of the role conflict between the duties of the nurse and the prevailing standards of proper behavior for "ladies." Some of her nurses, for example, were reluctant to view nudity or to be present at physical examinations (Freidson, 1970a).

However, in 1854 the Crimean War afforded Nightingale a much better opportunity to establish nursing as a formal occupation. She organized a contingent of nurses and, assisted by money raised by public subscription, she and her group sailed for the Crimea, where Great Britain, France, Sardinia, and Turkey were involved in war with Russia. Once there, Nightingale offered to the British military authorities the nursing services of her women for the sick and wounded troops.

At first the military refused to employ her nurses and she retaliated by refusing to allow any of the nurses to provide patient care on their own initiative. Instead the nurses worked only when their assistance was specifically requested by physicians. Eventually such requests were forthcoming and Nightingale's nurses received considerable publicity in the British press as "angels of mercy." In fact, Nightingale's nurses had captured the imagination of the British public and when Nightingale returned to England after the war she found herself hailed as a heroine. Capitalizing upon her fame and popularity, she instigated a successful fund-raising effort that brought in enough money to organize a nursing school at St. Thomas Hospital in London. Other schools were also established and within a few years the "Nightingale system" became the model for nursing education.

Nightingale's approach to nursing training emphasized a code of behavior that idealized nurses as being responsible, clean, self-sacrificing, courageous, cool-headed, hard-working, obedient to the physician, and possessing the tender qualities of the mother; this idealized portrayal of nurses saw them as nothing less than "disciplined angels" (Strauss, 1966). In reality, Nightingale had incorporated the best attributes of the mother and the housekeeper into her ideal nurse. This image did little to establish the view of nurses as having the qualities of leadership and independence necessary for true professional status. Although Nightingale had been able to establish nursing as a distinct and honorable occupation, her philosophy perpetuated the traditional social role of the nurse as a female supervised and controlled by a male physician. Perhaps in her time there was no other way to gain access to an official position within the male-dominated field of medicine, but the overall effect of subordination to the physician's orders weakened nursing's efforts in its struggle to achieve professionalization.

Nursing Education

Florence Nightingale's ideas formed the basis for establishing the first accredited schools of nursing in the United States. These schools, founded in 1873, were located at Bellevue Hospital in New York City, the Connecticut Training School in New Haven, and the Boston Training School. Although they were intended to be separately administered, the new nursing schools were affiliated with hospitals that provided financial support and required, in turn, that the students furnish much of the nursing services on the hospital wards. During the late nineteenth and early twentieth centuries, there was a rapid increase in the number of hospitals and hospital nursing schools. At the same time, increasing numbers of women entered the labor market due to immigration from abroad or migration from rural to urban areas. Nursing was an attractive occupation for many of these women because it afforded an opportunity for a woman to make a living and to also have a respectable position in the community.

But as Anselm Strauss (1966) and others have pointed out, many of the students in these early nursing schools did not receive the training that the Nightingale system required. Since there were only a few trained nurses available and money was often in short supply, many hospital administrators and physicians, perhaps also unaware of Nightingale's techniques for training nurses, used nursing students as inexpensive and exploitable sources of hospital labor. As a result, much of the effort of nursing educators during the first decades of the twentieth century was directed at securing less hospital service and more education for nursing students in hospital schools. They also sought a university-based nursing school, with the first one being formed at the University of Minnesota in 1909.

While nursing educators were able to improve the standards of education for their students, they failed to obtain centralized control over educational programs. Unlike medical schools, which follow a pre-scribed and generally similar program of education leading to the M.D., nursing has been characterized by a curious assortment of different types of educational experiences—all of which can qualify the student as a registered nurse. For example, there are currently three types of programs available for R.N.s: (1) two-year associate degree programs usually located in junior or community colleges; (2) hospital-based diploma schools requiring two and one-half to three years of study; (3) four-year and five-year university baccalaureate programs.

The most prestigious of the nursing education programs is the baccalaureate program, which is intended to provide training not only in nursing skills and theory, but also to provide the background for be-coming a nursing educator or leader. But, as Mauksch (1972:211) makes clear, the graduates of any nursing program—despite the differences in time, money, effort and, supposedly, intellect demanded by their pro-grams—are virtually identical in terms of the basic skills required for their jobs.

The major source of nurses in the United States has traditionally been the hospital-based diploma school. College-based programs, with their combination of occupational training and liberal arts education, have become increasingly popular with nursing students in the last few years, although diploma schools provide more day-to-day experience with patients. As Figure 7–1 shows, in 1961 diploma schools accounted for over 80 percent of all nursing graduates, but by 1970 this percentage had declined to 52.3 percent and the period between 1970 and 1974 witnessed a further rapid decline to 31.5 percent. Although the percentage of graduates from baccalaureate programs increased over the period covered by Figure 7–1, the primary beneficiary of declining numbers of diploma graduates had been the associate degree programs. With only 3 percent of the total number of nursing graduates in 1961, associate degree programs had grown to produce 43.3 percent of the total by 1974.

Typically the associate degree programs are relatively inexpensive, require only two years of training, and yet place their graduates on the same career track as graduates of diploma and baccalaureate degree

FIGURE 7-1. SCHOOLS OF NURSING (R.N.) BY TYPES OF SCHOOL AND PER-CENT OF GRADUATES (1961, 1965, 1970, 1974)

Type of School	1961 (N = 30,267)	1965 (N = 34,686)	1970 (N = 43,639)	1974 (N = 67,628)
Diploma	83.6	77.3	52.3	31.5
Associate Degree	3.0	7.2	26.8	43.3
Bachelor's Degree	13.4	15.5	20.9	25.2
TOTALS	100.0%	100.0%	100.0%	100.0%

SOURCE: National Center for Health Statistics, *Health Resources Statistics* (Washington, D.C.: U.S. Department of Health, Education and Welfare, 1975).

schools. Originally conceived as a middle-range level of nursing education somewhere between the training required to perform simple or assisting nursing tasks and that required for complex tasks, the work role of the associate degree graduate has expanded into supervisory and management functions. There has been some controversy concerning this trend since it requires associate degree nurses to function beyond their intended level of training, but the trend continues because of the expectations of nursing service administrators about the capabilities of AD graduates (Miller, 1974). Despite problems regarding the work role, AD programs have become the largest single source of nurses in the U.S.

Despite the remarkable growth of the associate degree programs and the growing acceptance of their graduates in nursing, their appearance has presented a special problem in terms of nursing's claims of professional status since the AD programs are essentially vocational rather than professional. A strategy to avoid this situation was to designate associate degree nurses as "technical" nurses and baccalaureate degree nurses as "professional" nurses, while advocating that all nurses be graduates of college programs at some time in the future. Although this became the official position of the American Nurses' Association in 1965, it was not accepted by the majority of its membership, who had graduated from diploma schools. These nurses replied that it would be a hardship for them to quit work and return to college and they pointed out that a liberal arts education did not help a nurse perform better nursing procedures (see Olesen and Whittaker, 1968). The end result was that among R.N.'s the baccalaureate nurses are regarded as the *most* "professional"—leaders of organized nursing—yet associate degree and diploma nurses still consider themselves to be "professionals."

A related problem that also affects nursing's claims to professionalism is the open recruitment of nurses (Strauss, 1966). While medical schools are highly selective in regard to the pre-professional qualifications of the students they accept, the variety of nursing programs and the lack of centralized control of these programs by organized nursing has meant that practically any person can gain admission to some type of nursing program. Usually only a high school education is necessary for admission to most programs leading to the R.N.; only two years of high school are often required to enter programs of practical nursing. Most professions obtain some degree of control over who is accepted and allowed to graduate into the profession's ranks in order to ensure that only the most desirable candidates are able to represent the profession. While such controls are never perfect, they nevertheless represent a profession's standards. The fact that nursing has relatively low standards of recruitment thus lowers its claim to professional status.

Nursing Students

In 1975, there were 1,359 schools of nursing offering programs leading to the R.N., with a total of 244,486 students enrolled in their courses (National Center for Health Statistics, 1975). Over 50,000 of these students will graduate annually through the 1970s with their total number increasing by a few thousand each year. Nursing students have traditionally been characterized as having lower-middle-class and working-class social origins, often from small towns or rural areas, who are attracted to nursing as a means of upward social mobility (Hughes et al., 1958). Although this pattern still persists today, there have been increasing numbers of students from upper- and upper-middle-class families and urban areas entering nursing schools (Davis, 1972; Mauksch, 1972), with the result that nursing, like teaching, has become a distinctly middle-class occupation.

There have been several studies of student nurses and their reasons for seeking training as a nurse. These studies, as summarized by Mauksch (1972), suggest that the objectives of a majority of nursing students are to be needed and to be engaged in personal helping relationships. However, some studies have suggested that a serious conflict often develops within new students concerning the lay image of the nurse as mother-surrogate (an image the students usually bring with them to the school) and the refusal of the nursing faculty to reinforce this image (Davis, 1972; Olesen and Whittaker, 1968; Psathas, 1968; Warnecke, 1973). Nursing faculties have tended to insist on students viewing their patients objectively, which has operated to de-emphasize an intimate nurse–patient relationship. The prevailing reward system also places greater emphasis upon removing the nurse from patient care and placing her in a supervisory position over auxiliary nursing workers.

In his study of nursing students in a major university school of nursing on the West Coast, Fred Davis (1972) observed that nursing students passed through six distinct stages of socialization. First was the stage of *initial innocence,* which consisted of the nursing students wanting to do things for patients within a secularized Christian-humanitarian ethic of care and kindness consistent with the lay (mother-surrogate) image of nursing. This stage was characterized, however, by feelings of inadequacy, worry, and frustration, as the nursing instructors failed to support the lay image of the nurse. Instead, the students were directed toward seemingly inconsequential tasks of patient care such as making beds and giving baths. These feelings of frustration, which usually came during the first semester of training, generated the second stage, which Davis called *labeled recognition of incongruity.* In this stage, the nursing students began collectively to articulate their disappointment and openly to question their choice of becoming a nurse. At this point a number of the students resigned from the school because they did not or could not adjust to the incongruity between lay expectations and actual training.

For those that remained, the third stage of *"psyching out"* began, in which the nursing students, like the medical students in the Becker et al. (1961) study, attempted to anticipate what their instructors wanted them to know and to concentrate upon satisfying these requirements. Whereas some students may have attempted to "psych out" the instructors from the very beginning, it now became a group phenomenon with the entire class collectively participating in the process. The fourth stage, termed *role simulation,* was characterized by students performing so as to elicit favorable responses from the instructors. The approved mode of behavior was the exhibition of an objective and "professional" (detached) attitude toward patient care, which included an understanding of the principles behind nursing techniques as well as mastery of those techniques. Many of the students felt they were "playing at acting like a nurse" and they questioned their lack of conviction about the role. But Davis points out that the more successful they became at convincing others that their performance was authentic, the more they began to gain confidence in themselves as nurses. This stage usually came at the end of the first year. The last two years of their program were characterized as the fifth stage of *provisional internalization* and the sixth stage of *stable internalization.* During these final two stages, the nursing students took on a temporary self-identity as a "professional" nurse, as defined by the faculty, and finally settled into a stable and consistent identification of self by the time of their graduation.

The same type of socialization was apparent in a later study at a large midwestern hospital school of nursing conducted by George Psathas (1968). Psathas found that while freshmen nursing students entered training with people-oriented attitudes, senior nursing students were more technique oriented. For example, when shown cards depicting situations concerning nurses and patients, freshmen were much more likely to respond that the patients needed emotional support, while the seniors were much more likely to see the situation involving simple technical or physical problems. All in all, the freshmen were considerably more idealistic about patient care than the seniors, who saw their work in a more unemotional and routine fashion. Psathas observed that as the work became more routine, it became less attractive and the training program took on the aspects of "something to get through." Psathas (1968:64) said, "that this result could occur in three years and while the girl is still in school—does not speak well for the development of an academic or professional interest or an increased dedication to the role."

Another problem with respect to the professional status of nursing is that, unlike medical students who desire a medical education as a terminal career, not all nursing students, perhaps not even a majority, view a career in nursing as their primary life goal. Davis (1972; Davis and Olesen, 1963) observed that many nursing students did not, either upon entry into nursing school or upon graduation, see themselves as being committed to a career in nursing. Their major life goal was that of marriage and family. This was so despite the influence of women's liberation and the encouragement of the nursing faculty to view nursing as a lifelong career. Davis (1972:46) found that the majority of students sought nursing training "as a kind of life insurance," should marriage and having a family not occur or should the marriage be less than ideal and result in "childlessness, divorce, premature widowhood, excessive financial burdens, or boredom with the home."

Therefore, the contingency of marriage became the decisive factor upon which all other career decisions were based. Davis noted that a student's announcement of an engagement to be married was a great occasion for both the student and her classmates. Not only did it indicate that the major concern was resolved in a positive manner for the engaged girl, but it also served to remind those not engaged of their less positive circumstances. Davis (1972:46) found that during the senior year there was "a veritable marital sweepstakes," in which the announcements of some engagements acquired the "theatrical overtones of a last minute rescue." Davis concluded:

In sum, the life perspective of these students was predominantly one in which a rather unpredictable set of contingencies lying well outside their sole determination and control—whether they would marry, when, to whom, with what resultant gains or losses—was seen as ruling over matters about which they could, if they chose, much more nearly exercise determination and control, that is, what to do about their careers in nursing.[1]

Other studies (Davis and Olesen, 1963; Psathas, 1968) have found that many nursing students anticipate that nursing school will provide them with the opportunity to meet physicians, medical students, or other young men working in health-related fields. This situation is further emphasized in the most readily available accounts of nurses in popular fiction, where marriage to the young doctor, not a commitment to a career, is portrayed as the heroine's ultimate goal (Richter and Richter, 1974).

On the West Coast, Davis and Virginia Olesen (1963) noted that many nursing students have difficulty adjusting to their categorization by male medical students primarily as "nurses" rather than as young, pretty, intelligent, and attractive females. In fact, nursing students had nothing to do with medical students in class or on the hospital wards. Friendships were formed largely around occupational lines, with the medical students tending to socialize with each other, leaving the nursing students to do likewise.

Psathas (1968) found similar trends in his study. Many freshmen nursing students arrived with the expectation of meeting and marrying a physician. Often they would describe themselves as having a "typical high school crush" on doctors and being satisfied just to be able to work beside them. Seniors, however, had a much greater interest in heterosexual activity and saw relationships with men, physicians or otherwise, as romantic or dating relationships to be consummated by marriage or an "affair." Relationships with interns and staff doctors were primarily described as "affairs," which Psathas interpreted as reflecting the reality of age and status differences between doctors and student nurses. It was unlikely that such relationships would lead to marriage. Instead, nursing seniors were much more likely than freshmen to describe orderlies and laboratory technicians, with equal or lower social status than themselves, as probable romantic interests.

The overall image of nursing projected by these studies is that of an occupation dominated by a small group of older, career-oriented R.N.s who serve as leaders, policy makers, and educators for a large and transient mass of younger nurses whose career aspirations are greatly weakened by outside influences such as marriage (see Freidson, 1970b). Thus nursing, like many other work roles for women, has been defined as

[1] Fred Davis, *Illness, Interaction, and the Self* (Belmont, Cal.: Wadsworth, 1972), p. 46.

a contingent role that can be assumed only to the extent that it does not interfere with the primary roles of wife and mother (Warnecke, 1973).

Furthermore, the motivation to work in such a role and to train for it often appears to be based upon factors (marriage and subsequent satisfaction) that are tangential or irrelevant to the intrinsic content of the role itself. Research by Richard Warnecke (1973) shows that a lack of commitment to the nursing role is the major nonintellectual factor of attrition from collegiate nursing programs; Davis (1966, 1972) has shown that among student nurses who graduate there is often a lack of commitment to the actual practice of nursing. The nursing degree thus often becomes an end in itself rather than the basis for a lifelong career, and this lack of professional commitment remains a most serious problem for the future development of nursing.

National Associations

Nurses have sought to improve the conditions of nursing practice and to gain professional status through the organization of national associations representing nursing interests. The most prominent of these organizations have been the National League of Nursing and the American Nurses' Association.

The National League of Nursing is composed mainly of nursing educators and formal agencies interested in nursing education. Its primary aim is to promote quality standards for nurses' training. The American Nurses' Association has become the major organization for registered nurses and is the official representative of nursing in relations with outside organizations. The ANA has not had the control over its membership, currently about 160,000 registered nurses, that has characterized the American Medical Association. Nor has membership in the ANA played an important role in the ability of individual nurses to establish important relationships with nursing colleagues. The overall effectiveness of ANA has been hampered by internal power struggles and lack of support of a unified membership. Only during the last few years has the ANA enjoyed the increasing support of a number of concerned nurses, who see in it the potential for positive group action (Bowman and Culpepper, 1974).

The "Doctor–Nurse Game"

It might be presumed from the literature examined thus far that nurses have generally been powerless and dependent practitioners. Some studies clearly suggest that nurses perceive themselves as pawns in most power struggles, that they have perhaps internalized the attitudes of subordination projected by physicians and hospital administrators. The attitudes of all participants are no doubt reinforced by the stereotypical roles of male dominance and female passivity. Mauksch (1972:223) has suggested, for example, that physician–nurse interaction "might be the last vestigial remains of the nineteenth-century relationship between the sexes."

Sex roles, however, are not the only social–psychological factors affecting the physician–nurse relationship. As Barbara Bates (1970) has noted, the full development of the nursing role has been limited both by pressures from without (physicians) and by timidity from within. In her review of the literature, Bates observed that few nurses have openly rebelled against physician authoritarianism and most have accepted a position of deference toward the physician. This attitude is also prevalent in nursing traditions where obedience to the physician has been emphasized (Strauss, 1966; Bates, 1970; Mauksch, 1972). Additionally significant in this regard is that physicians are often older than the nurses they work with, come from a higher socioeconomic background, are the socially recognized "experts" on medicine, and have been accorded greater rewards and higher prestige by the general public (Bates, 1970; Freidson, 1970a). Nor have medical schools provided experiences for medical students concerning the potential contribution of nurses (Becker et al., 1961).

Certainly the formal lines of authority that exist in the medical setting do operate to place nurses at a disadvantage in exercising and acting upon their judgments regarding medical treatment. Informally, however, nurses have been able to develop an extremely effective interactional style with physicians. This interaction has been described by Leonard Stein (1967) as the "doctor–nurse game" because it has all the features of a game—an object, rules, and scores. The object of the game is for the nurse to be bold, show initiative, and make significant recommendations to the doctor in a manner, however, that appears passive and totally supportive of the "super-physician." The central rule of the game is to avoid open disagreement between the players. This requires the nurse to communicate her recommendation without appearing to do so, while the physician, in seeking a recommendation, must appear not to be asking for it. Stein notes that the greater the significance of the recommendation, the more subtly it must be conveyed. Both participants must therefore be aware of each other's nonverbal and verbal styles of communication.

Stein illustrates the doctor–nurse game with an example of a nurse telephoning and awakening a hospital staff physician who is on call with a report about a female patient unknown to the doctor. The nurse informs the doctor that the patient is unable to sleep and had just been informed that day about the death of her father. What the nurse is actually telling the doctor is that the patient is upset and needs a sedative in order to sleep. Since the doctor is not familiar with the patient, the doctor asks the nurse what sleeping medication has been helpful to the patient in the past. What the doctor is actually doing is asking the nurse for a recommendation; however, the sentence is phrased in such a way that it appears to be a question rather than a request for a recommendation. The nurse replies that pentobarbital 100 mg has been effective for this particular patient, which Stein interprets as a disguised recommendation statement. The doctor then orders the nurse to administer pentobarbital 100 mg as needed and the nurse concludes the interaction by thanking the doctor for the order. The nurse has been successful in making a recommendation without appearing to do so, and the doctor has been successful in asking for a recommendation without appearing to do so.

While all of this may seem silly to persons unfamiliar with the physician–nurse relationship, it nonetheless represents a significant social mechanism by which the physician is able to utilize the nurse as a consultant and the nurse is able to gain self-esteem and professional satisfaction from her work. A successful game creates a doctor–nurse alliance and allows the doctor to have a good "score" by gaining the respect and admiration of the nursing staff; the nurse, in turn, scores by being identified by the physician as "a damn good nurse." If the doctor fails to play the game well, pleasant working relationships with the nurses may become difficult and the doctor may have problems of a trivial yet annoying nature when it comes to getting his work done. Nurses who do not play the game well (are outspoken in making recommendations) are either terminated from employment if they also lack intelligence, or are tolerated but not "loved" if they are bright. Nurses who do not play the game at all, according to Stein, are defined as dull and are relegated to the background in the social life of the hospital.

NURSING: FUTURE TRENDS

According to William Goode's (1957, 1960) analysis of the features of a profession (discussed in Chapter Six), the two core characteristics of a profession were those of a service orientation and control over a specialized body of abstract knowledge. Nursing, of course, has traditionally had a service orientation, which is inherent in the mother-surrogate role. But nursing's claims to a specialized body of knowledge do not seem to be justified in light of physician-defined and -created practices. Goode (1960), in fact, excluded nurses from consideration as professionals because he believed nursing training was nothing more than a "lower-level medical education." This same type of reasoning has prompted Freidson (1970a) to describe nursing as a paramedical occupation.

However, despite their lack of control over a unique body of specialized knowledge, nurses have continued to strive for a true professional position within the status and work hierarchy of medicine. The result has been a definite separation of nursing tasks; bedside care is accomplished by lower-echelon workers, while "professional" nurses, especially those R.N.s with baccalaureate degrees, have abandoned the mother-surrogate role in favor of roles as administrators and primary-care healers. This trend, which shows every sign of continuing, suggests that nurses may be likely to achieve a partial degree of professional status in the future social structure of medical care.

Hospital Administration

One significant change in the work role of nursing has been the evolution of the R.N. into an administrative role. Wilson (1970) has indicated that this development may be viewed as a response to blocked mobility. Competent nurses cannot be rewarded by promotion to the higher rungs of the medical profession; if the nurse is to reach the top of the medical structure, she is forced to leave nursing altogether and become a doctor. Since this is usually impractical, many nurses have sought a career in hospital administration because it allows them to be less subordinate to physicians and to assign traditional nursing tasks to less qualified health workers. Also, from the perspective of hospital administrators, registered nurses can be utilized more economically in managerial and supervisory positions because lower paid personnel are available for bedside tasks (Schulman, 1972).

The paradox in this development, however, is that while it allows the nurse to gain a somewhat more secure claim of professional status, it greatly reduces or eliminates the contact with patients for which nursing was organized in the first place. Yet it has been suggested that patients usually cannot tell one type of nurse from another and generally do not overtly request emotional support (Elder, 1963). Instead, patients typically request simple tasks—such as medications to ease pain or assistance in moving to a more comfortable body position—which can be accomplished by less qualified nursing aides. As Sam Schulman (1972:236) points out, in hospitals "mother-surrogateness is seldom encountered: in large measure, it is not asked for by patients nor is it given by nurses." It is Schulman's conclusion that, in an indirect sense, patients are supportive of the removal of most professional nurses from their bedsides because they want the most professional persons in charge of their care. Whether or not patients do approve of removing the best qualified nurses from their bedside is an arguable point; nevertheless, it is happening.

The Nurse Practitioner

The most recent change in nursing has been the emergence of another kind of nurse—the nurse practitioner or nurse clinician. This change is not intended to create a new type of health worker, but instead to utilize more fully the skills and capabilities of the well-trained nurse. The nurse practitioner is intended to occupy a work position similar to that of the new physician assistant role. The nurse practitioner is trained to assume many of the primary and routine tasks of patient care normally handled by the physician, such as giving physical examinations, taking medical histories, ordering laboratory tests and x-rays, providing health education to patients and their families, and making the decision as to whether or not the patient needs to consult with a physician. This role for the nurse allows the physician to assume the more realistic position of a highly trained specialist. It frees physicians from the routine tasks of medical practice and allows them to concentrate more fully· on the complex medical problems for which their training has prepared them.

Although the role of nurse practitioner has not been fully conceptualized in terms of the training, qualifications, and responsibilities, recent studies (Merenstein et al., 1974; Taller and Feldman, 1974) suggest that nurse practitioners have met with a high degree of acceptance among patients who have utilized their services and that patient care can indeed be made more efficient by involving paramedical personnel.

Hence, a formal role for nurses who practice medicine as well as nursing is beginning to develop within the context of patient care. In the future, nurse practitioners may even provide most or even all primary care for patients, leaving physicians to further consolidate their role as specialists. Although this would not effect a change in nursing's subordinate work role, it would allow the practitioners at least some share of the characteristics of professionalism. The primary concern, however, with this projection of an expanded role is that the nurse practitioner may simply be "consumed" by the medical profession as a "lesser" doctor or given only a more complex form of tasks delegated by the physician (Bates, 1970). Certainly this result is a distinct possibility and it relates to the point made earlier in this chapter by Wilson (1970) that nursing represents a case of blocked mobility; if "professional" nurses are to become anything more than supervisors of nursing care or practitioners of lower level medical care, they must leave nursing because the work role is inherently subordinate to the physician.

Current trends suggest that the new generation of R.N.s will play an expanded role in medicine through increased decision making and direct responsibility for decisions made as either administrator or practitioner. They will do so, however, within the overall structure of medical practice, and their position will remain subordinate to that of the physician. Direct bedside care of patients will increasingly come to be the domain of the practical nurse and the nurse's aide.

Physician's Assistant

While the concept of the nurse practitioner derives from the expansion of a traditional occupation, that of physician's assistant represents a new form of paramedical practitioner. This new occupation results from the recognition by American physicians that specialization has reduced them to narrower and narrower competencies and that the pressure of increasing case loads has reduced the time available for attending to many minor and routine patient demands. It has been charged that some physicians have relied upon excessive use of laboratory and diagnostic tests (thus increasing the costs of medical treatment) as a partial substitution for physician–patient interaction. It has also been suggested that decreased physician–patient time per visit has contributed to patient dissatisfaction and thus to malpractice suits. Ideally physician's assistants will handle many routine medical problems, thereby releasing the physician for increased physician–patient contact and more attention to difficult and complex problems. Although the exact duties and responsibilities of the physician's assistant have yet to be standardized, a general job description would be to provide a level of primary patient care similar to or higher than that of nurse practitioners.

In a survey of graduates of the eighteen physician's assistant training programs extant in 1972, Richard Scheffler and Olivia Stinson (1974) found that members of this new occupational group were primarily young white males, between the ages of twenty-five and thirty, who had a background in health care services prior to their qualification as physician's assistant. Their training was either in general medicine or in specialties, especially ophthalmology and orthopedics. Typically, they worked directly for physicians, either in private medical practices or in hospitals providing in-patient services. They indicated that they spent the largest part of their workday providing direct patient care, which was divided about equally between those tasks directly supervised and those indirectly supervised by physicians; considerably less time was spent in technical or laboratory work or in the supervision of other health workers.

However, the lack of a definitive role for physician's assistants has resulted in a problematic acceptance by other members of the health occupations, particularly nurses. Rodney Coe and Leonard Fichtenbaum's 1972 study of a small midwestern group practice and community hospital found that those persons who were initially supportive of the physician's assistant role had a clearer understanding of his duties than those opposed to the role. Physician's assistants viewed themselves as a "limited extension of the physician," but nurses ranked them below their own position but somewhat higher than practical nurses in the status hierarchy of the hospital. Nurses questioned the need for even having physician's assistants, especially in the hospital, and they were most concerned about those duties of the physician's assistant that overlapped their own assignments. Many nurses felt physician's assistants could be better utilized in rural communities that did not have a doctor in residence. Physicians, in contrast, generally agreed that the overall idea of a physician's assistant was a good one, but they expressed concern about the possible legal liabilities. They favored physician's assistants working under direct supervision in their own private offices. In sum, Coe and Fichtenbaum observed that in the beginning:

> The general attitude held by most hospital personnel (except physicians and administrators) was, at best, ambivalent. Much of it was negative. The ambivalence stemmed from "envy" of the physician assistant's close relationship with the physician, his freedom to make decisions (which most felt were the sole responsibility of the physician) and greater financial rewards with less formal training than most of the personnel with whom he worked.[2]

Yet, in a follow-up study six months later, Coe and Fichtenbaum detected the emergence of increasingly favorable attitudes toward physician's assistants (due in large measure, they believed, to the positive support of physicians). Earlier vehement criticisms were replaced with discussions about hiring more physician's assistants, and various other health personnel—registered nurses and laboratory technicians—were obviously motivated to become physician's assistants by the higher status and higher salaries. Coe and Fichtenbaum concluded that as long as physicians were willing to accept the responsibility for physician's assistants, problems were minimal.

Thus, it appears that if problems of role definition can be solved,

---

2 Rodney M. Coe and Leonard Fichtenbaum, "Utilization of Physician Assistants: Some Implications for Medical Practice," *Medical Care,* 10 (Nov.-Dec. 1972) , 500.

the physician's assistant is likely to become an established occupation within medicine. Although the new occupation is comprised primarily of men, it may become increasingly attractive to women not only because the status and pay are inviting, but also because the work role is asexual. It currently avoids both the female stereotype of nursing and the male stereotype of physicianship. (This may change, however, if males continue to dominate the ranks.) Most important for patient care, the physician's assistant, in conjunction with the nurse practitioner, may be able to resolve the significant issue of providing more primary care practitioners in the American system of health care delivery.

SUMMARY

Nursing as an occupation has evolved from being an informal exercise of charity ("sisterhood") into a formal occupational role subordinate to the authority and control of the physician. Many social factors have contributed to the maintenance of this situation, especially the stereotype of the mother-surrogate. It has also been noted that nurse's training is not necessarily viewed by nursing students as a means to a career, but as a kind of "life insurance" should they be disappointed in their primary goals of marriage and family. Nevertheless, nurses have continually struggled to achieve formal colleagueship with the physician and they may, to a certain extent, reach this goal as a result of their movement toward hospital administration and the nurse practitioner role.

The role of nurse practitioner seems particularly promising because it would enable nurses to gain some autonomy over what they do and to share more fully in medicine's specialized body of knowledge. Both the nurse practitioner and the physician's assistant roles result from a trend toward physician specialization that has made doctors less accessible to patients with minor and generalized ailments who nonetheless demand attention. Moreover, the emerging paramedical practitioners represent evidence that physicians have begun to modify their position in the medical work hierarchy by sharing once jealously guarded tasks of primary medical care. Perhaps the time may come, as Wilson (1970) has suggested, when the physician will lead a balanced team of health personnel who are involved in decision making and limited independent action.

PART III

HEALTH

INSTITUTIONS

8

THE HOSPITAL

Since many health problems require a level of medical treatment and personal care that extends beyond the range of services normally available in the patient's home or in the physician's office, modern society has developed formal institutions for patient care intended to help meet the more complex health needs of its members. The hospital, the major social institution for the delivery of health care in the modern world, offers considerable advantages to both patient and society. From the standpoint of the individual, the sick or injured person has access to centralized medical knowledge and technology so as to render treatment much more thorough and efficient. From the standpoint of society, as Talcott Parsons and Renée Fox (1952) suggest, hospitalization both protects the family from many of the disruptive effects of caring for the ill in the home and operates as a means of guiding the sick and injured into medically supervised institutions where their problems are less disruptive for society as a whole.

The purpose of this chapter is to consider the social role of the hospital. Besides serving the prescribed social function of providing medical treatment, hospitals can be viewed from the perspective of a functionally specific social world. This chapter will examine the organizational aspects of that world in the following order: (1) development of the hospital as a social institution; (2) the hospital system in the United States; (3) social organization of hospital work, including its effect upon the patient role; and (4) rising cost of hospital services.

THE DEVELOPMENT OF THE HOSPITAL
AS A SOCIAL INSTITUTION

The development of hospitals as institutions providing medical services for the general public proceeded apace with the prevailing needs, beliefs, values, and attitudes of the societies they served (Coe, 1970; Knowles, 1973; Rosen, 1963). Historically, hospitals have passed through four distinct phases of development: (1) as centers of religious practice, (2) as poorhouses, (3) as deathhouses, and (4) as centers of medical technology.

Hospitals as Centers of Religious Practice

Although the Romans were the first to establish separate medical facilities (for economic and military reasons) which have been described as hospitals, the origin of the institution we know today as the hospital has usually been associated with the rise of Christianity. Christian theology emphasized that human beings were duty bound to provide assistance to the sick and needy; this belief was reinforced by the notion that spiritual salvation could be obtained by whoever provided such a service. Consequently, the Roman Catholic Church encouraged its clergy to found hospitals and to locate these hospitals near churches as an integral feature of Christian religious endeavor. Furthermore, during the period of the Crusades between 1096 and 1291, many hospitals were established along the routes taken to the Holy Land by the Christian armies. Secular benefactors, such as kings, queens, other members of the nobility, wealthy merchants, artisan and craftsmen's guilds, and municipalities also founded hospitals. By the end of the fifteenth century, an extensive network of hospitals was known to have existed throughout Western Europe (Rosen, 1963).

The medieval hospital, however, was not a hospital by any modern standard. True, these hospitals were community centers for the care of the lower-class sick; yet the medical care, supervised and largely performed by clergy and nuns, consisted primarily of a rudimentary form of nursing. The primary functions of the medieval hospital were the exercise of religious practices and the extension of charity and welfare services to the poor, including both the able-bodied and the sick. These early hospitals, therefore, provided a wide spectrum of social tasks for the benefit of the lower classes, especially the provision of food, shelter, sanctuary, and prayer as well as nursing.

During the Renaissance and the Reformation, the religious character of the hospital began to disappear as increasing numbers of hospitals were placed under the jurisdiction of secular authorities. Nevertheless, as Rodney Coe (1970:236) has observed, three basic features of the modern hospital are derived from the influence of the Church. First, the concept of a service oriented toward helping others has become a guiding principle for the manner in which hospital personnel are required to approach their work. Second, hospitals are supposed to have a "universal-istic" approach—that is, to accept for treatment all persons who may be sick or injured. And third, the custodial nature of hospital care has been facilitated by housing patients within the confines of a single location.

Hospitals as Poorhouses

The secular control of hospitals marked a period of decline for the development of Europe's hospital system. Even though monks and nuns continued to work in hospitals, the removal of the centralized authority of the Church left hospitals under many separate administrations, usually those of municipal governments. Without general regulations pertaining to hospital administration, individual hospitals were free to pursue any course of action they desired. This situation encouraged abuse, partic-ularly in regard to neglect of facilities, misappropriation of funds, and the lowering of prevailing standards of patient care. In England the suppression of the monastery system in the mid-1500s led to the collapse of the English hospital system as many hospitals, left without personnel or money, were forced to close. The few remaining hospitals limited their services to persons who were actually sick and who could be cured. While this policy relegated the poor, both the incurably ill and the able-bodied, to poorhouses or to the streets for their support, it marked the beginning of a new definition of hospitals as institutions active in curing the sick and injured so that they could return to society.

However, by the end of the sixteenth century, as George Rosen (1963) explains, the economic and social conditions of the poor worsened to a considerable degree. Unemployment, higher prices, and the loss of land created a serious problem of vagrancy throughout Europe. Many vagrants likewise claimed to be sick or crippled, and they crowded whatever hospital facilities were available. In accordance with the new definition of social welfare as a community rather than a church responsi-bility, measures were eventually taken by city and national authorities to provide public assistance. Many hospitals were reopened, but they soon acquired the characteristics of boarding houses because they offered food and shelter to the poor, regardless of whether they were sick or healthy. Those persons living in hospitals who could work were required to pay for their lodging, while hospitals received further financial support through public taxation. Hospitals became little more than social "ware-houses," where invalids, the aged, orphans, and the mentally defective could be sent and thus removed from the mainstream of society. Even today in the United States, persons with chronic health problems requiring long-term hospitalization—the insane, the incurable, and individuals suffering from highly infectious diseases—tend to be sent to public institutions, while private hospitals tend to accept patients with acute disorders.

Hospitals as Deathhouses

Following the Renaissance and the Reformation, the outward character of hospitals appeared to change very little from that of a public institution whose purpose was to provide welfare services for the lower social classes on behalf of the communities in which they were located. Nonetheless, changes were taking place as physicians discovered that hospitals contained large numbers of sick and injured (and also generally powerless) persons whose health problems could be studied and upon whom the various evolving techniques of medical treatment could be practiced.

Physicians had first begun to associate themselves with hospitals during the fourteenth century; initially they had little influence because they were not members of the hospital staff and provided their services on a purely voluntary basis. By the seventeenth century, however, physicians acquired a virtual monopoly over the existing body of medical knowledge that placed them in the position of first advising and eventually directing all patient care within the hospital. As physicians became increasingly influential, non-medical hospital tasks gradually disappeared. By the early nineteenth century, hospitals had clearly assumed their present-day role as institutions for medical care, for medical research, and for the education of medical students.

Although medical treatment is recognized as the primary function of the hospital in the eighteenth century, the primitive level of that treatment produced few cures. Trained physicians were unable to achieve consistent results with their techniques and, accordingly, neither they nor hospitals were held in high esteem by the general population. Because so few patients survived treatment despite occasional heroic efforts, hospitals acquired an image as places where the poor went to die.

According to Coe (1970:245), the high death rate in hospitals was also related to the appalling living conditions provided patients. Typically, hospitals were dirty, poorly ventilated, and filled to capacity. Often more than one patient was placed in a single bed regardless of the patient's disorder, and treatment was usually carried out in a public fashion on the ward itself. Surgery, which Coe points out was limited at that time mostly to amputations and childbirth, plus the purging of fevers with various potions, bloodletting to eliminate "excess" blood, and the removal of the dead all occurred in the same general area where patients ate and slept. Nor did the attending physicians and surgeons practice even the most rudimentary standards of sanitation, moving from bed to bed and treating a great variety of disorders, including those that were infectious, without washing their hands or changing their clothes. Thus, it is not surprising that hospitals were regarded by most people as places where only the lower social classes went to die.

Hospitals as Centers of Medical Technology

Since the end of the nineteenth century, a new image of hospitals evolved as institutions where patients of all social classes could generally expect to find the highest quality medical care and could reasonably expect to be cured of their disorders. Three major factors were responsible for this change. First was the fact that medicine had indeed become a science in terms of employing the scientific method to seek out accurate medical knowledge and to develop successful techniques that could be employed in a consistent manner. Of particular importance was increased knowledge about human physiology and the development of the science of bacteriology; also important was the perfection of ether as an anesthetic that allowed surgery to be performed in a relatively painless fashion. Since the new medical technology required extensive and often expensive facilities, these facilities were centralized in hospitals in order that they could be available to most physicians. Hospitals eventually became places where physicians also referred their upper- and middle-class patients since the most advanced medical technology was located there. While the poor generally remained in a charity status as hospital patients, there came into being a new type of patient—the private patient—who required private accommodations, usually had a private physician, and who paid for hospital services.

A second important factor, concomitant with the development of medical technology, was the discovery and use of antiseptic measures in the hospital to help curtail infection. Hospitals were not only properly cleaned and ventilated, but patients with infectious diseases were isolated in special areas of the hospital, and hospital staffs were required to wash their hands and change their clothing after working with these patients. The use of such items as surgical masks, rubber gloves, and sterilized surgical instruments became commonplace. These procedures not only reduced the number of deaths among hospital patients, but also reduced the amount of time required for patient recovery.

Third, there was a significant improvement in the quality of hospital personnel. Especially important was the entry on the scene of the trained nurse and the laboratory technician, whose specialized skills were able to support the physician in his or her primary role of diagnostician and practitioner. In the twentieth century, the hospital has become the major institutional resource available to society for coping with problems of health and illness.

HOSPITALS IN THE UNITED STATES

The first hospitals were founded in the United States over two hundred years ago. Generally their development paralleled that of Western European institutions in the 1700s. The first such hospital was established by William Penn in Philadelphia in 1713, with the care of the sick being incidental to the main purpose of providing shelter for the poor. The well-known Charity Hospital in New Orleans was founded by the Catholic Church in 1737 for similar reasons. The first hospital to be established in the United States solely for the purpose of treating the sick was the Pennsylvania Hospital founded by Benjamin Franklin and a group of interested citizens in 1751. These early hospitals were not governmental undertakings, as Rosen (1963:24) points out, but were largely based on voluntary initiative by private citizens who wanted medical care available on a nonprofit basis. They were generally intended to provide treatment for those patients who had curable disorders.

Federal government participation in health care did not actually begin until 1798 with the U.S. Public Health Service hospital program for merchant seamen. State governments did not enter into health care delivery until the 1800s, and their efforts were largely confined to the establishment of state mental institutions. By 1873 there were only 178 hospitals of all types in the United States; this number grew to an estimated 7,481 hospitals in 1972.

Hospital Ownership

The ownership of hospitals in the U.S. may be classified into three major types: (1) voluntary (nonprofit), (2) proprietary (profit-making), or government (federal, state, or local). Figure 8-1 shows that of the total of 7,438 hospitals in 1973, the largest single type was the voluntary hospital.[1] This figure of 3,694 voluntary hospitals represents 50 percent of all U.S. hospitals.

[1] A hospital is defined as a facility with at least six beds that is licensed by the state as a hospital, or that is operated as a hospital by a federal or state agency and is therefore not subject to state or local licensing laws (National Center for Health Statistics, 1975:340).

Controlled by a board of trustees, nonprofit hospitals are exempt from federal income taxes and many other forms of state and local taxes. These hospitals have generally been characterized as emphasizing high quality care for the upper and middle social classes, while also allowing access to their facilities to lower-class patients primarily through clinics and teaching programs (Elling and Halebsky, 1961). Voluntary hospitals are highly dependent upon community physicians for membership on their staffs and for the referral of patients. According to data obtained from a 1969 American Hospital Association survey, Noralou Roos and her associates (1974) project that 59 percent of all capital funds for voluntary hospitals are derived from internal resources, mostly income from patient services. Other sources of capital funds for voluntary hospitals are philanthropic (24 percent) and government (17 percent). Large voluntary hospitals, however, are somewhat less dependent than smaller hospitals upon local physicians because of their greater prestige, more extensive facilities, and higher ratio of doctors requesting staff positions (see Roos et al., 1974).

Figure 8–1 shows that 980 hospitals (13 percent of the total) are classified as proprietary. These hospitals are usually small and are also

FIGURE 8–1. OWNERSHIP OF HOSPITALS, 1973

Ownership	Total hospitals	General medical and surgical	Specialty Total	Psychiatric	Chronic disease	Tuberculosis	Other[1]
Total	7,438	6,458	980	508	70	65	337
Government	2,744	2,239	505	321	45	60	79
Federal	397	365	32	27	—	—	5
State-local	2,347	1,874	473	294	45	60	74
Proprietary	1,000	818	182	104	7	—	71
Nonprofit	3,694	3,401	293	83	18	5	187
Church	840	788	52	12	3	1	36
Other	2,854	2,613	241	71	15	4	151

SOURCE: U.S. National Center for Health Statistics, *Health Resources Statistics* (Washington, D.C.: U.S. Department of Health, Education and Welfare, 1975).

[1] *Includes eye, ear, nose, and throat hospitals; epileptic hospitals; alcoholism hospitals; maternity hospitals; orthopedic hospitals; physical rehabilitation hospitals; and other hospitals.*

highly dependent upon local physicians for staff membership and patient referrals. The referral system is especially critical because generally the proprietary hospital's only source of capital funds is internal.

The number of government-owned hospitals shown in Figure 8–1 is 2744, which is 37 percent of the total. Roos estimates that government hospitals receive 56 percent of their capital funds from government sources, 36 percent from internal sources, and 8 percent from philanthropic contributions. Government hospitals tend to lack prestige in comparison to voluntary hospitals, perhaps because they fill the majority of their staff positions with interns and residents. They are the major source of health care for low-income persons, particularly in urban areas. Roos (1974) describes government hospitals as "hospitals of last resort" because it has been assumed that they place their greatest emphasis upon public access to their facilities rather than upon the quality of their care. Yet the increased affiliation of government hospitals with medical schools portends a shift in emphasis toward quality care and superior facilities.

Figure 8–2, a tabulation of the number of hospital beds by type of ownership in 1973, offers a further illustration of the distribution of hospital facilities in the United States. The figure reveals that voluntary

FIGURE 8–2. HOSPITAL BEDS BY OWNERSHIP OF HOSPITALS, 1973

| Ownership | Total beds | General medical and surgical | Specialty | | | | |
			Total	Psychiatric	Chronic disease	Tuberculosis	Other[1]
Total	1,449,062	1,030,432	418,630	338,574	22,350	10,215	47,491
Government	696,259	320,671	375,588	322,675	18,571	9,846	24,496
Federal	139,044	106,361	32,683	29,572	—	—	3,111
State-local	557,215	214,310	342,905	293,103	18,571	9,846	21,385
Proprietary	80,584	68,551	12,033	8,572	418	—	3,043
Nonprofit	672,219	641,210	31,009	7,327	3,361	369	19,952
Church	192,742	188,598	4,144	1,280	195	65	2,604
Other	479,477	452,612	26,865	6,047	3,166	304	17,348

SOURCE: U.S. National Center for Health Statistics, *Health Resources Statistics* (Washington, D.C.: U.S. Department of Health, Education and Welfare, 1975).

[1] *Includes eye, ear, nose, and throat hospitals; epileptic hospitals; alcoholism hospitals; narcotic hospitals; maternity hospitals; orthopedic hospitals; physical rehabilitation hospitals; and other hospitals.*

hospitals have 672,219 hospital beds, with most of these beds (641,210) located in general medical and surgical hospitals. Thus, voluntary hospitals (representing 50 percent of all hospitals) have approximately 46 percent of all hospital beds. Government hospitals (representing 37 percent of the total) have 696,259 beds or 48 percent of the total number of beds. Most beds (375,588) in government hospitals, however, are located in specialty hospitals. Proprietary hospitals (13 percent of the total number of hospitals) have 80,854 beds or 6 percent of the total. These beds are primarily in general hospitals.

The General Hospital

At this point it is important to distinguish between general and specialty hospitals, the two major categories of hospitals according to the type of service they offer. General medical and surgical hospitals provide diagnostic and treatment services for patients who have a great variety of health disorders. Most general hospitals are short-term care facilities. According to the U.S. Center for National Health Statistics (1975), there were approximately 6,458 general hospitals with over one million beds in 1973 (as shown in Figures 8–1 and 8–2). Although general hospitals are located throughout the United States, the South has the largest concentration of them. By state, California has the largest number (572) of general hospitals, followed by Texas (527). In 1973 there were 33 million admissions to general hospitals, representing a ratio of 158 admissions for every 1,000 Americans. Approximately 33 percent of these admissions were in the South, but two states, California and New York, had 17 percent of the total U.S. admissions to general hospitals. The U.S. Center for National Health Statistics also reports that in 1973 almost 2.7 million persons were employed either full- or part-time in general hospitals, with the majority (80 percent) working full-time. This figure represents a national average of 3.1 full-time general hospital workers for each hospital patient.

The Specialty Hospital

Specialty hospitals typically restrict their services to patients with specific disorders. Specialty hospitals are generally long-term care facilities and the majority are either psychiatric, chronic disease, or tuberculosis hospitals. The U.S. National Center for Health Statistics classified approximately 980 hospitals in the United States as specialty hospitals in 1973. Figure 8–2 indicates that psychiatric hospitals were the largest single type of specialty hospital, with a total of 508 hospitals. New York and Massachusetts are the two states with the largest number of specialty hospitals. Northeastern United States has more admissions to specialty hospitals than any other region of the country. There were 1.2 million admissions to specialty hospitals on a national basis in 1973 and nearly 83 percent of these admissions were to psychiatric hospitals. The number of patients in specialty hospitals during 1973 averaged 377,900 persons, or 1.8 patients per 1,000 citizens. About 398,798 persons, some 93 percent of them full-time, were employed in these hospitals. This figure represents an average of one full-time specialty hospital employee per patient.

THE ORGANIZATION OF THE GENERAL HOSPITAL

Certainly not all hospitals are alike in their organization of services, but general hospitals, as the most common single type of hospital in the United States, exhibit organizational features similar to most other types of hospitals. Figure 8–3 shows the typical organization of large general hospitals. As a social organization, the general hospital has been described as being formal, highly stratified, quasi-bureaucratic, and quasi-authoritarian (Croog and Ver Steeg, 1972; Georgopoulos and Mann, 1972). General hospitals have also been described as "multi-purpose institutions" in that they provide a variety of health-related functions for society such as: (1) treating patients, (2) conducting medical research, (3) training health practitioners, (4) providing laboratories and other medical facilities to the community, and (5) sponsoring health education and preventive medicine programs for the general public (Coe, 1970; Heydebrand, 1973). Robert Wilson (1963), for example, describes the hospital as a hotel, a school, a laboratory, and a stage for treatment. The *primary* goal of the hospital, however, is that of providing medical treatment to its patients within the limits of contemporary medical knowledge and technology and the hospital's available resources. The hospital thus qualifies as a formal organization in that it has developed to coordinate scarce resources to achieve stated goals in as efficient a manner as possible (Becker and Gordon, 1966).

In order to accomplish its tasks and coordinate its various activities, the hospital relies upon a prescribed hierarchy of authority (as shown in Figure 8–3), which is operationalized through formal rules, regulations, and administrative procedures. The key to hospital efficiency and overall effectiveness is coordination of the various departments and individuals. They represent a complex and highly specialized division of labor that is both interlocking and interdependent.

Consider what happens when a staff doctor prescribes medication for a patient. The doctor's order for medication is written in the patient's medical records by a floor clerk, and the clerk, or a nurse's aide or

FIGURE 8-3. TYPICAL LARGE GENERAL HOSPITAL ORGANIZED INTO FIVE DIVISIONS

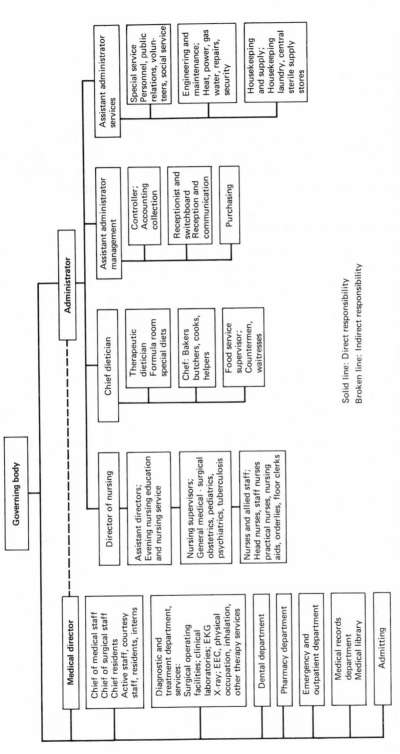

SOURCE: *Technology and Manpower in the Health Service Industry,* Manpower Research Bulletin, No. 14. Washington, D.C.: U.S. Department of Labor, Manpower Administration, May 1967.

Solid line: Direct responsibility
Broken line: Indirect responsibility

orderly, takes the request to the pharmacy. When the medication is sent by the pharmacy, it is most likely administered by a nurse. A record is then forwarded to the accounting office so that the proper charges for the drug can be entered upon the patient's bill; another written order might be sent from the pharmacy to purchasing (through the appropriate administrative channels) to reorder the medication and replace it for future use by another patient. So the rather routine activity of one particular member of the hospital staff (in this case a doctor) initiates a chain of events that affects the work of several other hospital employees.

The Hospital: Dual Authority

According to Figure 8-3, the overall supervision of the general hospital comes under the auspices of its governing body. In most non-federal hospitals, that governing body is a board of trustees. Figure 8-3 also shows that whereas the medical director and the hospital administrator are linked to the governing body by a direct line of responsibility, they are only indirectly responsible to each other. What this type of arrangement indicates is that the authority system of the general hospital operates on a dual level (see Coser, 1958; Durbin and Springall, 1974; Goss, 1963; Smith, 1955). This system is an outgrowth of the organizational conflict in the hospital between bureaucracy and professionalism.

Several sociologists (see Goss, 1963; Heydebrand, 1973) have noted that Max Weber's (Gerth and Mills, 1946) concept of bureaucracy appears incompatible with the norms of professional authority. Weber described bureaucracy as a rational and impersonal division of labor characterized by the principles of *office hierarchy* and levels of graded authority (lower offices are supervised by higher ones), and by *fixed and official areas of jurisdiction* governed by laws or administrative regulations. The essence of the conflict between bureaucracy and the professional consists of the professional's insistence on exercising an autonomous individual judgment within the limits prescribed by the profession itself. As Mary Goss (1963) points out, the work norms of the professional (in this case, the medical doctor) emphasize self-determination for each practitioner, that is, exclude control by those outside the profession. The bureaucrat (here, the hospital administrator), on the other hand, seeks to follow a rationalistic management approach that favors the efficient coordination of the hospital's activities through formal rules and impersonal regulations applicable to all persons in all situations.

Charles Perrow (1963) has traced the evolution of this conflict in his study of one voluntary general hospital he believes to be representative of most other hospitals of this type. Perrow noted that in the late 1800s and early 1900s the voluntary general hospital was dominated by its board of trustees, because this was an era when securing capital funds and gaining community recognition were critical hospital goals. Since community involvement was the pivotal factor, individual members of boards of trustees were usually laypersons selected at large from the community. Legally they were responsible for protecting the community's interests, but they also sought to incorporate hospital services into the general pattern of community life. Perrow believes this approach ultimately derives from seventeenth-century attitudes toward hospitals as state institutions operated on public funds, that is, as community welfare agencies and poorhouses.

In the 1930s trustee domination succumbed to medical domination. Perrow (1963:118) cites three major reasons for this change: First, the emphasis upon free care declined significantly as hospital services became oriented toward patients who could pay; second, the facilities to support a complex system of medical technology were developed and the quality of care provided patients was improved; and third, the hospital sought prestige through medical research in terms defined by physicians. Hence, medical domination went hand in hand with increasing medical knowledge. During this period, however, Perrow also noted the appearance of several abuses which could be attributed to the great personal power of the medical director and his department heads. Especially deficient was the out-patient care afforded to low-income persons; also conspicuous was the favoritism shown toward certain physicians in the use of hospital facilities and staff promotions. Perrow observed:

> There was little to prevent such abuses. The doctor is an individual entrepreneur, selling his services for a profit. His income is affected by the facilities he commands in the hospital, his freedom from scrutiny, and by the price he must pay in the form of reciprocal duties such as teaching or committee work. Reliance upon professional ethics, even butressed by the atmosphere created by teaching and research activities, is not sufficient in itself to guarantee a disinterested, ethical non-economic point of view. Nor will it prevent abuses stemming from the enormous concentration of power in the hands of the chief of staff and department heads who also control the hospital.[2]

What was needed, said Perrow, was a system to limit these powers, to establish objective criteria for promotion, and to provide for more effective representation of patient and organizational interests. That system gradually emerged during the 1940s and 1950s as the role of

2 Charles Perrow, "Goals and Power Structures: A Historical Case Study," in *The Hospital in Modern Society*, ed. E. Freidson (New York: Free Press, 1963), p. 123.

hospital administrator gained in importance; through a constitutional system, the administration was able to define the medical staff's official powers, standardize the hospital's administrative procedures, and establish a level of quality for the hospital's medical services. These early administrators were often physicians who could be expected to further the interests of the medical staff, but in doing so began to curtail their power. As authority became centralized in the administrator's office, there often developed a blockage of communication between the staff and the board of trustees. This period, according to Perrow, was characterized by a complex power struggle which eventually led, in the 1950s, to a system of multiple leadership common among general hospitals today.

Multiple leadership, at least in its hospital version, is actually a system of dual authority, one administrative and the other medical. Perrow notes the high probability of such a system developing in the hospital, because goals are generally multiple (trustees, administration, and medical staff often have diverse interests), the criteria for achieving them broad, and the power of each group to protect its interests is considerable. Since the physician's professional norms can set specific limits on the hospital administrator's authority and vice versa, the result has been to reconcile the physician-professional with the administrator-bureaucrat by establishing a system of dual authority.

The board of trustees still remains the nominal center of authority in the general hospital. It usually meets on a periodic basis, weekly or monthly, to review the hospital's operations and act upon those matters brought to its attention. Generally the trustees themselves are persons who are influential in the wider community and who tend to use their hospital board membership as a power base in the community and/or as a symbol of their contribution to the community's welfare (Holloway et al., 1972; Perrow, 1963). But despite their position as the hospital's ultimate source of authority, the trustees have only limited de facto authority over the medical staff, who usually make all health-related decisions (Georgopoulos and Mann, 1972). The board of trustees typically concerns itself with administrative matters and public relations while working closely with the hospital administrator, who acts as their agent in exercising authority and supervising the day-to-day routine of the hospital.[3]

[3] However, as Morton Creditor (1971:135) points out, large urban voluntary hospitals have problems defining the community (usually a polyglot of racial, religious, and socioeconomic groups originating from the hospital neighborhood, the broad metropolitan area, the suburbs, and beyond). Since its trustees cannot be truly representative of this undefinable community, there is considerable difficulty in setting hospital policy in response to community needs. Instead, hospital policy is usually most influenced by whatever is "good for the hospital."

The medical staff maintains control over medical matters. As Basil Georgopoulos and Floyd Mann (1972) point out, physicians are subject to very few non-medical restrictions because (1) private physicians are not employees of the hospital (they are "guests" with the privilege of practicing medicine there) ; (2) they have considerable social status and prestige in American society; and (3) they have supreme authority in all matters of patient care and medical professionalism. Nowhere in a hospital's bylaws are there statements denoting the responsibility of medical staff members to the administration; medical staff members are responsible to each other and to their patients, but not to the hospital (see Creditor, 1971). Thus occurs a rather curious situation where the primary function (medical treatment) of an organization (a hospital) is carried out by people (nurses and other health professionals) employed by the organization, but who are supervised by self-employed individuals (private practitioners). The primary "customer" of the hospital is the physician, who does not pay for its services. Eliot Freidson describes this situation by making the following comparison:

> It is as if all professors were self-employed tutors, sending individual pupils to universities where they can themselves administer some special training, but most particularly where they can count on having their pupils trained specially by lesser personnel employed by the university rather than by the professor.[4]

The occupational group in the hospital most affected by its system of dual authority are the nurses and auxiliary nursing workers who perform health care tasks on the hospital's wards. Nurses are responsible to the physician for carrying out the physician's orders, but they also are responsible to the nursing supervisors and the upper echelons of the hospital's administration. Even though the communication and allegiance of ward personnel tend to be channeled along occupational lines within and toward the "administrative channel of command," medical authority can and does cut across these lines (Wessen, 1972). While this system can at times cause interpersonal stress, inconsistency, overlapping of responsibility, and inadequate coordination (Henry, 1954, 1957), it also allows ward personnel to "play off" one authority against the other if one appears unreasonable (Wessen, 1972) and acts to reduce organizational inflexibility and authoritarianism (Georgopoulos and Mann, 1972). In fact, Georgopoulos and Mann further argue that the hospital's system of dual authority is virtually inevitable in light of its high degree of functional specialization and professionalism. Nonethe-

4 Eliot Freidson, *Professional Dominance* (Chicago: Aldine, 1970) , pp. 174–175.

less, hospital personnel share a common goal of providing quality patient care through competency, devotion to duty, and hard work, qualities Georgopoulos and Mann suggest have had the effect of producing many common norms, values, and complementary expectations. The hospital's normative system, they argue, underlies its administrative structure and:

> . . . enables the hospital to attain a level of coordination and integration that could never be accomplished through administrative edict, through hierarchical directives, or through explicitly formulated and carefully specified organizational plans and impersonal rules, regulations, and procedures.[5]

In a separate study of a psychiatric hospital, Anselm Strauss and his associates (1963) noted a similar process wherein the hospital rules governing the actions of the professionals who worked within its setting were far from extensive, clearly stated, or clearly binding. These researchers contended that the social order of the hospital was not fixed or automatically maintained, but was the result of continual negotiation between the administration, the medical staff and other hospital employees, and patients. The individuals involved had varying degrees of prestige and power, were at different stages in their careers, and had their own particular goals, reference groups, and occupational ideologies. In addition, hospital rules governing physicians' conduct were not clearly stated, extensive, or binding. The hospital administration tended to take a tolerant position toward institutional rules in the belief that good patient care required a minimum of "hard and fast" regulations and a maximum of "innovation and improvisation." Thus, there was continual negotiation of the medical rules—what they were and whether or not they applied in a particular situation. What held the hospital staff together was the sharing of a common goal to return their patients to the outside world in a better condition than when they entered the hospital. Strauss and associates explained:

> This goal is the symbolic cement that, metaphorically speaking, holds the organization together: the symbol to which all personnel can comfortably, and frequently point—with the assurance that *at least* about this matter everyone can agree! Although this symbol . . . masks a considerable measure of disagreement and discrepant purpose, it represents a generalized mandate under which the hos-

5 Basil F. Georgopoulos and Floyd C. Mann, "The Hospital as an Organization," in *Patients, Physicians and Illness,* 2nd ed., ed. E. Jaco (New York: Macmillan, 1972) , p. 308.

pital can be run—the public flag under which all may work in concert.[6]

Although it might appear from the Strauss study that the hospital was in a state of chaos, held together by only a single, idealistic agreement, actually the process of negotiation was observed to have a definite pattern. In following their own particular approach to their work, the physicians were able to originate relatively stable understandings with the nurses and other hospital employees; this resulted in efficient and standardized forms of behavior not dependent on special instructions for all contingencies. Consequently, the process of negotiation not only created new meanings, but also reinforced the significance of the more formalized rules through a process of periodic appraisal.

In summary, the hospital's organization consists of a varied group of professionals and allied health workers with different functions, training, and occupational values. In order to make this social organization function effectively, it has been necessary to construct a decentralized system of authority organized around a generally acceptable objective of service to the patient. While the administrator directs and supervises hospital policy, the medical staff retains control over medical decisions.

However, the reader should realize that the dual system of authority that currently exists in the hospital may be in jeopardy as a result of the famous precedent-setting Darling case in Illinois.[7] The Darling case involved a suit for damages sought by the plaintiff for alleged medical and hospital negligence. The patient, Dorrence Darling, broke his leg while playing football and was taken to the emergency room of Charleston Community Hospital. A general practitioner put the leg in the cast. The leg became discolored, pulseless, and a foul odor developed. The nursing staff complained to the administrator and the physician in charge. The cast was ventilated but the odor continued. Ultimately the leg was amputated. The physician settled out of court. The nurses were not held negligent because they followed the accepted guidelines and procedure. The hospital bylaws provided for the consultation of another physician upon the request of the administrator. The administrators maintained that the hospital had provided the "brick" and "mortar" (the facilities) in which health care took place and that they had acted as all other hospital administrators would have done. The court found the administrators negligent in their relationship to the patient by not requiring a

6 Anselm Strauss, Leonard Schatzman, Danuta Ehrlich, Rue Bucher, and Melvin Sabshin, "The Hospital and Its Negotiated Order," in *The Hospital in Modern Society*, ed. E. Freidson (New York: Free Press, 1963) , p. 154.

7 See *Darling v. Charleston Community Hospital*, 33 Ill. 2d 326, 211 N.E. 2d 253 (1965) , 50 Ill. APP 2d 253 Cert. denied, 383 U.S. 946 (1966) .

consultation as provided in the hospital bylaws. It held that hospitals do much more than just furnish treatment facilities; they also assume certain responsibilities for the care of the patient.

Therefore, as Richard Durbin and W. Herbert Springall (1974) have pointed out, if the hospital is going to be held liable for professional medical decisions, the administration will probably attempt to gain greater control over the practice of medicine within its facilities. Durbin and Springall predict that liability for patient care will result in the hospital's imposing more of its rules and regulations on the physician, raising the standards of qualification required for staff privileges, and generally reducing the amount of professional discretion and autonomy physicians have traditionally been allowed to exercise.

THE HOSPITAL–PATIENT ROLE

While hospital services are oriented toward a supportive notion of patient welfare, hospital rules and regulations are generally designed for the benefit of hospital personnel so that the work of treating large numbers of patients can be more efficient and easier to perform (Coe, 1970; Freidson, 1970a; Lorber, 1975). Consequently, sick and injured persons are organized into various patient categories (maternity–obstetrics, neurology, orthopedics, urology, pediatrics, psychiatry) that reflect the medical staff's definition of their disorder, and are then usually subject to standardized, staff-approved medical treatment and administrative procedures.

While it can be argued that standardizing patient care results in increased organizational efficiency—and ultimately serves the best interest of the patient—a prominent theme of the hospitalization experience noted by medical sociologists has been that of depersonalization. Erving Goffman (1961), for example, describes the status of mental hospital patients as akin to being a "non-person," while Coe (1970) believes that patients in general tend to be devalued by hospital personnel even before they are admitted to the hospital because they are old, sick, or defective in some way. In other words, hospital patients are more than just dependent upon other people, but they are also less than "ideal." H. Jack Geiger, an M.D., illustrates the feelings of depersonalization in hospital care by commenting on his own experience as a patient:

> I had to be hospitalized, suddenly and urgently, *on my own ward*. In the space of only an hour or two, I went from apparent health and well-being to pain, disability, and fear, and from staff to inmate

in a total institution. At one moment I was a physician: elite, technically skilled, vested with authority, wielding power over others, affectively neutral. The next moment I was a patient: dependent, anxious, sanctioned in illness only if I was cooperative. A protected dependency and the promise of effective technical help were mine—if I accepted a considerable degree of psychological and social servitude.[8]

Geiger was subsequently placed in the ward's only private room, which he believed was more for the unconscious benefit of the staff than for himself. He felt that had he been placed among the other patients, lending objective credence to physician "mortality," the patients might have used the situation to reduce status and role barriers between themselves and the staff. Furthermore, Geiger learned what he now believes is the major reason why physicians make such "notoriously terrible patients." It was not because their technical knowledge caused them to be more fearful of the consequences of their disorder or more critical of the way it was treated. Instead it was the loss of their professional role and authority in the medical setting, which Geiger surmises is an integral part of their self-concept.

Personnel in hospitals do not necessarily have the express goal of making their patients feel depersonalized, but the organization of the hospital's work does favor rules and regulations that reduce patient autonomy and encourage patient receptivity of the hospital routine. Another important factor is the work situation itself. Jeanne Quint Benoliel (1975:180) has pointed out that nurses who had difficulty tolerating the work in intensive or coronary care hospital units felt oppressed by "repetitive exposure to death and dying, daily contact with mutilated and unsightly patients, formidable and demanding work loads, limited work space, intricate machinery, and communication problems involving physicians, staff, and families." The intensive care ward is thus an example of a work situation that generates pressures of a dehumanizing nature as a result of staff attempts to cope with inherently intense psychological stress. Furthermore, Benoliel adds that on the surgical wards patients are so concerned about themselves that if the nurses do take a personal interest in them, they demand increasing amounts of the nurses' time and energy.

Yet it should be noted that the process of depersonalization is not just as a result of the manner in which large numbers of patients are managed or the work conditions, but it is also related to the patient's

8 H. Jack Geiger, "The Causes of Dehumanization in Health Care and Prospects for Humanization," in J. Howard and A. Strauss (eds.), *Humanizing Health Care* (New York: Wiley-Interscience, 1975), p. 13.

subjective experience of feeling sick. Howard Leventhal (1975) has explained that most reports of depersonalization commonly cite the experience of one's self as a physical object or thing. A second common experience is the feeling that one's own psychological self is isolated from other psychological selves (other people). Furthermore, Leventhal suggests that bodily symptoms such as pain can create a sense of separation within the individual of the physical self from the conscious psychological self. This inner alienation, in addition to the feeling of isolation from others, compounded by the doubt, uncertainty, and confusion that often accompany feelings of illness, can create for patients a sense of inadequacy and inability to control their lives. Leventhal's argument is that this attitude of incompetency is further intensified by the patient's having to assume an institutional role like the sick role, in which he or she is officially dependent and excluded from decision making (see also Bloom, 1963). The process of depersonalization is undoubtedly enhanced by the need of the physician or nurse to have access to the patient's body. However legitimate this may be, Coe (1970) points out that the exposure and giving over of one's body to strangers can be a degrading and humiliating experience, even though it is intended to be therapeutic.

Stripping, Control of Resources, and Restriction of Mobility

Coe (1970) states that patients are alienated from their usual lives and reduced to a largely impersonal status in the hospital through three basic mechanisms of hospital processing: (1) stripping, (2) control of resources, and (3) restriction of mobility. Coe explains that when patients present themselves for treatment in a hospital, they bring with them a particular social identity, what Goffman refers to as a "face" (see Chapter Three) ; this represents their attitudes, beliefs, values, concept of self, and social status, all of which form the basis for their manner of presenting themselves to the world. *Stripping* occurs when the hospital systematically divests the person of these past representations of self. The patient's clothes are taken away and replaced with a set of pajamas; regardless of whether the pajamas are the property of the hospital or the patient, the simple fact of wearing pajamas serves as a uniform that identifies that person as sick and restricts movement to those areas of the hospital in which pajamas (patient dress) are authorized. Personal belongings of value are taken away and locked up for safekeeping by the staff. Visiting regulations control not only when patients are allowed to have visitors, but also who is allowed to visit (children under age fourteen are typically excluded). In addition, the staff supervises the patient's diet, decides when the patient should be asleep or awake, and in essence controls the general conduct of the patient's social life in the hospital. The hospital routine for one patient is very similar to the routine of others having the same or similar health problems.

Another important feature of hospitalization is the *control of resources* by the staff. Coe includes under the control of resources not only physical items, like bedclothes, and toilet paper, but also the control of information about the patient's medical condition. For example, patients are normally not aware of their prognosis or the results of laboratory tests and x-rays unless the physician decides to inform them. On occasion doctors and nurses will even deliberately limit communication with patients if it interferes with their work or might lead to patients' discovering their mistakes and shortcomings (Brown, 1966; Lorber, 1975; Roth, 1963). Several studies indicate that a major complaint of patients is the difficulty they have in obtaining information about themselves from their doctors (Coe, 1970; Davis, 1972; Duff and Hollingshead, 1968; Shiloh, 1965), including patients who were dying (Glaser and Strauss, 1965; McIntosh, 1974; also see Chapter 12).

Fred Davis (1972) found, in a study of the interaction between the parents of children who were victims of paralytic poliomyelitis and their physicians, that four communication modes were possible: (1) communication, where the doctor could make a reasonable prognosis and communicated it to the parents; (2) dissimulation, where the doctor could not make a reasonable prognosis, but communicated one to the parents anyway; (3) admission of uncertainty, where the doctor could not make a reasonable prognosis and admitted this to the parents; or (4) evasion, where the doctor could make a reasonable prognosis, but chose not to communicate it. The most common form of communication was evasion; the doctors tended to answer the questions of the parents in terms that were either evasive or unintelligibly technical. One staff member rationalized that it was better for the parents to find out for themselves in a "natural sort of way." The "natural way," Davis (1972:97) observed, was often a painfully slow and prolonged reduction of the parents' expectations about a complete recovery for their children. The reason the physicians in the Davis study did not explicitly inform the parents that their child was likely to be crippled or significantly impaired was apparently fear of being confronted with an "unmanageable" emotional reaction on the part of the parents. Other physicians rationalized that the parents would not be able to understand the prognosis even if they were informed. Davis (1972:98) concluded that in being evasive, equivocating, and abruptly ending an interview with the parents, the doctor was able to avoid a possible "scene," in having to confront them. Such tasks were generally viewed by hospital personnel as unpleasant and time consuming.

Inability to understand what they are told and negative effects of the threatening information are the two most common reasons given by medical professionals for not communicating fully with their patients (see Howard and Strauss, 1975:238–239). However, even if patients are able to comprehend the medical ramifications of their disorder, should they always be told the full story? As Robert Cooke has pointed out, physicians need to know what the knowledge will do to the patient and the patient's family:

> I'm worried about the problem of the patient's knowing when he or she can't do anything about it, as is true for Huntington's Chorea. You may have a child who at 12 has serious deterioration of the central nervous system. . . . We can now make the diagnosis on this newborn sib, age one week; and you say to the family: "I can tell you with 100 percent certainty this child is going to be just like your older child and be deteriorating and dead in 5, 6, 7, 9, 10 years."[9]

The situation Cooke describes could cause considerable anguish, worry, frustration, and anxiety within a family. Most likely the hopelessness of this type of health disorder would compound the emotional trauma resulting from knowledge of the condition. Cooke implies, then, that perhaps in some circumstances it is better not to make a full disclosure and to spare a family's feelings for as long as is realistically possible. Thus, the dilemma remains unresolved. In general, however, all patients are entitled to full knowledge about their medical condition, and it is incumbent upon the doctor to help them cope with this information. Coe indicates that the denial of this information contributes to a sense of uncertainty among patients and lessens their perceived ability to control their own lives.

The third aspect of depersonalization outlined by Coe is the *restriction of mobility*. In most hospitals patients are not allowed to leave their wards without the permission of the head nurse, who is usually required to know the location of all patients at all times; when patients do leave the ward to travel to another area of the hospital, they are generally accompanied by a nurse, nurse's aide, or orderly. When patients are admitted to the hospital and also when discharged, they are taken in a wheelchair between the ward and the hospital entrance regardless of their ability to walk because the hospial is "responsible" for them whenever they are inside its walls. The result is that even the ability of patients to move about is supervised and controlled.

[9] As quoted in Jan Howard and Anselm Strauss (eds.), *Humanizing Health Care* (New York: Wiley-Interscience, 1975), p. 239.

Conforming Attitudes

Some patients may be so seriously ill that feelings of depersonalization do not enter the picture. All they desire is to get well and they are very happy to do or experience whatever is necessary to accomplish that goal. That is, they are quite willing to conform to the situation.

Yet this assumption may not be entirely correct. In a recent study of hospital patients in New York City, Judith Lorber (1975) found that conforming attitudes were common among cancer patients but not among patients hospitalized for very serious surgery. Lorber suggests that the cancer patients may have been scared by the ambiguities of the information they received. One woman, for example, refused to believe her doctor was telling her the truth after she had a tumor removed and it was found to be benign. Serious surgery patients, on the other hand, were much better informed about their illnesses, yet they behaved more "deviantly" (were troublesome, uncooperative, and complaining) than the cancer patients. Their somewhat lengthy stays in the hospital had not generally resulted in their complete acceptance of the staff's model of the "good" (obedient) patient. Thus, seriousness of a patient's illness was not a good predictor of whether or not a patient would conform to hospital routine.

The best attitude predictors, according to Lorber, were age and education: the younger and better educated the patient, the less likely was the patient to express highly conforming attitudes. Conversely, the older and more poorly educated patients were the least likely to express deviant attitudes. Yet among college-educated patients, Lorber found those patients over sixty years of age to be moderately conforming, while those under sixty tended to adopt "deviant" attitudes. This latter finding is consistent with other studies (Cartwright, 1964; Coser, 1956), which suggest that younger patients tend to be more aggressive about seeking information in the hospital and less conforming, while older patients tend to be more submissive to hospital rules.

Lorber (1975:220) also examined the attitudes of the doctors and nurses toward the patients, and her analysis of staff evaluations suggested the important finding that "ease of management was the basic criterion for a label of good patient, and that patients who took time and attention felt to be unwarranted by their illness tended to be labeled problem patients." Good patients were those who were uncomplaining, stoical, and cooperative. Although the staff expected patients with pain or other problems to make the staff aware of their needs, those who took up more of the staff's time than seemed appropriate were considered problem patients. "In short," Lorber (1975:220) says, "the less of a doctor's time the patient took, the better he or she was viewed." Patients who had a

tendency to complain or be uncooperative or overemotional were generally considered to be a problem only by the particular staff member
who had cause to interact with them. The key variable, therefore, in how
the doctors and nurses defined the patients was the amount of time from
the staff that the patient demanded. Interestingly enough, Lorber reported that some staff members labeled certain patients as "good" if they
couldn't remember them too well.

A question remains as to what actions physicians and nurses take to
deal with troublesome hospital patients. Some studies (Daniels, 1960;
Glaser and Strauss, 1965) suggest that staff members tend to avoid
patients who are not liked or who are uncooperative; sometimes particularly bothersome patients will be reprimanded or scolded. Lorber found
that the usual method of handling difficult patients in a New York City
hospital was to prescribe tranquilizers or sedatives. If drugs did not
accomplish the desired cooperation, then disruptive patients might on
occasion be sent home or transferred to a convalescent center with
trained psychiatric nurses. Lorber's general impression was that the hospital staff tended to treat the short-term, paying patients in a permissive
fashion and put up with the problems they caused. It remains to be seen
if the staff would have been as tolerant had the patients been hospitalized on a long-term, charity basis.

The Sick Role for Hospital Patients

To Parsons' (1951) concept of the sick role, which emphasizes
patient cooperation and striving to get well (see Chapter Five), we may
now add that of the hospitalized sick role, which apparently includes an
obligation to accept hospital routine without protest (Tagliacozzo and
Mauksch, 1972). Lorber (1975:214) notes the similarities between
Parsons' sick role and the role of the hospital patient. Both are universal-
istic, affectively neutral, functionally specific, and collectivity oriented.
However, a major difference between them, Lorber observes, is that the
idea of voluntary cooperation, one-to-one intimacy, and conditional
permissiveness (being temporarily excused from normal social activities
on the condition of seeking medical advice and care) applies primarily
to the relationship between an out-patient and a private physician.
In-patient care subjects the hospital patient to a role additionally characterized by submission to authority, enforced cooperation, and depersonalized status.

Coe (1970) has suggested that acquiescence is the most common
form of patient adjustment to hospital routine and the most successful
for short-stay patients in terms of the quality of their interaction with the

hospital staff. Basically, all the attitudes of the hospitalized sick role are results of the necessity for a well-established work routine for hospital staff. As Rose Laub Coser (1956) has pointed out, in meeting the medical needs of patients the hospital demands that its patients give up substantial rationality about the direction and nature of their personal activities in favor of the functional rationality of organizational life.

THE RISING COST OF HOSPITALIZATION

Any discussion of American hospitals would be incomplete without considering the financial cost of hospitalization, which has risen more sharply in recent years than any other aspect of medical care. For purposes of comparison, John Knowles (1973) indicates that in 1925 the cost of one day's stay as a patient at the Massachusetts General Hospial in Boston was $3.00, and the bill was paid entirely by the patient. By 1977, however, the average one-day cost of hospitalization had risen to nearly $225, with most of the expense paid by a third party such as a private health insurance company—Blue Cross, Blue Shield, or some other hospital-medical plan—Medicare, Medicaid, or a state welfare agency. Not only did costs increase significantly, but the manner of payment has also changed, as about 90 percent of all expenses for hospital services are now paid by third-party sources. In some cases, third-party coverage has led to increased hospital admission rates, since health needs which are met in the physician's office are often not covered by insurance. Hospitalization can therefore reduce the patient's direct cost of health care.

But this does not mean that patients escape paying hospital bills. Government expenditures are paid out of tax revenues, while private health insurance costs must also be covered and private companies are set up to make a profit. In 1969, health insurance companies paid $14 billion in benefit payments in return for $17 billion they received in insurance premiums from policy holders. In 1974, health insurance companies paid nearly $28 billion out of approximately $34 billion in premiums.

About sixty-one cents of every insurance claim dollar goes for hospital bills, thirty-one cents for physicians' services, three cents for dentists, three cents for drugs and drug sundries, and the remaining two cents for private-duty nursing, eye care, nursing home care, visiting nurse service, and other types of care.

Although most private health insurance payments are for hospital expenses, insurance benefits are not the largest source of hospital income. In 1976, public funds, primarily Medicare and Medicaid monies, accounted for 55 percent of all hospital care expenditures. Private insurance companies paid for an additional 36 percent, leaving the individual consumer to be responsible for direct payments covering 8 percent of hospital costs. Overall health expenditures in the United States in 1976 amounted to $139.3 billion, of which $55.4 billion was spent on hospital care. Thus, about 40 percent of all the money spent on health in the U.S. is spent on hospital services. Americans are spending about $215 a year per person for this one category of health care.

What does the hospital do with its income? Knowles explains that hospital expenses are categorized as either routine or ancillary costs. Routine costs are those expenses of providing room and board, including the provision of several different diets of three meals a day served in bed; the cost of non-medical supplies and equipment; the salaries of all members of the hospital's non-medical staff; and the salaries of medical technicians, nurses, auxiliary nursing workers, interns, and residents who are available to patients on a twenty-four hour basis, seven days a week. Ancillary expenses include the cost of laboratories, the pharmacy, operating rooms, x-ray rooms, cast rooms, and other specialized hospital facilities, plus the cost of all medical supplies. Even though patients do not get to see or even utilize all of a hospital's facilities, the cost of maintaining and operating these facilities for those patients who do use them continues regardless.

The most expensive hospitals in the United States are located in New England and on the Pacific Coast, while the least expensive are found in the South and in some of the Rocky Mountain states. Supposedly, regional differences in the cost of hospitalization are related to regional differences in the overall cost of living. Other factors (see Berry, 1974) that have been found to be important in determining hospital costs are the ratio of personnel to total expenses (the cost of labor is higher in high-cost hospitals) and the patient occupancy rate (low-cost hospitals tend to have relatively high occupancy rates). Even the type of hospital administrator may be a significant factor, as administrators with medical qualifications (M.D.s) may be able to negotiate to the administration's advantage in controlling the staff's demands for more and/or improved equipment and facilities.

It has also been found that one of the most significant factors affecting costs is the structure of the decision-making process. Edward Morse and his associates (1974) argue that decentralization of decision making tends to facilitate a hospital's adoption of modern medical technology. But while the application of new technology usually reduces the average length of stay and may increase the average occupancy rate, it has little direct impact upon the hospital's total expenses. Instead, Morse suggests that the more centralized the hospital's decision-making structure, the more efficient it will be in controlling expenses by selecting those organizational practices that facilitate goal achievement at the lowest cost. Inefficient hospital management has, needless to say, been a major factor in the rise in hospital costs.

Two other factors contributing to higher hospital expenses have been inflation and increased costs of hospital labor. Between 1967 and 1974, the overall cost of medical care in the United States rose by 50.5 percent, which ranked third behind the rise in the cost of food (61.7 percent) and the increase in the cost of housing (50.6 percent). The increase in the cost of all consumer items combined was 47.7 percent. Moreover, inflation has not only affected the cost of medical equipment, supplies, and new construction, but has also served to intensify the demands of hospital employees for higher salaries to meet the rise in the cost of living. Labor constitutes about 70 percent of a hospital's total expenses, and increased labor costs are therefore a highly significant component of rising hospital expenses (see Andersen and May, 1972).

On a national average, it cost about $130 for one day's stay in a hospital in 1974. Since a patient remains in a hospital for an average of 7.8 days, the average total cost of being hospitalized in the U.S. is approximately $1000 (Health Insurance Institute, 1976). This amount represents nearly a 12 percent increase over 1973, when the average hospital stay was also 7.8 days, but the average cost was $890. In 1968 a patient remained in the hospital for an average of 8.4 days with the cost being about $520. Thus, while the average length of stay in the hospital has declined somewhat since 1968, the cost of that stay has nearly doubled.

What can be done about controlling increases in hospital costs? Several measures might prove effective. For one thing, inflation is not the only cause. Knowles (1973) states that the decisive factor in controlling hospital costs is the full and appropriate utilization of hospital beds. Also important are improved management techniques, maximum use of computers, automatic machines, industrial engineers, and reduced turnover rates for hospital employees. Knowles states, for instance, that it costs the hospital between $1000 to $2000 to break in a new nurse, yet turnover rates for nurses in the U.S. today are as high as 70 percent per year. Knowles also urges the adoption of regional planning in order to utilize hospital facilities to their fullest and to avoid overduplication. In addition, he points out that health insurance programs are needed to promote low-cost services, health education, and programs of preventive medicine; especially helpful would be the further development of more prepaid comprehensive medical–hospital care programs, such as the Kaiser-Permanente system on the Pacific Coast.

One new measure undertaken to control hospital costs is the National Health Planning and Resources Development Act of 1974 (Public

Law 93–641). This act divides the United States into 202 Health Services Areas, each of which will contain a Health Systems Agency (HSA). The HSAs will be directed by a governing body of ten to twenty members with 50 to 60 percent of the members being health care consumers. The remainder will be comprised of health care providers and at least some locally elected government officials, as stipulated in the act.

The Health System Agencies are intended initially to survey hospital systems in their respective areas and to originate health care plans to eliminate the costly duplication of hospital services. The act also contains provisions to eventually give the HSA widespread control over all the hospitals in its area, both public and private. The primary objective of this new legislation is to prevent the kind of proliferation of medical care facilities that occurred in a number of metropolitan areas fifteen or twenty years ago. At that time, many hospitals were able to procure funds locally from various private and municipal sources, money that could be used to buy expensive technology or to expand facilities. Every hospital had to have a cobalt machine or a large modern maternity ward, or whatever. Thus a goal for planning agencies like HSAs is to bring about a consensus of which hospitals in large communities should be responsible for what. The idea is not to police the provision of hospital services but to coordinate all available services through efficient planning, thereby reducing the cost of having expensive specialized facilities at all hospitals. HSAs can tell hospitals whether to expand or close down services, how much to charge, and possibly even to shut down altogether.

There is currently some question as to whether HSAs will be responsive to local needs and issues, since they report directly to the U.S. Department of Health, Education, and Welfare, and what their authority will be in relation to county governments that currently provide much of an area's hospital services. It remains to be seen exactly whether the HSAs will be effective in controlling hospital costs; the concept does, however, reflect the public's demand that something be done to contain the rising costs of health services in the United States.

Yet, as Herman Somers (1970) points out, it would be illusory to believe that health care costs can be prevented from rising. So long as the prices of goods and services in general continue to increase, the cost of health care and hospitalization may be expected to proceed apace. The principle issue is whether or not increases can be contained in such a way that hospital care is kept within a reasonable relationship to the rest of the economy and that the highest quality of care can be provided for all Americans for the amount of money spent for that care. More satisfactory means of financing health services must be found, and this topic will be considered in the next chapter.

SUMMARY

This chapter has reviewed the hospital's evolving role as a community institution intended to serve the needs of sick and injured persons as a form of social responsibility. Passing through stages of being a center for religious practice, a poorhouse, and a deathhouse, the hospital has finally come to be a center for medical technology designed to handle the health problems of all members of society, not just the lower classes.

Today in the United States hospitals can be classified in terms of their type of ownership (voluntary or nonprofit, proprietary or profit-making, or government owned) and by their type of service (general medical–surgical or specialty). The largest single type of hospital in the U.S. is voluntary and general medical–surgical. These hospitals are nominally supervised by a governing body, such as a board of trustees, but actually exhibit a dual system of authority: administrative and medical. Although hospitals are supposedly oriented toward the welfare of the patient, a significant body of literature in medical sociology is concerned with the fact that treating large numbers of people has resulted in organizational procedures that tend to depersonalize the individual patient. The final section of the chapter dealt with the rising cost of hospitalization, which has become a major social issue.

9

HEALTH CARE DELIVERY
AND SOCIAL POLICY

The central issues in the public debate about health care delivery in the
United States are those of inflated costs and maldistribution of services.
No other single issue in medicine has attracted more public attention in
recent years than the rising cost of health care and the diminished ability
of certain segments of American society to obtain health services adequate for their needs. The paradoxical nature of this situation, as
Rodney Coe (1970:350) points out, is that the United States—one of the
wealthiest countries in the world—has developed a technology to provide
high quality health care and has the resources to implement it on a large
scale; yet a substantial portion of the population does without even
minimally adequate health care. The Americans most affected by the
sharply escalating costs of medical services are the white rural and urban
poor, ghetto blacks, the lower-middle class above the Medicaid income
maximum, and middle-class families unable to contend with the rising
costs (Alford, 1975).

An illustration of the increase and the magnitude of the cost of
health care in American society can be found in an examination of the
U.S. Consumer Price Index. As in most other nations of the world, the
cost of goods and services has been steadily rising. Figure 9–1 shows that
between 1935 and 1974 the cost of medical care increased *faster* than any
other major category of personal expense; between 1964 and 1974 alone,
medical costs rose by 72 percent. From 1968 to 1972, increases in the cost
of medical care were greater than those in all other categories, and in

FIGURE 9–1. CONSUMER PRICE IN THE UNITED STATES

Year	All items	Food	Apparel	Housing	Trans- portation	Medical care
1935	41.1	36.5	40.8	49.3	42.6	36.1
1940	42.0	35.2	42.8	52.4	42.7	36.8
1945	53.9	50.7	61.5	59.1	47.8	42.1
1950	72.1	74.5	79.0	72.8	68.2	53.7
1955	80.2	81.6	84.1	82.3	77.4	64.8
1960	88.7	88.0	89.6	90.2	89.6	79.1
1961	89.6	89.1	90.4	90.9	90.6	81.4
1962	90.6	89.9	90.9	91.7	92.5	83.5
1963	91.7	91.2	91.9	92.7	93.0	85.6
1964	92.9	92.4	92.7	93.8	94.3	87.3
1965	94.5	94.4	93.7	94.9	95.9	89.5
1966	97.2	99.1	96.1	97.2	97.2	93.4
1967*	100.0	100.0	100.0	100.0	100.0	100.0
1968	104.2	103.6	105.4	104.2	103.2	106.1
1969	109.8	108.9	111.5	110.8	107.2	113.4
1970	116.3	114.9	116.1	118.9	112.7	120.6
1971	121.3	118.4	119.8	124.3	118.6	128.4
1972	125.3	123.5	122.3	129.2	119.9	132.5
1973	133.1	141.4	126.8	135.0	123.8	137.7
1974	147.7	161.7	136.2	150.6	137.7	150.5
Percent of Change 1967– 1974	47.7	61.7	36.2	50.6	37.7	50.5

SOURCE: U.S. Department of Labor, as quoted in *Source Book of Health Insurance Data, 1975–1976* (New York: Health Insurance Institute, 1975).

* *1967 = 100.0*

1974 the cost of medical care was exceeded only by the rise in the price of food and was about equal to the rise in the cost of housing.[1]

Within the general category of medical care, Figure 9–2 shows the increase in the costs of various subcategories of items. The greatest single increase has been in semiprivate hospital room rates, which includes only the basic charge for room and board; this category is followed by in-

[1] Health expenditures for Americans increased an average of approximately 12 percent annually between 1965 and 1976. In 1965, Americans spent a total of $38.9 billion on health needs, as compared to fiscal year 1976 health expenditures of $139.3 billion. Also, in 1965 an average of $197.75 per person in the U.S. was spent on health; by 1976 this figure had risen to $637.97.

FIGURE 9–2. CONSUMER PRICE INDICES FOR MEDICAL CARE ITEMS IN THE UNITED STATES

Year	All medical care items	Physicians' fees	Dentists' fees	Optometric examination and eyeglasses	Semiprivate hospital room rates	Prescriptions and drugs
1947	48.1	51.4	56.9	67.7	23.1	81.1
1950	53.7	55.2	63.9	73.5	30.3	88.5
1955	64.8	65.4	73.0	77.0	42.3	94.7
1960	79.1	77.0	82.1	85.1	57.3	104.5
1961	81.4	79.0	82.5	87.8	61.1	103.3
1962	83.5	81.3	84.7	89.2	65.3	101.7
1963	85.6	83.1	87.1	89.7	68.6	100.8
1964	87.3	85.2	89.4	90.9	71.9	100.5
1965	89.5	88.3	92.2	92.8	75.9	100.2
1966	93.4	93.4	95.2	95.3	83.5	100.5
1967	100.0	100.0	100.0	100.0	100.0	100.0
1968	106.1	105.6	105.5	103.2	113.6	100.2
1969	113.4	112.9	112.9	107.6	128.8	101.3
1970	120.6	121.4	119.4	113.5	145.4	103.6
1971	128.4	129.8	127.0	120.3	163.1	105.4
1972	132.5	133.8	132.3	124.9	173.9	105.6
1973	137.7	138.2	136.4	129.5	182.1	105.9
1974	150.5	150.9	146.8	138.6	201.5	109.6
Percent of Change 1967– 1974	50.5	50.9	46.8	38.6	101.5	9.6

SOURCE: U.S. Department of Labor, as quoted in *Source Book of Health Insurance Data 1975–1976* (New York: Health Insurance Institute, 1975).

Note: *In 1972, a composite index of Hospital Service Charges was developed. This index rose from 102.0 in 1972 to 115.1 in 1974.*

creases in physicians' fees and dentists' fees. Since 1964, the cost of a semiprivate hospital room has nearly tripled and physicians' fees have more than doubled.

Besides the increased cost of health care, the maldistribution of existing health services is also a significant problem in American society. It is a problem felt not just by the poor, but also by individuals and families who have enough income or health insurance to pay for the services they desire. For this group of people the problem is to get the kind of care they need when they need it (Fuchs, 1974). What prevents them from accomplishing this has to do with (1) the geographical dispersion of physicians and (2) the decline in number of primary care practitioners.

A major factor in obtaining adequate medical care for some people is the numerical shortage of physicians serving patients in rural areas and urban slums. Physicians generally prefer to practice medicine in urbanized settings where they are close to cultural, educational, and recreational facilities. Another advantage of an urban practice is its proximity to extensive technological resources in the form of well-equipped hospitals, clinics, and laboratories staffed by well-trained personnel. Also important are the relationships with colleagues which tend to enhance professional life, and these relationships are more readily available in urban areas where there are greater opportunities for professional recognition. And finally, it should be recognized that the more financially rewarding medical practices are those in large cities.

Data from the American Medical Association (1973) substantiate that physicians are in relatively short supply in rural areas. The AMA indicates that there are about 2.3 times more physicians available in urban areas than in rural sections of the country. In other words, there is one doctor for every 500 people in large cities, compared to only one doctor for every 2,000–2,500 persons in nonmetropolitan locales. Despite the fact that small communities often advertise and try actively to recruit physicians, many doctors remain attracted to urban life.

The physician shortage is not limited to rural areas, however; it also extends into certain urban locales. Physicians in private practice are seldom found in neighborhoods characterized by large numbers of poor and non-white residents. Cities whose residents have relatively low levels of education and income tend to have proportionately fewer medical doctors in private practice than cities with a more "favorable" population profile (see Reskin and Campbell, 1974:995).

Shortages in the number of physicians in certain areas are not the only factor contributing to physician maldistribution. The overspecialization of medical doctors has further reduced the access of patients to primary care or general practitioners. The number of primary care practitioners has declined substantially from 112,000 in 1950 to about 50,000 in 1973. At the present time, there is one physician for every 645 Americans, but there is only one primary-care practitioner for every 4,771 people. A major reason for the trend in specialization has to do with the complexities of modern medicine. At Cornell Medical School, Patricia Kendall and Hanan Selvin (1957) noted that as the medical students progressed through medical school, more and more of them began to express a preference for specialized training. Kendall and Selvin found that the reason for the tendency to specialize was the desire on the part of the students to restrict themselves to a particular area of knowledge with which they could be highly skillful, rather than trying to deal with an insurmountable body of knowledge. In addition, a specialized and more manageable area of medicine may be less demanding of personal time, has more prestige, and provides a greater income (Fuchs, 1974; Magraw, 1975).

There are twenty-two specialty boards affiliated with the American Medical Association that certify physicians to practice in some fifty-two medical specialities such as internal medicine, pediatrics, anesthesiology, obstetrics, gynecology, dermatology, psychiatry, general surgery, orthopedic surgery, urology, ophthalmology, and neurology. While medical specialization has produced positive benefits by allowing physicians to concentrate their efforts upon treating certain parts of the body, it has produced negative side effects in that it has become increasingly difficult to find a physician to take on continuing responsibility for the "whole" patient. Victor Fuchs describes the situation as follows:

> What the typical patient wants is easy, quick, reliable access to a source of care seven days a week, twenty-four hours a day. Moreover he wants this source of care to know him, have all his records, care about him, take continuing responsibility for him, and guide him through the labyrinth of whatever specialty care may be available. Such access is indeed rare. Instead, the medical care industry offers him a multitude of highly trained specialists, each of whom can provide better care than was previously available—but only within his specialty and only during office hours.[2]

It is clear that the continuing decline in the number and availability of primary care practitioners inhibits the access of patients to the health care delivery system in the U.S. (Rogers, 1973). Hospital emergency rooms are increasingly becoming centers of primary care because of the lack of primary care practitioners, the reluctance of physicians to make house calls, and the unavailability of private physicians in the urban inner-city (Gibson et al., 1970). Also significant is the fact that hospital emergency rooms are accessible, have a minimum of administrative barriers, and have the resources of an entire hospital behind them (Satin and Duhl, 1972). Generally, the people who tend to utilize emergency rooms for primary care are the underprivileged who have minimal social ties and no other regular source of medical care (Satin, 1973).

[2] Victor R. Fuchs, *Who Shall Live?* (New York: Basic Books, 1974), pp. 68–69.

The medical specialty that has drawn the greatest amount of criticism in recent years is surgery. Some 25 percent of all beginning physicians enter surgical training programs which, in the face of the growing shortage of primary care physicians, is too large a percentage. Not only are there too many surgeons, but the question has also arisen whether all the surgical operations ordered are necessary. John Bunker (1970), writing in the *New England Journal of Medicine,* compared the number of surgeons and surgical operations performed in the United States, England, and Wales. He found that there are twice as many surgeons in proportion to the population in the United States as in England and Wales, and that they perform twice as many operations. He could not determine if American surgeons operated too often and British surgeons too infrequently, yet he noted that surgery in Great Britain was closely regulated, involved more frequent use of consultants, and included restrictions in facilities and in the number of surgeons.

Another study by Rita Nickerson et al. (1976) found that too many non-specialist physicians perform surgery, while the work loads of surgical specialists tends to be relatively modest. This study, based upon hospital operations performed in 1970 by some 2,700 practitioners, noted that approximately one-half of the physicians performed one operation or less a week. Only one percent of the total physician population operated ten or more times a week. The obvious conclusion of this study was that there are far too many physicians of all kinds who perform surgical operations.

OVERVIEW OF HEALTH CARE DELIVERY

The existing health care delivery system in the U.S. is a conglomerate of health practitioners, agencies, and institutions, all of which operate on a more or less independent basis. The greatest portion of all patient services, approximately 80 percent, is provided in the offices of private physicians, who sell their services on a fee-for-service arrangement. About 75 percent of the 250,000 active nonfederal physicians involved in direct patient care work in an office-based practice, while the remainder are mostly interns, residents, or full-time staff members of hospitals. Of these office-based physicians, some 80 percent are either solo practitioners or are part of a two-physician partnership. The other 20 percent are organized into group practices which usually comprise three to four physicians each. Thus, the predominant organizational form of private medical practice in the U.S. is the solo or two-person office-based partnership providing services to patients in return for a monetary fee. In 1976, direct payments by patients represented 35 percent of all expenditures for physicians' services; private insurance paid 39 percent, and the government paid 26 percent. The total amount of expenditures for physician services in 1976 was $26.3 billion or about $122 for every man, woman, and child in the U.S.

The next most prominent form of health care delivery consists of services provided by hospitals. With the exception of tax-supported government institutions, hospitals, like physicians, charge patients according to a fee-for-service system. Voluntary (nonprofit) hospitals charge patients for hospital services from the standpoint of recovering the full cost of services provided, the determination of which, as economist Uwe Reinhardt (1973:172) has observed, "is at best an imprecise matter." Proprietary hospitals calculate not only the cost of services rendered, but also function to realize a profit from those services. Voluntary and proprietary hospitals rely heavily on third-party sources, either private health insurance or government agencies, to pay most or all of a patient's bill. As noted in the preceding chapter, Americans spent $55.4 billion or about $258 per person on hospital services in 1976.

Besides office-based medical practices and hospitals, the other types of organizations involved in the delivery of health care to the American public are official agencies, voluntary agencies, health maintenance organizations, neighborhood health centers, and allied health enterprises in the business community.

Official agencies are public organizations supported by tax funds, such as the U.S. Department of Health, Education, and Welfare, the U.S. Public Health Service, and the Food and Drug Administration, which are intended to support research, develop educational materials, and provide services designed to minimize public health problems. Official agencies also have the responsibility for the direct medical care and health services required by special populations like reservation Indians, the military, veterans, the mentally ill, lepers, tuberculosis patients, alcoholics, and drug addicts.

Voluntary agencies are charitable organizations, such as the Multiple Sclerosis Society, the American Cancer Society, and the March of Dimes, who solicit funds from the general public and use them to support medical research and provide services for disease victims.

Health maintenance organizations (HMOs) are prepaid group practices, like the Kaiser-Permanente program, in which a person pays a monthly premium for comprehensive health care services. HMOs are oriented toward preventive and ambulatory services intended to reduce hospitalization. Under this arrangement, HMOs derive greater income from keeping their patients healthy and not having to pay for their hospital expenses than they would if large numbers of their subscribers were hospitalized. There is some evidence that HMOs do reduce hospital use and produce overall lower medical care costs than the traditional open-market fee-for-service pattern (see Roemer and Shonick, 1973). But HMOs are difficult to organize (see Saward, 1973), and the mode of treatment tends to be more impersonal (patients do not have their "own" doctor but are treated by whomever is on duty).

Neighborhood health centers (NHCs) are clinics financed by the federal government to provide ambulatory care in low-income areas where health services are either nonexistent or inadequate. NHCs are supposed to provide health care that is financially and physically accessible to all members of the community and to be particularly sensitive to meeting the health needs of the poor. NHCs have apparently been able to reduce the barriers to access among lower income persons and blacks; however, their drawbacks include inequitable distribution of service among poor communities, difficulty in attracting physicians and other health personnel (thereby implying a substandard level of care), and suspicion of promoting a two-class health care system by segregating the poor from other channels of health care (see Reynolds, 1976).

Allied health enterprises are the manufacturers of pharmaceuticals and medical supplies and equipment; these enterprises belong to an industry, whose business totals over $11 billion per year (see Goddard, 1973).

Despite the existence of HMOs, NHCs, and direct patient care programs supported by official agencies, the majority of patient care services in the United States are still delivered upon the traditional fee-for-service system. This is the case whether the consumer pays the bill himself or whether the bill is paid indirectly through a third party. Reinhardt (1973:172) points out that Americans probably accept this arrangement as quite normal within the total pattern of consumerism in the U.S. However, this method has resulted in a number of undesirable side effects, the most undesirable of which is, according to Robert Alford (1975:1), that health care in the U.S. is fragmented, unresponsive, uncoordinated, costly, and inefficient. All of this is consistent with the charge that the American system of health care delivery is actually a "nonsystem."

David Rutstein illustrates the American "nonsystem" of health care delivery by depicting it as a "tangled web." Rutstein says:

> The catch-as-catch-can structure of our unplanned medical care system is comprised of conflicting and duplicating activities on one hand and gaps in service on the other. Doctors settle where they will with large numbers in the suburbs and few, if any, in the country or in the slums of our large cities. Hospital centers tend to be self-centered. Their growth in buildings and equipment is usually not determined by community need but by financial resources, the

interest and demands of the medical staff, and the pride and drive of the board of trustees. Public health and social service resources appear to grow with the social outlook of the community, with more and better services in the wealthier communities and fewer and poorer services in the low-income areas where they are most needed. All of these discrepancies persist even though our federal government through legislation and financial allocations attempts to equalize services throughout the country.[3]

The Argument for the Fee-for-Service System

Advocates of the fee-for-service system of health care delivery agree that under that system there is no single pathway to health care nor any determination by a single coordinating authority as to the extent of health care services and the placement of health personnel and facilities. However, as James Appel (1970) argues, an organized system of health care delivery has developed nonetheless and is based upon the voluntary decisions of both health care providers and consumers. Appel says that a "line of drift" exists in which persons in need of medical treatment are attracted to private physicians on the basis of their reputations within specific geographic areas. These private physicians represent "portals of entry" into the health care delivery system as they either provide the needed services in their offices or direct the patients into hospitals or to other health practitioners where those services can be obtained.

Furthermore, advocates of the fee-for-service system propose that if the quality of American health care is to be improved, an expansion should be undertaken in the diversity of medical facilities, the number of physicians, the competition between health facilities, and the quantity and quality of private health insurance (Alford, 1975:1-3). This notion derives from the concept of the open market, in which the consumers of health care, like the consumers of other products, are supposedly free to choose which health care provider offers the best services at the best price. The assumed benefit is an improvement in services as a result of competition between the providers. Theoretically, physicians who are incompetent or who charge excessive prices and hospitals with inferior or duplicated facilities would be driven out of the market by the more competent, reasonably priced, and more efficient physicians and the better hospitals. The fee-for-service system also includes the proviso that the cost of quality health care for the indigent will be assumed by the government.

Thus, the open-market fee-for-service thesis rests on the belief in free choice both for the physician as provider and the patient as consumer. To

[3] David Rutstein, *The Coming Revolution in Medicine* (Cambridge, Mass.: MIT Press, 1967), p. 49.

eliminate or reduce free choice would, according to this argument, undermine the incentive of the physician to satisfy the patient; the eventual result would be treatment that is not only inferior but also depersonalized.

The fee-for-service system is a highly attractive situation for physicians, and it is obviously no coincidence that it is the dominant form of private practice. It allows physicians to decide what branch of medicine they should specialize in, where they should practice medicine, how many patients they should have, how many hours they should work per week, and how much money they should charge for their services. Professional ethics are supposed to block any desire they might have to try to make as much money as possible.

The Argument Against the Fee-for-Service System

But, as Reinhardt (1973) explains, health care delivery is not a good example of a perfectly competitive marketplace because of the very nature of the physician–patient relationship. Physicians define what patients need and then provide the service; patients themselves do not select those services based upon fully knowledgeable consent. In addition, Alford points out that critics of the prevailing system argue that:

> . . . the choices allegedly provided by the plurality of health care providers are not real for most people, that the economic incentives to physicians result in much over-doctoring, over-hospitalization, and over-operating, and that the alleged intimate and humane quality of most doctor–patient relationships is a myth.[4]

Specific misgivings about the fee-for-service system have been summarized by Reinhardt (1973:172–174) into four principal arguments. These arguments are as follows:

1. The existing system of health care delivery lacks effective planning and coordination. This has resulted in
   a. widespread duplication of expensive facilities that unnecessarily increase the cost of health care
   b. maldistribution of medical resources with a relative abundance of resources in affluent urban areas and a corresponding lack in poorer urban and rural areas
   c. a lack of comprehensiveness and continuity of care
2. While current licensure laws and restrictions on medical practice protect consumers from unqualified personnel, this benefit is dubious because they also

---

[4] Robert R. Alford, *Health Care Politics* (Chicago: University of Chicago Press, 1975), p. 3.

     a. tend to discourage the use of paramedical personnel for tasks they could accomplish as well as and cheaper than physicians

     b. tend to discourage entry of candidates into the paramedical occupations because of the lack of opportunity for upward mobility

3. The fee-for-service system, combined with the fact that consumers are usually more fully insured for in-patient rather than out-patient care, tends to

     a. deter consumers not covered by private health insurance or other third-party sources from seeking out preventive care in the early stages of a health problem

     b. encourage consumers and physicians to use insured hospital services rather than uninsured ambulatory care

     c. block some consumers, particularly the lower-middle class, from access to health care

     d. encourage physicians to overtreat those consumers who can afford to pay for the treatment

4. Hospital reliance on the full-cost recovery formula, combined with the fact that a hospital's prestige increases in relation to the more complex types of cases it handles, tends to encourage the purchase of expensive and "superfluous" equipment. The result of unwarranted capital outlays is higher cost passed on to the consumer.

Reinhardt concludes:

> Even a cursory reading of the literature on health care, both academic and popular, convinces one that there is widespread disenchantment with the nation's existing health-care system. It is argued that the present system fails to deliver what is needed, where it is needed, and at the right time. Furthermore, there is persuasive empirical evidence that such services as are made available to consumers are often produced inefficiently and are therefore unnecessarily costly. As a result, even those individuals who can afford the price of normal health-maintenance services are constantly exposed to the risk of financial ruin through illness.[5]

At the very least, Reinhardt contends that existing health care delivery be consolidated and coordinated, that less expensive paramedical personnel be substituted for more expensive physicians, and that the fee-for-service system be replaced with a system of prepaid capitation (per capita) fees for comprehensive health care.

In sum, the United States is the only major industrial country that

---

[5] Uwe E. Reinhardt, "Proposed Changes in the Organization of Health-Care Delivery: An Overview and Critique," *Milbank Memorial Fund Quarterly*, 51 (Spring 1973), 208–209.

has no comprehensive program for making health care available to all its citizens. The suggestion of Appel (1970) of the merits of a "line of drift" of consumers to health care providers based upon the "reputation for excellent performance" by those providers is clearly idealistic, oversimplified, and fails to account for the needs of consumers whose economic and social disadvantages preclude them from drifting toward the best health care available in American society. If such a "line of drift" does exist, then it appears that affluent patients drift toward the better physicians and facilities, leaving the less affluent to drift toward less adequate sources of care, while physicians themselves tend to gravitate toward well-to-do urban areas featuring a wide range of prestigious social activities. Moreover, rising costs of medical care have not resulted in improved quality of care, and the growth of public resentment in this regard has forced and is forcing regulation in the American system of health care delivery, despite the opposition of the medical profession.

SOCIAL LEGISLATION IN HEALTH CARE

The medical profession in the United States, as Ernest Saward (1973) has pointed out, has a consistent record of resistance to social legislation seeking to reduce the authority, privileges, and income of physicians. With the exception of some individuals, the profession as a group has opposed workmen's compensation laws, social security and voluntary health insurance in their initial stages, Medicare and Medicaid, and the creation of Professional Standards Review Organizations (PSROs) to review the work of those physicians involved in federally funded programs. The medical profession has also opposed the expansion of health maintenance organizations and strongly resisted proposals for national health insurance, even in the light of overwhelming evidence of their inevitability. "In short," Saward (1973:129) states, "the organized medical profession has repeatedly been on the negative side of social issues where the general public has been on the affirmative side."

Medicare and Medicaid: Passage and Programs

For more than forty years, the American Medical Association fought successfully to block the passage of any federal health care legislation that threatened the fee-for-service system or which advocated national health insurance. By the early 1960s, however, it was clear to most segments of society that private health insurance had not met the needs of the aged and the poor (see Saward, 1973:131). A considerable portion of the literature in medical sociology during the 1950s and 1960s, for instance, documented the disadvantaged position of the elderly and the poor in obtaining adequate health care in American society. Several sociological and political factors thus combined to influence the drafting of laws to provide hospital insurance for the aged—the commitments of Presidents John F. Kennedy and Lyndon B. Johnson; the changed composition of the U.S. Senate in 1962 and the U.S. House of Representatives in 1964; the lack of past effective health care legislation; the continuing increase in the cost of medical care; and perhaps the lessening credibility of the AMA, which claimed that "physicians cared for the elderly" and "knew their health needs better than anyone else" or that federal health insurance was incompatible with "good" medicine (Stevens, 1971:438–439).

Despite the strong resistance of the medical profession, Congress passed the Medicare and Medicaid amendments of the Social Security Act in 1965. Although these amendments were compromises between what was ideal and what was politically feasible, their passage marked a watershed in the history of medical politics in the United States as the general public for the first time emerged as a dominant voice in health care delivery and demonstrated that the direction of medical practice might no longer be the sole prerogative of organized medicine (Marmor, 1973; Saward, 1973; Stevens, 1971). In addition, the resistance of the medical profession to Medicare brought home the point to the general public that the medical profession could not always be relied upon to place the public's interest ahead of the profession's interest.

Medicare. Medicare is a federally administered program providing hospital insurance (part A) and supplemental medical insurance (part B) for persons sixty-five years or older, regardless of financial resources; disabled persons under the age of sixty-five who receive cash benefits from social security or railroad retirement programs and certain victims of chronic kidney disease are also eligible for Medicare benefits. Hospital insurance benefits include (1) in-patient hospital services for up to ninety days for an episode of an illness, plus a lifetime reserve of sixty additional days of hospital care after the initial ninety days have been used; (2) care in a nursing home for up to one hundred days after a period of hospitalization; and (3) up to one hundred home health visits after hospitalization.

Supplementary Medicare insurance benefits include (1) physicians' and surgeons' services, certain non-routine services of podiatrists, limited services of chiropractors, and the services of independently practicing physical therapists; (2) certain medical and health services, such as diagnostic services, diagnostic x-ray tests, laboratory tests, and other services, including ambulance services, some medical supplies, appliances, and equipment; (3) out-patient hospital services; (4) home health services (with no requirement of prior hospitalization) for up to one hundred visits in one calendar year; and (5) out-patient physical and speech therapy services provided by approved therapists.

There are specified deductible and coinsurance amounts for which the beneficiary is responsible. The current deductible on the hospital insurance (part A) is $84 and on the medical insurance (part B) is $60, with a 20 percent coinsurance amount also required for most part B services. The hospital insurance is financed primarily through social security payroll deductions, while the medical insurance plan, whose participation is voluntary, is financed by premiums paid by the enrollees and from federal funds. The medical insurance premium in 1977 was $7.70 a month.

The Medicare program is under the overall direction of the Secretary of Health, Education, and Welfare and is supervised by the Bureau of Health Insurance of the Social Security Administration. Most of the day-to-day operations of Medicare are performed by commercial insurance companies and Blue Cross/Blue Shield plans that review claims and make payments. Requests for payment are usually submitted by the provider of services and signed by the beneficiary; reimbursement is made on the basis of reasonable charges as determined by the private insurance companies who issue the payments. In 1974, a total of $12.4 billion in Medicare benefits were paid under coverage that extends to about twenty-two million people.

Medicaid. Medicaid, as Rosemary Stevens (1971) points out, is technically a welfare program. It provides for the federal government sharing in the payments made by state welfare agencies to health care providers for services rendered to the poor. Medicaid provides, to the states, federal matching funds ranging from 50 to 83 percent, depending on the per capita income of the states involved. Each state is required to cover all needy persons receiving cash assistance. Eligible health care services include in-patient and out-patient hospital services, laboratory and X-ray services, skilled nursing home services, and physicians' services, plus other forms of health care covered at the option of the individual states. For instance, it permitted states to include not only the financially needy, but also the medically needy, the aged, blind, and disabled poor, as well as their dependent children and families. Medicaid is administered by the states, not the federal government, and as such is subject to wide variation.

Medicare and Medicaid: Evaluation

Medicare and Medicaid were not designed to change the structure of health care in the United States. These programs did not place physicians under the supervision of the federal government nor attempt to control the distribution or quality of medical practice. Instead they were based on preexisting patterns of insurance coverage, involving the participation of private health insurance companies, and they allowed physicians to continue to set their own fees and conduct business as "usual."

In fact, Medicare and Medicaid turned out to be a financial "boon" to organized medicine and to hospitals as they channeled federal monies into health care and helped the industry become a $139 billion a year business in the United States, grossing three times more in 1976 than it did in 1965. It can also be argued that Medicare and Medicaid contributed to rising prices in health care as they provided the opportunity to pass excessive demands for payment on to insurance companies instead of to the patients themselves. Of course, the general public does not really escape from paying higher prices, as the costs of the insurance companies have to be met. And to make matters worse, in some states the Medicaid program was beset by serious problems of fraud, abuse, scandal, and administrative inefficiency. In 1976 in New York City, for example, it was estimated that 10 to 20 percent of a total $2 billion annual Medicaid benefits were overpayments.

However, as Stevens (1971) notes, if the only problems in American health services were poor management and high incomes for physicians, there would not be the sense of massive urgency that has pervaded the U.S. health care situation in recent years. The problems in fact go to the very core of medical practice—its purpose to provide quality medical care for the entire population. What Medicare and Medicaid have accomplished on a national scale are basically two highly important measures. First, these programs may have been expensive and may not have met all the needs of the aged and the poor for which they were intended, but they have provided needed health services for the old and poverty-stricken where these services were not previously available.

Second, Medicare and Medicaid established the precedent of the federal government's involvement in the administration of health care, and this involvement is the key to future health care planning and reorganization. And, according to Stevens, the time has long passed in the United States when the question of whether or not the federal government should intervene in health care delivery is debated. Federal government involvement in health care is now an important and substantial reality, and whatever happens in the future organization and scope of health care services in the U.S. is now dependent on federal government decisions.

As for the present effects of Medicare and Medicaid upon the elderly and indigent, two studies, one by Karen Davis (1975b) and one by Lu Ann Aday (1976), provide relevant indicators. Davis, in a study of

U.S. Department of Health, Education, and Welfare data pertaining to Medicare services provided in 1968, concluded that Medicare had helped some elderly persons but had not been sufficient to guarantee equal access to health care for all. She found that the poor, blacks, and residents of the South tended to utilize the program least frequently; these persons also tended to have the poorest health. Elderly persons with incomes above $15,000 annually received twice the payments for physician services (and were also more likely to seek care from higher priced physicians) than those received by persons with family incomes below $5,000. Whites received 30 percent more payments for hospital services than blacks, 60 percent more payments for physician services, and more than twice the payments for posthospital extended care services. This disparity between the races was particularly evident in the South. The South as a whole received the lowest proportion of payments of any region of the country, some 40 percent lower than the West, the highest recipient.

Davis explains that geographical variations in Medicare benefits are primarily a reflection of regional patterns of availability of medical resources and differences in the cost of medical care. Thus, greater uniformity among geographical regions is not likely without a better distribution of medical resources, particularly physicians. But since Medicare payments are based upon prevailing costs and charges, physicians practicing in scarcity areas and charging lower prices will continue to receive lower levels of payment, thus discouraging the new generation of physicians from opening practices there.

Davis also found that differences in Medicare utilization were not solely attributable to those aspects of higher income associated with having more education and living near a greater concentration of medical resources. Conversely, the lower utilization of services by blacks was not attributable to a lower average income or poorer education. Instead, the data suggested that structure of the Medicare program itself was largely responsible for the greater use of its services by higher income persons (who also tended to be white) because of the requirement for cost-sharing. Davis found that the deductible and coinsurance provisions of the medical insurance portion (part B) of Medicare were a significant deterrent for many low-income elderly persons.

Davis suggested four improvements in Medicare:

1. adjusting the cost-sharing structure according to income, with all elderly persons below the poverty line exempted from deductible and coinsurance amounts
2. improving the access of minority persons to medical care
3. reforming the financing of Medicare
   a. to eliminate the premium for supplementary medical insurance

  b. to extend coverage of both parts of Medicare to all elderly persons even if they are not eligible for social security benefits

  c. to change the structure of payroll deductions to help lower income workers

 4. improving reimbursement policies, not the least of which would be to set a nationally uniform reimbursement schedule for physicians to ensure that physicians working in under-served areas would be paid the same as those in affluent areas.

Aday's (1976) study was based upon 1963–70 nationwide surveys of access to medical care, prior to and after the introduction of Medicare and Medicaid. Aday suggested that there should be "guarded optimism" in regard to the success of Medicare and Medicaid in narrowing the differential between income groups. She found that low-income persons, in contrast to previous patterns, now visit a doctor more often than do high- or middle-income level persons (see Chapter Four). In 1970, 65 percent of low-income persons saw a physician compared to only 56 percent in 1963. However, considering the use of services by the poor relative to their needs, low-income persons were still found to be at a disadvantage because of their higher ratio of disability.

Aday concluded:

> Changes in the financing of care have apparently enhanced low-income people's ability to get care when the need arises—especially among those who have a regular point of entry to the system. For those who do not, however, significant inequities in access persist.[6]

National Health Insurance

The major public issue now in health care delivery is to move beyond Medicare and Medicaid toward the development of some form of national health insurance that would provide coverage to all Americans. At the present time there are several different plans for national health care before Congress, but regardless of whether one of these plans is adopted or a new plan is envisioned as more satisfactory, most of these programs are concerned with three important goals: (1) ensuring that all persons have financial, geographic, and social access to medical care; (2) eliminating the financial hardship of medical bills; and (3) limiting the rise in health care costs (see Davis, 1975a).

Exactly how these goals should be pursued, however, is a matter of

---

[6] Lou Ann Aday, "The Impact of Health Policy on Access to Medical Care," *Milbank Memorial Fund Quarterly*, 54 (Spring 1976), 228.

serious disagreement and debate. The form of national health insurance to be adopted may be either one or a combination of major proposals. The plans most commonly discussed are the Kennedy-Mills proposal, the Kennedy-Griffiths Health Security Act, and the Long-Ribicoff Catastrophic Insurance Plan. The Kennedy-Mills proposal is a two-part bill that provides a national health insurance plan for the general population and a revised Medicare program for the aged and disabled. The plan would abolish Medicaid and would be funded on the basis of a graduated payroll tax on the first $20,000 of earned income. All persons eligible for social security benefits, working full-time or covered under other programs now in existence, would be extended coverage under this plan. The Kennedy-Griffiths Health Security Act would cover all Americans and would be financed by payroll deductions and general federal revenues. The entire cost of care would be covered, and there would be no limit on the number of claims that could be made. The Long-Ribicoff Catastrophic Insurance Plan would (1) cover the general population with a provision for catastrophic cost coverage when medical expenses exceed a certain limit, and (2) provide an assistance plan for the poor and the medically indigent. This plan would cover persons of all ages who are covered by social security and would be financed by a special tax on wages.

None of these plans appears to be totally adequate when its coverages, costs, and system of administration are carefully reviewed (for an extensive discussion of current national health care plans, see Davis, 1975a; U.S. Department of Health, Education, and Welfare, 1976). The most pressing issue does not concern coverage and implementation but finance: how to keep the costs down and obtain the money to pay for the services. It is idle to speculate at this time about which plan is best or which will probably be adopted because as this book goes to press, many of the key issues in the formulation of a national health insurance plan have yet to be decided.

But as a framework for assessing whatever plans may be advanced for a program of national health insurance, the Committee on Public Policy of the Medical Sociology Section of the American Sociological Association has urged that such a plan recognize:

> that the people of the nation have a right to comprehensive health care
> that such health care should be effective and of high quality
> that financial and other barriers should not limit its availability
> that it should be provided at times and places that render it accessible
> that it should be coordinated with other programs relating to health and the prevention of disease

that it should offer continuity of care for individuals and families
that health care, including the production and distribution of drugs
and medical supplies should be regarded as service to the community
and to the nation, rather than as profit-making enterprises
that the people have the right and responsibility to participate in
shaping health policies and programs
that the government has the duty to assure that these health rights
are fulfilled

Finally, it should be noted that national health insurance will
probably not change the structure of medical care. Organized medicine
still has a professional monopoly over medical knowledge, techniques,
and procedures and can define most clearly and authoritatively what
health care should entail in the United States. Therefore, regardless of
what program is chosen, public control of medical practice in the United
States will probably remain relatively indirect, that is, unless there is a
fundamental reconstruction of the social and economic structure of
American society—which seems rather unlikely (see Alford, 1975).

As Stevens (1971) points out, it would be unrealistic to assume that
a total sweep of traditions and institutions will take place over night; instead any future health care system is likely to be profoundly influenced
by the pattern of American medicine developed over the past three centuries. The result is likely to be a compromise of public interests and
medical professional interests, with organized medicine retaining direct
control over medical practice, education, research, and health care
delivery, but with sizable inroads upon professional autonomy that
should render the medical profession more responsive to public needs.

In the final analysis, what we are really talking about is the issue of
whether medical care is a *right* of all Americans or whether it is a
privilege. Some people have maintained that health care is a privilege
not a right, and if people want medical treatment they should pay for it.
At least this is a position that has been advocated by certain parties in
the American Medical Association (Julian, 1977). This type of statement
should not necessarily be construed to mean that the poor are unworthy
to receive medical care. Behind this argument is a generalized opposition
to the welfare state; it is felt that the best way to help the poor is to
provide them with jobs so that they can *buy* medical care like everybody
else. To give the poor the highest quality of medical care available without improving the conditions of poverty within which they live is thought
to be an exercise in futility. Although it does make sense to increase the
overall purchasing power of the poor and to bring medical care within
their reach financially, this utopian view would also allow the medical
profession to maintain its current system of fee-for-service oriented toward financial gain.

A more socially responsible argument is that medical care does represent a special case. More in the nature of an opportunity rather than a commodity, quality health care should be available as a right of all Americans, regardless of living conditions or financial status. But, as Victor Fuchs (1974) points out, the "right" to health is a misleading concept. It implies that society has a supply of "health" on hand, which it can pass on to those individuals who have access, either privately or publicly secured, to the system of health care providers. Fuchs suggests that the notion that we can spend our way to health is an oversimplification. There is very little that medical care can accomplish for some conditions, for example, fatal wounds resulting from homicide or automobile accidents, or advanced cases of cirrhosis of the liver resulting from an excess of alcohol, or lung carcinoma due to smoking. In fact, we may be reaching the point where there is no longer a significant relationship between spending money on health and getting improved results (Burger, 1974; Forbes, 1967). It has been suggested that the complete eradication of heart disease, cancer, and stroke would extend the average life expectancy at birth by only six or seven years (Kass, 1976). Thus, medicine's contribution to longer life may reach a natural limit. William Forbes (1967) points out that when life expectancy is considered, cultural factors may now be more important than medical factors in countries where infectious diseases are no longer the major causes of death.

Forbes states that:

> . . . improvement in our average remaining lifetime is more likely to result from the study and control of factors not commonly thought of as medical ones than from further efforts along strictly medical lines. Examples of such factors follow the organization of modern life as determined by urbanization, the automobile and television; diet as determined by industrial pressures and requirements; and interpersonal relations as influenced by crowding and by industry.[7]

What Forbes is telling us is that we may be reaching the point of diminishing returns with regard to health care expenditures. More significant for the future than medical technology may be the effects of life style and physical environment on our health, especially such things as chemical pollution and insecticides in our food. Forbes may be correct in his assessment of the limitations of medicine to provide the American public with "health," but at this point, the central issues are finding answers to the questions of how we can stop rising health care costs and how we can see that every American at least has the opportunity to obtain quality health services. Until such time as there is a major change

[7] William H. Forbes, "Longevity and Medical Costs," *New England Journal of Medicine,* 277 (July 13, 1967), 77.

in our present system of health care delivery, certain preliminary measures can be undertaken to reach these goals. These measures (see also Fuchs, 1974:149–151; Julian, 1977:3–44) include:

1. Provide universal comprehensive health insurance for all Americans.
2. Increase the supply of physicians and encourage medical schools to train more primary care practitioners.
3. Make greater use of physicians' assistants and nurse practitioners in order to offset shortages of primary care physicians.
4. Train physicians to be more sensitive to the needs of the poor and racial/ethnic minority groups.
5. Require public and private health insurance agencies to be more critical in assessing physician and hospital fees; refuse to pay unreasonable charges and set lower maximum payments for services.
6. Expand hospital out-patient facilities in order that illnesses can be detected and treated at earlier stages, and make these facilities readily accessible to all members of the community.
7. Insure that adequate health care facilities and practitioners are available in rural areas and urban slums.

SUMMARY

This chapter has examined the significant social debate regarding the rising cost of health care and the unequal distribution of health services in the United States which has been a focal point of concern in the interface between medicine and society. Although organized medicine has consistently opposed social legislation that might affect the fee-for-service system of medical practice and the entrepreneurial role of the physician, the passage of Medicare and Medicaid signified the emergence of public awareness that the medical profession's interests were not always those of the general public. It now appears to be a foregone conclusion that in the near future there will be some form of national health insurance. It is likely, however, that such an insurance plan will not be a radical departure from the past, but will reflect a compromise of medical and public interests.

PART IV

HEALTH AND
SOCIAL PROBLEMS

10

MENTAL DISORDERS

Mental disorders rank with heart disease, cancer, and accidents as the greatest threats to health for Americans. Fully reliable statistics describing the incidence and prevalence of mental disorders in the United States do not exist, but the best evidence to date suggests that about 10 percent of the American population, over twenty million people, suffer from some form of mental illness and only about one-seventh of those afflicted ever receive some type of psychiatric treatment (National Institute of Mental Health, 1975:3). Because of its immense importance and because of the significant relationship between mental disorder and social conditions, the study of mentally disturbed behavior is a major area of sociological inquiry and analysis.

It is the purpose of this chapter, accordingly, to examine the social processes involved in the onset, experience, and consequences of being mentally ill in American society. The discussion will focus on three selected topics as an introduction to the field. These topics are (1) theoretical models of mental disorder, (2) the social epidemiology of mental disorders, and (3) the social process of mental hospitalization—pre-patient, in-patient, and post-patient phases.

THEORETICAL MODELS OF MENTAL DISORDER

Attempts to understand and explain disordered mental behavior and to cope with the psychological and social problems that result from such behavior have been confounded by a pronounced inability to define mental disorder in accurate and scientific terms. Generally, mental disorders are considered a form of deviant behavior (see Chapter Five). However, as Robert Spitzer and Paul Wilson (1975:827) explain, the lack of consensus among psychiatrists about what actually constitutes a mental disorder concerns three issues: (1) whether a given mental condition is undesirable; (2) the degree of undesirability; and (3) whether the condition, no matter how undesirable, is a problem properly treated by psychiatry or by some other discipline. Noting that none of the standard psychiatric textbooks and neither the first nor second edition of the American Psychiatric Association's *Diagnostic and Statistical Manual of Mental Disorders* define mental disorder, Spitzer and Wilson (1975:831–833) point out that psychiatrists have worked since the mid-1800s to formulate an objective diagnostic system in an area that is inherently subjective and not amenable to precise explanations of cause and effect that apply to many physical illnesses. Before discussing the four major theoretical approaches to mental disorder—the medical model, the psychoanalytic model, the societal reaction model, and the social learning model—the reader should first take a glimpse at the present classification system employed by psychiatry to conceptualize mental disorders.

Major Types of Mental Disorders

The American Psychiatric Association's *Diagnostic and Statistical Manual of Mental Disorders* (DSM-II) published in 1968 lists eleven major classifications of mental disorders:

1. *mental retardation* (subnormal general intellectual functioning)
2. *organic brain syndromes* (psychotic or nonpsychotic disorder caused by impaired brain tissue)
3. *psychoses* not attributed to physical conditions listed previously (mental disorder characterized by impaired capacity to recognize reality, communicate, relate to others, and cope with ordinary demands of life; includes *schizophrenia*, a psychosis characterized by disturbances in mood, thinking, and behavior manifested by distortions of reality, particularly delusions and hallucinations)
4. *neuroses* (mental disorder characterized by anxiety)
5. *personality disorders* and certain other nonpsychotic mental disorders (mental disorders characterized by maladaptive patterns of adjustment to life; also includes sexual deviation, alcoholism, and drug dependence)

6. *psychophysiological disorders* (mental disorder characterized by physical symptoms of psychic origin)
7. *special symptoms* (speech disturbance, learning disturbance, sleep disorder, etc.)
8. *transient situational disturbances* (mental disturbance characterized by temporary, acute stress related to a specific situation)
9. *behavior disorders of childhood and adolescence* (hyperkinetic reaction, runaway reaction, unsocialized aggressive reaction, etc.)
10. *conditions without manifest psychiatric disorder and nonspecific conditions* (marital maladjustment, social maladjustment, dyssocial behavior, etc.)
11. *nondiagnostic terms for administrative use*

The Medical Model

The medical model conceives of mental disorders as a disease or disease-like entity that can be treated through medical means. It seeks to attribute all mental dysfunctions to physiological, biochemical, or genetic causes. The medical model can be said to have originated from the efforts of physicians during the Renaissance and post-Renaissance to combat the notion, prevalent during the Middle Ages, that mental disorder was caused by supernatural forces: the devil, demons, and spirits of the underworld. Persons exhibiting bizarre or unorthodox behavior were often considered to be possessed by or under the influence of the devil. Many of these people were persecuted and even put to death because of strong popular beliefs in demonology and witchcraft, when in actuality they were nonconformists, victims of religious persecution, or were suffering from a mental disorder (see Alexander and Selesnick, 1966; Mora, 1975; Szasz, 1970).

Yet by the end of the seventeenth century, considerable progress had been made by the medical profession in separating explanations of mental disorder from the realm of theology and placing them instead within the field of medicine. Physicians looked to the study of human anatomy for evidence that abnormal behavior was caused by pathological organic processes within the body, but with exceptions, such as syphilis of the brain, such evidence was not forthcoming. Nevertheless, in the latter half of the nineteenth century the idea that mental disorders were caused by mental diseases had been widely accepted by the medical profession, despite the lack of proof to support this assumption. Since physicians were held responsible for the treatment of mental disorders, their views were generally shared by the lay public.

However, in the twentieth century, it has become clear that most mental disorders cannot be attributed to physiological factors. As Spitzer and Wilson (1975:826–827) note, most psychiatric conditions do not meet the four presumed criteria for a physiological dysfunction: (1) having a specific etiology (such as a germ); (2) being qualitatively different from some aspect of normal functioning; (3) showing a demonstrable physical change; and (4) being internal processes which, when once initiated, proceed somewhat independently of environmental conditions outside the body.

In defense of the medical model as it applies to mental disorder, Spitzer and Wilson point out that some physical disorders, such as essential hypertension, endocrine disorders, and vitamin deficiencies, likewise fail to meet all the criteria for the medical model and that these disorders are treatable through medical means. They argue that the appropriateness of the medical model cannot be derived from the requirements of logic but should be based upon how well the model works in practice. And even when it works poorly, they insist that it should not be abandoned until another model is shown to be more effective.

In some situations, the medical model has proven effective. Several studies have shown, for example, that the use of psychoactive drugs like the phenothiazines has promoted greater improvement among mental hospital in-patients than among similar patients administered a placebo or given no treatment at all (Ray, 1972). Furthermore, the introduction of psychoactive drugs into psychiatric treatment programs on a large scale in the mid-1950s has been regarded as the major factor in the decline of the U.S. mental hospital population. Prior to that time, the mental in-patient population in this country had been steadily increasing.

In addition, current research on brain chemicals, focusing upon those compounds responsible for neurotransmission, has shown that an increase in the supply of norepinephrine (believed important in the control of emotions) can have a significant effect upon increasing the rate of recovery from the depressive disorders. Haloperidol, chlorpromazine, and the tranquilizing drugs of the phenothiazine group have been found to be effective in the treatment of schizophrenia. These latter drugs apparently are able to block the action of dopamine, another neurotransmitter, whose hyperactivity is thought to be important in the production of paranoid delusions and auditory hallucinations.

Other research in the area of behavior genetics has produced strong evidence that genetic factors are important in the transmission of schizophrenia, thus providing an explanation of why certain people appear to be prone to schizophrenia and why schizophrenia tends to be prevalent in certain families and not in others. The exact genetic factors involved in this process are not fully understood at present, and it is also not known what conditions actually "trigger" schizophrenia in a genetically susceptible person, but the evidence does indicate that a genetic mechanism has something to do with the onset of schizophrenia in some individuals (Kety, 1975; Kohn, 1974; Rainer, 1975).

While such research efforts as these offer considerable promise for the understanding and treatment of mental disorders, the emphasis of the medical model upon drug therapy can be severely criticized. This approach, as Albert Bandura (1969:16) has explained, has "led to heavy reliance upon physical and chemical intervention, unremitting search for drugs as quick remedies for interpersonal problems, and long-term neglect of social variables as influential determinants of deviant response patterns." Therefore, while they may provide an effective short-term solution to many mental problems, drugs obviously cannot change social situations that act to precipitate a mental disorder. Studies of patients diagnosed as acute schizophrenics have shown that drug therapy provides better short-term results in the hospital setting than psychotherapy alone, and that treatment by drugs combined with effective planning for the patient's future after discharge from the hospital is more effective than drugs alone; after discharge, however, psychotherapy, public health nursing, and social case work may be more effective than drug therapy (see May, 1975:972).

Despite its inadequacies, the medical model of mental disorder has been and continues to be a pervasive influence upon the practice of psychiatry. This should not be too surprising since all psychiatrists are first trained as medical doctors and are thereby socialized into a medical perspective. The medical profession, of course, regards medical training as the optimal preparation for working with mentally disturbed persons.

The Psychoanalytic Model

The psychoanalytic approach to mental problems is analogous to the medical model in that it also focuses attention on internal factors that affect the human being. In its concern with psychic rather than physiological conditions, however, the psychoanalytic model views human beings as driven in a seemingly irrational manner by powerful internal forces. Not only is the individual unable to control these forces, but he or she is even unaware of their existence.

The psychoanalytic model is based upon the work of Sigmund Freud (1856–1939), who lived most of his life in Vienna, and upon the work of others whom he influenced, such as Erik Erikson, Carl Jung, Alfred Adler, Adolf Meyer, Karen Horney, Otto Rank, and Wilhelm Reich—to name only a few of the important figures in psychoanalytic literature. The scope of this chapter does not permit an extensive discussion of Freud's theories, which psychoanalists regard as the most comprehensive and profound explanation of human behavior (Meissner et al., 1975) and which many behavioral scientists, particularly sociologists, view as interesting, but theoretically incorrect (Swanson, 1972). Despite conflicting assessments of Freud's life work, the reader should be aware that the psychoanalytic approach has dominated the training and practice of psychiatry in that it constitutes a fundamental aspect of psychiatric terminology, ideology, and understanding of human behavior.

Freud's Concept of the Personality. Briefly stated, Freud views the human organism as a complicated energy system with all of the energy needed to perform the work of the personality being obtained from instincts, which Freud defines as mental stimuli arising from within the organism itself. However, instincts are seen as a special type of stimulus because they do not have a single or momentary impact, but are a constant force within the personality. The *id,* one of the three major components in Freud's structure of the personality, functions as the discharger of any energy or tension brought about by internal or external stimulation. It is guided by the primary process which produces a memory image of the tension-reducing object. The id uses its energy for instinctual gratification by fulfilling the pleasure principle (avoiding pain and finding pleasure) through the means of reflex action—eating, having sex, wish fulfillment.

The failure of the id to obtain satisfaction gives rise to the *ego,* the second major part of the personality, which represents the energizing of new processes of memory, judgment, perception, and reason that are intended to bring harmony to a person's psychological system by synchronizing the subjective inner world with the objective outer world of social reality. The ego is governed by the reality principle, whose function is to postpone the release of energy until the actual object has been located that will satisfy the need; the ego tolerates or opposes tension until it can be discharged by an appropriate form of behavior. Thus, to the primary process of memory is added the secondary process of finding the correct solution (reality) through thought and reason. Sometimes the solution is not found until various realities have been tested and discovered to provide suitable fulfillment. Hence, the ego is primarily a product of interaction with the external environment.

The third major aspect of the personality, the *superego,* can be described as the moral or judicial branch of the personality. Freud hypothesizes that the superego evolves from the ego as the child assimilates the moral authority of his or her parents by patterning behavior after that of the parents' own overt behavior or motives and the parents' aspirations for the child. The internalization of parental values in the child is accomplished through fear of punishment and desire for parental approval, which cause the child to control his or her own behavior in accordance with the wishes of the parents. The superego represents what is ideal rather than what is real, and its aim is to strive for perfection instead of reality (the function of the ego) or pleasure (the function of the id). Through its two subsystems, the ego-ideal and the conscience, the superego has the power both to reward and to punish the organism psychologically through feelings of pride (ego-ideal) or of guilt and inferiority (conscience).

Seen in its basic form, Freud's concept of the personality is a system of psychic energy consisting of the id striving for pleasure in order to satisfy fundamental instincts and the superego striving for perfection while leaving the ego to balance the two drives with a sense of reality. Obviously, the personality would be maladjusted should the ego fail and either the id or the superego become dominant.

Psychosexual Development and Adult Ego Defense. A basic premise of psychoanalytic theory is that "the child is psychologically father to the adult." What Freud means by this is that the events of infancy and childhood persist in the personality throughout all subsequent life. The impairment of adult behavior can therefore be systematically traced to early childhood experiences, particularly the manner in which sexually oriented urges for bodily pleasure were resolved by the parents during the oral, anal, phallic, latency, and genital stages of psychosexual development. These stages last from birth through adolescence and present the child with a series of developmental crises such as obtaining oral gratification, developing trust and a sense of external reality, becoming toilet trained, acquiring the appropriate sex role identity, and gaining a sense of social competency. Successful resolution of these tasks results in a mature adult.

Freud's concept of ego defense is based upon the premise that at each stage of psychosexual development the ego builds up appropriate defense mechanisms to defend against the conflicts, anxieties, and frustrations that disturb normal psychological functioning. The ego is responsible for this defense because, as the personality's center of narcissism or self-love, it attempts to escape from any situation that threatens its sense of well-being and integrity. Threats that summon up the ego's defenses come from essentially three sources: (1) the id as it tries to overwhelm the ego with pressure for instinctual gratification, (2) the superego as it attempts to punish the ego through feelings of guilt, and (3) external danger perceived as being directed toward the ego. All ego defense mechanisms operate at an unconscious level and are activated on a more or less automatic basis; therefore, the individual is not even aware of their existence. Some of the most common ego defense mechanisms are sublimation, repression, projection, denial, rationalization, regression, and reaction formation.

Psychoanalysis and Psychoanalytic Therapy. According to psychoanalytic theory, emotional problems are likely to be revealed in one of four general ways. The person (1) develops a personality disorder (displaces conflicts toward the external world), (2) becomes neurotic (develops excessive ego defenses), (3) develops a psychophysiologic disorder (tension is experienced within the body and eventually produces an organic pathology), or (4) becomes psychotic (the ego disintegrates with a loss of the ability to cope with reality).

The forms of treatment used to eliminate or reduce the effects of unconscious pressures upon the personality are psychoanalysis and psychoanalytic therapy. Psychoanalysis is a one-to-one relationship between the therapist and the patient which utilizes free association as its primary technique. In free association the patient is encouraged to say whatever comes to mind, while the analyst ensures that the sequence of the undirected thought remains unchanged and that the patient does not withhold any information, no matter how trivial or distressing. Psychoanalysis is a lengthy process and takes about two to five years to complete, but its proponents believe that sooner or later the patient will direct the underlying disorder toward the therapist in a process known as transference. Once this happens and the unconscious tendencies are revealed, the patient can be made aware of the source of the problem and counseled upon ways to deal effectively with it.

Psychoanalysis is used most often with patients who are suffering from a neurosis and who have some ego strength. Besides being time-consuming, it is expensive and does not lend itself to the treatment of large numbers of patients simultaneously. In addition, there is evidence that neuroses tend to be self-limiting, that psychoanalysis is no more successful than other psychotherapeutic methods, and that recovery obtained through ordinary life experiences and nonspecific treatment may work as well for neurotics as all other forms of psychotherapy, including psychoanalysis (Eysenck, 1961).

Psychoanalytic therapy is a modified form of psychoanalysis. The major difference is that psychoanalytic therapies focus on current conflicts instead of attempting to work through the entire history of a person's psychosexual development; however, prior to treatment, an extensive psychiatric diagnosis seeks to obtain as much information as possible about the patient's history. This therapy also involves a moderately superficial transference reaction and relies more upon interviewing and discussion than upon free association. The principal types of psychoanalytic therapy are insight therapy (resolution of selected conflicts), relationship therapy (assisting growth of an immature personality), and supportive therapy (assistance in adjusting to difficult situations) .[1]

Assessment of the Psychoanalytic Model. One of the most striking criticisms of the psychoanalytic model is that it is based largely upon myth. Advocates of the model are required to accept as dogma the unproven assumptions of Freudian thought in much the same way that persons living in the Middle Ages accepted on faith the idea that mental disorder was caused by the devil. There is no evidence that the human personality has a tripartite structure consisting of an id, ego, and superego. A second major criticism of the psychoanalytic model is that it portrays human beings as being propelled by instincts without taking into account the individual's ability to will his or her own behavior. Some behavioral scientists argue, for example, that the mind is not a structure but a process. This concept arises from the unique human ability to engage in reflexive thinking, an ability that makes possible the control and organization of conduct by the individual in relation to the environment. Third, most research does not support the view that "the child is psychologically father to the adult." There is no conclusive evidence linking personality problems of adults with specific experiences of pleasure or frustration during a particular developmental stage of childhood. Fourth, the psychoanalytic approach has been accused of underemphasizing the importance of cognitive development and overemphasizing emotional development. Alfred Lindesmith and his associates (1975:319) point out that the separation of emotional experience from cognition neglects "the fact that emotional experiences do not exist as pure states, but are shot through with cognitive elements." And the fifth major criticism of psychoanalytic theory is that it is vague, difficult to test empirically, and does not lend itself to predictive assessments. For instance, it does not offer any guidance to parents about what they can do to protect their children from experiencing an inadequate psychosexual development in advance of that development.

Why then has the psychoanalytic perspective been so influential? Primarily for two reasons: First, no other theoretical approach has provided so many insights into the development and functioning of the

1 Another type of treatment influenced by the psychoanalytic model includes group therapy. Group therapy is popular in the United States and consists of gathering selected mentally disordered patients together with a trained therapist for the purpose of the patients helping each other to confront problems and achieve personality change. Group therapy emphasizes values of rugged individualism and a collective approach to problems, while at the same time allowing for the expression of deviant behavior. There are many different types of group therapy, but most of them rely on a psychoanalytic perspective (see Sadock, 1975) .

human personality.[2] Even though the central propositions of psychoanalytic theory are not empirically verifiable, neither are many of the theories of the classic masters of sociological thought—Emile Durkheim, George Herbert Mead, Georg Simmel, and Max Weber among others—or, ultimately, other branches of human behavior. "Freud is provocative," states Guy Swanson (1972:41), "because he provides a rich set of differentiations readily interpretable as variations in mind which, in turn, are particularly significant consequences of social organization's impact on individuals." Furthermore, psychoanalytic theory proposes explanations for some of the subtle features of human behavior that have been overlooked elsewhere in psychology and addresses itself to the presence of unconscious influences upon the individual.

Second, psychoanalytic theory is important because it offers a model that is inseparable from physiological concepts and is therefore an ideal psychology for the physician. It provides the physician with an objective structure of the personality and a prescribed mode of treatment, as well as a nosology by which physicians can communicate about, attempt to control, and comprehend mental disorders. In the absence of other models that can be proven more effective *when applied to the care and treatment of patients,* the quasi-medical psychoanalytic model and the medical model dominate the practice of psychiatry.

The Societal Reaction Model

Szasz: The Myth of Mental Illness. The societal reaction model of mental disorder is derived from the suggestion by Thomas Szasz that mental illness is clearly not an "illness" and should not be regarded as such. In his book *The Myth of Mental Illness* (1964, 1974), Szasz proposed the following argument: (1) only symptoms with demonstrable physical lesions qualify as evidence of disease; (2) physical symptoms are objective and independent of sociocultural norms, but mental symptoms are subjective and dependent upon sociocultural norms; (3) mental symptoms result from problems in living; therefore, (4) mental disorders are not diseases, but are conflicts resulting from differing social values that the medical profession disguises as illnesses through the use of medical terminology.

For example, Szasz says that a man's belief that he is Napoleon or is being persecuted by communists cannot be explained by a defect or disease of the nervous system. Statements such as these are considered to be symptoms of a mental disorder only if the observer (the audience) believes that the patient is not Napoleon or is not being persecuted by

[2] For a more comprehensive discussion of Freud's work, see Freud, 1953–1966; Meissner et al., 1975.

the communists. Thus, the statement that X is a symptom of a mental disorder involves rendering a social judgment. The observer must match the person's ideas and beliefs with those held by the observer and the rest of society. In other words, a person's behavior is judged by how well his or her actions "fit" a concept of normality held by a social audience. It is upon this basis then that Szasz insists that mental illness cannot be defined in a medical context. Mental illness should be defined within a social and ethical context, with psychiatrists recognizing that in actual practice they are dealing with problems in living rather than illnesses.

In rebuttal, David Ausubel (1961) has disputed Szasz's perspective by arguing that (1) mental symptoms do not have to be physical lesions to be defined as a disease (subjective pain, for instance, can be regarded as a disease state) ; (2) psychological symptoms can be classified as evidence of disease if they impair the personality and adversely affect behavior; (3) there is no contradiction in regarding psychological symptoms both as evidence of illness *and* problems in living; and (4) deviant behavior (such as engaging in an immoral act) and mental illness are clearly different types of conditions.

As a result, Szasz's argument is regarded by many psychiatrists as representing a radical position in psychiatry—interesting but not terribly relevant to actual psychiatric practice, since it is not more useful in treating mental disorders than the medical model Szasz attacked (Spitzer and Wilson, 1975) . However, among behavioral scientists and laypersons who object to the medical orientation toward mental disorder, and especially among sociologists who subscribe to the approach of labeling theory, Szasz's work has become very influential.

Scheff: A Societal Reaction Theory of Mental Disorder. The leading spokesman of the societal reaction or labeling theory approach to mental disorder in sociology is Thomas Scheff (1966, 1974, 1975) . Scheff (1966) agrees with Szasz that the social situation is of primary importance in understanding mental disorders; he further suggests that social stereotypes profoundly shape the symptoms of mental disorder in American society. Scheff maintains that the stereotyped image of mental disorder is learned in early childhood. The meaning of "crazy" is grasped by grade school children and becomes part of our culture, as illustrated by the general understanding of phrases like, "The boogie man will get you." Scheff goes on to point out that the cultural stereotype of insanity stays with us even in adulthood and is continually reinforced through social interaction; in fact, it is often the basis for our manner of reacting to people who have already been labeled insane. Furthermore, this stereotype is available to the patient and becomes part of the patient's orientation for guiding his or her own "crazy" behavior. Thus, in brief,

Scheff considers mental disorder a social role whose behavior conforms to society's expectations about people who are "crazy."

Scheff argues that for various reasons some people will occasionally engage in residual rule-breaking. Residual rule-breaking is based upon the idea that most social conventions are fairly clear-cut. Violations of these social conventions tend to be regarded as violations of morality—people who kill are murderers, people who steal are thieves, people who think they are better than others are called snobs. But Scheff says there is a residual area of social convention that goes beyond just violating norms and is assumed to be so natural that it is part of "human nature." These residual social conventions include such behaviors as looking at the person you are talking to or responding to someone who calls your name. To violate these residual norms, that is, to act "unnatural" is to do something that is very disturbing. People can understand why someone would kill under certain circumstances like a war, or why someone might steal or be a snob, but to break residual rules is considered to be doing something for which there may be no other explanation than a mental disorder.

Depending upon certain contingencies, such as the identity of the rule breaker, the rule broken, and the social context in which the rule-breaking behavior takes place, the residual rule breaker may be publicly labeled as being "mentally ill." Once a person has been so labeled, society reacts so as to stabilize the abnormal behavior. The process of stability results from the stereotype of mental disorder, learned and culturally reinforced since childhood, which governs the expectations about being "mentally ill" both for the rule breaker and for the social audience. The rule breaker is thus constrained to behave as a crazy person in order to conform to the popular conception. Also, once labeled as mentally ill, the rule breaker is rewarded for playing the stereotyped deviant role because, as will be discussed, one of the first actions of psychotherapy in mental hospitals is to get patients to recognize that they are mentally ill and need help. If patients conform to the stereotype of what their mental problems are supposed to represent, then they are regarded as "good" patients. If the labeled person tries to return to a conventional role instead of accepting the stereotyped deviant role, he or she is punished for it; witness the 1972 case of a U.S. Senator who was not allowed to continue as a vice-presidential candidate after it was publicly disclosed that he had once been under psychiatric care. Once the labeling of a person as deviant (in this case, being mentally ill) has taken place and society responds toward the person in accordance with that particular label, Scheff contends that a deviant has been created by society. And this process is confirmed for both society and the individual when the person accepts the label of mental illness as correct. Through the agency of labeling, such a person "is launched on a career of 'chronic' mental illness" (Scheff, 1975:10).

In a subsequent article, Scheff (1974) refuted criticism from Walter Gove (1970) that certain existing studies did not clearly support Scheff's explanation of mental illness. Scheff showed that a majority of studies dealing explicitly with the societal reaction or labeling theory approach did provide supportive evidence of his views. Scheff's defense, however, rested upon the assumption that only those studies that explicitly test labeling theory can provide relevant evidence, and this may not necessarily be a correct assumption (see Gove, 1975). Nevertheless, additional criticisms have been forthcoming that point to serious weaknesses in the labeling theory of mental illness as proposed by Scheff. These criticisms argue (1) that Scheff has not adequately taken into account the implications for labeling theory of recent advances in drug therapy (Gove, 1975), and (2) that a person may not be irreparably stigmatized ("launched on a career of chronic mental illness") by friends and family as a result of once being labelel mentally ill (Clausen and Huffine, 1975; Gove and Howell, 1974). Nor for that matter does the labeling theory of mental illness explain what actually causes mental disorders other than societal reaction to residual rule-breaking. It likewise fails to offer a systematic model of therapy for mentally disordered persons.

The merit of Scheff's work is that it emphasizes the common conceptions of mental disorder shared by people and that these ideas significantly affect the manner in which members of a society regard mental abnormality. This process can thus have very definite social consequences for the person being so labeled.

The Social Learning Model

Another alternative to the medical and psychoanalytic models of mental disorder is the social learning model, based chiefly upon theories of learning and techniques of behavioral conditioning derived from the classical conditioning experiments of Ivan Pavlov and Edward Thorndike. The underlying premise of this model is that social behavior is learned and that what can be learned, can also be unlearned and replaced with more appropriate behavior (Bandura, 1969; Brady, 1975). The therapeutic technique of the social learning model, known as behavior modification, emphasizes that treatment should be centered upon behavior that is externally observable and measurable. Preferred techniques include those of symptom desensitization (learning to approach feared situations or objects without anxiety), positive reinforcement (reward), aversive conditioning (punishment), extinction (eliminating a stimulus), conditioned avoidance (electric shocks or drugs paired with situational stimuli), and contingency contracting (agreeing with others to engage in certain behavior in return for a similar response).

Social learning theory, like labeling theory, overlooks those mental disorders related to genetic and physiological factors; unlike labeling theory, social learning theory does suggest specific forms of therapy. However, behavior modification appears to be subject to four major limitations. First, there are serious questions as to whether human beings can actually be "conditioned" to the extent that they respond more or less automatically to the play of stimuli upon their cerebral functions. Second, even if such conditioning is possible, there are questions concerning the duration of the effects and their strength in real world, nonclinical settings. Third, behavior modification may not be a totally sufficient form of therapy for many types of mental disorders in which the complexity of the disorder may require much more than just learning new behaviors. And fourth, behavior modification requires that patients be willing and able to learn, have a certain amount of willpower, and recognize and cope with reality at least somewhat consistently—prerequisites many mental patients may not have.

Still it can be argued that behavior modification does have certain strengths. Its grounding in experimental psychology lends itself more readily to verifiable research techniques, and some studies have shown it to be an effective approach (see Bandura, 1969), especially for short-term results and simple symptom configurations such as bedwetting. This therapy may also be more appropriate for the treatment of lower-class persons, both because it is less expensive than psychoanalysis and because it does not demand a high degree of self-analysis. Just how effective behavior modification actually is has yet to be determined.

Defining Mental Disorder

The intent of this section has been to give an overview of the various definitions of mental disorder based upon the competing perspectives of the medical, psychoanalytic, societal reaction, and social learning models. None of these models provides a satisfactory overall explanation of mental disorder, but if one such model were to be selected for its potential significance for future psychiatric practice, it is likely that model would be the medical model. This is so because the medical profession has high expectations for drug therapy and studies of brain chemistry. This trend seems likely regardless of the fact that such an approach ignores most psychological and sociological correlates of mental disorder and does not adequately deal with the nonchemical causes or the external environments that foster behavioral abnormalities. The psychoanalytic model will also remain somewhat influential, though less influential than in the past, because its definitions, terms, and conceptualizations still dominate the psychiatric perspective of mental disorder. The social learning model, perhaps in combination with the medical model, is likely to remain important, but the societal reaction model appears to have the least influence outside sociology itself.

Spitzer's (Spitzer and Wilson, 1975:829) definition of a mental disorder appears to offer mental health professionals the most realistic assessment of such conditions in terms of both adequately explaining and treating them. Spitzer defines mental disorder as follows: (1) it is a condition that is primarily psychological and involves alterations in behavior, including changes in physiological functioning if such changes can be explained by psychological concepts, such as personality, motivation, or conflict; (2) it is a condition which, in its "full-blown" state, is regularly and intrinsically associated with subjective stress, generalized impairment in social functioning, or voluntary behavior the person would like to stop because it is associated with threats to physical health; and (3) it is a condition distinct from other conditions and responds to treatment.

Of the three criteria described by Spitzer, the first separates psychiatric from nonpsychiatric conditions. The second specifies that the disorder may be recognizable only in a later stage of its development ("full-blown") and that its identification depends on consistent symptomatology ("regularly associated with"). Spitzer also says that the disorder must arise from an inherent condition, and not from the manner in which society reacts to the condition, and that the impairment in functioning not be limited to a single form, such as heterosexual relationships, but include an inability to function in several social contexts ("generalized impairment in social functioning"). Criterion two also includes "voluntary behavior," for example, such conditions as compulsive eating or smoking. The third criterion places the definition within the confines of the medical model as a distinct condition that is treatable.

SOCIAL EPIDEMIOLOGY OF MENTAL DISORDERS

One of the major contributions of medical sociology to the practice of psychiatry has been its investigation of the extent of mental illness in the general population and the identification of significant sociodemographic variables. Since many of these studies have focused upon patients admitted to psychiatric treatment facilities, they have helped to describe the relationship between social factors and rates of mental disorders. In 1971, for instance, the rate of admissions to all psychiatric in-patient and out-patient services in the United States was 1,239.6 admissions per 100,000 persons (National Institute of Mental Health, 1975). Figure 10–1 shows that the largest single diagnostic category for admissions to psychiatric services is that of "other," which includes a wide variety of disorders such as neuroses and psychophysiological disorders; but when more specific categories are considered, schizophrenia ranks highest with 258.0 admissions per 100,000 persons in the U.S., followed by the depressive disorders (216.9), and alcoholism (127.9).

Although studies of admissions to psychiatric treatment programs are important in the planning of such services, rates of patients in treatment fail to indicate the "true" distribution of mental disorders, which includes both treated and untreated cases. In an extensive review of the literature, Bruce and Barbara Dohrenwend (1974; also see Bruce Dohrenwend, 1975) have noted that since 1900 some sixty investigators in eighty different studies conducted in several countries have attempted to assess the "true" prevalence of mental disorders among their respective populations. Most of these studies were based upon large samples of the general public and included few persons who had ever been mental patients. Although direct comparisons were difficult because of differences in methodology, cultures, time periods, locations, and contrasting defini-

FIGURE 10–1. ADMISSION TO PSYCHIATRIC IN-PATIENT AND OUT-PATIENT SERVICES PER 100,000 PEOPLE IN THE UNITED STATES, 1971

Type of Disorder	Admission per 100,000 People
Schizophrenia	258.0
Depressive disorders	216.9
Alcoholism	127.9
Organic brain syndromes	54.9
Drug abuse	43.1
Mental retardation	28.9
Other psychotic disorders	18.9
Undiagnosed	88.9
All other diagnoses, including, for example, child behavior disorders, neuroses, and psychophysiological disorders	401.1

SOURCE: *National Institute of Mental Health,* Summary Report of the Research Task Force of the National Institute of Mental Health (Washington, D.C.: U.S. Department of Health, Education and Welfare, 1975).

tions of mental disorder, the most impressive feature of all these studies was the consistent finding of significant relationships between mental disorder and three specific sociodemographic variables: sex, rural versus urban location, and social class. Race, which is often a significant factor in explaining human behavior, is apparently not a strong predictor of mental disorder (see, for example, Warheit et al., 1975).

Sex

The majority of studies of the "true" prevalence of mental disorder by sex clearly indicate (see Dohrenwend and Dohrenwend, 1974, 1976; Bruce Dohrenwend, 1975) that: (1) there are no consistent differences by sex in rates of functional psychoses in general and schizophrenia in particular; however, manic-depressive disorders are generally higher for women; (2) rates of neuroses are consistently higher for women regardless of time and place; and (3) rates of personality disorders are consistently higher for men regardless of time and place.

Obviously, then, these findings refute contentions that more mental disorder is found among women than men and that changing sex roles in American society promote more mental disorder among women. Instead, as the Dohrenwends indicate, sexual differences are consistent and apparent only in specific types of mental disorders—women being more likely to have manic-depressive psychoses and neuroses, and men being more likely to have personality disorders. Significant also is that these findings apply throughout the twentieth century, regardless of changing sex roles. According to the Dohrenwends, we should:

> . . . discard undifferentiated, unidimensional concepts of psychiatric disorder and with them false assumptions about whether women or men are more prone to "mental illness." In their place we would substitute an issue posed by the relatively high female rates of neurosis and manic-depressive psychosis, with their possible common denominator of depressive symptomatology, and the relatively high male rates of personality disorders with their possible common denominator of irresponsible and antisocial behavior. The important question then becomes, What is there in the endowments and experiences of men and women that pushes them in these different directions?[3]

Differences by sex in certain types of mental disorders seem to relate to both biological and sociocultural factors. States of depression and

[3] Bruce P. Dohrenwend and Barbara Snell Dohrenwend, "Sex Differences and Psychiatric Disorder," *American Journal of Sociology*, 81 (May 1976), 1453.

neuroses in women may be influenced by hormonal changes in the body, such as those occurring during menstruation and menopause. Research on animals has suggested that the male hormone androgen stimulates aggression (Mazur and Robertson, 1972), while there is limited and inconclusive evidence that the Y (male) sex chromosome is an "aggression" gene. Data supporting such a premise are derived from studies of XYY genotypes (males with an extra male chromosome), who tend to be somewhat overrepresented in penal and mental institutions; nevertheless, the sample of such individuals is small in relation to the total population (Hook, 1973).

There is also evidence that the sexes may differ in the way they think, perceive, aspire, daydream, experience anxiety, and play competitive games (see Hochschild, 1973b). In school, girls appear to start out ahead of boys in nearly all subject areas and then fall behind boys in some subjects beginning in the late high school years. Studies comparing sex differences in intelligence, for example, show that, despite a more or less equal distribution of boys and girls in terms of superior performance, there are substantial differences between the sexes in specific ability areas (see Boocock, 1972). Males tend to outperform females on mathematical reasoning, judgment, manipulation of spatial relations, and mechanical aptitudes. Females tend to outperform males on vocabulary, verbal fluency, and memorization tasks. Eleanor Maccoby (1966) has found that sex differences in scholastic performance may be attributed to the more aggressive and active behavior of boys, while girls exhibit greater dependency, anxiety, and passivity. These tendencies could also be significantly related to increased depression and neurotic behavior for women and increased personality disorders, which are often characterized by active and antisocial behavior, for men. However, whether these behavioral differences between males and females are mostly the result of innate biological qualities or of sociocultural influences is not known.

When sociocultural factors are considered, sex-based differences in behavior appear to be the result of socialization into the socially prescribed roles for men and women. Sex-specific behavior in human society is strongly influenced through the process of sex typing, in which boys are taught to be men, and girls to be women, with all that these roles imply in terms of masculine or feminine attributes. The sex role for men clearly offers an advantage in self-direction and professional opportunities, yet may lend itself to increased susceptibility to personality disorders. Conversely, the sex role for women may lend itself to increased depression and anxiety. Walter Gove and Jeannette Tudor (1973), for instance, have summarized some pertinent assumptions concerning the role of adult American women: (1) most women are restricted to a single occupational and social role—that of being a housewife—and this severely limits their sources of gratification; (2) being a housewife is frustrating because it requires limited skill and has low prestige; (3) the role of the housewife is relatively unstructured and invisible; (4) when a woman is employed outside the home, she is typically in a less satisfactory position than a married male; and (5) the expectations confronting women in American society lack specificity.

From a social standpoint, sex can thus be depicted as an enduring ascribed characteristic that cuts across all social classes and racial/ethnic groups to affect the evaluation of persons and social positions and to form the basis for a persisting sexual division of labor and sex-related inequalities (Acker, 1973:940). These differences, combined with biological differences, undoubtedly contribute to the varying incidence between men and women of certain mental disorders. The task currently before sociologists, as the Dohrenwends (1976; Bruce Dohrenwend, 1975) point out, is to assist in isolating the relative contributions of male-female biological differences and social differences in those mental disorders in which gender is an important variable.

Rural versus Urban Living

The widely held assumption that the stress of urban living is responsible for high rates of mental disorder and that rural areas are relatively free of such problems is not entirely accurate. In their review of relevant studies, the Dohrenwends (1974; Bruce Dohrenwend, 1975) found that psychoses in general and manic-depressive psychoses in particular are more prevalent in rural areas. Schizophrenia was an important exception in that it appears to be much greater in urban areas. Neuroses and personality disorders are also more common in urban areas.

Although these trends are clearly evident in the bulk of the research investigating the relationship of residence upon mental disorder, it is not at all certain what causes them. The relatively high incidence of manic-depressive psychoses in rural areas may be related to feelings of physical isolation. Schizophrenia, the neuroses, and personality disorders, on the other hand, may be related to the stress of urban living, but this is also a purely speculative conclusion. One of the most significant demographic shifts in the U.S. during this century has been the move from rural to urban areas, so that perhaps some of these rural migrants brought their mental disorders with them to the city. Obviously this would inflate the rates of mental disorder for urban areas. Whatever the exact cause(s) of the urban-rural differences in the proportion of certain mental disorders, the differences seem to be there nonetheless.

Socioeconomic Status

The basic finding of most studies that the highest overall rates of mental disorder are found among members of the lowest socioeconomic group has, according to Bruce Dohrenwend (1975:370), "remained remarkably persistent in the 'true' prevalence studies conducted since the turn of the century." The lower social class has been observed to have both the greatest prevalence of mental disorder in general and personality disorders and schizophrenia in particular. Neuroses and manic-depressive psychoses, however, tend to be more prevalent among the upper classes (see Dohrenwend and Dohrenwend, 1974; Bruce Dohrenwend, 1975).

Three of the best known studies of the relationship between social class and mental disorder have been those of Robert Faris and H. Warren Dunham (1939), August Hollingshead and Frederick Redlich (1958), and Leo Srole et al. (1962). The first systematic study of the distribution of mental disorder in a community was conducted in Chicago by Faris and Dunham in the mid-1930s. Using large maps to trace the addresses of some 35,000 persons who had received psychiatric care from both public and private mental hospitals, Faris and Dunham found that the highest rates for psychoses, especially schizophrenia, were clustered in the slum areas of town. They hypothesized that persons living in conditions of poverty were more isolated from "normal" social contacts and therefore more vulnerable to developing a "seclusive" personality, which they believed was the key trait of schizophrenia. Although impaired social relationships are a characteristic of schizophrenia, we know now that they are usually the result of the disorder rather than its cause. Nevertheless, the Faris and Dunham study does point to isolation from significant others as an important factor in the experience of becoming schizophrenic (see Clausen, 1975), and the process of isolation apparently becomes more pronounced as the progress of the disorder becomes more advanced.

The Hollingshead and Redlich study was conducted in New Haven, Connecticut, in the 1950s and involved a comparison of public and private mental patients with a sample of the general non-patient population. The study employed Hollingshead and Redlich's influential Index of Social Position, which correlated race, ethnicity, and religion with location of residence, occupation, and education to determine a person's socioeconomic status. The study found that upper- and upper-middle-class persons were more aware of psychological problems and more perceptive of conflict and the nature of personal difficulties. This was in direct contrast to lower-class persons, who were much slower to attribute personal problems to mental disorder or to label someone as "crazy" because of the serious consequences of such a label (arrest, confinement in a mental hospital). This study likewise found that the lower the social class, the greater the prevalence of mental disorder. Particularly significant was the finding that the prevalence of schizophrenia was over eleven times greater in the lower class than in the upper class.

The Srole study, also conducted in the 1950s, involved an investigation of the "true" prevalence of mental disorder among a cross-section of persons living in the midtown Manhattan area of New York City. Some 1,660 persons were interviewed and data were obtained on their personal background, past history of psychopathology and psychotherapy, and their acknowledgment of current symptoms of mental disorder. The respondents were also rated by the interviewer in terms of their level of tension at the start of the interview. All of the information was then provided to a team of psychiatrists who assessed the respondent's psychiatric status. Once again it was found that mental disorders were more prevalent among the lower class than among the other socioeconomic groups. In addition, it was found that those persons who were upwardly social mobile showed fewer signs of emotional disturbances than those remaining at the same socioeconomic level or who were downwardly mobile.

The Faris and Dunham study in Chicago and the Hollingshead and Redlich study in New Haven can, of course, be criticized for investigating only treated cases of mental disorder, and the midtown Manhattan study of Srole and associates can be faulted for relying upon subjective and somewhat incomplete judgments by psychiatrists. Yet the results of these three studies relating mental disorder to social class position have been confirmed by several other investigators to the extent that the trend is clear: there is greater prevalence of mental disorder among the lower class. However, once having established this point, it is necessary to move beyond a description of what seems to exist to an explanation of why it exists.

Three rationales have generally been advanced to explain this significant relationship. First is the *genetic* explanation, which holds that there is a greater predisposition to mental disorders among the lower social classes as a result of genetic inheritance. But recent studies of monozygotic twins and adopted twins have shown that genetics alone cannot account for the onset of schizophrenia, a mental disorder prevalent among the lower classes. It is therefore apparent that, while genetic mechanisms are significant, sociocultural factors are also important (Dohrenwend, 1975; Kohn, 1972, 1974). Second is the *social stress* explanation, which notes that members of the lower class are subjected to greater stress as a result of living in a deprived life situation and having to cope with this deprivation with fewer resources. This explanation may also contribute much to our understanding of mental disorders if its validity can be determined. However, in a review of studies of individual reactions to extremely stressful situations (war and natural disasters) and a review of studies dealing with the relationship between mental disorder and ordinary stressful life events, Barbara Dohrenwend (1975) has indicated that the existing evidence is inconclusive. Third is the *social selection* explanation, which maintains that more mental disorder is located in the lower class because mentally ill persons tend to "drift" downward in the social structure (the "drift" hypothesis) or, conversely, mentally healthy individuals in the lower class tend to be upwardly mobile, thus leaving behind a "residue" of mentally ill persons (the "residue" hypothesis). While there is evidence to support a relationship between social mobility and mental disorder (see Bruce Dohrenwend, 1975; Kohn, 1972, 1974; Srole et al., 1962), social mobility in itself does not seem to be a fully adequate explanation. As Melvin Kohn explains in the case of schizophrenia, the weight of the evidence

> . . . clearly indicates either that schizophrenic individuals have been no more downwardly mobile (in fact, no less upwardly mobile) than other people from the same social backgrounds, or at minimum, that the degree of downward mobility is insufficient to explain the high concentration of schizophrenia in the lowest socioeconomic strata.[4]

The social selection approach, along with the genetic and social stress explanations, are all very likely contributing factors in the prevalence of mental disorder among the lower classes. Considered separately, none of these hypotheses has at present sufficient explanatory power, but all appear to warrant serious consideration in future research.

Kohn's (1974) alternative explanation to the class-schizophrenia relationship appears to be a highly promising line of inquiry. His hypothesis is that the constricted conditions of life experienced by people in the lower socioeconomic classes encourages the formation of limited and rigid conceptions of social reality that inhibit such persons' ability to deal effectively with problems and stress. His earlier research (Kohn, 1969) noted that the lower a person's social class position, the more likely that person was to value conformity to external authority and to believe that such conformity was all that his or her own capacities and external resources would allow. The social–psychological orientation of the lower-class person was therefore one that appeared to feature a rigidly conservative view of life involving fear, distrust, and "a fatalistic belief that one is

[4] Melvin L. Kohn, "Social Class and Schizophrenia: A Critical Review and a Reformulation," in *Explorations in Psychiatric Sociology*, ed. P. Roman and H. Trice (Philadelphia: F. A. Davis, 1974), p. 118.

at the mercy of forces and people beyond one's control, often, beyond one's understanding" (Kohn, 1974:129).

Kohn does not argue that this orientation is held by all members of the lower class or that it is a philosophy to which lower-class people subscribe exclusively, but simply that the perception of social reality he has described is more prevalent in the lower class. Kohn suggests that the family is particularly important in this scheme because of its role in transmitting its unique conception of social reality to the young. By transmitting a learned conception of reality that is too limited and too rigid to deal effectively with complex and changing stress-inducing situations, lower-class families may well contribute to the onset of schizophrenia among those genetically susceptible persons who experience great stress. Kohn suggests, accordingly, that future investigations of social class and schizophrenia look at the social psychology that underlies class-based conceptions of social reality. This suggestion appears to be highly appropriate when it is remembered that (1) most schizophrenia occurs in the lower class, (2) the lower class contends with the harshest and most discomforting forms of social reality, and (3) schizophrenia is a mental disorder characterized by *withdrawal from reality,* accompanied by delusions, hallucinations, ambivalence, and bizarre activity.

THE SOCIAL PROCESS
OF MENTAL HOSPITALIZATION

Another focal point of medical sociology's investigation into mental disorders has been the examination of the social processes by which an individual becomes committed to a mental institution and the effect of this experience upon the patient. This literature will be discussed from the standpoint of the pre-patient, in-patient, and post-patient phases of hospitalization.

The Pre-patient Phase

The initial decision that a particular person is mentally disordered usually takes place within the context of the social groups such as family or friends in which that person participates. The lack of clear guidelines for defining mental illness, both among mental health professionals and laypersons in the United States (see Townsend, 1975) often creates a problem. Generally a person is started on the route to becoming defined as "mentally ill" when that person's inability to respond "normally" in a given situation becomes a consistent pattern of behavior; at other times the person himself recognizes a dysfunction when he compares his performance or behavior with that of others. Usually, however, the person's behavior is defined as abnormal by others in the community; the difficulty here is not only the lack of objective guidelines, but also the fact that there are vast differences among people, both individually and as a group, in their capacity to tolerate difficult behavior. The strong tendency of others, particularly relatives, to "normalize" difficult behavior patterns through rationalization until those patterns can no longer be tolerated is a major reason why delay in psychiatric treatment often occurs.

The reluctance to label a family member as having a mental problem is aptly illustrated in studies of the wives and husbands of mental patients. M. Yarrow and associates (1955), in their study of the process by which wives attempted to cope with their husband's mental illness, found that it usually involved five major stages: (1) an initial recognition that the husband's behavior was not understandable or was unacceptable; (2) the wife would adjust her own expectations about her husband to account for his deviant responses; (3) the wife's interpretation of the husband would vary, sometimes the husband was seen as normal and at other times abnormal; (4) the wife would try to adapt to the husband's behavior and would become very defensive about it with other people and (5) finally the wife would no longer be able to sustain a definition of normality or be unable to cope with the husband's behavior. The fifth stage would generally be the prelude to intervention by outside authorities.

A study by Harold Sampson and associates (1964) found that husbands displayed a somewhat similar series of responses to their wife's abnormal behavior. First was the development of a pattern of accommodation by the husband to the wife's behavior. Often a husband would simply withdraw from his wife and develop new interests elsewhere—another woman, a second job, a hobby, or sports. Second, this pattern of accommodation would eventually be disrupted as the pattern of withdrawal by the husband became intolerable to one or both of the parties involved. Either the husband would suggest that the wife seek help or the wife would realize that she could not go on as things were. Sometimes the husband would just get rid of the "problem" by divorcing his wife. This was particularly true for men about the age of forty who looked at the future and decided they did not want to spend the remainder of their active years with their present spouse. Some husbands would develop a pattern of resistance to their wife's demands for involvement. These husbands would either appear indifferent if the wife sought help from a minister or psychiatrist or, if other persons became interested in their wife's problems, they would usually respond negatively. Often the husband did not become involved as a responsible party in the wife's mental condition until the wife was actually hospitalized, and usually this event would result from some extreme act of deviance on the part of the wife, such as burning the house down, that called attention to her needs.

Sampson and associates point out that many mental patients come to the attention of mental health professionals only during the course of an unmanageable crisis. Without such an emergency, the wife's problem was likely to continue to be ignored. This situation is consistent with Howard Becker's (1973) assertion that many people are willing to tolerate deviance or ignore it until someone actually makes a complaint about it and forces society to act against the deviant.

Erving Goffman (1961) explains that when a person is launched on a "career" of being a mental patient, that career involves a round of agents and agencies that mark the progress of the individual's passage from the status of a "civilian" to that of a mental patient. Goffman identifies the agent roles involved in this process as next-of-relation, complainant, and mediators. The next-of-relation, usually a relative, is the person whom the patient expects to be the last to doubt his or her sanity and the first to save the patient from being committed to a mental hospital. The complainant is the person who actually starts the patient on his or her way to the mental hospital. Since this person may also be the next-of-relation, the emotions the patient experiences during the commitment sequence are compounded. The mediators are a sequence of agents and agencies through which the individual is relayed until he or she is actually committed to the mental hospital. These persons are typically lawyers, police, social workers, clergy, physicians, and psychiatrists. Eventually, one agent (the judge in proceedings for involuntary commitment) will have the legal mandate to sanction commitment and may exercise it. If this happens, all of the mediators will retire and the pre-patient now becomes an in-patient.

Goffman points out that this passage to the mental hospital is often characterized by feelings of betrayal on the part of the patient. Goffman found that the potential patient is encouraged to cooperate with others to the extent that it was possible for the patient to travel the whole circuit from home to hospital without forcing anyone to look directly at him or her or to deal with raw emotion. Upon reflection, the patient may realize that everybody else's comfort was being maintained while his or her long-range welfare was being undermined. Often the next-of-relation will handle the patient's affairs while he or she is in the hospital. This person thus serves as a useful identity to whom the hospital can point for justification for its method of treatment. The staff's action is therefore in the patient's best interest both because of their superior training and knowledge *and* because of the authorization by the next-of-relation (who supposedly has the patient's best interests at heart) to work on behalf of the patient. Paradoxically, as Goffman notes, the next-of-relation is the person to whom the patient turns for support in being discharged from the hospital and also the person to whom the hospital turns for authorization to treat the patient.

The passage to commitment as a mental patient as described by Goffman may not apply to all potential mental patients, especially those who seek voluntary admission to a mental hospital or those who are arrested by the police and for whose commitment the state assumes responsibility. However, the import of Goffman's research is that in many cases passage to the mental hospital is a process of alienation; the patient is removed from "normal" society to a setting in which he or she is clearly regarded as being mentally unacceptable.

Voluntary Commitment. Voluntary commitment results when individuals present themselves for admission to a mental hospital on their own accord. Elliot Mishler and Nancy Waxler (1968) have found that the most important variable in whether a mental hospital will accept a person who volunteers for treatment is a referral by a physician. Physician requests to admit a person were viewed as more "legitimate." Other significant factors were the presence of a relative at the admission interview, the age of the patient (younger patients were preferred), and the patient's past history of mental hospitalization (there was a low acceptance rate of ex-patients). Other research has indicated that upper-class and married persons are more likely to be hospitalized than persons who are lower class or unmarried (Gove and Howell, 1974).

A well-publicized study of voluntary admission procedures conducted by David Rosenhan (1973) consisted of a group of eight supposedly normal persons—a psychiatrist, a pediatrician, a painter, a housewife, a psychology graduate student, and three psychology professors—who presented themselves for admission as schizophrenics at twelve different mental hospitals located in five different states on both the East and West coasts. All were admitted, and once in the hospital they immediately reverted to their usual normal behavior. Yet despite their show of sanity after some initial nervousness over actually being a mental patient, the pseudo-patients were never detected by the hospital staffs as being "fakes." Rather it was the "real" patients who correctly identified the pseudo-patients as imposters. For example, all of the pseudo-patients took extensive notes about their confinement experiences in an obvious fashion. This writing was viewed by the staffs as being just another aspect of their pathological behavior, while the real patients accused the pseudo-patients of being either journalists or college professors who were "checking up" on the hospital.

Goffman (1961) makes the highly significant point that there are no objective and universally applicable standards for admission to mental hospitals, and such studies as those by Mishler and Waxler (1958) and Rosenhan (1973) seem to confirm Goffman's observation. Mishler and Waxler found that factors external to the mental disorder itself, such as the presence of a relative or a letter of referral by a physician, were relevant in being admitted to a mental hospital on a voluntary basis. The Rosenhan study suggests that practically anyone, sane or insane, can in fact gain admission to a mental hospital; once in the hospital, what appeared to be important was not so much the patient's behavior, but the general acceptance by the staff of the diagnosis given at admission. There was even evidence that the history of past behavior taken during interviews was somewhat distorted to be consistent with theories of mental disorder held by the interviewer. *Thus, past circumstances did not shape the diagnosis, but instead the diagnosis appeared to shape the diagnostician's perceptions of past circumstances.* Rosenhan believed that the failure of the hospital staffs to discover the pseudo-patients (length of hospitalization ranged from seven to fifty-two days, with an average of nineteen days) illustrates the power of labeling in psychiatric assessment. Once labeled as a schizophrenic, there was nothing the pseudo-patients could do to overcome an identification that profoundly affected the perceptions of other people about them and their behavior. Their release from the mental hospital was contingent upon the staff's accepting the idea that the nonexistent schizophrenia was in "remission."

This discussion is not intended to convey the impression that all mental hospitals are unable to tell real patients from phony ones or that factors not directly relevant to a person's mental status are always highly significant in admission procedures. But it is intended to convey the idea that without objective standards for admission, decisions made by mental hospital staffs concerning admissions are subjective in nature and are clearly prone to error—yet result in significant consequences for the person who becomes a patient.

Involuntary Commitment. Involuntary commitment results when a state uses its power and authority to involuntarily confine an individual to a mental hospital. Involuntary commitment proceedings are of two types: those dealing with criminal offenses, in which insanity is claimed as a defense, and those which are civil (noncriminal) in nature. Scheff (1964) observed the legal psychiatric screening procedures for civil cases in a midwestern state. There were five steps in this procedure, which consisted of (1) three citizens making an application to the court, (2) an intake examination conducted by a hospital psychiatrist, (3) an examination conducted by two court-appointed psychiatrists, (4) an interview by a court-appointed lawyer to represent the patient, and (5) a judicial hearing conducted by a judge. The primary legal rationales for depriving patients of their civil liberties was that they represented a danger to themselves, to others, or to property. Scheff found that a majority (63 percent of the patients) were not necessarily dangerous. It was his conclusion that the evidence in such cases was somewhat arbitrary (there were no objective standards for admission) ; that the patients were often prejudged (it was assumed that all who appeared were in need of being admitted, otherwise they would not have been there) ; that the examinations were both careless and hasty (the interviews by the lawyer and the examinations by psychiatrists lasted about ten minutes on the average) ; and that sometimes there was really no "evidence," but people were committed anyway (there was an assumption that psychiatric treatment would either help or was neutral—it would not hurt—and that it was better to risk unnecessary hospitalization than have the patient be in a position to hurt himself or others) .

In criminal cases, the claim of mental disorder is employed as an excusing condition that relieves the individual from criminal responsibility for his or her act. The logical model for an excusing condition in Anglo-American law is the accident, and it defines a class of persons who fall outside the boundaries of blame (Goldstein, 1967; Simon, 1967; Szasz, 1963). A finding of insanity by a judge or jury, based upon the testimony of psychiatrists as expert witnesses, is a matter of opinion, as the law, like psychiatry, does not have objective standards for ascertaining mental disorder. A verdict of insanity does not release the individual to return to society, for in most jurisdictions that person is involuntarily committed to a mental hospital.

For civil commitment of an involuntary nature, the mere designation of a mental disorder is not sufficient justification for the confinement of an individual to a mental hospital. There usually must also be a finding that the mental disorder is of such degree or character that if the individual in question were allowed to remain at large, that person would constitute a danger to self, others, or property. Despite the fact that these criteria for civil commitment are widely recognized, few concepts in the law are as elusive and undefined as dangerousness. Decisions are normally rendered by judges on a case-by-case basis, based upon the opinions of psychiatrists who assess the probability of the individual's committing a dangerous act. Actions ranging from murder to writing bad checks have all been found to be dangerous enough to warrant confinement. To determine dangerousness, courts look to the severity of the harm, the likelihood that the action will occur, and the behavior of the person that gave rise to the prediction of dangerousness. There is no judicial consensus on any but the most obvious acts of dangerousness, such as murder and direct physical harm, and the issue remains one of the most unsettled areas of the law.

As in the Mishler and Waxler study of voluntary commitment, a study of the assessments used to determine dangerousness in cases of involuntary commitment by Richard Levinson and M. Zan York (1974) also found evidence that factors external to the disorder itself were influential in the decision-making process. This study, based on the files of a large mental health program in Atlanta, Georgia, found that being male, young, unmarried, with a past history of previous psychiatric treatment, and a person for whom help was solicited by a caller outside the person's household were all factors contributing to a diagnosis as dangerous, provided the person demonstrated disorderly behavior in the presence of the mental health professional making the assessment. Levinson and Zan York concluded that since standards are imprecise, criteria unrelated to the pathological condition may unduly influence the attribution of dangerousness to a particular person and the decision to commit that person to a mental hospital.

Therefore, as Goffman explains, whether or not a person is actually launched on a career as a mental patient depends upon a number of contingencies—for example, the visibility of the offense, the socioeconomic status of the patient, the availability of treatment, the convenience of authorities, the opinion of judges and perhaps jurors (in criminal proceedings), and so forth. Becoming a mental patient is a highly arbitrary process.

The In-patient Phase

The last step in the pre-patient phase is the recognition by the individual that he or she has been turned out by society and subjected to the restrictions of living in an institution under the authority of others. Goffman (1961:xiii) has described the mental hospital as being a "total institution," which he defines "as a place of residence and work where a large number of like-situated individuals, cut off from the wider society for an appreciable period of time, together lead an enclosed, formally administered round of life." The central feature of the total institution, which also includes prisons, monasteries, homes for the blind, and military camps, is a breakdown of barriers normal to most people. All aspects of life are conducted in the same place, under the same authority, and in the immediate company of others who are treated alike and who do the same thing together. All phases of activities are scheduled to fulfill the aims of a rational plan supposedly designed to meet the official goals of the institution, which in the case of the mental hospital is therapy and/or custodial care.

Goffman explains that a major characteristic of all total institutions is the existence of some form of deference between or among its group members. In mental hospitals this deference refers to the status of the staff as superior and righteous and the status of the patients as inferior and guilty of failure in the so-called "normal" world. This type of perspective, however, lends itself to a process of dehumanization that makes it easier for the staff to tend to disregard the inmates to achieve greater efficiency without a great expenditure of personal energy and emotional involvement. While not all mental patients in all mental hospitals may experience depersonalization, the dependent status of the patient does lend itself to that type of situation. Furthermore, Goffman points out that the ease with which an inmate can be managed by the staff is likely to increase the degree to which that inmate is dehumanized.

In his study of normal people posing as patients, Rosenhan (1973) found that being a mental patient involved the recognition that powerlessness was evident everywhere. Mental patients lacked credibility in what they said by virtue of their mental disorder. They could not initiate contact with the staff but could only respond to overtures from them. Furthermore, there was only minimal personal privacy, and personal thoughts and history were open to inspection by any staff member, no matter what the reason. Rosenhan stated:

> At times, depersonalization reached such proportions that pseudopatients had the sense they were invisible, or at least unworthy of account. Upon being admitted, I and other pseudopatients took the initial physical examinations in a semipublic room, where staff members went about their own business as if we were not there.
>
> On the ward, attendants delivered verbal and occasionally serious physical abuse to patients in the presence of other observing patients, some of whom (the pseudopatients) were writing it all down. Abusive behavior, on the other hand, terminated quite abruptly when other staff members were known to be coming. Staff were credible witnesses. Patients are not.
>
> A nurse unbuttoned her uniform to adjust her brassiere in the presence of an entire ward of viewing men. One did not have the sense she was being seductive. Rather, she didn't notice us. A group of staff persons might point to a patient in the dayroom and discuss him animatedly, as if he were not there.[5]

Rosenhan attributed the origins of depersonalization to two major factors: (1) the attitudes held by society toward the mentally ill, includ-

---

[5] David L. Rosenhan, "On Being Sane in Insane Places," *Science,* 179 (January 19, 1973) , 256.

ing those who treat them, as "some*thing* that is unattractive" despite benevolent intentions toward them; and (2) the hierarchical structure of the mental hospital, which facilitated depersonalization in that those at the top had the least contact with patients and their behavior was a model for the rest of the staff. Rosenhan found that patients spent very little time with hospital physicians (an average of 6.8 minutes a day for six pseudo-patients over a total of 129 days of hospitalization) and that the physicians, in turn, influenced the behavior of the nurses and ward attendants, who likewise tended to reduce the time they spent with patients. Heavy reliance upon drug therapy also seemed to contribute to the process of depersonalization by allowing the staff to rationalize that treatment was being conducted and that additional contact with the patient was not needed.

Goffman has pointed out that mental patients actually have very little choice but to adapt to the social environment of the hospital. He identifies four different types of adjustment to the total institution: (1) situational withdrawal, (2) intransigence (rebellion), (3) colonization (using experiences of life in the outside world to demonstrate the desirability of life on the inside), and (4) conversion (living up to the staff-sponsored ideal model). Goffman tells us that typically the inmates will not follow any one particular mode of adaptation completely, but will most likely adopt a somewhat opportunistic combination of conversion, colonization, and loyalty to the inmate group. Instead of making what Goffman calls a primary adjustment of "giving in" to the system, the patient will make a secondary adjustment, which is to appear to conform to the system while gaining hidden satisfactions wherever possible. One of the primary functions of inmate society is to help maintain a sympathetic and supportive atmosphere in the hospital ward and to serve as a vehicle by which the patient can assert a self-identity and perhaps some independence within an overall context of dependence and forced association (Smith and Thrasher, 1963). Apparently one of the prominent activities that takes place in these patient "societies" is the expression of face-saving rationalizations for each other's presence in the hospital. Goffman explains that such stories as the following are given:

> I was going to night school to get an M.A. degree and holding down a job in addition, and the load got too much for me.
>
> I got here by mistake because of a diabetes diagnosis and I'll leave in a couple of days. (The patient had been in seven weeks.)
>
> The others here are sick mentally but I'm suffering from a bad nervous system and that is what is giving me these phobias.[6]

6 Erving Goffman, *Asylums* (New York: Anchor, 1961), pp. 152–53.

As Goffman notes, an entire social role in the patient community may be constructed upon the basis of these fictions; thus what we see in these exchanges is the classic function of a network of equals to serve as audiences for each other's self-supportive statements. But while the patient may be denying that he or she is mentally ill, that same patient may at other times show evidence of mental disorder. And, as Goffman indicates, there is still that official sheet of paper to confirm the patient's illness. Regardless of the patient's attempts to rationalize his or her fate, being admitted as a mental patient seriously inhibits the credibility of the rationalizations. Goffman states:

> Certainly the degrading conditions of the hospital setting belie many of the self-stories that are presented by patients, and the very fact of being in the mental hospital is evidence against these tales. And of course there is not always sufficient patient solidarity to prevent patient discrediting patient, just as there is not always a sufficient number of "professionalized" attendants to prevent attendant discrediting patient. As one patient informant repeatedly suggested to a fellow patient:
> If you're so smart, how come you got your ass in here?[7]

Thus, despite the possible supports provided by inmate society, the influence and power of the hospital staff is pervasive. Sometimes the staff will even deliberately discredit a patient's story in order that the patient be encouraged to adopt the hospital's view of himself or herself. What is that view? Generally, the "good" patient is expected to (1) believe that recovery is possible, (2) recognize that he is mentally ill and needs treatment, (3) trust and have faith in the therapist, (4) conform willingly to hospital life, and (5) accept the treatment that is prescribed (Denzin, 1968). If a patient follows this prescription, then, to use Goffman's terminology, that patient is "converted." And since the patient's release from the hospital (in cases of noncriminal confinement) is dependent upon the staff's assessment of how well he or she conforms to the staff's expectations of behavior, the staff has tremendous leverage in their influence over the patient.

Recent studies, however, indicate that many mental patients do not necessarily think of themselves as mentally ill and that conversion is mostly an acceptance of hospital life and the status of mental patient—not an acceptance of the institution's definition of themselves (Braginsky et al., 1969; Townsend, 1976). As Goffman explains in his general approach to institutionalization, inmates, over time, will make opportu-

[7] *Ibid.*, p. 154.

nistic adjustments to the institution. Townsend (1976) points out that mental patients are in a special situation. They know that their subjective and personal feelings are under observation and that the outcome of this observation helps determine their fate. Thus, they adjust their behavior to the situation, depending on what they perceive is the purpose of that situation. Townsend explains:

> . . . Given the mental patient's special situation, it may not be a meaningful question to ask what he "really" thinks of himself. His responses will not necessarily match his actual feelings at the moment and, in any case, both feelings and responses tend to vary with context. At times the patient may feel good about himself; at other times, bad. Some may suspect at times that they are insane and yet not admit these suspicions. At other times, things may be going well and they consequently feel healthy. Even so, they might still fear leaving the hospital, and, as a result, do poorly during a staff evaluation. Patients, like anyone, are also capable of deceiving themselves. They may inwardly suspect they are insane, yet ward off confrontation with these feelings by rationalizing their presence in the hospital and denying that they are mentally ill.
>
> It thus appears that it is difficult to define exactly what a patient thinks of his condition at any one time, and it may be that this is not an empirically useful question.[8]

Nevertheless, a number of medical sociologists and other persons interested in the treatment of mental patients have expressed concern about the effects of the mental hospital as a total institution upon the attitudes and self-concepts of the inmates. The major focus of this concern has to do with the effect of prolonged living in a state of enforced dependency. It is feared that this process may influence the patient to become so dependent on the hospital and its routines that it becomes well-nigh impossible for the patient to leave. As William Eaton (1974:252) describes it, the patient "gradually learns to play the chronic sick role, to reduce aspirations, and to find friends within the hospital instead of outside." The literature is clear that the longer a person stays at a mental hospital, the less likely that person is to leave (Eaton, 1974; Townsend, 1976). One of the focal points of Ken Kesey's well-known novel on a mental hospital, *One Flew Over the Cuckoo's Nest,* is the effort of the patient McMurphy to organize inmate society and to literally force it to recognize that life outside the hospital is much more

---

[8] J. Marshall Townsend, "Self-Concept and the Institutionalization of Mental Patients: An Overview and Critique," *Journal of Health and Social Behavior,* 17 (September 1976) , 269.

attractive. Two of the studies most often cited to depict the effects of institutionalization are those of Ailon Shiloh (1971) and John Wing (1968). Shiloh investigated the attitudes of mental patients toward the outside world in a veterans' hospital in Illinois and found basically two groups, whose goals were diametrically opposed. He classified about 40 percent of the patients as being "institutionalized" and not wanting to leave the hospital, while 25 percent were classified as "noninstitutionalized" in that they had a reasonable expectation of getting out. The remaining 35 percent of the patients could not be classified either way. The key difference between the institutionalized and noninstitutionalized patients was that the former group was generally poorly educated, single or divorced, and lower class; the noninstitutionalized patients were mostly middle-class, married, and well educated. Noninstitutionalized patients saw being hospitalized as a temporary but unfortunate state. In contrast, the institutionalized patients considered themselves as simply cut off from the outside world, yet were well aware of the hospital's comforts—food, warm beds, television, movies. The goal of the institutionalized inmates was very plainly that of security.

Wing studied the patients in two mental hospitals in London and found that the syndrome of institutionalization is dependent upon three factors. First is the social perspective of the patient. Patients who lacked strong family and community ties were usually not too concerned with restrictions on personal liberty. Second, the disease process itself may be significant, as many mental disorders foster social withdrawal. And third, the influence of the institution itself, particularly over a long period of time, may gradually affect the patient by making him more dependent upon institutional life and unable to adapt to other living situations.

Eaton (1974) has investigated the influence of the mental hospital upon institutionalization by proposing four theoretical models to account for a number of times a person is hospitalized for schizophrenia. The positive reinforcement model holds that the hospital positively reinforces the individual at each episode and is consonant with institutionalization. The negative reinforcement model takes the opposite position, that the hospital experience causes individuals not to want to return. The heterogeneity model proposes that individual differences between people explain the variation, and the pure random model assigns a strictly random cause for recurrent stays in mental hospitals. Eaton suggested that all four models represent processes that occur to some degree; however, the heterogeneity model was found to be the most satisfactory in explaining the data.

Although institutions may be able in some cases to positively reinforce an individual's attitudes toward accepting hospital life, the most relevant factor, as suggested by Eaton's work, is apparently that people exhibit psychological and social characteristics that lend themselves in different degrees to acceptance of enforced dependency. Some people are apparently very attracted to situations in which their needs are provided for with little effort or risk on their part.

The Post-patient Phase

A considerable portion of the research on the post-patient phase of the mental hospital experience has been concerned with the effect of stigma upon these individuals. Charles Whatley (1959) found, for example, that strong tendencies to shun mental patients were most prevalent in personal situations. ("Would you want your daughter to marry an ex-mental patient?"). The greatest tolerance was exhibited in impersonal situations. Other research has indicated that feelings of stigma are low among a majority of family members, but that upper-class and middle-class families have a greater tendency to detect such stigmatic attitudes even when unintended (Freeman and Simmons, 1961). More recently, however, it has been found that if former mental patients manage to function well in their work and get along well with their family, feelings of stigma apparently diminish over time and neither patient, family, nor friends will tend to characterize them as former mental patients (Clausen and Huffine, 1975). In general, Americans tend to reject unequivocally persons classified as mental patients, but they also tend to accept the authoritative judgments of psychiatrists that a person has recovered and is "normal" (Olmsted and Durham, 1976).

The key to adequate readjustment to the outside world for most mental patients probably is being able to construct a social–psychological framework in which the ex-patient can show a strong degree of competence. In a study of over one thousand former mental patients in California, Dorothy Miller (1971) identified four elements as being significant factors in the patient's ability to stay out of the mental hospital. First, an adequate source of material support was needed. Second, the presence of someone who cared about the patient and provided close support for the patient's attempts to cope with the outside world was very important. Third, the patient needed to experience a series of spontaneous positive relationships with other people. And fourth, the ability to define a new situation as one in which the patient was able to exercise some degree of control was helpful. If any of the above four elements was missing, Miller believed that ex-patients were likely to fail outside the hospital.

Community Psychiatry

Since the mid-1950s there has been a steady decline in both the number of people admitted to mental hospitals in the U.S and the average length of confinement. The most significant change in mental health policy in recent years has been the development of community mental health centers to provide therapy in the community setting. In 1963, Congress passed the Mental Retardation and Facilities and Community Mental Health Centers Construction Act as a commitment on the part of the federal government to help support easily accessible and locally controlled mental health centers. This law reflected the philosophy that the objective of modern treatment should be to support mental patients in their own communities as much as possible so that they can lead relatively normal lives. Advocates of community psychiatry cite four major concerns as the rationale behind community mental health programs (see Cohen, 1974). First is the idea that the mental patient's entire social environment be viewed as a "therapeutic community" that offers resources for treatment to mental health professionals. The second concern, clearly related to the first, is that some means must be found to use the patient's relationships with family and friends to improve therapy and to prevent recurrence of a mental disorder. The third concern is to develop and organize local community control over these mental health centers so that center policies are both community based and oriented. Fourth is the desire to reduce the patient "load" at state mental hospitals by providing prompt response and twenty-four hour service.

In 1972 there were nearly three hundred community mental health centers in the U.S. and the number has steadily increased since. In order to meet federal funding requirements, community mental health centers are required to provide both in-patient and out-patient services, day care services, a twenty-four hour emergency service, and educational services for community agencies and professional personnel.

Several studies have confirmed the utility of home treatment (see, for example, Freeman and Simmons, 1963). When this method works, it provides the advantage of being more personalized and less expensive than hospitalization. But is home treatment the answer? It all depends upon which environment—hospital or community—is best for the patient. David Mechanic (1969) has observed that when mental patients do show impressive signs of remission during hospitalization these symptoms often reappear when the patient returns home. This seems to be indicative of difficulties in the home environment, which may remain unchanged. Also, one of the benefits of hospitalization is that it affords a respite—both to the patient and to the family—from the turmoil that may have been a major causal factor in the onset and progress of the disorder. This respite can provide a period of reassessment and redefinition leading to a hopeful outlook (Clausen and Huffine, 1975). Sampson and associates (1964) have found that a significant effect of hospitalization upon marital ties is to separate the disputants, block final action, and defer formalization of the end of the marriage so that other solutions can be attempted. Often hospitalization may create conditions under which a relationship can be resumed.

The decision whether to opt for hospital care or community (home) care, therefore, seems to depend on the situation. Merely to conclude that institutional life is dehumanizing, and therefore necessarily bad, is to overlook those situations in which it may be the better alternative.

SUMMARY

This chapter has reviewed selected aspects of the sociology of mental health from the standpoint of theoretical models of mental disorder, social epidemiology of mental disorder, and social processes of mental hospitalization. The medical model has been enhanced in recent years by successful research in brain chemistry, which the medical profession believes will offer the greatest potential for treating abnormal behavior. Although the medical model will, in all probability, retain its preeminent position in determining theory, therapy, and policy, the contributions of sociology toward our understanding of what mental disorders are and what causes them are gaining ever greater acceptance. Research in the social epidemiology of mental disorder has clearly pointed to three variables—sex, rural versus urban location, and social class—that demonstrate significant differences among groups of people. Because the relationships among these variables have remained consistent over time, they will prove useful in clarifying causes of mental difficulties. Studies of hospitalization in mental institutions have illustrated some of the problems; and one meaningful reaction has been the development of community psychiatry to provide a more humane treatment situation.

11

AGING

A number of health-related factors, including improved medical care, nutrition, sanitation, and housing, have combined in the twentieth century to help promote longer lives for most Americans. In 1974, for example, the average infant at birth in the United States could expect to live 72.9 years. This figure represents an increase in longevity of nearly 50 percent since 1900, when life expectancy at birth in the U.S. was 47.3 years. Furthermore, in the decade between 1960 and 1970, the number of persons aged 75 and over increased three times as fast as the number in the 65–74 age category. Today, there are over 20 million persons in the United States age 65 and over, of whom about one-third are 75 and over.

Thus, the present century in the U.S. can be described as a period of exceedingly rapid growth of the aged population. Not only are more persons living to reach older ages, but also since 1958 the fertility rate in the U.S. has been in a period of decline. The lower death rate coupled with the lower birth rate has thus produced a much higher proportion of older Americans in relation to the total population. Figure 11–1 illustrates this trend by showing that in 1900 only some 4 percent of the total U.S. population was age 65 or over. By 1970, however, older Americans constituted 9.7 percent of the total population and by 2020 it is projected that 13.4 percent of all Americans will be in this age bracket.

Another way to illustrate the growing proportion of elderly persons in America is to recognize that in 1977 about one in ten Americans is

FIGURE 11–1. PERCENT OF TOTAL U.S. POPULATION AGE 65 AND OVER FOR SELECTED YEARS

	1900	1930	1950	1960	1970	2000 (pro-jected)	2020 (pro-jected)
Percent Age 65 and Over	4.0	5.4	8.1	9.2	9.7	10.2	13.4

SOURCE: U.S. Department of Health, Education and Welfare, *Facts and Figures on Older Americans: An Overview, 1971* (Washington, D.C.: U.S. Government Printing Office, 1971); U.S. Bureau of the Census, *Current Population Reports: Projections of the United States by Age and Sex, 1970 to 2020* (Washington, D.C.: U.S. Government Printing Office, 1970).

over sixty-five; by the year 2020, this ratio will have increased to one in six.

The increasing longevity of Americans has helped foster a growing interest among both social and medical scientists in the biological and behavioral aspects of the aging process and the social role of the elderly person. Accordingly, the study of gerontology has increased in scope and importance in recent years, and many medical sociologists are specializing in social gerontology, that is, the study of aging as a social and psychological experience.

AGING AND THE LIFE CYCLE

In the United States, age sixty-five years has generally marked that point in life when a person is "officially" old—largely because of its arbitrary selection by the Social Security Administration as the age of eligibility for old age benefits. Except for its bureaucratic significance, however, being sixty-five has no other particular relevance. This is because chronological age is an inconsistent indicator of the aging process. Just as physical and intellectual capabilities mature at different times in different people so can aging be said to begin at different points in time for different people. It is possible to be a "young" sixty-five or an "old" fifty-five-year-old person.

Also, it is interesting to note that individual perceptions of whether or not a certain age is "old" can vary according to the variables of age and sex (Drevenstedt, 1976). Older persons and women tend to perceive middle and old age as occurring chronologically later in life than do younger persons and men. Or as one senior citizen once put it: "To me old age is always fifteen years older than I am" (Rosow, 1974:11).

One way to "explain" the social and psychological aspects of the aging experience is to categorize that experience into phases or stages denoting the human life cycle (Atchley, 1972; Birren, 1964; Neugarten and Moore, 1968). Although the stages of the life cycle are based upon chronological age and do not account for variations among individuals, they are nevertheless indicative of the general life course most people follow. Implicit in the idea of a life cycle is a common set of social experiences through which all members of a society are expected to pass. For instance, childhood is the time when a person generally receives a primary education; adolescence and young adulthood are usually the time of courtship and marriage; the period of later maturity is typically the time of retirement.

Thus, as Vern Bengston (1973) points out, age is a dimension of social organization because the divisions of the life cycle are those prescribed by the culture of a society in order to lend stability and predictability to the typical sequence of life events. Implied in this arrangement is the idea that individuals also undergo a change in behavior as they pass from one stage of life into a subsequent stage. Infants, children, young adults, middle-age adults, and older persons are all expected by other people to behave in a manner characteristic of their age group; social judgments of their maturity are dependent upon how close their behavior approximates the corresponding age-related norm. Furthermore, at each stage of life a person takes on new social roles and the responsibilities that accrue to those roles, while the person's status and relationships with other people are modified accordingly.

The typical stages of the human life cycle and the approximate ages they represent are shown in Figure 11-2. Although a person can be regarded as aging from the moment of conception or from the moment the individual reaches full maturation (there is some disagreement on this point), for the purposes of our discussion, the stages of middle age, later maturity, and old age are most relevant.

As previously noted, the onset of old age varies among individuals. Although aging is known to occur as a result of changes in the body's cells, the exact cause of the process is still a mystery. The two most widely accepted theories state that aging may be due in large part to deterioration in the integratory homeostasis that exists between cells of the same tissue and those of other tissues, or it may be the result of some form of preset genetic program for cell aging. Whatever the cause, the interaction of biological, genetic, and social–psychological factors seems to be involved. Aging can also be of a primary or a secondary nature. Primary

FIGURE 11–2. THE LIFE CYCLE

Stage	Approx-imate Age
Infancy	2
Preschool	2–5
Childhood	5–12
Adolescence	12–17
Early Maturity	17–25
Maturity	25–40
Middle Age	40–55
Later Maturity	55–75
Old Age	75

aging occurs over time, while secondary aging occurs through disease or trauma and may be temporally premature. The single most obvious indication of aging is the appearance of the skin, which tends to dry out and wrinkle. The person's capacity for sight and hearing are reduced and the brain begins to shrink, losing about 100,000 cells a day. Muscles also shrink and become weaker, joints stiffen and swell, while the heart, lungs, kidneys, and bladder begin to operate at reduced levels of effectiveness, and the body's output of hormones begins to diminish. The body becomes increasingly susceptible to stress, infection, and especially to the degenerative diseases of cancer, arteriosclerosis, and diabetes.

According to Robert Atchley (1972), *middle age* is the period of life when a person initially becomes aware of the fact that he or she is aging. Middle age is the time when the person recognizes a reduction of energy and often begins to favor intellectual activities over physical endeavors. Usually the person's work career more or less reaches a plateau, and the great majority of a couple's children will have left home in order to lead their own lives. As Atchley (1972:7) explains, middle age is when most people realize that they are aging and that death is very real, not just something that happens to somebody else. Robert Kastenbaum (1971), for example, has found that a characteristic of old age is a foreshortened time perspective. The older person avoids thoughts of the future because of the limited time left and instead dwells on the past. Kastenbaum suggests that a majority of people are past-oriented by the age of forty and virtually all people are by age fifty-five.

Later maturity is characterized by a marked reduction in energy, vision, and hearing. Chronic health disorders are commonplace and poor health can join with reduced income, retirement, and the deaths of friends and relatives to curtail social interaction. By the time they are in their mid-sixties, most women are widows. But, as Atchley notes, the period of later maturity can be a pleasant one for those persons who plan for it, retain a good measure of physical vigor, and perhaps wish to enjoy a time of lessened responsibilities. Also, the aged individual may continue to be a highly productive member of society. Charles Bowden and Alvin Burstein (1974:212) point out, for example, that the "myth that age necessarily involves an inability to produce is challenged by the numbers of second careers and examples of influence maintained by prominent individuals late into their lives."

Old age, in contrast to other stages of life, is more likely to be a rather unpleasant period as there is a higher probability of loneliness, boredom, and loss of self-esteem. Also it can be a time when mental processes are diminished. Whereas it seems clear that the aged brain takes longer to respond to a stimulus and the recall of recent events may be impaired (probably due to the tendency toward increased distractability on the part of the older person), remote memory of past events is usually quite good. If there is considerable memory loss, it can be a sign of organic brain damage. But it should be realized that while such brain damage may be likely to occur with increasing age, it does not occur in all elderly persons. Besides reduced mental activity in very old age, another problem peculiar to the elderly is that of physical frailty and the possibility of being disabled such that physical mobility is highly restricted or denied.

Physical and mental infirmities and the reality of being tired, ill, and less able to cope with problems—all set in a framework of the recognition of impending death—can and do produce severe problems of adjustment and depression for the elderly. With reduced resources, the elderly person is less able to cope with stress and adapt to new conditions. Old age is thus a period in life many people fear and wish to avoid, yet, as in the period of later maturity, the key to success in old age is obviously to maintain an optimal level of physical strength and mental awareness.

SOCIAL GERONTOLOGY: THEORIES OF AGING

There are several theories of aging in social gerontology, but three of these—disengagement, activity, and continuity theory—that have generally been accepted as the most influential to date will be considered here.

Disengagement Theory

Disengagement theory, which stems from the functionalist perspective in sociology, is probably the most influential and controversial theory in social gerontology. According to two of its proponents, Elaine Cumming and William Henry (1961), disengagement theory contains three basic propositions: (1) a process of mutual withdrawal of aging individuals and society from each other is a usual occurrence; (2) this process of withdrawal is inevitable; and (3) it is also necessary for "successful" aging. Disengagement theory tells us that all people die eventually, yet it is necessary for society's institutions to survive in order to maintain social stability and cohesive social functioning. It follows then that it is necessary to have an orderly means of transferring power from the older members of society to the younger. Disengagement theory supports the notion that it is to society's benefit to phase out those individuals whose deaths would disrupt the smooth functioning of the social order. The process of phasing out older persons from the mainstream of society thus becomes institutionalized, as stable and routine norms are developed to indicate which individuals should be disengaged and what forms of behavior should occur at this time. Accordingly, societies develop norms requiring that an individual retire from work at a certain age and a rite of status passage—for example, a retirement ceremony—often marks the occasion. However, as Atchley (1972) notes, disengagement is not usually a single event, but instead a gradual process that involves the separation of an individual from several of his or her regular social roles and activities.

As a functionalist perspective, disengagement theory is similar to the Kingsley Davis and Wilbert Moore (1945) theory of social stratification. Davis and Moore held that in order to attract the best qualified persons to compete for the positions that fill society's most important needs, it is necessary to offer society's greatest rewards and inducements (money, power, prestige, status) to those persons. Disengagement theory extends the Davis-Moore thesis by explaining that the work of people in key positions must continue uninterrupted if social order is to be preserved. Therefore, society must be able to replace persons whose ability to perform adequately in an important position becomes questionable through old age or otherwise. If old age is a problem (which disengagement theory says it is), then it is necessary for society to be able to move the aged person out of the key position and into a less important one.

However, the disengagement of society from the individual is only half of disengagement theory. The other half of the theory, according to Cumming and Henry (1961), maintains that individuals themselves select to withdraw from certain social roles when they become old. The more roles an older person withdraws from, the less that person is bound to society's norms. The disengaged person is thus able to play a particular social role (the retired person) that allows him or her to become increasingly more self-centered and more preoccupied with personal interests. To the extent that the disengagement process allows the aged person to assume such a role, the more successful the aged person will be in retirement.

There are, as should be obvious to the reader, some significant weaknesses in disengagement theory. As Atchley (1972) points out, societal disengagement does not seem to occur in all social institutions. He explains that if societal disengagement were a functional necessity, then it should apply to political officeholders as well. However, the relatively older ages of U.S. senators and particularly U.S. Supreme Court justices (who have an average age of sixty-four) seem to bespeak a flaw in the propositions advanced by Cumming and Henry.

Additionally, as Atchley notes, disengagement theory does not adequately account for individual disengagement. From this perspective, there are essentially three major difficulties with disengagement theory: (1) individual disengagement is most probably a much more complex process than the theory allow; (2) preliminary research has shown that once an individual has internalized a norm, more than simply the absence of interaction is required to extinguish it; and (3) the assumption that people will desire to be disengaged (to pursue their own self-centered world) does not explain the desire that many individuals have toward continued engagement.

In a study of university and college professors emeritus, Paul Roman and Philip Taietz (1967) were able to observe a post-retirement position that allowed retired professors to continue working in their pre-retirement activities of research, teaching, administration, or public service. Roman and Taietz believed that disengagement was not a feature of all social systems, and they questioned the assumption of disengagement theory that individuals naturally want to disengage as they perceive themselves getting old. Roman and Taietz found that, given the opportunity to continue their activities, most of the professors emeritus remained engaged. What is indicated by this study and others (Carp, 1968; Tallmer and Kutner, 1969) is the importance of the social situation (see, for example, Atchley, 1972:223–224). Some people may disengage because the rules of the institution force them to or because of the impact of physical and social stress. But given the opportunity and the means to remain engaged, they might well choose to do so. The assumption of disengagement theory that disengagement is both natural and positive for the aged person cannot be conclusively demonstrated.

Why then is disengagement theory important? Chiefly because it is able to describe the social processes that occur when older persons withdraw from their usual roles as a result of age. The theory is particularly applicable to situations of forced disengagement according to predetermined rules of an institution or organization and to situations of mutual disengagement, where both society and the individual define disengagement as positive. The strength of disengagement theory lies in the realization that at some point in time the interests of society intersect with the rule performance of older persons in key positions, and the result is often the disengagement of that older person. By setting a specific age, usually sixty-five, as the time of retirement, disengagement becomes institutionalized and orderly and inevitable, just as aging itself is inevitable. Some degree of disengagement appears to be inherent in the aging process for many people and disengagement theory helps to explain what happens in certain specific situations. Overall, then, disengagement theory can be described as a promising theory that remains to be reformulated if it is to attain a greater measure of universal validity.

Activity Theory

Activity theory, as suggested by Robert Havighurst (1963), is primarily an action theory for successful aging. It consists of three basic premises: (1) that the majority of normally aging persons will maintain fairly constant levels of activity; (2) that the amount of engagement or disengagement will be influenced by past life styles and by socioeconomic considerations rather than by some intrinsic and inevitable process; and (3) that it is necessary to maintain or develop substantial levels of social, physical, and mental activity if the aging experience is to be successful (see Palmore, 1969).

What constitutes successful aging? According to Havighurst, the norms for old age are the same as those for middle age; therefore, successful aging is how close a person in the stages of later maturity or old age approximates the norms and activities of middle-aged persons. In other words, activity theory is an approach to understanding the social behavior of elderly persons in terms of how well those persons deny the fact that they are elderly. Successful aging consists of being or behaving as much as possible like a middle-aged person.

There is research that clearly supports the basic propositions offered by activity theory. In a longitudinal study at Duke University carried out over a ten-year period, Erdman Palmore (1968, 1969) found that older men tended to show almost no overall reduction in their activities or in life satisfaction, while older women tended to have a small (but statistically significant) reduction in both activities and life satisfaction.

Temporary decreases in activities due to illness were usually followed by subsequent increases so that there was little or no overall change.

Palmore noted that his data were obtained from persons who were relatively healthy and, therefore, disengagement may be more typical of the less healthy. His point was, however, that disengagement by the elderly is not an inevitable product of aging. There were consistently high levels of activity by the respondents throughout the ten-year period of the study. Furthermore, it was found that activity was significantly related to high morale and life satisfaction. The more active a person was, the more likely that person was to be happy. Palmore concluded that continued engagement rather than disengagement was typical of the normal, healthy older person, and the amount of that person's activity was strongly related to his or her past life style. If disengagement occurred among these elderly persons, it usually did so only just prior to death.

What activity theory essentially tells us is that some persons (perhaps a majority) do not disengage from society when they become old. If they do retire from their occupational role, they compensate for its loss by engaging in some other type of activity which provides satisfaction. Bernice Neugarten (1971), for example, cites the case of a 75-year-old retired school teacher who made the most money of his life selling insurance as a second career after retirement. This is not to forecast, however, that most elderly persons will seek a second career, but rather that they are likely to remain active in some fashion if their past lives were characterized by being active.

Yet as a theory explaining the social behavior of the aged, activity theory suffers from two basic inadequacies. First, it rests upon the assumption that older persons judge themselves according to norms common to middle-aged activity and behavior, but it does not explain what happens when the elderly do not subscribe to such norms. And second, it does not explain what happens to those older persons who cannot, for physical, mental, or socioeconomic reasons, maintain a middle-aged standard of living regardless of how they judge themselves. Thus, activity theory, like disengagement theory, fails to account for the behavior of all individuals.

Continuity Theory

Continuity theory, a third major theoretical approach to the social experience of aging, is somewhat more recent than the others (Atchley, 1972; Neugarten, 1964). It is based upon the premise that the various stages of the life cycle are characterized by a high degree of continuity. As a person grows to maturity and passes on to the stages of later maturity and old age, continuity theory holds that the individual develops rather stable values, attitudes, norms, habits, that become an integral part of his or her own personality. The manner in which an individual will react to the aging process will thus be influenced by that person's attempts to maintain characteristic traits and predispositions.

Continuity theorists do recognize, however, that predispositions to act in certain ways are always subject to change or modification because of the ongoing and sometimes complex forms of interaction people have with others and with the environment during all stages of the life cycle. Although there will be a tendency toward consistency, continuity theory admits that people also change by adapting to new situations. For instance, a person who looked forward to retirement might not like it after all, and might instead be forced to accommodate to an unwelcome situation. Continuity theory thus admits of a wide range of different reactions to the aging experience, each dependent upon a variety of factors.

The merit of continuity theory is that it might be able to explain several aspects of aging in a much fuller sense than disengagement or activity theory is now able to do. But conversely, the theory seems extremely difficult to conceptualize, to make operational for research studies, and to analyze in ways that indicate its relevance for our understanding. It is too early to tell what contributions continuity theory may produce to explain aging, but the theory does offer considerable promise.

Theories of Aging: An Overview

For the present, two theoretical approaches—disengagement theory and activity theory—dominate the research literature in social gerontology. These theories have attempted to systematize the existing social and psychological data on aging so as to serve as a predictive model of the behavior that accompanies old age. Disengagement theory views old age as a distinct phase of life decidedly different from middle age; it is a time when specific social and psychological forces come to bear upon the person to make him or her aware of a reduced ability to contend with stress. Furthermore, disengagement theory suggests that disengagement of the elderly from society's important functions is not only beneficial for society, but also for the elderly person, who is freed from the stresses of the pre-retirement role. While an overall decrease in social activity is generally observable in old age, disengagement theory does not account for the fact that many older people remain active (engaged) in some fashion and that such activity is significantly related to life satisfaction. So it is not at all clear that disengagement is inevitable nor is it as personally satisfying an experience as the theory would suggest.

Activity theory, on the other hand, strongly supports the notion of a positive relationship between activity and life satisfaction. Yet its weakness lies in not explaining what happens to people who cannot be active or who do not believe that being active is the only way to keep happy in old age. The proposition that high levels of activity are necessary for "successful" aging has not been conclusively demonstrated. The promise of continuity theory is that it tells us people age according to a general life pattern which, with adaptations, continues to the end of life. Thus, aging persons may not necessarily be dependent upon the social environment, but are seen as capable of making adaptations to social and biological changes in their lives. Continuity theory is, however, still in the nature of a hypothesis.

It is obvious that all theories of social gerontology are still in the formative stage. There are two major reasons for this situation. First, social gerontology is a relatively new field that marks its beginning with a study of aging conducted by Robert Havighurst and Ruth Albrecht in 1953; as such it awaits the accumulation of an extensive body of research data that can only come with a considerable amount of work in the field. Second, research concerning the aging experience should include studies of people as they age if social gerontology is going to be able to explain and perhaps to predict the changes in behavior that come with aging. Such research is not only expensive, but, if done correctly, is going to take several years of data collection before adequate theories can be formulated.

IMAGE OF THE AGED:
SELECTED RESEARCH FINDINGS

Society's View of the Aged

A major theme underlying the social psychology of aging is the anxiety with which many adults face old age. According to Neugarten (1971), most people have an irrational fear of aging based on negative stereotypes of what it is like to be old. Palmore (1971), for example, studied attitudes toward aging as suggested by humor. Humor can be an important indicator of social attitudes since it often reflects widely held social stereotypes. Some 264 jokes were singled out and analyzed to indicate prevalent societal attitudes. Over half of the jokes reflected a negative view of aging, the most disparaging being those whose principal subject matter was physical ability, appearance, age concealment, mental abilities, and being an "old maid." The majority of jokes about being a male "old-timer" and still having sexual ability were either positive or ambivalent. Jokes dealing with old men generally tended to be much more positive than those dealing with old women; in fact, most of the age concealment jokes referred to women. In addition, jokes that could be related to the activity theory of aging were more positive than those related to disengagement theory. This study suggested: (1) the popular culture generally devalues old age, and (2) a double standard may exist in which aging women are viewed more negatively than aging men.

The common stereotypes of old age in American society are that it is characterized by economic insecurity, poor health, loneliness, rigid attitudes, and failing physical and mental powers (Tuckman and Lorge, 1953; Neugarten, 1970, 1971). Despite the fact that many elderly persons are not lonely, poor, and in bad health, nor do they become overtly senile or mentally ill (Neugarten, 1970, 1971), negative stereotypes of aging are both pervasive (Atchley, 1972) and highly resistant to change (Tuckman and Lorge, 1952). The end result of these stereotypes is their use as a psychological barrier by the young to separate themselves from the old and to ascribe an inferior social status to being elderly.

The group in society that appears to hold the most negative views of old people are young and middle-aged adults. By contrast, studies involving children find little evidence of devaluation of old age. In a review of children's literature between 1870 and 1960, Mildred Seltzer and Robert Atchley (1971) concluded that there was little evidence of negativity toward aging in the readings. More recently, Elizabeth Thomas and Kaoru Yamamoto (1975) have found a rather positive attitude toward the aged in a study of children and adolescents. There was general agreement that older persons were "good" and "wise," while the qualities of being "pleasant," "happy," and "exciting" were seen to decrease with age but were nonetheless present in old age. Only on the qualities of being "active" and having "power" were the elderly rated negatively. Thomas and Yamamoto suggest that rather than developing negative attitudes toward aging in childhood, what apparently happens is that people acquire negative stereotypes of aging as they themselves begin to feel threatened by old age.

Thus, older persons must not only confront the fact of biological decline, but they must also cope with being relegated to a relatively inferior social status. In pointing out that perhaps the most important impact of aging is that it may cause an individual to lose eligibility to occupy a valued social position, Atchley aptly summarizes society's view of the aged:

> To put the position of older person into proper perspective, one need only to ask: do people get wealthy, revered, or influential simply by growing old? The answer must be a resounding "no." As a matter of fact, if anything happens to a person as a result of

getting old, it will probably be that wealth, influence, or prestige of his other positions will *decrease*. Being defined as old may cause him to be *removed* from some of his other positions.[1]

The Aged's View of Themselves

A review of the research literature comparing the way the aged view themselves with societal stereotypes of the elderly both supports and refutes the proposition that older people view themselves in a negative context. For example, in a comparison of institutionalized older persons and noninstitutionalized older and younger persons, Evelyn Mason (1954) found that the aged institutionalized group viewed its self-worth in a significantly more negative fashion than did either of the noninstitutionalized groups. Within this latter group, however, the noninstitutionalized aged viewed their self-worth more negatively than a similar group of young adults. Irving Rosow (1967) has suggested that the stress of daily living, especially alienation resulting from the loss of preferred adult statuses, tended to lower feelings of self-worth and well-being among the aged. In a later work, Rosow (1974) held that the ambiguity associated with the role of older persons affects psychological stability and promotes depression, anxiety, anomie, and refusal to view one's self as old. This condition is attributed to role loss and society's failure to develop clear norms pertaining to the role of the elderly.

Other research, however, has indicated that older persons have a generally positive impression of themselves. In a comparison of the attitudes of retired and nonretired older persons, Caroline Preston (1967) found no significant differences between the two groups in terms of life satisfaction and suggested that the aged may indeed feel more positive about themselves than had been previously assumed. In a recent study of teachers and telephone company employees, Atchley (1976) found that the great majority of his subjects liked retirement. Earlier, Atchley (1972) had noted that retirement per se has little psychological effect on the individual (the greatest problem may be reduced income), and other research (Riley and Foner, 1968) had concurred that negative orientations toward the self tend to decrease with age.

Why is the research about the self-perceptions of the elderly so contradictory? A basic problem has to do with the attempts of many researchers to generalize that most old people are either unhappy or happy. These gross generalizations fail to take into account considerable variance between individuals in the manner in which they cope with the aging experience. Neugarten (1971) has made the important point that

[1] Robert C. Atchley, *The Social Forces in Later Life* (Belmont, Cal.: Wadsworth, 1972), p. 100.

the aged in American society are not a homogeneous group. As Neugarten explains, a consistent finding of studies of happiness, intelligence, personality, and the health of adults have shown that age is a poor index of the way in which people differ from each other. At the University of Chicago, for instance, Neugarten and her colleagues carried out a longitudinal study lasting some fifteen years of the adaptational patterns of about 2,000 persons aged seventy to seventy-nine. Three principal areas of life among the aged were examined—personality, life satisfaction, and extent of social-role activity. As a result of their data, they were able to construct four major types of personalities common to the aged: (1) integrated, (2) defended, (3) passive-dependent, and (4) disintegrated.

The majority of these respondents were classified as having an *integrated* personality, that is, they were characterized as being high in life satisfaction, mature, open to new experiences, having good cognitive abilities and a view of themselves as competent. The integrated personality consisted of three subtypes, each of which was based upon the person's role activity. One subtype, termed the *reorganizers,* included those aged persons who engaged in a wide variety of activities, such as business and community affairs. The second subtype was classified as the *focused;* these were persons who remained active, but only in a few select roles. The other subtype was the *disengaged,* persons with well-integrated personalities who experienced satisfaction with their lives but demonstrated low activity. Members of this latter group had high self-esteem and appeared to be complex, self-directed individuals, yet they had voluntarily withdrawn from role commitments to be content with the "rocking-chair" approach to old age.

The second major personality category was the *defended.* These were hard-driving, ambitious, achievement-oriented individuals who were very defensive about aging. The defended personality consisted of two major subtypes. First was the *holding-on* group, which continued to work hard and maintain relatively high levels of activity as means of obtaining satisfaction from life. Next were those defended personalities described as *constricted.* Constricted individuals combated aging by trying very hard to maintain their health through diet and general activities, while also being oriented toward maintaining a youthful physical appearance.

The third major personality was identified as *passive-dependent.* There were two subtypes common to this group. *Succorance-seeking* individuals had strong needs to be dependent and have other people respond to them. They were somewhat active and seemed to adjust to aging in a positive manner so long as they had some other person or persons to depend upon for assistance and support. The second subtype, of whom only a small number were found, was the *apathetic*. The primary characteristic of this person was passivity. These people had little interaction with others, engaged in few activities, and seemed to have little interest in what went on around them.

The fourth major personality type was the *disintegrated*. Very few persons qualified for this category. The disintegrated personality consisted of persons who demonstrated gross psychological disorganization and who were generally only able to maintain themselves outside an institution because of family arrangements or the tolerance of other people in their social network.

While recognizing that other personality types common to patterns of aging may exist, Neugarten has suggested two important conclusions about aging in American society. First, she has pointed out that older people deal with aging in a number of ways. She is impressed by the fact that variation rather than similarity seems to be the rule among the aged, and she further indicates that such variation may become even more pronounced in the future. This is so because current data on the aged are derived from persons who tend to be poor, foreign-born, and poorly educated. As Americans who have enjoyed the financial affluence and higher standards of education characteristic to the mid-twentieth century become old, she believes these people will have even greater freedom in selecting their life styles. And second, as an advocate of continuity theory, she suggests that people age in accordance with the behavior that is generally typical of lifelong patterns of responses. Though lacking conclusive data, she believes that the general image of aging is one of personality continuance over time.

However, besides personality, some other variables have been found to affect the way in which older people view themselves. The most significant of these variables, which seem to be related to each other as well as important in themselves, are: (1) level of health, (2) sex, and (3) socioeconomic status.

Regardless of one's personality, a most significant variable affecting an individual's adjustment to old age is level of health. George Maddox (1962), for example, has found that the most important single determinant of an elderly person's self-assessment is that person's health status. Pessimism about one's health was associated with anxiety and poor adjustment to the environment, while optimism about one's health was associated with an absence of these problems. Preston (1968) studied aged persons who were about to retire. She found that those aged respondents who reported more chronic health disorders and more incapacity due to illness showed a greater tendency to think of themselves as being "old" than aged persons who did not report such health problems. In another study, Arthur Schwartz and Robert Kleemeier (1965) examined two groups of elderly people and two groups of young people who were categorized upon the basis of age and state of health (sick or well). They noted that among those who were sick, illness tended to have a greater effect upon the self-perceptions of the aged rather than the young, but the relationship was due to the effects of illness and age, and not just to age alone.

Sex-based differences in attitudes toward aging constitute another important variable. A past assumption in some of the research literature on aging has been that the retired role is much more difficult for men than for women because men are considered to be more strongly attached to their occupational role and relationship with the external social structure (see Cumming and Henry, 1961). In Atchley's (1976) sample of aged school teachers and telephone company employees, however, it was the women rather than the men who had the most difficulty facing retirement. In comparison to the men (who seemed reasonably content with retirement), the women were more likely to be lonely, anxious, unstable in self-concept, highly sensitive to criticism, and highly depressed; the men were more susceptible to anomie and more likely to identify themselves as "old."

Denial of aging appears to be a characteristic more typical of women than men. As noted earlier (Drevenstedt, 1976), women generally perceive the onset of old age later than men. This tendency may be related to sex role stereotypes in American society which equate female beauty and sexuality with youth. With very few exceptions, aged women are not generally depicted in the popular culture as "beautiful," but aged men can be considered "handsome" or "distinguished." Instances of older men marrying young women, for example, tend to be more common than older women marrying young men. All in all, the fact that women live longer than men does appear to be a mixed blessing, as old age for women presents serious difficulties of adjustment.

The third variable that needs to be mentioned is socioeconomic status. As Arlie Russell Hochschild (1973a) has observed, the assumption that old age is the great leveler because it affects the rich and poor alike is not necessarily true. It is much better to be old and rich than to be old and poor. Chapter Two on social epidemiology showed that the upper social classes tend to have a longer life expectancy than the lower classes and, in effect, what Hochschild is saying is that the shorter a person's life expectancy, the poorer that person's health and morale. Therefore, lower-class persons may begin to "feel" old at progressively earlier ages than upper-class persons. For instance, Caroline Preston and Karen Gudiken (1966) have found that indigent older persons expressed significantly more negative than positive traits about themselves when they compared themselves to "others my age." Negative self-reporting among the indigent aged appeared to be a manifestation of depression. Maddox (1962) also noted that social class position is related to optimism and pessimism about health. Older persons of high social status were much more likely than other persons to be optimistic about their health. Older persons of low social status tended to be pessimistic about their health, even when they were medically assessed to be in good health.

Besides the effect of poverty upon the health status and general outlook of the aged, the aged poor are more likely to be socially isolated. Rosow (1967) found in Cleveland that middle-class older persons tended to have more good friends in old age than working-class older persons. Hochschild summarizes this situation as follows:

> Removed from the economy, the old have been cast out of the social networks that revolve around work. Lacking work, they are pushed down the social ladder. Being poor, they have fewer social ties. Poverty reinforces isolation. To eliminate enforced isolation, we have to eliminate poverty, for the two go together.[2]

The significance of race in the aging experience is generally a result of the fact that aged persons who belong to racial minority groups are also more likely than aged whites to be poor. There has been a suggestion (see Palmore, 1969) that perhaps old age provides some relative advantage to blacks because aged blacks do not suffer as great a reduction in income as whites (whether or not this is an advantage is certainly questionable, because the income of blacks is more likely to be low anyway) and because older blacks receive more acceptance and support from their children. This latter assumption has recently been challenged, however, in a study of black and white widowed women by Helena Znaniecki Lopata (1973) in a large northern metropolis. Contrary to the common belief that older black widows live rich and full lives surrounded by their kin, Lopata found that black widows appear to be just as isolated in old age as white widows. In fact, it may be that the psychological stresses of being a member of a racial minority group in the U.S. is further compounded when that minority person becomes old. Regardless of race, old age itself seems to confer no particular advantage upon the elderly person except that of lessened responsibilities.

The Aged as a Minority Group

A controversial issue in social gerontology is whether or not the aged in American society constitute an emerging minority group (see Palmore, 1969). It has been pointed out that many older persons experi-

2 Arlie Russell Hochschild, *The Unexpected Community* (Englewood Cliffs, N.J.: Prentice-Hall, Inc., 1973), p. 140.

ence negative stereotyping, relegation to an inferior social status, discrimination, and segregation. A common reaction of persons exposed to these social and psychological stresses is the formation of a group identity with a specific group-oriented belief and value system reflecting the needs and goals of group members. It has therefore been proposed that such a group identity in the form of a distinct subculture has been developing among the aged. This subculture is thought to be an increasingly important phenomenon as the proportion of older persons in American society increases (Rose and Peterson, 1965).

One of the most engaging studies on the subculture of the aged is Hochschild's (1973a) research among the residents of Merrill Court, a small apartment building in San Francisco, comprised mostly of sixty-, seventy-, and eighty-year-old widows. The forty-three residents of Merrill Court had developed their own social community, which Hochschild suggested was founded on a particular kind of relationship—the "sibling bond." What was special about this community was not that it was an old age subculture, but that membership in the sisterhood at Merrill Court offered these social siblings a full and meaningful social life based on adult autonomy. Unlike the institutionalized elderly, the widows at Merrill Court took care of themselves and made their own decisions. By sharing a social life of coffees, lunches, shopping, activities in the service club, bowling, and by being related to the other residents in terms of belonging to the same age stratum with its common rewards, problems, desires, and abilities, the widows were tied to each other by a bond characteristic of siblings.

Hochschild believes that certain periods of life, specifically adolescence and old age, are better for forming sibling bonds as they are times when people seem to be in particular need of "back-up" social relationships. In these periods—just before and after raising a family—and entering and leaving the economy—many people tend to forge friendship solidarity within their own generation. These are also times when social change is most pronounced in a person's life. Hochschild explains that the sisterhood at Merrill Court was no substitute for the love of children and family, but that it did provide a social life independent of the family and added a measure of meaningful and enjoyable activity not otherwise obtainable. While recognizing that the residents of Merrill Court may not be typical of most old people, Hochschild suggests that this type of community may be a forecast of what is to come among the aged because it is a positive adjustment to an unpleasant social condition: the tendency of aged persons in modern, industrialized societies to be socially isolated.

To describe elderly persons in general, however, as constituting a genuine minority group is a dubious assumption. The best description

(Barron, 1961) is that the aged represent a "quasi-minority group" because they do not currently function as a socially organized subgroup in American society. Yet as Palmore (1969) explains, the extent to which the aged represent a distinct minority group is apparently a matter of degree, as elderly persons organize and develop social and political power to reduce discrimination and win benefits for their specific needs. Social action groups for the aged are becoming more commonplace in the U.S., and the future may see the aged emerge as a powerful interest group in American society mobilized to effect social changes in favor of the elderly.

SUMMARY

This chapter has reviewed the major theories and selected research findings that currently comprise the field of social gerontology. The most influential of these theories is disengagement theory, which views the withdrawal of the older person from society as being beneficial both to society and to the individual. Disengagement theory encounters a serious challenge, however, in activity theory, which holds that activity itself keeps older persons happy. A relatively recent theory, continuity theory, offers another perspective. People act in accordance with their past activities and personalities, but are amenable to a certain degree of change in new situations. Thus, the elderly person may have a wider range of choice than had previously been recognized. Further refinement of these theories is needed before their validity can be fully assessed.

A major problem confronting older people is their devaluation by the young, as reflected in numerous negative stereotypes ascribed in the elderly. Yet older people do not necessarily agree with these stereotypes; in fact, research was cited by Neugarten (1971) to suggest that most older persons are relatively happy and satisfied with their lives. Life satisfaction in old age, however, seems to be affected by the variables of health, sex, and socioeconomic status. At the present time, it cannot be claimed that a distinctive subculture appears among the elderly or that they constitute a genuine minority group in terms of political and social organization to benefit group membership. However, the number and proportion of older persons in the U.S. is continuing to increase and the time may come when the aged represent a much greater social force in American society than they currently do. Overall, the literature has revealed that there is no homogeneous self-concept among the aged; older Americans do not all think alike about aging and themselves as aged people.

12

DEATH AND DYING

Death is a characteristic of human existence and all societies have developed social arrangements for containing its impact. Yet despite the obviousness of this personal and social phenomenon, it has only been in the last decade that the study of death as a social process has been given considerable attention in medical sociology and also in psychology, medicine, psychiatry, and law. Death as a topic of investigation had been generally avoided because of the unpleasantness of the subject matter. Yet attempts to define death as something so indeterminate that it can be denied or easily avoided have not been successful strategies in coping with both the meaning and process of dying, either on an individual or societal level. Death is an inevitable biological and social experience of all persons and as such is a dominant part of the process of living. Its effect upon human behavior cannot be ignored.

Beginning in 1965 with Barney Glaser and Anselm Strauss' seminal work, *Awareness of Dying*, there has been an increasing interest on the part of medical sociologists to study the process of death and dying in contemporary society. The result has been that the study of death has become one of the most active areas of research in medical sociology. The study of attitudes toward death have also made that topic one of the most recent sources of significant theoretical and applied insight into human behavior.

Initially, most of the research concerning death dealt with the problem of death as a solitary and perhaps cruel experience in modern hospitals where the dying patient was often found to be socially and psychologically isolated. Hospital staff and the dying patient's family appeared inhibited in their attempts to interact with the patient in an open and socially meaningful manner. The process of dying was itself hidden as much as possible in order to minimize the effect of death upon all concerned, especially the living. Now it seems that our attitudes toward death may be changing, not only in the academic disciplines, but in American society generally. While it remains to be confirmed that we are actually in a period of a "death revolution," which some writers suggest will see the elimination of the fear of death in advanced industrialized societies, the contemporary approach toward death is to deal with it as a natural part of the human condition. Hopefully, this approach will help us to understand our own lives and ease our fears about the inevitability of mortality in a more open, honest, and satisfying manner.

DEATH AND THE INDIVIDUAL

The basic problem that humans have in dealing with death is one of fear. In a review of traditional attitudes toward death, Elisabeth Kübler-Ross (1969) points out that death has been and remains a fearful and frightening event to human beings and that fear of death is universal throughout the human species. Many studies in psychology and psychiatry have documented the fact that this strong, deep-rooted fear motivates many persons to seek secure environments and to avoid activities and situations that could result in premature death. Sigmund Freud, for example, believed that fear of death was a primary motivation for social cohesion as people sought security and strength from group membership. Even though some persons may not overtly express a fear of death and dying, Herman Feifel and Allan Branscomb (1973) have suggested that nearly everyone fears death. In a survey, Feifel and Branscomb noted that over 70 percent of their respondents verbally denied they were afraid of death. However, at a second level of testing, which involved reactions to images of death, the respondents began to demonstrate ambivalent attitudes. At a third level of testing, involving word and color-word associations, nearly 95 percent of the respondents revealed a subconscious fear of death. Even persons who characterized themselves as extremely religious indicated "a demonstrable fear of death" on the subconscious level.

Fear of Death

Although many fears have been identified in connection with death, the primary fear is fear of the unknown—the dread of not knowing what happens when you die and after you die. Barney Glaser and

Anselm Strauss (1968) say that when death occurs slowly, the dying patient is forced to cope with death by overcoming the fear of loss of self and the fear of dying as physical, and perhaps mental, disintegration. No one can share his or her experiences of death with the living; yet reports are available from persons who have nearly died of a heart attack or from an accident of some kind. Although such reports do give clues about the experience of life's final moments, the reader should be cautioned about accepting the validity of such accounts because they obviously cannot be verified.

A study by Russell Noyes, Jr. (1972) of the process of dying found that many persons who report being close to death have similar experiences. Based upon descriptions of dying experiences, both autobiographical and clinical, Noyes developed a model of the death experience consisting of three stages: resistance, review, and transcendence.

The initial stage of *resistance* to death begins when a person struggles for survival, realizing that death may be imminent. This resistance is characterized by marked anxiety but not disabling panic. If even the slightest possibility of survival remains, the person often feels an enormous surge of energy that may enable him or her to survive by alert mental activity and possible feats of strength. But, conversely, this upsurge of energy is countered by a powerful desire to surrender and the person is caught between the impulse to fight and the impulse to surrender. If the person is dying gradually, Noyes claims that as energy wanes, life seems to be dependent upon an inner struggle to maintain it. He (1972:177) states: "It is as though their will to live sustains them and as though without it they might simply let themselves go and, in a sense, will their deaths."

The second stage of *review* appears after all hope of survival has apparently disappeared and the person surrenders to his fate. Death is faced calmly, perhaps with a sense of tranquility. At this particular point, Noyes says that the person begins to review past life experiences from a detached perspective, as if the ego had become an entity capable of observing itself act out the past. The present author has interviewed persons who reported similar experiences after being close to death as a result of automobile and industrial accidents. These persons believed that they, in fact, left their hospital beds and "hovered" about the room able to view themselves and others as a detached consciousness. Parapsychologists term this experience an "out-of-the-body" phenomenon, which may be a negation of death on the part of the dying person. Here the subject views his body as near death, but exists outside it, thus becoming a detached witness. Some persons, according to Noyes, report viewing scattered scenes or all the important events in their lives in this "detached" state. He suggests that the certainty of loss of future may necessitate a return to the past in order to make their existence real in a final grip on life. The phenomenon of the ego splitting from the body may also lessen personal anxiety by reducing death to solely bodily annihilation.

The final phase is *transcendence*. Here the person's perspective becomes more distant and he experiences himself as outside of time or beyond the past and future. This altered sense of time represents complete immersion in the present moment. Another characteristic feeling is a sense of loss of control as if held by a superior power. At this point the person experiences feelings of oneness or unity with other human beings and the universe. Death is near.

While providing some interesting insights, Noyes' analysis of the death process cannot be considered conclusive by any means. His descriptions were rendered by persons generally in good health who were suddenly threatened with death. We do not know if these experiences are typical or how accurately most people identify their dying moments. Then, too, the mystical state of consciousness reported during transcendence may not be shared by all dying persons, but just those persons who have a tendency toward such modes of perceiving. Other variables, such as age, sex, personality, and culture, may also be very important. Still, the similarities among those cases reported by Noyes seem to suggest important guidelines for future research into the experience of dying.

The first stage of resistance in Noyes' typology raises an important sociological question regarding death. This question concerns the extent to which the "will to live" is responsible for length of life. Although researchers are not aware of what physiological mechanisms may be at work in this process, there is a body of literature in psychology which suggests that perhaps rats, chickens, monkeys, human beings, and even cockroaches become unusually susceptible to death when they discover that they have no control over what is happening to them and that further action is futile (Seligman, 1974). The experience of American prisoners-of-war during the Korean and Vietnam wars who simply lay down and died, although apparently in good physical health, are examples of this phenomenon.

Research by David Phillips and Kenneth Feldman (1973) has found evidence that there are fewer deaths than usual before important ceremonial occasions such as a birthday (a domestic ceremony), a presidential election (a political ceremony), and the Jewish Day of Atonement (a religious ceremony). According to data derived from biographies of famous persons, Phillips and Feldman suggest, in accordance with Emile Durkheim's (1961) description of social integration and ceremonies, that persons who are strongly integrated into a society feel an obligation to participate in the ceremonies of that society. Thus, persons strongly attached to society postpone death in order to participate in meaningful social ceremonies; persons detached from society and uninvolved with its ceremonies may die prematurely by committing suicide or by just "letting go." Admittedly speculative, this hypothesis does offer interesting possibilities for future sociological research concerning the will to live and the social processes that might either reinforce or possibly negate that will.

The other major fear of the unknown is fear of what happens after death. Beliefs about existence after death are common in most cultures, and one of the primary functions of religion is to reduce anxiety by providing answers concerning life after death. However, research to date about the effects of religion in allaying fear of death has been inconclusive (Dumont and Foss, 1972). Kübler-Ross (1969) found in her research with terminally ill patients that religious patients seemed to differ little from those who were not religious. Very few patients could be identified as being truly religious or as confirmed atheists. Most held beliefs somewhere between the two extremes and their philosophical perspectives were usually not strong enough to relieve them of the fear of dying. Kübler-Ross observed that persons with less education, little sophistication, and few professional obligations or social ties had the least difficulty in facing death. Those persons experiencing the greatest difficulty were characterized as ambitious by virtue of attempting to strive for control of their environment and accumulation of material goods. Although they had many social ties, they exhibited few meaningful personal relationships and usually faced death alone.

But fear of the unknown is not the only fear related to the experience of dying. At least five other significant fears have been identified: (1) fear about not being able to pursue or to complete certain goals; (2) fear of what will happen to dependents; (3) fear of the loss of self-mastery or control over one's destiny; (4) fear of punishment for sins; and (5) fear of isolation and separation from loved ones and treasured objects. All of these fears, either singly or in combination, can produce a considerable degree of anxiety in an individual concerned about death.

Strategies for Dealing with Death:
Childhood, Adolescence, Adulthood

Since fear of death is universal—defined by existentialist philosophers as the human being's "most profound awareness"—numerous strategies have been employed by individuals and society for coping with death anxieties. In very early *childhood,* there is generally no conception of what death means, and the discovery of the phenomenon of death is not typically accompanied by great emotion (Anthony, 1968, 1972).

Often the child's discovery of death occurs as a simple incident in day-to-day living when the child explores his or her environment and perhaps finds a dead object such as a bird or insect. Sylvia Anthony (1968) tells us that usually there is a definite interval between a child's first questions about death and the arousal of emotion connected with the idea of dying. Death is commonly associated with the child's understanding of his or her world and may be viewed as going to sleep, going on a trip, or going up in the sky.

Relevant research suggests that anxieties regarding death do not appear until around the ages of three to five when the child realizes the possibility of loss of someone upon whom the child depends or the loss of one's own self (Prugh et al., 1953; Knudson and Natterson, 1960; Natterson and Knudson, 1960; Anthony, 1968; Spinetta, 1974). D. G. Prugh and associates found that among hospitalized children, types of death anxiety varied according to age; children under the age of six were thought to be highly anxious about separation from other people. The other studies cited above agree that death disturbs the very young child mostly in regard to the thought of separation, loneliness, or abandonment.

Many young children, however, do not develop death anxieties. They are usually able to control their fears about death because they do not perceive death as the end of life. The dead may be viewed as being simply another category of the living who are less than alive or who live somewhere else, such as in heaven. Many children are taught that there is an after-life as a defense against death anxiety. Often the perception of young children regarding death may involve a close relationship between death and birth—someone dies and then returns as a baby. Many games that children play also include a death theme in which death is not defined as a permanent or finite state. Children who are "killed" while playing "soldier" or "cowboys and Indians" are expected to come back to life at an appropriate time. This view of death is reflected in children's literature, where death is seen as an event that can be undone; the dead hero can be returned to life by magic or the intervention of good fairies and spirits (Wahl, 1965).

While there is general agreement in the research literature concerning three- to five-year-olds' fears of death as separation, there has been serious disagreement about the characteristics of death anxieties in the six- to ten-year-old age group. Much of the initial research consisted of data collected from observations of terminally ill children that found that this age group lacked the intellectual ability to develop an extensive concept of death (see, for example, Debuskey, 1970; Evans and Edin, 1968; Ingalls and Salerno, 1971). These children apparently experienced little anxiety about dying unless adults intervened to point out to the child the seriousness of the illness. Other research suggested that while six-to ten-year-olds could not fully conceptualize death, nonetheless they were aware that something very serious was wrong with them (see, for example, Binger et al., 1969; Easson, 1970). John Spinetta (1974) has strongly criticized this research, however, on the grounds that their conclusions rested largely on observations of parents and hospital staff rather than on direct observation of the children; also, when they were based upon observations of the child, the studies lacked objective measures, with little or no use of control groups for purposes of comparison.

Recent studies, however, strongly suggest that six- to ten-year-olds are aware of what death means. E. H. Waechter (1971) asked a set of four matched groups of children—children who were fatally ill, children with chronic but not fatal illnesses, children with temporary illnesses, and normal, nonhospitalized children—to construct stories about themselves using a set of pictures. Waechter found a greater number of overtly expressed death themes among the fatally ill children. She concluded that this age group is not only subjectively aware of dying, but also able objectively to express that awareness.

Spinetta and associates (1974) tested Waechter's conclusion in an experiment involving a group of twenty-five children fatally ill with leukemia with a control group of twenty-five chronically ill children with nonfatal diseases. The six- to ten-year-olds were matched not only by age group, but also by sex, race, grade in school, and amount of medication. The children were asked to tell a story about a sick friend in the hospital by placing dolls representing a sick child and significant adults (nurse, doctor, mother, father) in their *usual* places in a model of a hospital room. Later the children were asked to repeat the story by putting the dolls in places they would *like* them to be. Since the dying children placed the adult dolls at such a significantly greater distance from the doll of the sick child, Spinetta and associates inferred that the placement of the dolls by the dying children was reflective of a growing sense of psychological separation from both the people and the circumstances of the hospital environment. In interviews with parents and hospital staff, they found additionally that adults reported a decrease in the frequency, intensity, and quality of interaction with the dying child. Although the parents wished for the child's recovery and attempted to provide great affection, they also wished to withdraw from the child in order to protect themselves emotionally when the child died. The hospital staff likewise reported a reluctance to become emotionally involved for similar reasons.

Accordingly, Spinetta and associates ask some important questions: Does the dying child reflect the unresponsive feelings of adults or does the child try to prepare for death by separating from parents? Does the dying child prefer to be left alone for reasons of his own choosing or because he senses embarrassment on the part of adults?[1] Spinetta does not provide answers to these questions, but he does suggest that whatever the reason, the fatally ill child is aware of death and perhaps dies psychologically isolated from other people.

Spinetta concludes:

> It seems clear . . . that the fatally ill 6–10-year-old child is concerned about his illness and that even though this illness may not always take the form of overt expressions about his impending death, the more subtle fears and anxieties are nonetheless real, painful, and very much related to the seriousness of the illness that the child is experiencing.[2]

Jean Piaget (1959), the noted Swiss psychologist, has observed that children do not recognize the generality and impersonality of death until somewhere between the ages of six and twelve. Piaget considers this recognition of major importance in the development of mature concepts of causality. It signifies that the child is changing his perception from the idea that all events and existence can be attributed to personal motivation to an acknowledgement of the action of impersonal causal forces.

Once children near *adolescence*, around the age of ten or so, they develop adult concepts of death which recognize that death is not only inevitable, but also final. Yet adolescents generally fear death less than other age groups because death is not an immediate threat and they are reasonably sure of a full life ahead of them (Dumont and Foss, 1972). Actually, the outward aspects of death often appear very funny to them. They construct jokes and rhymes about death and enjoy laughing at movie and television scenes containing exaggerated expressions of bloody mayhem. Anthony (1968) calls the adolescent's mockery of death "a halfway house" to the defenses against death anxiety available to the adult.

Human beings like to think that somehow the individual personality is not meant to die and that something personal about themselves is able to survive death. However, the strategies that exist, for use by the *adult* in the desire for eternal survival are limited to those of (1) sexual reproduction, (2) belief in an after-life, or (3) belief in reincar-

---

[1] Judith Miller (1975), reporting on the research of Richard Lansdown, a British child psychologist, notes that the most difficult problem for the dying child was the anxiety of the child's parents. Although considered as "callous" by those who were not intimately familiar with the situation, Lansdown found when the parents stopped visiting the child, the child was happiest, sensing that the parents were no longer worried or extremely upset about him. This finding is counter to the implications of Spinetta et al. (1974) regarding the unpleasantness of the dying child's psychological isolation.

[2] John J. Spinetta, "The Dying Child's Awareness of Death: A Review," *Psychological Bulletin*, 81 (April 1974), 259.

nation. Sexual reproduction allows adults at least to imprint themselves genetically upon succeeding generations. Belief in an after-life is derived either from religion or a personal philosophy of existence. Some persons embrace religion and try to live the kind of life that "qualifies" for life after death in heaven. Other people have their own perhaps nonreligious belief in a life or existence of some type after death, perhaps as a spirit or energy form in the cosmos. Or the adult may believe in reincarnation. Several accounts have been written by persons who are convinced they were born, lived, and died at a time in the past and have returned to the present to live another life. Otherwise, the adult must cope with the idea of death as the total end of experience and an eternity of nothingness.

Strategies for Dealing with Death: The Dying Patient

Despite the particular strategy an individual selects to contain the fear of death, the time arrives for most people (except for infants, comatose patients, or those persons dying sudden and unexpected deaths) to confront the process of dying. Two of the most noted studies describing this process are those of Kübler-Ross (1969) and Glaser and Strauss (1965). Kübler-Ross has identified five stages of coping with dying: (1) denial and isolation, (2) anger, (3) bargaining, (4) depression, and (5) acceptance. The first stage of *denial and isolation* consists of the patient's shock and dismay at the disclosure of impending death. Often the initial awareness of death is accompanied by resentment against other people who are not dying or against fate itself. Sometimes patients in the stage of denial will "shop around" for another physician in order to disprove a previous diagnosis of terminality. Most patients, according to Kübler-Ross, demonstrate at least partial denial of their deaths at some point in their efforts to cope with the dying process.

Glaser and Strauss also found attempts at denial in their study of terminal patients. Some of these attempts included refusal to seek further information from physicians, refusal to discuss their illness and death with anyone, favorable comparisons of themselves with other dying patients, emphasis upon the future, resumption of activity with a passion, and juggling time. This last strategy consisted of setting a particular point in time as a survival goal and, after reaching that time, selecting another future time, and so on.

Throughout all of the stages oulined by Kübler-Ross, dying patients expressed hope that death could somehow be averted. Usually this hope was based upon the possible discovery of a new drug or sometimes upon the skill of physicians. Stewart Alsop (1973), a journalist dying of cancer, said that such hope allowed the dying person to die more easily. While the patient may be told he *may* die or *probably* will die, Alsop thought that the patient should not be told he *will* die.

Kübler-Ross observed that very few patients are able to maintain a "make-believe world" in which they are healthy up until the final moments of living. When denial of one's death could no longer realistically be maintained in the face of medical evidence, the second stage of anger appears. Often this anger is displaced upon family, friends, the hospital staff, or upon God. Kübler-Ross said this can be a very difficult time for those who must interact with the dying patient. The next stage, *bargaining,* usually does not last very long. This stage represents an attempt to postpone death by good behavior or good deeds. Perhaps in return for some special service, dying patients hope they will be granted an extension of life. The fourth stage of *depression* occurs usually prior to the acceptance of death. Here the patient knows definitely that absolutely nothing can be done to change his fate. The great majority of patients, according to both Kübler-Ross and Glaser and Strauss, come to terms with their depression sufficiently enough to go on to the final stage of *acceptance.*[3]

If the patient has had enough time and perhaps assistance in working through the other stages of reaction to dying, Kübler-Ross found that the patient usually reaches the stage of acceptance. During this stage the patient is no longer angry or depressed, but recognizes the inevitability of death. This is not a happy period, but one characterized by Kübler-Ross as "almost devoid of feelings." Pain and struggle may be over and all that usually remains is the wait for death. Glaser and Strauss, however, tell us that acceptance may be either active or passive. Passive acceptance consists of calm resignation as described by Kübler-Ross, but active acceptance involves preparing for death by becoming philosophical about life and death, settling personal and financial affairs, becoming very religious, or eliminating the distressing prospect of dying a painful and lingering death by committing suicide. Some patients accept the fact of their dying, but decide to fight it by intensive living, seeking out marginal or "quack" doctors for miracle cures, or by volunteering to participate in medical research and experiments that might produce a cure.

[3] Lansdown (Miller, 1975) discovered in his research with children dying of leukemia that the parents of these children underwent a stage of mourning during the acceptance of death. This "anticipatory mourning" occurred prior to the death of the child and was similar to post-death mourning. He also found that since leukemia is a disease characterized by remission periods during which the children appeared healthy, parents who had reached the stage of acceptance sometimes returned to the stage of denial, and the entire process of accepting death was repeated several times. Remissions, according to Lansdown, make leukemia "one of the more psychologically complex diseases."

Alsop (1973) has provided a particularly insightful account of the acceptance of death in his book *Stay of Execution*. Although he did not welcome the prospect of dying, it was difficult to accept a life of pain and weakness with a dependency upon medication and blood transfusions like a "vampire." To be without the possibility of ever returning to a normal life and to feel very, very sick made the thought of death far less terrible to him. He (1973:23) finally reached the point where he believed that just as a sleepy man needs to sleep, a dying man needs to die, and that a time comes when it is both wrong and useless to resist.

DEATH AND SOCIETY

Like individuals, societies develop attitudes toward death which are reflected in the establishment of normative practices designed to contain death's presence. To assess the contemporary American perspective regarding death, it is useful to compare its evolution from the social thought of Western Europe during the Middle Ages to the present. According to Philippe Ariés (1974), the French social historian, death in Western society in the twelfth century could be characterized as "tamed death" because it seemed to lack the anxieties common to the twentieth century. People in the Middle Ages did not desire to die, or at least they were in no hurry to do so, but when they realized that death was near, the art and literature of the period suggests that they usually died very simply, as if death was a familiar aspect of living. Death was supposedly viewed as the collective destiny of the species and the simplistic, perhaps naive, acceptance of death was acceptance of the order of nature.

Except for sudden or unexpected death, the deaths that occurred during the Middle Ages usually involved a familiar ritual. First, the dying person was supposed to lie down in bed, if at all possible, in order to die. Then, the actual process of dying consisted of a ceremony organized by the dying person, who was expected to follow a prescribed sequence of behaviors intended to conclude life. The dying person was supposed to express sorrow about the end of life and to recollect beloved persons, events, and things. He or she was expected to pardon the usually numerous companions who gathered around the deathbed for any disapproved acts, followed by a final prayer in which the dying person requested forgiveness of sins. After a priest administered absolution, all that remained was the wait for death. Dying was a public and familiar act, and the dying person's room was a social setting to be entered freely by relatives, friends, and neighbors. For example, as Ariés points out, no portrayal of the deathbed scene between the twelfth and eighteenth centuries failed to include the appearance of children. Usually there was no great show of emotion at the deathbed because behavior was guided by the dying person in the formally prescribed death ritual.

In modern society people no longer experience death in this simple, ceremonial manner. Instead the modern version of dying has been characterized by fear, anxiety, and social isolation. What happened? What caused our attitudes toward death to change? Ariés claims that from the Middle Ages on, death in Western society was subtly modified into a pervasive dread. One source of this change, as noted by Ariés and others, is found in Christianity. Walter Kaufmann (1959:61) states that "although some early Christian martyrs died fearlessly, in eager anticipation of eternal bliss, Christianity has on the whole used its vast influence to make men dread death." Inspired by the book of Matthew, the Christian death scene during the Middle Ages emphasized the idea of judgment; that is, the weighing of souls by Christ the Judge according to the deeds, both good and bad, committed during a person's lifetime. The eternal destination of heaven or hell for the dying person was at issue and, notwithstanding its cosmic essence, judgment was peculiar to each individual. Thus, the security of death as a collective rite was joined by the anxiety of interrogation and personal trial.

Medieval Christianity was certainly not wholly responsible for the changing attitudes toward death, but it was influential. During the eighteenth century, romanticism, with its emphasis on love of nature and the expression of strong emotion, viewed death as a painful rupture from the beauty of nature and the joy of living things. Acute anxiety over death was a norm sanctioned by a society strongly aware of the pain of separation from persons and objects that were loved and valued. Another important attitude that first emerged full-blown in the nineteenth century, the Age of Rationalism, was the notion of guilt about personal failure to accomplish certain goals. Ariés (1974:105) summarizes this latter attitude as "a passion for being, an anxiety at not sufficiently being."

The twentieth century marked the efforts of society to control death by making it as unobtrusive a social process as possible. Emphasis was placed upon the "acceptable" death, which was a death that could be tolerated by the survivors. This idea had its origin in the belief of the Middle Ages that there was a close relationship between death and an individual's personal biography. It was thought that each person's life flashed before his eyes at the moment of death; the dying person's attitude at that time would thus provide his biography with its conclusion and final meaning. Death was believed to be the occasion when human beings were most able to know themselves. Consequently, to die well or to experience a good death became very important. The twentieth century interpretation of this attitude, however, was concerned not with the benefit of the individual but with society. The antithesis to an "acceptable" death was the graceless, fearful, and embarrassing death that caused strong emotions and revulsion among other people and a disruption of social life. Therefore, modern society sought to control death and to make it as acceptable as possible by hiding it.

Societal control of the impact of death was significantly assisted by two contemporary phenomena: (1) the occurrence of dying generally among persons furthest removed from the mainstream of social life and (2) the displacement of the traditional site of dying from the home to the hospital. Approximately two-thirds of all deaths in industrialized societies are the result of biological decay and the infirmities of old age. Deaths associated with the aging process occur largely among persons who have retired from work and who no longer have parental responsibilities. These deaths rarely interrupt the smooth functioning of society.

Hospitals have become the places to die because the care provided there is usually not possible in the home. Today in American society only a minority of people die at home and the number is decreasing rapidly. Exact figures on the number of persons actually dying in hospitals are difficult to obtain, but a review of available data suggests that about one-half of all deaths occur in large general hospitals and a smaller but increasing number occur in nursing homes (Morison, 1973). Probably fewer than one-third of the deaths in American society take place at home, at work, or in public places. The removal of most deaths from the home has caused the traditional death ritual to disappear. Death in the hospital is controlled not by the dying person or his family, but by the physician and the hospital staff, who define not only the circumstances of death, but the exact moment of dying.[4] Access by family and friends to the dying patient can also be controlled by the hospital, so that death occurs under the jurisdiction of relative strangers to the dying person. Such a controlled death is disruptive neither to the general functioning of the hospital nor to society at large.

The Social Organization of Dying

Two major studies on death in medical sociology, that of David Sudnow (1967) and Glaser and Strauss (1965) provide illustrations of the death environment in contemporary American society. Sudnow (1967) studied the organization of dying by utilizing participant obser-

---

[4] The medical and legal definition of death is no longer the traditional criterion of heart stoppage because of the possible restoration of heart action, even when there is no longer the remotest possibility of the patient's recovering consciousness and brain functions (Hirsh, 1974). The new basis for defining death is that of a "flat" or isoelectric electroencephalogram denoting "brain death," which is taken after signs of respiratory and circulatory failure.

vation in two hospitals: a large, urban West Coast charity institution and a private, general hospital in the Midwest. Most of Sudnow's observations took place in the charity hospital, which he described as a setting for the concentration of death. Three-fourths of the patients were over sixty years old and there was an average of three deaths daily. Most of the deaths occurred on the medicine and surgery wards. The personnel on these wards encountered death so frequently that it was considered routine. The routinization of dying was made easier, both at the charity and at the private hospital, because almost all of the deaths were preceded by a coma. Comatose patients were regarded as being essentially dead and they could be disattended as a social object.[5] Of the some two hundred deaths he witnessed, Sudnow noted that not a single death was of the "Hollywood" variety where the dying person's last sentence was interrupted by a final breath.

Those persons having the most contact with death in the hospitals were generally lower echelon employees. Once a patient died, except for the autopsy, the physician lost interest in the body. The higher one's position in the status hierarchy of the hospital as a nurse or a physician, the less likely was one to witness dead bodies or physically handle corpses. The handling of corpses was considered "dirty work" in the value system of the hospital, and whenever possible ward personnel would leave a body to be processed by the next work shift. Usually the morgue attendants and orderlies performing these unpleasant tasks were blacks.

Sudnow saw the hospital as an environment of occurrences, with death being an occurrence mainly definable in reference to its similarity to other deaths experienced by the personnel. Although any given death could give pause for retrospective comment on the part of staff members, the mention of deaths was usually routine except for those involving unusual events, such as obtrusive settings or styles of dying, accidents, diagnostic or treatment errors, or the high social status of a patient. The age of the dead person could also cause comment, especially the deaths of children. General philosophical consideration by the staff of death and dying did not naturally occur.

While the staff sought to minimize and routinize death as much as possible for themselves, the organization of dying was constructed in such a way as to hide the fact of dying from patients and visitors. Most

---

[5] As suggested by Erving Goffman, Sudnow (1967:74–75) has made a distinction between "clinical death" (signs of death based upon physical examination), "biological death" (cessation of cellular activity), and "social death" (the point at which a person is treated like a corpse although still alive clinically or biologically). "Social death" was not simply the asocial treatment of a dying patient by the hospital staff, but was the beginning of social activities commonly associated with death: planning the autopsy, grieving, preparing obituary notice, contacting insurance companies, disposing of personal effects, arranging for the funeral, etc.

hospitals, for example, locate the morgue in a relatively inaccessible part of the hospital basement. Sudnow (1967:51) quotes a text in hospital administration: "The hospital morgue is best located on the ground floor and placed in an area inaccessible to the general public. It is important that the unit have a suitable exit leading onto a private loading platform which is concealed from hospital patients and the public." Often the patient whose death was imminently expected was moved to a private room to avoid troubling other patients, and bodies were not removed from these rooms during visiting hours to avoid upsetting visitors.

There was, however, a difference between the charity and private hospitals in regard to the presence of family and friends at the dying patient's bedside. At the private hospital, relatives were considered entitled to be present at the bedside at the moment of death. The dying person did not preside over the gathering as in the traditional death ritual; nonetheless, the experience of death was not as solitary as it was in the charity hospital. Dying patients were shielded from relatives at the charity hospital in order to minimize disruption of hospital routine and processing of the body. The justification for this action was in terms of protecting the relatives from the "unpleasantness of seeing someone die." Family members were urged by the staff to go home and await further news if death was regarded as imminent or, at least, to wait in waiting rooms or in the corridors and not in the patient's room. The result was that relatives were usually not present at the time of death and were summoned only after the staff had completed its processing duties.

Awareness Contexts

Glaser and Strauss developed a typology of awareness contexts based upon both participant observation and personal interviews in six hospitals in the San Francisco Bay area. These awareness contexts—closed awareness, suspected awareness, mutual pretense awareness, and open awareness—were all derived from observing the social settings and the control of information about dying in the hospital. Glaser and Strauss found that the physicians were reluctant to disclose impending death to the patient, and nurses were not expected to do so without the consent of the responsible physician. Thus, patients were generally required to take action in order to get information about the extent of their illness and were often prevented from asking questions about dying by the staff. Awareness contexts were not relevant if the patient was comatose, an infant, someone whose knowledge of death was not important to the staff, or in emergency situations. Awareness contexts pertained when the patient was conscious and the staff managed knowledge of the patient's dying.

Closed awareness is a social condition where the staff knows the patient is dying but the patient is unaware of that fact. It is based upon the following structural conditions: (1) inability of the patient to recognize the signs of dying; (2) reluctance of the staff to discuss dying with the patient; (3) reluctance of family members to discuss the patient's condition with the patient; (4) organization of the hospital itself, which is designed to conceal information and records, and the skill of the hospital staff at not disclosing information; and (5) lack of anyone to help the patient find out the facts, including other patients. When any of the above conditions was lacking, then other awareness contexts were possible. *Suspected awareness* is a situation in which the patient is suspicious but does not know that an illness is terminal. The patient is then forced to draw information from whatever sources are available to confirm his or her suspicions. *Mutual pretense* is a somewhat more comfortable situation; the patient is aware of a terminal condition and refuses to talk about it, and the staff is under no obligation to discuss dying. This arrangement usually worked to contain emotions unless either party to the interaction broke down while trying to maintain the pretense. *Open awareness* is a condition in which everyone knows and openly acknowledges the terminal situation. The patient is held responsible for his or her behavior and is expected by the staff to face death with dignity, to sustain responsibilities to family and friends, and to cooperate with the staff. This last condition was most acceptable to the staff. Although there are no formal norms for the "ideal" death, Glaser and Strauss make the important point that people just can't help judging other people.

The Glaser and Strauss study differs somewhat from Sudnow's research because most of the patients observed by Glaser and Strauss were not comatose, paid for their own hospital care, and were of a higher social status. Unlike patients in the Sudnow study, they were in a better position to negotiate the dying process. Nevertheless, in both studies the staff saw death as inconvenient and managed interaction with the dying patient so as to minimize disruption.

Desensitizing Death: Coroners and Physicians

The implications of the Sudnow and the Glaser and Strauss studies contribute to an understanding of the social psychology of those persons whose occupations and professions require routine exposure to death. The findings of other attitudinal studies should also be noted. For example, Kathy Calkins Charmaz (1975) reported that county coroner's deputies employed self-protective strategies in order to avoid the emotion of the death scene and to maintain the routine character of their work (ascertaining the cause of death, establishing the identity of the deceased, protecting the property of the deceased, and locating the relatives of the deceased to whom the announcement of death could be made). In making the announcement to relatives, most deputies expressly avoided using the word "dead" and substituted the words "fatally injured" or "passed away," if they made any direct reference to death at all. Sometimes they just gave progressively meaningful cues in the conversation so that the relatives would realize what had happened and would themselves say the word "dead." The deputies were also prompt to turn the situation around by asking about funeral and burial arrangements, so that the responsibility for the occasion was thus symbolically shifted to the relatives.

According to Charmaz, one of the most striking features of the attitudes shown by the deputies was the extent to which they reflected typical cultural taboos. The deputies demonstrated an avoidance of death, were uncomfortable during the expression of grief by survivors, and showed an absence of personal philosophy either about death in general or about their own deaths in particular. Instead, they subjectively interpreted death as being a by-product of their work rather than the focus of it. This approach was exemplified by the comment of one deputy (Charmaz, 1975:304), who stated: "That's not a body lying there. It's an *investigation*. You have to look at it as an investigation, not as a person lying there." The deputies supported an occupational ideology that militated against their becoming involved in the situation on the grounds that they would then be unable to perform their work properly.

Studies of physician attitudes have found a similar reluctance to deal with the emotions surrounding death. In a study of over two hundred physicians on the staff of Michael Reese Hospital in Chicago, Donald Oken (1961) found that 90 percent of the doctors stated a preference for not telling cancer patients that their condition was terminal. In discussing their diagnosis with the patient, the use of euphemisms was the general rule. Patients would be told they had a "lesion," a "mass," or perhaps a "tumor," but terms like "cancer" and "malignancy" were avoided. Yet regardless of the patient's condition or the doctor's mode of discussing that condition, the doctor would invariably try to sustain and bolster the patient's hope of a recovery.

Despite this strong reluctance to level with a cancer patient, there was essentially unanimous agreement among the physicians that some family member must be told. Not only were legal and ethical considerations important in disclosing the diagnosis to some relevant person, but Oken believed that there was also a strong need on the part of the physician to share the burden of knowledge that someone was going to die.

The primary reason cited by the doctors for not wanting to tell the patients they had terminal cancer was "clinical experience." "Clinical experience" consisted of the opinion of the physicians that most people did not want to know, that they know already, or that they should not be told so that they would not give up or become depressed. However, Oken found that the real determinant for avoiding the disclosure of a terminal diagnosis was an emotion-laden, a priori judgment related to a fear of how the patient would react to the information (become angry, commit suicide) and the physician's underlying feelings of pessimism and futility about cancer.

Oken further explained that the physicians interviewed generally agreed that patients feared cancer because its diagnosis was equated with suffering and certain death. What was impressive was that the physicians themselves felt very much the same way and these feelings were in conflict with their strong desire to prevent suffering and save lives. Oken stated:

> Situations of this kind, associated with intense charges of unpleasant emotions, call forth a variety of psychological defenses which reduce the intensity of feelings to manageable proportions. Among such defenses are those which involve the avoidance, negation, or denial of the existence of some unpleasant fact, and acting as if it were not real.[6]

Robert Coombs and Pauline Powers (1975) have characterized medical school and the teaching hospital as the locale in which medical students and physicians learn to cope with death in an objective manner (while at the same time denying its subjective implications). Coombs and Powers identified five developmental stages in this process: (1) idealizing the doctor's role, (2) desensitizing death symbols, (3) objectifying and combating death, (4) questioning the medical model, and (5) dealing with personal feelings. In the initial stage, medical students tend to demonstrate the same emotional attitudes toward death that are common among laypersons; for example, they found the "coolness" of the qualified physician's approach to death to be "offensive." Nevertheless, they generally realized that they themselves needed to control their emotions about death if they were to become good physicians. In the second stage, they began to become desensitized to the symbols of death as a result of their experience dissecting cadavers, attending autopsies, and working in the pathology laboratory. In addition, they began to acquire the knowledge and medical terminology that allowed them to adopt an intellectual perspective toward disease. The third stage of objectifying and combating death came when the medical students started

6 Donald Oken, "What to Tell Cancer Patients: A Study of Medical Attitudes," *Journal of the American Medical Association*, 175 (April 1961), 1127.

working in the hospital and were exposed to dead and dying patients. They realized more fully at this time the necessity of detaching themselves from the trauma associated with death in order to protect themselves from their own personal feelings and be able to work effectively as a doctor. An important desensitizing technique at this time, which was modeled by the clinical faculty, was the student's denial of the subjective features of death. Coombs and Powers explained it this way:

> In other words, the clinician learns to view dying patients not as people with feelings, but as medical entities, specimens, or objects of scientific interest. By adopting a scientific frame of mind, utilized so effectively in their previous work with dead bodies, clinicians can effectively avoid the uncomfortable inner feelings which occur when they are exposed to dying patients.[7]

Some (but apparently not all) of the medical students and physicians in the Coombs and Powers study experienced a fourth stage of socialization to death which questioned the medical model. As they perceived it, the medical (scientific) model of treatment tended to dehumanize patients and to define doctors as little more than technicians. From this perspective, it became unrealistic to think that all patients could be cured; thus in some cases it might be inappropriate to prolong life unnecessarily. Some physicians apparently did not experience this fourth stage; their ego was easily inflated when they were cast in the role of a healer who had powers over death. "When his self-esteem was involved," stated Coombs and Powers (1975:262-263), "it is imperative that he prevent death from occurring, for death makes him feel vulnerable. But if he can keep the 'corpse' alive for a few more days or weeks, his mastery over death is demonstrated." This so-called "God complex," regarded by many physicians as incompatible with good medical practice, was nonetheless an observable phenomenon.

What socialization had generally accomplished up to the time of the fifth stage of dealing with their own personal feelings about death was that the doctors had been conditioned to repress their personal anxieties and fears. However, Coombs and Powers (1975:263-264) found: "Our interviews with physicians revealed rather dramatically how much repressed emotionality exists among medical practitioners." When pressed to discuss their own feelings about death, several of the physicians revealed serious psychological problems. One interviewer noted that the interviews were becoming increasingly difficult because the physicians were having a "horrible time" discussing death and dying, both on a

---

[7] Robert H. Coombs and Pauline S. Powers, "Socialization for Death: The Physician's Role," *Urban Life,* 4 (October 1975), 258.

professional and a personal level. The most common strategy employed by the physicians to cope with their own fears was that of avoidance. In a comment reminiscent of the Sudnow (1967) and Glaser and Strauss (1965) studies, Coombs and Powers stated:

> Typically every effort is made in the hospital to shield oneself from mourning relatives. In the emergency room quiet crying is tolerated, but if any kind of emotional outburst occurs, relatives are usually hustled off to the chapel as fast as possible. "We isolate them so that their grief is not so obvious," a physician said. "It isn't done cruelly, but, frankly, it is done more to protect the emergency room staff than to help the family."[8]

What is suggested by the Charmaz (1975), Oken (1961), and Coombs and Powers (1975) studies is a tendency of persons who confront death regularly to develop a self-protective psychology, which consists of a behavioral and cognitive pattern of avoidance and negation of the death experience through the process of objectification. Dead and dying persons come to be defined as "cases" or "investigations" rather than as people. Meanwhile, personal fears and anxieties about the subjective meaning of death are suppresed. The objectification of death is justified on the grounds that the professional be able to carry on—"do a good job." Yet despite an outward appearance of control over emotions, both Oken and Coombs and Powers report that the process does not always function smoothly and some physicians do experience a considerable amount of subjective stress about death.

CHANGING ATTITUDES TOWARD DEATH

Death in the wider context of American society has not been socially disruptive because, as Robert Blauner (1966) explained, the impact of death has been controlled through bureaucratization. Hospitals care for the terminally ill and manage the crisis of dying; mortuaries attend to the problem of disposal of the dead and the transition ritual of the funeral. The handling of death by these specialists and the isolation of the dying experience in hospitals and nursing homes has minimized the average person's exposure to death.[9] Blauner describes the modern hospital as a "mass reduction" system because it tends to reduce the individuality of its dying patients. Yet, as Blauner has noted, this system cannot be fully achieved because of the tension between death and a bureauc-

---

[8] *Ibid.*, p. 265.

[9] Dumont and Foss (1972) estimate that the average American experiences a death in his family once every twenty years.

racy. Bureaucracies are committed to routine and unemotional administrative procedures. Death, on the other hand, is laden with considerable
emotionality, not only the deep-rooted fear of one's own dying, but also
the grief and bereavement of survivors which can elicit some of the
strongest emotions of human existence. No matter how much effort and
control is exerted by a society to contain and routinize death and dying
through bureaucratic procedures, such procedures are not in themselves
satisfying alternatives for handling a strongly emotional and inevitable
event.[10]

Attitudes toward death in American society have reached the point
of change. The fundamental cause of this change is the recognition of the
failure of efforts to hide and deny the process of dying, which had resulted
from death becoming a depersonalizing and lonely experience. The humanistic approach appears to be slowly but steadily returning. Also, as
Diana Crane (1975a, 1975b) has observed, there is an increasing desire to
exert autonomy in areas where formerly the individual had allowed others
to make decisions. Consequently, many individuals desire not only to control their own life, but also their own death and the factors contributing
to it. Furthermore, Crane notes that the development of certain life-
sustaining machines and techniques, such as dialysis for kidney disease
and organ transplantation, have stimulated questions about the use of
medical technologly and the quality of the lives that are thus prolonged.

There is considerable evidence to support the contention that attitudes toward death in American society are changing. In just the last few
years there has been a tremendous amount of material on death produced and presented in the mass media, particularly in the form of
books. Colleges, universities, and schools of medicine, nursing, and public
health are adding courses on the social and psychological aspects of
death. Ten years ago, practically none of these courses existed; in fact,
medical schools offered courses dealing only with clinical facets of death.
There has also been recognition in the last few years that large general
hospitals have not been very good places to die. In order to cope with this
problem, numerous clinics and seminars have been established to train in-
service hospital personnel to handle dying patients more humanely. One

10 In studies of two retirement communities, Victor Marshall (1975a, 1975b) found that
the residents of one particular community (Glen Brae) organized themselves as a community of dying to legitimatize death as an appropriate (although not always positive)
event because they had "lived their lives." The residents were able to socialize each
other to their impending deaths through frequent conversations about it and the
presence of role models with which to anticipate their own dying. All in all, when
a death occurred, the residents of Glen Brae managed a "low-key" approach to the
way in which that death was observed. Marshall agreed with Arlie Hochschild (1973)
that individuals are better able to face their deaths if they can observe, in a kind of a
role-modeling process, that the deaths of others take place within a taken-for-granted
framework.

particular approach is to encourage physicians and nurses to deal with the reality of their own deaths and their own personal philosophies about life and death. If health practitioners are unable to change the medical outcome of a disease, yet have faced the possibility of their own deaths, then it is believed that they can perhaps be supportive of the dying patient in that patient's search for meaning during the remaining portion of his or her life (see also Coombs and Powers, 1975).

Crane (1975a:10) has summarized changing attitudes toward death as providing the context for the emergence of a loosely coordinated, norm-oriented social movement with two major goals: (1) improvement in the quality of interaction between dying persons and those who come into contact with them and (2) enactment of legislation to support the patient's right to refuse treatment. In line with this second goal, there is growing interest in euthanasia, as evidenced by increasing numbers of persons who have joined organizations advocating the legality of "mercy killing."

In 1973 the American Hospital Association approved a patient's "bill of rights" which included the provision for the patient to be able to choose death by rejecting lifesaving treatment.[11] A 1974 Gallup Poll showed that 53 percent of those polled, compared to a response rate of 35 percent in 1950, approved of the physician being allowed to induce painless death for an incurable patient if requested by both the patient and the patient's family. Most of the respondents responsible for this shift in public opinion were young and college-educated.

However, the legality of directly ending a life is highly questionable. In the widely publicized Karen Ann Quinlan case of 1975–76, the parents of a comatose girl sued the hospital and physicians attending their daughter in order to require them to cease their life-prolonging measures in a hopeless situation. There was medical evidence that Miss Quinlan had suffered brain damage thought to be due to the combined effects of alcohol and sleeping pills (exactly what happened has never been fully determined) and was not likely to ever regain consciousness. The hospital staff refused to cease treatment and deliberately allow their patient to die. Eventually the parents won the right to have their daughter removed from the hospital to a nursing home, where the parents had the choice whether or not to continue extraordinary life-prolonging measures. This case illustrates the moral and legal differences between directly killing a patient or allowing the patient to die by

[11] Crane (1975a, 1975b) has found that physicians themselves may decide whether or not to "actively" treat a patient. The criteria used, however, were more social than physiological, since those patients defined as most treatable were those the physicians judged to be capable of engaging in meaningful social interaction.

withholding lifesaving treatment. On a moral level there might be a distinction between directly killing a dying patient or simply stopping treatment. But in either case, the result is the same in that the patient dies (Veatch, 1972).

At the core of this dilemma is the position of the physician, who has a special ethical duty to preserve life. So long as the patient is legally competent to make a decision to die, then it is arguable that the patient has the right to do so. But what happens when the patient is not legally competent by virtue of being comatose or insensible due to pain or drugs? At the present time there is no answer to this question and no policy, other than the decision of a physician to terminate treatment made on a case-by-case basis. Robert Veatch (1972) suggests that the best policy would be legislation based upon the right of a patient to refuse treatment. If the patient is not competent, an agent, such as the next-of-kin, could be appointed to make the decision on the patient's behalf to authorize cessation of treatment. The physician would therefore be protected from having to make a moral (and nonmedical) judgment about what is best for the patient, and the responsibility would accrue instead to the family or some court-appointed agent who would be regarded as representing the patient's interest. Veatch (1972:10) says, "At some time the decision must be made that the dying process has been tampered with long enough and that there is nothing more that man can or should do."

In contrast, supporters of the "hospice" concept insist that the right to die involves a corresponding duty to kill and that euthanasia should not be allowed. Instead, the hospice, a hospital that specializes in the care of the terminally ill, offers an alternative approach. Tried with some success in Great Britain and currently being introduced in the United States, the hospice involves a complete change in the priorities of the physician and nurse. The aim is no longer to cure the patient, but to make the patient more comfortable and his or her dying days more meaningful. The hospice stresses companionship, sense of security, and control of physical symptoms through medical and nursing techniques. The control of pain is very important in order to allow the patient to be as active as possible for as long as possible.

Because modern society has attempted to be more open and intellectual concerning death does not mean that the fear and anxiety of dying can be rationalized away. It simply suggests that the process of dying may become less impersonal and dehumanizing. Perhaps death in the future will return to a modern version of Ariés' notion of "tamed death." In the final analysis, however, death will probably remain an experience characterized by various forms of fear.

SUMMARY

This chapter has examined death and dying from the perspective of both the individual and society. The primary problem death presents for society is that of coping with the fear of death, particularly fear of the experience itself and of its consequences. While everyone has difficulty in managing these fears, most persons eventually reach a stage of acceptance of death.

Presently, death is contained by the larger social system in hospitals, nursing homes, and mortuaries by specialists who ensure that death is not disruptive for society. The result of these practices has been the dehumanization of death in modern society; evidence is now beginning to mount, however, that attitudes in American society are evolving toward a more humanistic interpretation of the dying experience.

EPILOGUE

This book has discussed basic social issues confronting American medicine today. By necessity, much of the material was framed within a social problems context. The reason for this, quite simply, is two-fold: *medicine is both a solution and a cause of many social and individual problems.*

The paradox inherent in this statement derives from the medical profession (with society's blessing) having assumed an ever increasing responsibility for control of a wide variety of social concerns. Physicians not only actively intervene in identifiable disease processes such as atherosclerosis, cancer, and diabetes, but they also deal with complaints not necessarily associated with disease—for example, dangerousness, hyperactive behavior in school, anxiety related to being in love, and television programming for children. There are few areas of daily life not touched by a medical opinion intended to make that life better. Conversely, medicine itself is a social problem as a result of a combination of several negative factors—failure to provide quality care or even adequate care to all segments of society, high cost of health services, maldistribution of these services, and a tendency toward impersonalization in the physician-patient relationship.

Attempts to change the existing structure of health care delivery in the United States have met with strong resistance from organized medicine. Such change threatens not only the fee-for-service or profit-making aspect of medical practice in a free enterprise system, but also might diminish the professional control physicians currently enjoy over their own work and the work of a vast health care industry. Unfortunately, an adversary relationship between the medical profession and some elements of the general public has developed, as evidenced by the rise in malpractice litigation, public demand for national health insurance, and public outrage over the high cost of health care. This has been exacerbated by cases of fraud perpetrated by physicians in Medicare and Medicaid overpayments. Statements such as one made as recently as 1977 by a leading official of the American Medical Association that physicians alone should make decisions regarding health care delivery because the public is unable to understand the complexity of the situation, only serve to underscore a growing credibility gap between the medical profession and the lay public.

Regardless of the position of organized medicine, current trends (as noted in Chapter Six) point toward substantial modification of the physician's role in the future. The power dependency role of the physician-patient will most likely be changed into more of a provider-consumer relationship. The emergence of paramedical practitioners like the physician's assistant and the nurse practitioner may further modify the physician's professional dominance as these occupations assume an increasing share of responsibility for primary medical care. However, it is unlikely that any radical change is forthcoming that would limit the physician's ability to perform effectively in the provision of medical services.

By and large, physicians appear to be dedicated, hard-working individuals whose highest priority is the welfare of their patients. American medicine has produced technology and expertise second to none in the quality and quantity of health care it is capable of delivering to society. Disenchantment with the medical profession refers not so much to the quality of its work (although errors are sometimes made—as they are in all professions), but to the inequality and expense of existing services and the growing suspicion that organized medicine does not always place the public interest ahead of professional interest.

On the other hand, even if quality health care becomes readily available to all Americans, we may be reaching a point of diminishing returns in health care expenditures. At present, much of the money invested in medical research is spent on ailments like heart disease, cancer, and stroke, which are primarily diseases of old age. If, in fact, these diseases could be eliminated from society, how much would life expectancy be increased? Some estimates are that, at most, only one or two years would be added to the average life span. The human body supposedly has a natural limit on longevity, thought to be about seventy-seven years for most people—even if optimal health conditions exist. Thus, there is a point when the body is going to succumb to the degenerative effects of aging, whether cancer or otherwise; that is, the body just wears out.

Assuming that quality health care is available, what may become more significant for increasing life expectancy in the future than medical technology alone is the effect of life style (urbanization, interpersonal relations, occupational pressures) , and physical environment (pollution) on health. This confirms the inescapable notion that medicine is indeed a social science, as advocated by the eminent nineteenth-century German pathologist Rudolf Virchow.

Good health is one of the most cherished benefits available to humankind and good health is based upon an intricate relationship between mind, body, and the social and physical environment. This is why knowledge of the principles of sociology, psychology, and anthropology is essential in the practice of contemporary medicine. Accordingly, the contribution of the social sciences to medicine represents tremendous potential for the improvement of life and the treatment of socially related disorders. What makes people sick, how they experience being sick, and what they do about it are all bound up in the prevailing social and cultural expectations of behavior and definitions of disease. Research and theory development are needed. The medical sociologist is in the enviable position of participating in and influencing the course of an exciting, challenging, and important field whose application to human life can provide beneficial results.

BIBLIOGRAPHY

ACKER, JOAN.
  1973 "Women and social stratification: A case of intellectual sexism."
  American Journal of Sociology, 78 (January) :936–945.
ADAY, LOU ANN.
  1976 "The impact of health policy on access to medical care." *Milbank
  Memorial Fund Quarterly,* 54 (Spring) :215–233.
ALEXANDER, FRANZ G., and SHELDON T. SELESNICK.
  1966 *The history of psychiatry.* New York: Mentor.
ALFORD, ROBERT R.
  1975 *Health care politics.* Chicago: University of Chicago Press.
ALLEN, MICHAEL A., and MICHELLE TOLLIVIER.
  1974 "Medical delivery system for urban Indians: Consumer and providers'
  perceptions." Paper presented to the Southwestern and Rocky Mountain
  Division of the American Association for the Advancement of Science
  Meeting, April, 1974, Laramie, Wyoming.
ALSOP, STEWART.
  1973 *Stay of execution.* Philadelphia: J. B. Lippincott.
ALVAREZ, W. C.
  1931 "How early do physicians diagnose cancer of the stomach in themselves?" *Journal of the American Medical Association,* 97 (July 11) :77–83.
AMERICAN MEDICAL ASSOCIATION.
  1951 *Guide to services.* Chicago: AMA.
  1973 *Measuring physician manpower.* Chicago: AMA
ANDERSEN, RONALD, and J. JOEL MAY.
  1972 "Factors associated with increased costs of hospital care." *The Annals
  of the American Academy of Political and Social Science,* 401 (January) :
  62–72.

ANDERSON, JAMES G., and DAVID E. BARTKUS.
1973 "Choice of medical care: A behavioral model of health and illness behavior." *Journal of Health and Social Behavior,* 14 (December): 348–362.

ANDERSON, ODIN W., and RONALD M. ANDERSEN.
1972 *"Patterns of use of health services."* pp. 386–406 in *Handbook of medical sociology,* 2nd ed., H. Freeman, S. Levine, and L. Reeder (eds.). Englewood Cliffs, N.J.: Prentice–Hall, Inc.

ANDERSON, O. W., and P. B. SHEATSLEY.
1967 *Hospital use—A survey of patients' and physicians' decisions.* Research Series No. 24. Chicago: University of Chicago Center for Health Administration Studies.

ANTHONY, SYLVIA.
1968 "The child's idea of death," pp. 315–328 in *The world of the child,* Toby Talbot (ed.). New York: Anchor.
1972 *The discovery of death in childhood and after.* New York: Basic Books.

ANTONOVSKY, AARON.
1972 "Social class, life expectancy and overall mortality," pp. 5–30 in *Patients, physicians and illness,* 2nd ed., E. Gartly Jaco (ed.). New York: Free Press.

APPEL, JAMES Z.
1970 "Health care delivery," pp. 141–166 in *The health of Americans,* B. Jones (ed.). Englewood Cliffs, N.J.: Prentice-Hall, Inc.

APPLE, DORRIAN.
1960 "How laymen define illness." *Journal of Health and Social Behavior,* 1 (Fall):219–225.

ARIÉS, PHILIPPE.
1974 *Western attitudes toward death.* Trans. P. M. Ranum. Baltimore: Johns Hopkins University Press.

ATCHLEY, ROBERT C.
1972 *The social forces in later life.* Belmont, Cal.: Wadsworth.
1976 "Selected social and psychological differences between men and women in later life." *Journal of Gerontology,* 31 (March):204–211.

AUSUBEL, D. P.
1961 "Personality disorder is a disease." *American Psychologist,* 16 (February):69–74.

BACK, KURT W., and MORTON D. BOGDONOFF.
1964 "Plasma lipid responses to leadership, conformity, and deviation," pp. 24–42 in *Psychological approaches to social behavior,* P. Leiderman and D. Shapiro (eds.). Stanford: Stanford University Press.

BANDURA, ALBERT.
1969 *Principles of behavior modification.* New York: Holt, Rinehart, and Winston.

BARRON M. L. (ed.).
1961 *The aging american.* New York: Crowell.

BATES, BARBARA.
1970 "Doctor and nurse: Changing roles and relations." *New England Journal of Medicine,* 283 (July 16):129–134.

BAUMANN, BARBARA.
1961 "Diversities in conceptions of health and physical fitness." *Journal of Health and Social Behavior,* 2 (Spring):39–46.

BECKER, HOWARD S.
   1963 *Outsiders: Studies in the sociology of deviance.* New York: Free Press.
   1973 "Labeling theory reconsidered," pp. 177–208 in *Outsiders: Studies in the sociology of deviance,* 2nd ed. New York: Free Press.
BECKER, HOWARD S., and BLANCHE GREER.
   1958 "The fate of idealism in medical school." *American Sociological Review,* 23 (February) :50–56.
BECKER, HOWARD S., BLANCHE GREER, EVERETT C. HUGHES, and ANSELM STRAUSS.
   1961 *Boys in white: Student culture in medical school.* Chicago: University of Chicago Press.
BECKER, MARSHALL H. (ed.).
   1974 *The health belief model and personal health behavior.* San Francisco: Society for Public Health Education, Inc.
BECKER, MARSHALL H., and LOIS A. MAIMAN.
   1975 "Sociobehavioral determinants of compliance with health and medical care recommendations." *Medical Care,* 13 (January) :10–24.
BECKER, S., and G. GORDON.
   1966 "The entrepreneurial theory of formal organizations, part I: Patterns of formal organization. *Administrative Science Quarterly,* 2, no. 3:315–344.
BELLIN, SEYMOUR S., and H. JACK GEIGER.
   1972 "The impact of a neighborhood health center on a patient's behavior and attitudes relating to health care: A study of low income housing." *Medical Care,* 10 (May-June) :224–239.
BENGTSON, VERN L.
   1973 *The social psychology of aging.* New York: Bobbs-Merrill.
BENOLIEL, JEANNE Q.
   1975 "The realities of work: Commentary on Howard Leventhal's information-processing model," pp. 175–188 in *Humanizing health care,* J. Howard and A. Strauss (eds.). New York: Wiley-Interscience.
BEN-SIRA, ZEER.
   1976 "The function of the professional's affective behavior in client satisfaction: A revised approach to social interaction theory." *Journal of Health and Social Behavior,* 17 (March) :3–11.
BERGER, EDWARD J.
   1974 "Health and health services in the United States: A perspective and discussion of some issues." *Annals of Internal Medicine* 80: 645–650.
BERGER, PETER L., and THOMAS LUCKMANN.
   1967 *The social construction of reality.* New York: Anchor.
BERKANOVIC, EMIL.
   1972 "Lay conceptions of the sick role." *Social Forces,* 51 (September) : 53–63.
BERKANOVIC, EMIL, and LEO G. REEDER.
   1974 "Can money buy the appropriate use of services? Some notes on the meaning of utilization data." *Journal of Health and Social Behavior,* 15 (June) :93–99.
BERRY, RALPH E., JR.
   1974 "Cost and efficiency in the production of hospital services." *Milbank Memorial Fund Quarterly,* 52 (Summer) :291–314.
BICE, T. W., R. L. EICHHORN, and P. D. FOX.
   1972 "Socioeconomic status and use of physician services: A reconsideration." *Medical Care,* 10 (May-June) :261–271.

BINGER, C. M., A. R. ABLIN, R. C. FEUERSTEIN, J. KUSHNER, S. ZOGER, and C. MIKKELSEN.
1969 "Childhood leukemia: Emotional impact on patient and family." *New England Journal of Medicine*, 280 (February 20) :414–418.

BIRREN, JAMES F.
1964 *The psychology of aging*. Englewood Cliffs, N.J.: Prentice-Hall, Inc.

BLACKWELL, LOUISE.
1967 "Upper middle class adult expectations about entering the sick role for physical and psychiatric dysfunctions." *Journal of Health and Social Behavior*, 8 (June) :83–95.

BLAUNER, ROBERT.
1966 "Death and social structure." *Psychiatry*, 29 (November) :378–394.

BLOOM, SAMUEL W.
1963 *The doctor and his patient*. New York: Free Press.
1973 *Power and dissent in the medical school*. New York. Free Press.

BOOCOCK, SARANE S.
1972 *An introduction to the sociology of learning*. New York: Houghton Mifflin.

BOURNE, PETER.
1970 *Men, stress, and Vietnam*. Boston: Little, Brown.

BOWDEN, CHARLES L., and ALVIN G. BURSTEIN.
1974 *Psychosocial basis of medical practice*. Baltimore: Williams & Wilkins.

BOWMAN, ROSEMARY AMASON, and REBECCA CLARK CULPEPPER.
1974 "Rx for change." *American Journal of Nursing*, 74 (June) :1054–1056.

BRADY, JOHN P.
1975 "Behavior therapy," pp. 1824–1831 in *Comprehensive textbook of psychiatry*, Vol. II, 2nd ed., A Freedman, H. Kaplan, and B. Sadock (eds.). Baltimore: Williams & Wilkins.

BRAGINSKY, B. M., D. BRAGINSKY, and K. RING.
1969 *Methods of madness: The mental hospital as a last resort*. New York: Holt, Rinehart, and Winston.

BROWN, ESTHER L.
1966 "Nursing and patient care," pp. 176–203 in *The nursing profession*, F. Davis (ed.). New York: Wiley.

BUNKER, JOHN P.
1970 "Surgical manpower: A comparison of operations and surgeons in the United States and in England and Wales." *New England Journal of Medicine*, 282 (January 15) :135–144.

BURGER, EDWARD J.
1974 "Health and health services in the United States." *Annals of Internal Medicine*, 80:645–650.

BURROW, JAMES G.
1963 *AMA: Voice of American medicine*. Baltimore: Johns Hopkins University Press.

CANNON, WALTER B.
1932 *The wisdom of the body*. New York: Norton.

CARP, FRANCES M.
1968 "Some components of disengagement." *Journal of Gerontology,* 23 (July) :382–386.

CARTWRIGHT, ANN.
1964 *Human relations and hospital care.* London: Routledge and Kegan Paul.

CHALFANT, H. PAUL, and RICHARD KURTZ.
1971 "Alcoholics and the sick role: Assessments by social workers." *Journal of Health and Social Behavior,* 12 (March) :66–72.

CHARMAZ, KATHY C.
1975 "The coroner's strategies for announcing death." *Urban Life,* 4 (October) : 296–316.

CLARK, MARGARET.
1959 *Health in the Mexican-American culture.* Berkeley: University of California Press.

CLAUSEN, JOHN A.
1975 *"Sociology and psychiatry,"* pp. 373–382 in *Comprehensive textbook of psychiatry,* Vol. I, 2nd ed., A. Freedman, H. Kaplan, and B. Sadock (eds.). Baltimore: Williams & Wilkins.

CLAUSEN, JOHN A., and CAROL L. HUFFINE.
1975 "Sociocultural and social/psychological factors affecting social responses to mental disorder." *Journal of Health and Social Behavior,* 16 (December) :405–420.

COCKERHAM, WILLIAM C.
1975 "Drinking attitudes and practices among Wind River Reservation Indian youth." *Journal of Studies on Alcohol,* 36 (March) :321–326.
1977 "Patterns of alcohol and multiple drug use among rural white and American Indian adolescents." *International Journal of the Addictions,* 12 (2-3) :271–285.

COCKERHAM, WILLIAM C., MORRIS A. FORSLUND, and ROLLAND M. RABOIN.
1976 "Drug use among white and American Indian high school youth." *Interntional Journal of the Addictions,* 11 (2) :209–220.

COE, RODNEY M.
1970 *Sociology of medicine.* New York: McGraw-Hill.

COE, RODNEY M., and LEONARD FICHTENBAUM.
1972 "Utilization of physician assistants: Some implications for medical practice." *Medical Care,* 10 (Nov.-Dec.) :497–504.

COHEN, ROSALIE.
1974 "Neglected legal dilemmas in community psychiatry," pp. 69–82 in *Sociological perspectives on community mental health,* P. Roman and H. Trice (eds.). Philadelphia: F. A. Davis.

COLE, STEPHEN, and ROBERT LEJEUNE.
1972 "Illness and the legitimation of failure." *American Sociological Review,* 37 (June) :347–356.

COLUMBOTOS, JOHN.
1969 "Social origins and ideology of physicians: A study of the effects of early socialization." *Journal of Health and Social Behavior,* 10 (March) : 16–29.

COOLEY, CHARLES H.
1962 *Social organization.* New York: Schoken.
1964 *Human nature and the social order.* New York: Schocken.

COOMBS, ROBERT H., and PAULINE S. POWERS.
1975 "Socialization for death: The physician's role." *Urban Life,* 4 (October) :250–271.
COSER, ROSE L.
1956 "A home away from home." *Social Problems,* 4 (July) :3–17.
1958 "Authority and decision-making in a hospital." *American Sociological Review,* 23 (February) :56–63.
CRANE, DIANA.
1975a *The sanctity of social life: Physicians' treatment of critically ill patients.* New York: Russell Sage.
1975b "Decision to treat critically ill patients: A comparison of social versus medical considerations." *Milbank Memorial Fund Quarterly,* 53 (Winter) :1–34.
CREDITOR, MORTON C.
1971 "If doctors owned the hospitals." *New England Journal of Medicine,* 284 (January) :134–139.
CROOG, SYDNEY H., and DONNA F. VER STEEG.
1972 *"The hospital as a social system,"* pp. 274–314 in *Handbook of medical sociology,* H. Freeman, S. Levine, and L. Reeder (eds.) . Englewood Cliffs, N.J.: Prentice-Hall, Inc.
CUMMING, ELAINE, and WILLIAM E. HENRY.
1961 *Growing old: The process of disengagement.* New York: Basic Books.
DANIELS, M. J.
1960 "Affect and its control in the medical intern." *American Journal of Sociology,* 61 (November) :259–267.
DAVIS, FRED.
1966 "Problems and issues in collegiate nursing education," pp. 138–175 in *The nursing profession,* F. Davis (ed.) . New York: Wiley.
1972 *Illness, interaction, and the self.* Belmont, Cal.: Wadsworth.
DAVIS, FRED, and VIRGINIA OLESEN.
1963 "Initiation into a women's profession: Identity problems in the status transition of coed to student nurse." *Sociometry,* 26 (March) : 89–101.
DAVIS, KAREN.
1975a *National health insurance.* Washington, D.C.: The Brookings Institution.
1975b "Equal treatment and unequal benefits: The Medicare Program." *Milbank Memorial Fund Quarterly,* 53 (Fall) :449–488.
DAVIS, KINGSLEY, and WILBERT MOORE.
1945 "Some principles of stratification." *American Sociological Review,* 10 (April) :242–249.
DAWBER, THOMAS R., WILLIAM B. KANNEL, and LORNA P. LYELL.
1963 "An approach to longitudinal studies in the community: The Framingham study." *Annals of the New York Academy of Sciences,* 107:539–566.
DEBUSKEY, M. (ed.) .
1970 *The chronically ill child and his family.* Springfield, Ill.: Thomas.
DENZIN, NORMAN K.
1968 "The self-fulfilling prophecy and patient-therapist interaction," pp. 349–358 in *The mental patient: Studies in the sociology of deviance,* S. Spitzer and N. Denzin (eds.) . New York: McGraw-Hill.

DeWolff, P., and J. Meerdink.
    1954 "Mortality rates in Amsterdam according to profession," pp. 53–55 in Proceedings of the World Population Conference, Vol. I. New York: United Nations.
Dodge, David L., and Walter T. Martin.
    1970 *Social stress and chronic illness.* South Bend, Ind.: University of Notre Dame Press.
Dohrenwend, Barbara S.
    1973 "Life events as stressors: A methodological inquiry." *Journal of Health and Social Behavior,* 14 (June) :167–175.
    1975 "Group differences in the anticipation and control of stressful life events." Paper presented at the Conference of the Society for Life History Research in Psychopathology, University of Rochester Medical School, Rochester, New York, May 21–23.
Dohrenwend, Bruce P.
    1974 "Problems in defining and sampling the relevant population of stressful life events," pp. 275–310 in *Stressful life events: Their nature and effects,* B. S. Dohrenwend and B. P. Dohrenwend (eds.). New York: Wiley.
    1975 "Sociocultural and social-psychological factors in the genesis of mental disorders." *Journal of Health and Social Behavior,* 16 (December) : 365–392.
Dohrenwend, Bruce P., and Barbara Snell Dohrenwend.
    1969 *Social status and psychological disorders.* New York: Wiley.
    1974 "Social and cultural influences on psychopathology." *Annual Review of Psychology,* 25:417–452.
    1975 "The conceptualization and measurement of stressful life events: An overview of the issues." Paper presented at the Conference of the Society for Life History Research in Psychopathology, University of Rochester Medical School, Rochester, New York, May 21-23.
    1976 "Sex differences and psychiatric disorder." *American Journal of Sociology,* 81 (May) :1447–1454.
Dozier, E.
    1966 "Problem drinking among American Indians." *Quarterly Journal of Studies on Alcohol,* 27 (March) :72–87.
Drevenstedt, Jean.
    1976 "Perceptions of onsets of young adulthood, middle age, and old age." *Journal of Gerontology,* 31 (January) :53–57.
DuBos, René
    1969 *Man, medicine, and environment.* New York: Mentor.
Duff, Raymond S., and August B. Hollingshead.
    1968 *Sickness and society.* New York: Harper & Row.
Dumont, Richard G., and Dennis C. Foss.
    1972 *The American view of death.* Cambridge, Mass.: Schenkman.
Durbin, Richard L., and W. Herbert Springall.
    1974 *Organization and administration of health care.* St. Louis, Mo.: Mosby.
Durkheim, Emile.
    1950 *The rules of sociological method.* New York: Free Press.
    1951 *Suicide.* New York: Free Press.
    1956 *The division of labor in society.* New York: Free Press.
    1961 *The elementary forms of religious life.* New York: Collier.

EASSON, W. M.
1970 *The dying child: The management of the child or adolescent who is dying.* Springfield, Ill.: Thomas.

EATON, WILLIAM W., Jr.
1974 "Medical hospitalization as a reinforcement process." *American Sociological Review,* 39 (April) :252–260.

ELAM, L.
1969 "What does the ghetto want from medicine?" pp. 33–42 in *Medicine in the ghetto,* J. C. Norman (ed.) . New York: Meredith.

ELDER, R. G.
1963 "What is the patient saying?" *Nursing Forum,* 2:25–37.

ELLING, RAY, and SANDOR HALEBSKY.
1961 "Organizational differentiation and support: A conceptual framework." *Administrative Science Quarterly,* 6 (September) :185–209.

ENGEL, GEORGE L.
1977 "The need for a new medical model: A challenge for biomedicine." *Science,* 196 (April 8) :129–135.

EVANS, A. E., and S. EDIN.
1968 "If a child must die." *New England Journal of Medicine,* 278 (January 18) :138–142.

EYSENCK, HANS J.
1961 "The effects of psychotherapy," pp. 697–725, *Handbook of abnormal psychology,* H. Eysenck (ed.) . New York: Basic Books.

FARIS, ROBERT E., and H. WARREN DUNHAM.
1939 *Mental disorders in urban areas.* Chicago: University of Chicago Press.

FBI.
1975 *Crime in the United States.* Washington, D.C.: U.S. Department of Justice.

FEIFEL, HERMAN, and ALLAN B. BRANSCOMB.
1973 "Who's afraid of death?" *Journal of Abnormal Psychology,* 81 (June) : 282–288.

FEIFEL, HERMAN, SUSAN HANSON, ROBERT JONES, and LAURI EDWARDS.
1967 "Physicians consider death." *Proceedings,* 75th Annual Convention, American Psychological Association.

FELDMAN, J.
1966 *The dissemination of health information.* Chicago: Aldine.

FISHBEIN, MORRIS.
1947 *A history of the American Medical Association, 1847–1947.* Philadelphia: W. B. Saunders.

FORBES, WILLIAM H.
1967 "Longevity and medical costs." *New England Journal of Medicine,* 277 (July 13) :71–78.

FOX, RENÉE.
1957 "Training for uncertainty," pp. 207–241 in *The student-physician,* R. K. Merton, G. Reader, and P. L. Kendall (eds.) . Cambridge, Mass Harvard University Press.
1974 "Is there a new medical student," pp. 197–220 in *Ethics of health care,* L. R. Tancredi, Washington, D.C.: National Academy of Sciences.

FREDERICKS, MARCEL A., PAUL MUNDY, and JOHN KOSA.

1974 "Willingness to serve: The medical profession and poverty programs." *Social Science and Medicine*, 8 (January) :51–57.

FREEBORN, DONALD K., and BENJAMIN J. DARSKY.

1974 "A Study of the power structure of the medical community." *Medical Care*, 12 (January) :1–12.

FREEMAN, HOWARD E., SOL LEVINE, and LEO G. REEDER.

1972 "Present status of medical sociology," pp. 501–522 in *Handbook of medical sociology*, 2nd ed., H. Freeman, S. Levine, and L. Reeder (eds.). Englewood Cliffs, N.J.: Prentice-Hall, Inc.

FREEMAN, HOWARD E., and OZZIE G. SIMMONS.

1961 "Feelings of stigma among relatives of former mental patients." *Social Problems*, 8:312–321.

1963 *The mental patient comes home.* New York: Wiley.

FREIDSON, ELIOT.

1960 "Client control and medical practice." *American Journal of Sociology*, 65 (January) :374–382.

1970a *Profession of medicine.* New York: Dodd, Mead.

1970b *Professional dominance.* Chicago: Aldine.

1975 *Doctoring together.* New York: Elsevier.

FREUD, SIGMUND.

1953–1966 *Standard edition of the complete psychological works of Sigmund Freud.* London: Hogarth Press.

FUCHS, ESTELLE, and ROBERT HAVIGHURST.

1972 *To live on this earth: American Indian education.* New York: Anchor.

FUCHS, VICTOR R.

1974 *Who shall live?* New York: Basic Books.

FUNKENSTEIN, DANIEL H.

1971 "Medical students, medical schools, and society during three eras," pp. 229–281 in *Psychosocial aspects of medical training*, R. H. Coombs and C. E. Vincent (eds.). Springfield, Ill.: Thomas.

GALVIN, MICHAEL L., and MARGARET FAN.

1975 "The utilization of physician's services in Los Angeles County, 1973." *Journal of Health and Social Behavior*, 16 (March) :75–94.

GEERTSEN, REED, MELVILLE R. KLAUBER, MARK RINDFLESH, ROBERT L. KANE, and ROBERT GRAY.

1975 "A re-examination of Suchman's views on social factors in health care utilization." *Journal of Health and Social Behavior*, 16 (June) :226–237.

GEIGER, H. JACK.

1975 "The causes of dehumanization in health care and prospects for humanization," pp. 11–36 in *Humanizing health care*, J. Howard and A. Strauss (eds.). New York: Wiley-Interscience.

GEORGOPOULOS, BASIL F., and FLOYD C. MANN.

1972 "The hospital as an organization," pp. 304–311 in *Patients, physicians and illness*, 2nd ed., E. Jaco (ed.). New York: Macmillan.

GERTH, H. H., and C. WRIGHT MILLS (eds.).

1946 *From Max Weber: Essays in sociology.* New York: Oxford University Press.

GIBBS, JACK.
  1971 "A critique of the labeling perspective," pp. 193–205 in *The study of social problems,* Earl Rubington and Martin S. Weinberg (eds.) . New York: Oxford University Press.
GIBSON, GEOFFREY, GEORGE BUGBEE, and ODIN W. ANDERSON.
  1970 *Emergency medical services in the Chicago area.* Chicago: University of Chicago, Center for Health Administration.
GLASER, BARNEY G., and ANSELM M. STRAUSS.
  1965 *Awareness of dying.* Chicago: Aldine.
  1968 *Time for dying.* Chicago: Aldine.
GOCHMAN, D. S.
  1971 "Some correlates of children's health care beliefs and potential behavior." *Journal of Health and Social Behavior,* 12 (June) :148–154.
GODDARD, JAMES L.
  1973 "The medical business," pp. 121–125 in *Life, death, and medicine,* San Francisco: W. H. Freeman.
GOFFMAN, ERVING.
  1959 *The presentation of self in everyday life.* New York: Anchor.
  1961 *Asylums.* New York: Anchor.
GOLDMAN, LEE.
  1974a "Doctors' attitudes toward national health insurance." *Medical Care,* 12 (May) :413–423.
  1974b "Physicians' medical and political attitudes." *Journal of Health and Social Behavior,* 3 (September) :177–187.
GOLDMAN, LEE, and A. EBBERT, JR.
  1973 "The fate of medical student liberalism: A prediction." *Journal of Medical Education,* 48 (December) :1095–1103.
GOLDSTEIN, ABRAHAM S.
  1967 *The insanity defense.* New Haven: Yale University Press.
GOODE, WILLIAM J.
  1957 "Community within a community." *American Sociological Review,* 22 (April) :194–200.
  1960 "Encroachment, charlatanism, and the emerging profession: Psychology, sociology, and medicine." *American Sociological Review,* 25 (December) : 902–914.
GOODRICH, CHARLES H., MARGARET C. OLENDZKI, and GEORGE G. READER.
  1972 *Welfare medical care: An experiment.* Cambridge, Mass.: Harvard University Press.
GORDON, GERALD.
  1966 *Role theory and illness.* New Haven: College and University Press.
GOSS, MARY E.
  1963 "Patterns of bureaucracy among hospital staff physicians," pp. 170–194 in *The Hospital in modern society,* E. Freidson (ed.) . New York: Free Press.
GOVE, WALTER A.
  1970 "Societal reaction as an explanation of mental illness: An evaluation." *American Sociological Review,* 35 (October) :873–884.
  1975 "The labelling theory of mental illness: A reply to Scheff." *American Sociological Review,* 40 (April) :242–248.

GOVE, WALTER R., and PATRICK HOWELL.
1974 "Individual resources and mental hospitalization: A comparison and evaluation of the societal reaction and psychiatric perspectives." *American Sociological Review,* 39 (February) :86–100.

GOVE, WALTER R., and JEANNETTE F. TUDOR.
1973 "Adult sex roles and mental illness." *American Journal of Sociology,* 78 (January) :812–835.

GRAHAM, DAVID, J. D. KABLER, and FRANCIS K. GRAHAM.
1962 "Physiological responses to the suggestion of attitudes specific for hives and hypertension." *Psychosomatic Medicine,* 24 (March–April) :159–169.

GRAHAM, SAXON.
1972 "Cancer, culture, and social structure," pp. 31–39 in *Patients, physicians and illness,* 2nd ed., E. Jaco (ed.) . New York: Free Press.

GRAHAM, SAXON, and LEO G. REEDER.
1972 "Social factors in the chronic illness," pp. 63–107 in *Handbook of Medical Sociology,* 2nd ed., H. Freeman, S. Levine, and L. Reeder (eds.) . Englewood Cliffs, N.J.: Prentice-Hall, Inc.

GRINKER, ROY.
1953 *Psychosomatic research.* New York: Norton.

HALL, OSWALD.
1946 "The informal organization of the medical profession." *Canadian Journal of Economics and Political Science,* 12 (February) :30–44.
1948 "The stages of a medical career." *American Journal of Sociology,* 53 (March) :327–336.

HARE, A. PAUL.
1976 *Handbook of small group research,* 2nd ed. New York: Free Press.

HAVIGHURST, ROBERT A.
1963 "Successful aging," pp. 299–320 in *Processes of aging,* R. Williams, C. Tibbitts, and W. Donahue (eds.) . New York: Atherton.

HAVIGHURST, ROBERT J., and RUTH ALBRECHT.
1953 *Older people.* New York: Longmans, Green.

HAYES-BAUTISTA, DAVID E.,
1976 "Termination of the patient-practitioner relationship: Divorce, patient style." *Journal of Health and Social Behavior,* 17 (March) :12–21.

HEALTH INSURANCE INSTITUTE.
1976 *Source book of health insurance data, 1975–76.* New York: Health Insurance Institute.

HEINZELMANN, F.
1962 "Determinants of prophylaxis behavior with respect to rheumatic fever." *Journal of Health and Human Behavior,* 3:73–81.

HENRY, JAMES P., and JOHN G. CASSEL.
1969 "Psychosocial factors in essential hypertension: Recent epidemiologic and animal experimental evidence." *American Journal of Epidemiology,* 90 (September) :171–200.

HENRY, JULES.
1954 "The formal structure of a psychiatric hospital." *Psychiatry,* 17 (May) : 139–151.
1957 "Types of institutional structure." *Psychiatry,* 20 (February) :47–60.

HEYDEBRAND, WOLF V.
1973 *Hospital bureaucracy.* New York: Dunellen.

HINES, RALPH.
   1972 "The health status of black Americans: Changing perspectives,"
   pp. 40–50 in *Patients, physicians and illness*, 2nd ed., E. Jaco (ed.).
   New York: Free Press.
HIRSH, HAROLD L.
   1974 "Death: A medical status or legal definition." *Case & Comment*,
   (Sept.-Oct.) 27–30.
HOCHSCHILD, ARLIE RUSSELL.
   1973a *The unexpected community*. Englewood Cliffs, N.J.: Prentice-Hall,
   Inc.
   1973b "A review of sex role research." *American Journal of Sociology*, 78
   (January) :1011–1929.
HOLLINGSHEAD, AUGUST B.
   1973 "Medical sociology: A brief review." *Milbank Memorial Fund
   Quarterly*, 51 (Fall) :531–542.
HOLLINGSHEAD, AUGUST B., and FREDERICK C. REDLICH.
   1958 *Social Class and Mental Illness*. New York: Wiley.
HOLLOWAY, ROBERT G., JAY W. ARTIS, and WALTER E. FREEMAN.
   1972 "The participation pattern of 'economic influentials' and their control
   of a hospital board of trustees," pp. 312–324 in *Patients, physicians, and
   illness*, 2nd ed., E. Jaco (ed.). New York: Macmillan.
HOLMES, THOMAS.
   1962 "Psychosocial and psychophysiological studies of tuberculosis," pp.
   239–255 in *Physiological correlates of psychological disorders*, R. Roessler
   and N. Greenfield (eds.). Madison: University of Wisconsin Press.
HOLMES, T. H., and R. H. RAHE.
   1967 "The social readjustment rating scale." *Journal of Psychosomatic
   Research*, 11 (August) :213–225.
HOOK, ERNEST.
   1973 "Behavioral implications of the human XYZ genotype." *Science*, 179
   (January) :139–150.
HOUGH, RICHARD L., DIANNE TIMBERS FAIRBANKS, and ALMA M. GARCIA.
   1976 "Problems in the ratio measurement of life stress." *Journal of Health
   and Social Behavior*, 17 (March) :70–82.
HOUSE, JAMES S.
   1974 "Occupational stress and coronary heart disease." *Journal of Health
   and Social Behavior*, 15 (March) :12–27.
HOWARD, JAN, and BARBARA L. HOLMAN.
   1970 "The effects of race and occupation on hypertension mortality."
   Milbank Memorial Fund Quarterly, 48 (July) :263–296.
HOWARD, JAN, and ANSELM STRAUSS (eds.).
   1975 *Humanizing health care*. New York: Wiley-Interscience.
HUDGENS, R. W.
   1974 "Personal catastrophe and depression: A consideration of the subject
   with respect to medically ill adolescents, and a requiem for retrospective
   life-event studies," pp. 119–134 in *Stressful life events: Their nature and
   effects*, B. S. Dohrenwend and B. P. Dohrenwend (eds.). New York:
   Wiley.
HUGHES, EVERETT C., HELEN MacGILL, and IRWIN DEUTSCHER.
   1958 *Twenty thousand nurses tell their story*. Philadelphia: Lippincott.

HUNTINGTON, MARY J.
1957 "The development of a professional self-image," pp. 179–187 in *The student-physician*, R. K. Merton, G. Reader, and P. L. Kendall (eds.). Cambridge, Mass.: Harvard University Press.

HURLEY, ROGER.
1971 "The health crisis of the poor," pp. 83–112 in *The social organization of health*, P. Dreitzel (ed.). New York: Macmillan.

HYDE, DAVID R., and PAYSON WOLFF.
1954 "The American Medical Association: Power, purpose and politics in organized medicine." *Yale Law Journal*, 63 (May) :938–1022.

INGALLS, A. J., and M. C. SALERNO.
1971 *Maternal and child health nursing*. St. Louis, Mo.: Mosby.

JANIS, IRVING L.
1958 *Psychological stress*. New York: Wiley.

JESSOR, R., T. GRAVES, R. HANSON, and S. JESSOR.
1968 *Society, personality and deviant behavior: A study of a tri-ethnic community*. New York: Holt, Rinehart, and Winston.

JULIAN, JOSEPH.
1977 *Social problems*. Englewood Cliffs, N.J.: Prentice-Hall, Inc.

KAPLAN, HAROLD I.
1975 "History of psychophysiological medicine," pp. 1624–1631 in *Comprehensive textbook of psychiatry*, Vol. II, 2nd ed., A. Freedman, H. Kaplan, and B. Sadock (eds.). Baltimore: Williams & Wilkins.

KASL, S., and S. COBB.
1966 "Health behavior, illness behavior, and sick role behavior." *Archives of Environmental Health*, 12 (February) :246–266.

KASS, LEON R.
1976 "Medical care and the pursuit of health," pp. 1–22 in *New directions in public health care: An evaluation of proposals for national health insurance*. San Francisco: Institute for Contemporary Studies.

KASSEBAUM, G., and B. BAUMANN.
1965 "Dimensions of the sick role in chronic illness." *Journal of Health and Social Behavior*, 6 (Spring) : 16–27.

KASTELER, JOSEPHINE, ROBERT L. KANE, DONNA M. OLSEN, and CONSTANCE THETFORD.
1976 "Issues underlying prevalence of 'doctor-shopping' behavior." *Journal of Health and Social Behavior*, 17 (December) :328–339.

KASTENBAUM, ROBERT.
1971 "Age: Getting there." *Psychology Today*, 5 (December) :53–54, 82–83.

KAUFMANN, WALTER.
1959 "Existentialism and death," pp. 39–69 in *The meaning of death*, H. Feifel (ed.). New York: McGraw-Hill.

KEGELES, S. S.
1963 "Why people seek dental care: A test of a conceptual formulation." *Journal of Health and Social Behavior*, 4 (Fall) :166–173.

KENDALL, PATRICIA L., and HANAN C. SELVIN.
1957 "Tendencies toward specialization in medical training," pp. 153–174 in *The student-physician*, R. Merton, G. Reader, and P. Kendall (eds.). Cambridge, Mass.: Harvard University Press.

KENNEDY, DONALD A.
1973 "Perceptions of illness and healing." *Social Science and Medicine,* 7 (October) :787–805.

KETY, SEYMOUR S.
1975 "Biochemistry of the major psychoses," pp. 178–187 in *Comprehensive textbook of psychiatry,* Vol. I, 2nd ed., A. Freedman, H. Kaplan, and B. Sadock (eds.). Baltimore: Williams & Wilkins.

KIRSCHT, JOHN P.
1974 "The health belief model and illness behavior," pp. 387–408 in *The health belief model and personal health,* M. H. Becker (ed.). San Francisco: Society for Public Health Education, Inc.

KNOWLES, JOHN H. (ed.).
1963 *Hospitals, doctors, and the public interest.* Cambridge, Mass.: Harvard University Press.
1972 "Introduction to the second edition," pp. xvii–xxii in *Handbook of medical sociology,* 2nd ed., H. E. Freeman, S. Levine, and L. G. Reeder (eds.). Englewood Cliffs, N.J.: Prentice-Hall, Inc.
1973 "The hospital," pp. 91–102 in *Life and death and medicine,* San Francisco: W. H. Freeman.

KNUDSON, A. G., and J. M. NATTERSON.
1960 "Participation of parents in the hospital care of their fatally ill children." *Pediatrics,* 26 (September) :482–490.

KOHN, MELVIN L.
1969 *Class and conformity: A study in values.* Homewood, Ill.: Dorsey Press.
1972 "Class, family, and schizophrenia." *Social Forces,* 50 (March):295–304.
1974 "Social class and schizophrenia: A critical review and a reformulation," pp. 113–137 in *Explorations in psychiatric sociology,* P. Roman and H. Trice (eds.). Philadelphia: F. A. Davis.

KOOS, EARL.
1954 *The health of Regionsville.* New York: Columbia University Press.

KOSA, J., and L. S. ROBERTSON.
1969 "The social aspects of health and illness," pp. 35–68 in *Poverty and health,* John Kosa, Aaron Antonovsky, and K. Zola (eds.). Cambridge, Mass.: Harvard University Press.

KOSA, JOHN, AARON ANTONOVSKY, and IRVING K. ZOLA (eds.).
1969 *Poverty and health.* Cambridge, Mass.: Harvard University Press.

KÜBLER-ROSS, ELISABETH.
1969 *On death and dying.* New York: Macmillan.

LARSON, DONALD E., and IRVING ROOTMAN.
1976 "Physician role performance and patient satisfaction." *Social Science and Medicine,* 10 (January) :29–32.

LAUER, ROBERT.
1974 "Rate of change and stress." *Social Forces,* 52 (June) :510–516.

LESHAN, L.
1966 "An emotional life history pattern associated with neoplastic diseases." *Annals of the New York Academy of Sciences,* 125:780–793.

LEVENTHAL, HOWARD.
1975 "The consequences of personalization during illness and treatment: An information-processing model," pp. 119–162 in *Humanizing health care,* J. Howard and A. Strauss (eds.). New York: Wiley-Interscience.

LEVENTHAL, H., G. HOCHMAN, and I. ROSENSTOCK.
1960 "Epidemic impact on the general population in two cities," pp. 14–23 in *The impact of Asian Influenza on community life.* Washington, D.C.: U.S. Department of Health, Education, and Welfare.

LEVINE, SOL, and NORMAN SCOTCH.
1970 *Social stress.* Chicago: Aldine.

LEVINSON, RICHARD M., and M. ZAN YORK.
1974 "The attribution of 'dangerousness' in mental health evaluations." *Journal of Health and Social Behavior,* 15 (December) :328–335.

LEVY, JERROLD, and STEPHEN KUNITZ.
1973 "Indian drinking: Problems of data collection and interpretation," pp. 217–235 in *Proceedings* of the First Abuse Alcoholism Conference of the National Institute on Alcohol Abuse and Alcoholism, M. Chafetz (ed.). Washington, D.C.: U.S. Government Printing Office.
1974 *Indian drinking: Navajo practices and Anglo-American theories.* New York: Wiley-Interscience.

LIEBER, CHARLES S.
1971 "The magnitude of the problem," pp. 3–5 in *Proceedings* of the First Annual Alcoholism Conference of the National Institute on Alcohol Abuse and Alcoholism, M. Chafetz (ed.). Washington, D.C.: U.S. Government Printing Office.

LIEF, HAROLD I.
1971 "Personality characteristics of medical students," pp. 44–87 in *Psychosocial aspects of medical training,* R. H. Coombs and C. E. Vincent (eds.). Springfield, Ill.: Thomas.

LINDESMITH, ALFRED, ANSELM STRAUSS, and NORMAN DENZIN.
1975 *Social psychology,* 4th ed. Hinsdale, Ill.: Dryden Press.

LIPOWSKI, Z. J.
1970 "Physical illness, the individual and the coping process." *Psychiatry in Medicine,* 1 (April) :91–101.

LOPATA, HELENA Z.
1973 "Social relations of black and white widowed women in a northern metropolis." *American Journal of Sociology,* 78 (January) :1003–1010.

LORBER, JUDITH.
1975 "Good patients and problem patients: Conformity and deviance in a general hospital." *Journal of Health and Social Behavior,* 16 (June) :213–225.

LOWENTHAL, M. F., and C. HAVEN.
1968 "Interaction and adaptation: Intimacy as a critical variable." *American Sociological Review,* 13 (February) :20–30.

LUDWIG, ALFRED O., BENJAMIN J. MURAWSKI, and SOMERS H. STURGIS.
1969 *Psychosomatic aspects of gynecological disorders.* Cambridge, Mass.: Harvard University Press.

McGRATH, JOSEPH E. (ed.).
1970 *Social and psychological factors in stress.* New York: Holt, Rinehart, and Winston.

McGRAW, R. M.
1966 *Ferment in medicine: A study of the essence of medical practice and of its new dilemmas.* Philadelphia: W. B. Saunders.

McIntosh, Jim.
1974 "Processes of communication, information seeking and control associated with cancer: A selective review of the literature." *Social Science and Medicine,* 8 (April) : 167–187.

McKinlay, John B.
1971 "The concept 'patient career' as a heuristic device for making medical sociology relevant to medical students." *Social Science and Medicine,* 5 (October) :441–460.
1972 "Some approaches and problems in the study of the use of services—an overview." *Journal of Health and Social Behavior,* 13 (June) :115–152.
1973 "Social networks, lay consultation and help-seeking behavior." *Social Forces,* 51 (March) :275–291.

McNeil, Elton B.
1970 *Neuroses and personality disorders.* Englewood Cliffs, N.J.: Prentice-Hall, Inc.

Maccoby, Eleanor (ed.).
1966 *The development of sex differences.* Stanford: Stanford University Press.

Maddox, George L.
1962 "Some correlates of differences in self-assessment of health status among the elderly." *Journal of Gerontology,* 17 (April) :180–185.

Madsen, William.
1973 *The Mexican-Americans of south Texas,* 2nd ed. New York: Holt, Rinehart, and Winston.

Magraw, Richard M.
1975 "Medical specialization and medical coordination," pp. 588–606 in *Medical Behavioral science,* T. Millon (ed.). Philadelphia: W. B. Saunders.

Major, Ralph A.
1954 *A history of medicine,* Vols. I and II. Springfield, Ill.: Thomas.

Makofsky, David.
1977 "Malpractice and medicine." *Society,* 14 (Jan.-Feb.) :25–29.

Marks, Renee.
1967 "A review of empirical findings," in *Social stress and cardiovascular disease,* S. L. Syme and L. G. Reeder (eds.). *Milbank Memorial Fund Quarterly,* 45 (April) :95.

Marmor, Theodore R.
1973 *The politics of Medicare.* Chicago: Aldine.

Marshall, Victor W.
1975a "Socialization for impending death in a retirement village." *American Journal of Sociology,* 80 (March) :1124–1144.
1975b "Organizational features of terminal status passage in residential facilities for the aged." *Urban Life,* 4 (October) :349–368.

Mason, Evelyn P.
1954 "Some correlates of self-judgments of the aged." *Journal of Gerontology,* 9 (July) :324–337.

Matsumoto, Y. Scott.
1971 "Social stress and coronary heart disease in Japan," pp. 123–149 in *The social organization of health,* H. Dreitzel (ed.). New York: Macmillan.

MAUKSCH, HANS.
1972 "Nursing: Churning for a change?" pp. 206–230 in *Handbook of medical sociology*, 2nd ed., H. E. Freeman, S. Levine, and L. G. Reeder (eds.). Englewood Cliffs, N.J.: Prentice-Hall, Inc.

MAY, PHILIP R. A.
1975 "Schizophrenia: Evaluation of treatment methods," pp. 955–982 in *Comprehensive textbook of psychiatry*, Vol. I, 2nd ed., A. Freedman, H. Kaplan, and B. Sadock (eds.). Baltimore: Williams & Wilkins.

MAZUR, ALLAN, and LEON S. ROBERTSON.
1972 *Biology and social behavior*. New York: Free Press.

MEAD, GEORGE HERBERT.
1934 *Mind, self, and society*. Chicago: University of Chicago Press.

MECHANIC, DAVID.
1962a "The concept of illness behavior." *Journal of Chronic Diseases*, 15 (February):189–194.
1962b *Students under stress: A study in the social psychology of adaptation*. New York: Free Press.
1964 "The influence of mothers on their children's health attitudes and behavior." *Pediatrics*, 33:444–453.
1968 *Medical sociology: A selective view*. New York: Free Press.
1969 *Mental health and social policy*. Englewood Cliffs, N.J.: Prentice-Hall, Inc.
1972 *Public expectations and health care*. New York: Wiley-Interscience.

MECHANIC, DAVID, and EDMUND H. VOLKART.
1961 "Stress, illness behavior, and the sick role." *American Sociological Review* 25 (February):51–58.

MEISSNER, W. W., JOHN E. MACK, and ELVIN V. SEMRAD.
1975 "Classical psychoanalysis," pp. 482–566 in *Comprehensive textbook of psychiatry*, Vol. I, 2nd ed., A. Freedman, H. Kaplan, and B. Sadock (eds.). Baltimore: Williams & Wilkins.

MELICK, D. W.
1959 "What a staff doctor expects of the hospital administrator." *Hospitals*, 33 (May 1):30–33.

MERENSTEIN, JOEL H., HARVEY WOLFE, and KATHLEEN M. BARKER.
1974 "The use of nurse practitioners in a general practice." *Medical Care*, 12 (May):437–444.

MERTON, ROBERT.
1938 "Social structure and anomie." *American Sociological Review*, 3 (October):672–682.

MERTON, ROBERT K., GEORGE G. READER, and PATRICIA KENDALL.
1957 *The student-physician*. Cambridge, Mass.: Harvard University Press.

MILLER, DOROTHY H.
1971 "Worlds that fail," pp. 102–114 in *Total institutions*, S. Wallace (ed.). Chicago: Aldine.

MILLER, JUDITH.
1975 "Study of death draws interest of psychologists." *APA Monitor*, 6 (February):1, 5.

MILLER, MICHAEL H.
1973 "Who receives optimal medical care?" *Journal of Health and Social Behavior*, 14 (June):176–182.

1974 "Work roles for the associate degree graduate." *American Journal of Nursing,* 74 (March) :468–470.

MILLER, STEPHEN J.

1970 *Prescription for leadership: Training for the medical elite.* Chicago: Aldine.

MILLMAN, MARCIA.

1977 "Masking doctors' errors." *Human Behavior,* 6 (January) :16–23.

MISHLER, ELLIOT G., and NANCY E. WAXLER.

1968 "Decision processes in psychiatric hospitalization: Patients referred, accepted, and admitted to a psychiatric hospital," pp. 262–276 in *The mental patient: Studies in the sociology of deviance,* S. Spitzer and N. Denzin (eds.). New York: McGraw-Hill.

MONTEIRO, LOIS.

1973a "Expense is no object . . .: Income and physician visits reconsidered." *Journal of Health and Social Behavior,* 14 (June) :99–115.

1973b "After heart attack: Behavioral expectations for the cardiac." *Social Science and Medicine,* 7 (July) :555–565.

MOORE, JOAN.

1970 *Mexican-Americans.* Englewood Cliffs, N.J.: Prentice-Hall, Inc.

MORA, GEORGE.

1975 "Historical and theoretical trends in psychiatry," pp. 1–75 in *Comprehensive textbook of psychiatry,* Vol. I, 2nd ed., A. Freedman, H. Kaplan, and B. Sadock (eds.). Baltimore: Williams & Wilkins.

MORISON, ROBERT S.

1973 "Dying," pp. 39–45 in *Life and death and medicine.* San Francisco: W. H. Freeman.

MORIWAKI, SHARON Y.

1973 "Self-disclosure, significant others, and psychological well-being in old age." *Journal of Health and Social Behavior,* 14 (September) :226–232.

MORSE, EDWARD V., GERALD GORDON, and MICHAEL MOCH.

1974 "Hospital costs and quality of care: An organizational perspective." *Milbank Memorial Fund Quarterly,* 52 (Summer) :315–346.

MOSS, GORDON E.

1973 *Illness, immunity, and social interaction.* New York: Wiley.

MOUSTAFA, A. TAHER, and GERTRUD WEISS.

1968 *Health status and practices of Mexican-Americans,* Advanced Report II, Mexican-American Study Project. Los Angeles: University of California.

NATIONAL CENTER FOR HEALTH STATISTICS.

1975 *Health resources statistics.* U.S. Department of Health, Education and Welfare.

1976 *Monthly Vital Statistics Report, Advance Report—Final Mortality Statistics, 1974,* Vol. 24, no. 11 (February 3). U.S. Department of Health, Education and Welfare.

NATIONAL INSTITUTE OF MENTAL HEALTH.

1975 *Research in the service of mental health: Summary report of the Research Task Force of the National Institute of Mental Health.* Washington, D.C.: Department of Health, Education, and Welfare.

NATTERSON, J. M., and A. G. KNUDSON.

1960 "Observations concerning fear of death in fatally ill children and their mothers." *Psychosomatic Medicine,* 22 (Nov.–Dec.) :456–465.

NEUGARTEN, BERNICE.
  1964 *Personality in middle and later life.* New York: Atherton.
  1970 "The old and young in modern societies." *American Behavioral Scientist,* 14 (Sept.–Oct.) :13–24.
  1971 "Grow old with me. The best is yet to be." *Psychology Today,* 5 (December) :45–48, 79–81.

NEUGARTEN, BERNICE, and JOAN W. MOORE.
  1968 "The changing age-status system," pp. 5–21 in *Middle age and aging,* B. Neugarten (ed.) . Chicago: University of Chicago Press.

NICKERSON, RITA J., THEODORE COLTON, OSLER L. PETERSON, BERNARD S. BLOOM, and WALTER W. HAUCK, JR.
  1976 "Doctors who perform operations: A study of in-hospital surgery in four diverse geographic areas." *New England Journal of Medicine,* 295 (October 21) :921–926, (October 28) :982–989.

NISBET, ROBERT A.
  1966 *The sociological tradition.* New York: Basic Books.
  1974 *The sociology of Emile Durkheim.* New York: Oxford.

NOYES, RUSSELL, JR.
  1972 "The experience of dying." *Psychiatry,* 35 (May) :174–184.

OKEN, DONALD.
  1961 "What to tell cancer patients: A study of medical attitudes." *Journal of the American Medical Association,* 175 (April 1) : 1120–1128.
  1967 "The psychophysiology and psychoendocrinology of stress and emotion," pp. 43–76 in *Psychological stress,* M. Appley and R. Trumbull (eds.) . New York: Appleton-Century-Crofts.

OLESEN, VIRGINIA L., and ELVI W. WHITTAKER.
  1968 *The silent dialogue.* San Francisco: Jossey-Bass.

OLMSTED, DONALD W., and KATHERINE DURHAM.
  1976 "Stability of mental health attitudes: A semantic differential study." *Journal of Health and Social Behavior,* 17 (March) :35–44.

PALMORE, ERDMAN.
  1968 "The effects of aging on activities and attitudes." *Gerontologist* 8 (Winter) :259–263.
  1969 "Sociological aspects of aging," pp. 33–69 in *Behavior and adaptation in later life,* E. Busse and E. Pfeiffer (eds.) . Boston: Little, Brown.
  1971 "Attitudes toward againg as shown by humor." *Gerontologist,* 2 (Autumn) :181–186.

PAPPWORTH, M. H.
  1971 *A primer of medicine.* New York: Appleton-Century-Crofts.

PARSONS, TALCOTT.
  1951 *The social system.* Glencoe, Ill.: Free Press.
  1975 "The sick role and role of the physician reconsidered." *Milbank Memorial Fund Quarterly,* 53 (Summer) :257–278.

PARSONS, TALCOTT, ROBERT F. BALES, and EDWARD A. SHILS.
  1953 *Working papers in the theory of action.* Glencoe, Ill.: Free Press.

PARSONS, TALCOTT, and RENÉE FOX.
  1952 "Illness, therapy and the modern urban American family." *Journal of Social Issues,* 8:31–44.

PAUL, JOHN R.
  1966 *Clinical epidemiology.* Chicago: University of Chicago Press.

PERROW, CHARLES.
1963 "Goals and power structures: A historical case study," pp. 112–146 in *The hospital in modern society*, E. Freidson (ed.). New York: Free Press.

PFLANZ, MANFRED, and JOHANN J. ROHDE.
1970 "Illness: Deviant behavior or conformity." *Social Science and Medicine*, 4 (December) :645–653.

PHILLIPS, DAVID P., and KENNETH A. FELDMAN.
1973 "A dip in deaths before ceremonial occasions: Some new relationships between social integration and mortality." *American Sociological Review*, 38 (December) :678–696.

PIAGET, JEAN.
1959 *The language and thought of the child*, 3rd ed. New York: Humanities Press.

PRESTHUS, ROBERT.
1962 *The organizational society*. New York: Vintage.

PRESTON, CAROLINE.
1967 "Self-reporting among older retired and non-retired subjects." *Journal of Gerontology*, 22 (October) :415–418.
1968 "Subjectively perceived agedness and retirement." *Journal of Gerontology*, 23 (April) :201–204.

PRESTON, CAROLINE E., and KAREN S. GUDIKEN.
1966 "A measure of self-perception among older people." *Journal of Gerontology*, 21 (January) :63–67.

PRUGH, D. G., E. M. STAUB, H. H. SANDS, R. M. KIRSCHBAUM, and E. A. LENIHAN.
1953 "A study of the emotional responses of children and families to hospitalization and illness." *American Journal of Orthopsychiatry*, 23 (January) :70–106.

PSATHAS, GEORGE.
1968 "The fate of idealism in nursing school." *Journal of Health and Social Behavior*, 9 (March) :52–64.

RAINER, JOHN D.
1975 "Genetics and psychiatry," pp. 89–104 in *Comprehensive textbook of psychiatry*, Vol. I, 2nd ed., A. Freedman, H. Kaplan, and B. Sadock (eds.). Baltimore: Williams & Wilkins.

RASMUSSEN, HOWARD.
1975 "Medical education—revolution or reaction." *Pharos* 38 (April) :53–59.

RAY, OAKLEY S.
1972 *Drugs, society, and human behavior*. St. Louis, Mo.: Mosby.

READER, GEORGE G.
1976 "Should medical schools require a sociology background?" *AAMC Education News*, 4 (December) :3, 8.

REEDER, LEO G.
1972 "The patient-client as a consumer: Some observations on the changing professional-client relationship." *Journal of Health and Social Behavior*, 13 (December) :406–412.

REEDER, LEO G., and EMIL BERKANOVIC.
1973 "Sociological concomitants of health orientations: A partial replica-

tion of Suchman." *Journal of Health and Social Behavior,* 14 (June) :134–143.

REINHARDT, UWE E.

1973 "Proposed changes in the organization of health-care delivery: An overview and critique." *Milbank Memorial Fund Quarterly,* 51 (Spring): 169–222.

REISSMAN, LEONARD, and RALPH PLATOU.

1960 "The motivation and socialization of medical students." *Journal of Health and Human Behavior,* 1 (Fall) :174–182.

RESKIN, BARBARA, and FREDERICK L. CAMPBELL.

1974 "Physician distribution across metropolitan areas." *American Journal of Sociology,* 79 (January) :981–998.

REYNOLDS, ROGER A.

1976 "Improving access to health care among the poor—the neighborhood health care center experience." *Milbank Memorial Fund Quarterly,* 54 (Winter) :47–82.

RICHTER, LUCRETIA, and ELIZABETH RICHTER.

1974 "Nurses in fiction." *American Journal of Nursing,* 74 (July) :1280–1281.

RILEY, MATILDA W., and ANN FONER.

1968 *Aging and society,* Vol. I. New York: Russell Sage.

ROBBINS, G. F., J. D. MACDONALD, and G. T. PACK.

1953 "Delay in diagnosis and treatment of physicians with cancer." *Cancer,* 6 (May) :624–626.

ROEMER, MILTON I., and WILLIAM SHONICK.

1973 "HMO performance: The recent evidence." *Milbank Memorial Fund Quarterly,* 51 (Summer) :271–318.

ROGERS, D. E.

1973 "Shattuck lecture—the American health-care scene." *New England Journal of Medicine,* 288 (June 28) :1377–1383.

ROGOFF, NATALIE.

1957 "The decision to study medicine," pp. 109–129 in *The student-physician,* R. K. Merton, G. Reader, and P. L. Kendall (eds.). Cambridge, Mass.: Harvard University Press.

ROMAN, PAUL, and PHILIP TAIETZ.

1967 "Organizational structure and disengagement: The emeritus professor." *Gerontologist,* 7 (September) :147–152.

ROOS, NORALOU P., JOHN R. SCHERMERHORN, and LESLIE L. ROOS, JR.

1974 "Hospital performance: Analyzing power and goals." *Journal of Health and Social Behavior,* 15 (June) :78–92.

ROSE, M. P., and W. A. PETERSON (eds.).

1965 *Older people and their social world.* Philadelphia: F. A. Davis.

ROSEN, GEORGE.

1963 "The hospital: Historical sociology of a community institution," pp. 1–36 in *The hospital in modern society,* E. Freidson (ed.). New York: Free Press.

1972 "The evolution of social medicine," pp. 30–60, in *Handbook of medical sociology,* 2nd ed., H. Freeman, S. Levine, and L. Reeder (eds.). Englewood Cliffs, N.J.: Prentice-Hall, Inc.

ROSENHAN, DAVID L.
1973 "On being sane in insane places." *Science,* 179 (January 19) :250–258.
ROSENSTOCK, IRWIN.
1966 "Why people use health services." *Milbank Memorial Fund Quarterly,* 44 (July) :94–127.
ROSOW, IRVING.
1967 *Social integration of the aged.* New York: Free Press.
1974 *Socialization into old age.* Berkeley, Cal.: University of California Press.
ROTH, J. A.
1962 "The treatment of the sick," pp. 214–243 in *Poverty and health,* J. Kosa, A. Antonovsky, and I. Zola (eds.). Cambridge, Mass.: Harvard University Press.
1963 "Information and the control of treatment in tuberculosis hospitals," pp. 293–318 in *The hospital in modern society,* E. Freidson (ed.). New York: Free Press.
ROUECHÉ, BERTON.
1967 *Annals of epidemiology.* Boston: Little, Brown.
RUESCHMEYER, DIETRICH.
1972 "Doctors and lawyers: A comment on the theory of professions," pp. 5–19 in *Medical men and their work,* E. Freidson and J. Lorber (eds.). Chicago: Aldine.
RUTSTEIN, DAVID.
1967 *The coming revolution in medicine.* Cambridge, Mass.: MIT Press.
SADOCK, BENJAMIN J.
1975 "Group psychotherapy," pp. 1850–1877 in *Comprehensive textbook of psychiatry,* Vol. II, 2nd ed., A. Freedman, H. Kaplan, and B. Sadock (eds.). Baltimore: Williams & Wilkins.
SALLOWAY, JEFFREY C.
1973 "Medical utilization among urban gypsies." *Urban Anthropology,* 2 (Spring) :113–126.
SAMPSON, HAROLD, SHELDON L. MESSINGER, and ROBERT L. TOWNE ET AL.
1964 "The mental hospital and marital family ties," pp. 139–162 in *The other side: Perspectives on deviance,* H. Becker (ed.). New York: Free Press.
SATIN, GEORGE D.
1973 "Help?: The hospital emergency unit patient and his presenting picture." *Medical Care,* 11 (July–August) :328–337.
SATIN, GEORGE, and FREDERICK J. DUHL.
1972 "Help?: The hospital emergency unit as community physician." *Medical Care,* 10 (May–June) :248–260.
SAWARD, ERNEST W.
1973 "The organization of medical care," pp. 129–135 in *Life, death, and medicine.* San Francisco: W. H. Freeman.
SCHEFF, THOMAS J.
1964 "The societal reaction to deviance: Ascriptive elements in the psychiatric screening of mental patients in a midwestern state." *Social Problems,* 11 (Spring) :401–413.
1966 *Being mentally ill.* Chicago: Aldine.

1974 "The labelling theory of mental illness." *American Sociological Review*, 39 (June) :444–452.

1975 *Labeling madness.* Englewood Cliffs, N.J.: Prentice-Hall, Inc.

SCHEFFLER, RICHARD M., and OLIVIA D. STINSON.
1974 "Characteristics of physician's assistants: A focus on specialty." *Medical Care*, 12 (December) :1019–1030.

SCHULMAN, SAM.
1972 "Mother surrogate—after a decade," pp. 233–239 in *Patients, physicians and illness*, E. Jaco (ed.). New York: Free Press.

SCHWAB, ROBERT S., and JOHN S. PRITCHARD.
1950 "Situational stresses and extrapyramidal disease in different personalities," pp. 48–61 in *Life, stress and disease*, Proceedings of the Association for Research in Nervous and Mental Diseases, No. 29. Baltimore: Williams & Wilkins.

SCHWARTZ, ARTHUR, and ROBERT W. KLEEMEIER.
1965 "The effects of illness upon some aspects of personality." *Journal of Gerontology*, 20 (January) :85–91.

SEGALL, ALEXANDER.
1976 "The sick role concept: Understanding illness behavior." *Journal of Health and Social Behavior*, 17 (June) :162–168.

SELIGMAN, MARTIN E. P.
1974 "Submissive death: Giving up on life." *Psychology Today*, 7 (May) : 80–85.

SELTZER, MILDRED M., and ROBERT C. ATCHLEY.
1971 "The concept of old age: Changing attitudes and stereotypes." *Gerontologist*, 11 (Autumn) :226–230.

SELYE, HANS.
1956 *The stress of life.* New York: McGraw-Hill.

SHAPIRO, D.
1965 *Neurotic styles.* New York: Basic Books.

SHILOH, AÏLON.
1965 "Equalitarian and hierarchical patients: An investigation among Hadassah Hospital patients." *Medical Care*, 3 (April-June) :87–95.
1971 "Sanctuary or prison—responses to life in a mental hospital," pp. 9–24 in *Total institutions*, S. Wallace (ed.). Chicago: Aldine.

SHINDELL, SIDNEY, JEFFREY C. SALLOWAY, and COLETTE M. OBEREMBT.
1976 *A coursebook in health care delivery.* New York: Appleton-Century-Crofts.

SHORTELL, STEPHEN M.
1973 "Patterns of referral among internists in private practice." *Journal of Health and Social Behavior*, 14 (December) :335–348.

SIGERIST, HENRY E.
1960 "The special position of the sick," pp. 10–11 in *Henry E. Sigerist on the sociology of medicine*, M. Roemer (ed.). New York: MD Publications.

SIMON, RITA JAMES.
1967 *The jury and the defense of insanity.* Boston: Little, Brown.

SMITH, H. L.
1955 "Two lines of authority: The hospital's dilemma." *Modern Hospital*, 84 (March) :59–64.

SMITH, HARVEY L., and JEAN THRASHER.
    1963 "Roles, cliques and sanctions: Dimensions of patient society." *Journal of Social Psychiatry,* 9:184–191.
SOMERS, HERMAN M.
    1970 "Health care cost," pp. 167–203 in *The health of Americans,* B. Jones (ed.). Englewood Cliffs, N.J.: Prentice-Hall, Inc.
SORENSON, JAMES R.
    1974 "Biomedical innovation, uncertainty, and doctor-patient interaction." *Journal of Health and Social Behavior,* 15 (December) :366–374.
SPARER, GERALD, and LOUISE M. OKADA.
    1974 "Chronic conditions and physician use patterns in ten urban poverty areas." *Medical Care,* 12 (July) :549–560.
SPINETTA, JOHN J.
    1974 "The dying child's awareness of death: A review." *Psychological Bulletin,* 81 (April) :256–260.
SPINETTA, JOHN J., DAVID RIGLER, and MYRON KARON.
    1974 "Personal space as a measure of a dying child's sense of isolation." *Journal of Consulting and Clinical Psychology,* 42 (December) :751–756.
SPITZER, ROBERT L., and PAUL T. WILSON.
    1975 "Nosology and the official psychiatric nomenclature," pp. 826–845 in *Comprehensive textbook of psychiatry,* Vol. I, 2nd ed., A. Freedman, H. Kaplan, and B. Sadock (eds.). Baltimore: Williams & Wilkins.
SROLE, LEO, T. S. LANGNER, S. T. MICHAEL, M. K. OPLER, and T. A. C. RENNIE.
    1962 *Mental health in the metropolis: The midtown Manhattan Study,* Vol. I. New York: McGraw-Hill.
STEIN, LEONARD I.
    1967 "The doctor-nurse game." *Archives of General Psychiatry,* 16 (June) : 699–703.
STEVENS, ROSEMARY.
    1971 *American medicine and the public interest.* New Haven: Yale University Press.
STEWART, OMAR.
    1964 "Questions regarding American Indian criminality." *Human Organization,* 23 (Spring) :61–66.
STOUFFER, SAMUEL A., EDWARD A. SUCHMAN, LELAND C. DeVINNEY, SHIRLEY A. STAR, and ROBIN M. WILLIAMS, JR.
    1949 *The American soldier,* Vol. I. Princeton: Princeton University Press.
STRAUS, ROBERT.
    1957 "The nature and status of medical sociology." *American Sociological Review,* 22 (April) :200–204.
STRAUSS, ANSELM.
    1966 "Structure and ideology of the nursing profession," pp. 60–104 in *The nursing profession,* F. Davis (ed.). Wiley.
    1970 "Medical ghettos," pp. 9–26 in *Where medicine fails,* A Strauss (ed.). Chicago: Aldine.
    1971 *Professions, work and career.* San Francisco: The Sociology Press.
    1975 *Chronic illness and the quality of life.* St. Louis, Mo.: Mosby.
STRAUSS, ANSELM, LEONARD SCHATZMAN, DANUTA EHRLICH, RUE BUCHER, and MELVIN SABSHIN.
    1963 "The hospital and its negotiated order," pp. 147–169 in *The hospital in modern society,* E. Friedson (ed.). New York: Free Press.

STRIMBU, JERRY, LYLE SCHOENFELDT, and O. SIMS.
1973 "Drug usage in college students as a function of racial classification and minority group status." *Research in Higher Education,* 1 (3) :263–272.
SUCHMAN, EDWARD A.
1965a "Social patterns of illness and medical care." *Journal of Health and Human Behavior,* 6 (Spring) :2–16.
1965b "Stages of illness and medical care." *Journal of Health and Human Behavior,* 6 (Fall) :114–128.
SUDNOW, DAVID.
1967 *Passing on.* Englewood Cliffs, N.J.: Prentice-Hall, Inc.
SUSSER, M. W., and W. WATSON.
1971 *Sociology in medicine,* 2nd ed. New York: Oxford University Press.
SWANSON, GUY E.
1972 "Mead and Freud: Their relevance for social psychology," pp. 23–43 in *Symbolic interaction,* 2nd ed., J. Manis and B. Meltzer (eds.). Boston: Allyn and Bacon.
SYME, LEONARD.
1975 "Social and psychological risk factors in coronary heart disease." *Modern Concepts of Cardiovascular Disease,* 44 (April) :17–21.
SZASZ, THOMAS S.
1963 *Law, liberty, and psychiatry.* New York: Collier.
1964 *The myth of mental illness.* New York: Harper & Row.
1970 *The manufacture of madness.* New York: Dell.
1974 *The myth of mental illness,* rev. ed. New York: Harper & Row.
TAGLIACOZZO, DAISY, and HANS O. MAUKSCH.
1972 "The patient's view of the patient's role," pp. 172–185 in *Patients, physicians and illness,* 2nd ed., E. Jaco (ed.). New York: Macmillan.
TALLER, STEPHEN L., and ROBERT FELDMAN.
1974 "The training and utilization of nurse practitioners in adult health appraisal." *Medical Care,* 12 (January) :40–48.
TALLMER, MARGOT, and BERNARD KUTNER.
1969 "Disengagement and the stresses of aging." *Journal of Gerontology,* 24 (January) :70–75.
TAYLOR, D. GARTH, LU ANN ADAY, and RONALD ANDERSEN.
1975 "A social indicator of access to medical care." *Journal of Health and Social Behavior,* 16 (March) :38–49.
THOMAS, ELIZABETH C., and KAORU YAMAMOTO.
1975 "Attitudes toward age: An exploration in school-age children." *International Journal of Aging and Human Development,* 6:29–40.
TOWNSEND, J. MARSHALL.
1975 "Cultural conceptions, mental disorders and social roles: A comparison of Germany and America." *American Sociological Review,* 40 (December) : 739–752.
1976 "Self-concept and the institutionalization of mental patients: An overview and critique." *Journal of Health and Social Behavior,* 17 (September) :263–271.
TUCKMAN, JACOB, and IRVING LORGE.
1952 "The influence of a course on the psychology of the adult on attitudes toward old people and older workers." *Journal of Educational Psychology,* 43 (November) :400–407.
1953 "Attitudes toward old people," *Journal of Social Psychology,* 37 (May) :249–260.

Twaddle, Andrew.
    1969 "Health decisions and sick role variations: An exploration." *Journal of Health and Social Behavior,* 10 (June) :105–114.
    1973 "Illness and deviance." *Social Science and Medicine,* 7 (October) : 751–762.

U.S. Department of Health, Education, and Welfare.
    1976 *National Health Insurance Proposals.* Washington, D.C.: U.S. Government Printing Office (February).

Veatch, Robert M.
    1972 "Choosing not to prolong dying." *Medical Dimensions* 1 (December) : 8–10, 40.

Volkart, E. H. (ed.).
    1951 *Social behavior and personality.* New York: Social Science Research Council.

Waddell, Jack O.
    1973 "Drink friend! Social contexts of convivial drinking and drunkenness among Papago Indians in an urban setting," pp. 237–251 in *Proceedings of the First Annual Alcoholism Conference of the National Institute on Alcohol Abuse and Alcoholism,* M. Chafetz (ed.). Washington, D.C.: U.S. Government Printing Office.

Waechter, E. H.
    1971 "Children's awareness of fatal illness." *American Journal of Nursing,* 71 (June) :1168–1172.

Wahl, C. W.
    1965 "The fear of death," pp. 56–66 in *Death and identity,* R. Fulton (ed.). New York: Wiley.

Waitzkin, Howard.
    1971 "Latent functions of the sick role in various settings." *Social Science and Medicine,* 5 (February) :45–75.

Wan, Thomas T. H., and Scott J. Soifer.
    1974 "Determinants of physician utilization: A causal analysis." *Journal of Health and Social Behavior,* 15 (June) :100–108.

Warheit, George J., Charles E. Holzer III, and Sandra A. Arey.
    1975 "Race and mental illness: An epidemiologic update." *Journal of Health and Social Behavior,* 16 (September) :243–256.

Warheit, George J., Charles Holzer III, and John J. Schwab.
    1973 "An analysis of social class and racial differences in depressive symptomatology." *Journal of Health and Social Behavior,* 14 (December) : 291–298.

Warnecke, Richard B.
    1973 "Non-intellectual factors related to attrition from a collegiate nursing program." *Journal of Health and Social Behavior,* 14 (June) :153–167.

Welch, Susan, John Comer, and Michael Steinman.
    1973 "Some social and attitudinal correlates of health care among Mexican-Americans." *Journal of Health and Social Behavior,* 14 (September) : 205–213.

Wessen, Albert F.
    1972 "Hospital ideology and communication between ward personnel," pp. 325–342 in *Patients, physicians and illness,* 2nd ed., E. Jaco (ed.). New York: Macmillan.

WEXLER, MURRAY.
   1976 "The behavioral sciences in medical education." *American Psychologist* 31 (April) :275–283.
WHATLEY, CHARLES D.
   1959 "Social attitudes toward discharged mental patients." *Social Problems,* 6:313–320.
WHITE, KERR L.
   1972 "Health care arrangements in the United States: A.D. 1972," pp. 17–40 in *Medical cure and medical care,* S. Andreopoulos (ed.). *Milbank Memorial Fund Quarterly,* 50 (October) :17–40.
WILSON, ROBERT N.
   1963 "The social structure of a general hospital." *Annals of the American Academy of Political Science,* 346:67–76.
   1970 *The sociology of health.* New York: Random House.
WING, J. K.
   1969 "Institutionalism in mental hospitals," pp. 219–238 in *Mental illness and social processes,* T. Scheff (ed.). New York: Harper & Row.
WOLF, STEWART, and HELEN GOODELL (eds.).
   1968 *Harold G. Wolff's stress and disease,* 2nd ed. Springfield, Ill.: Thomas.
WOLF, STEWART, and HAROLD G. WOLFF.
   1943 *Human gastric function: An experimental study of a man and his stomach.* New York: Oxford University Press.
WYSS, DIETER.
   1973 *Psychoanalytic school from the beginning to the present.* New York: Aronson.
YARROW, M., C. SCHWARTZ, H. MURPHY, and L. DEASY.
   1955 "The psychological meaning of mental illness in the family," *Journal of Social Issues,* 11 (October) :12–24.
ZBOROWSKI, MARK.

INDEX

AUTHOR INDEX

SUBJECT INDEX